Revival and Nationbuilding

A Biblical Guide for Black Nationbuilding

Richard G. Walker

Contents

A Special Word To The Reader

This is a book about the spiritual solution to oppression. Oppression robs its victims of justice, disfiguring their souls in the process. The only real solution to oppression is God acting on behalf of the oppressed, nullifying its effects and restoring the souls of the afflicted. This process begins by the new birth, by salvation through faith in Jesus Christ. Jesus came and gave his life to set people free from slavery to sin and to the devil [Ephesians 2.1]. By believing upon Christ as the one who paid for your sins with his own blood, you will receive forgiveness and eternal life, the basis for genuine freedom in every other area of life.

John 3:16–18 (KJV 1900) 16 For God so loved the world, that he gave his only begotten Son, that whosoever believeth in him should not perish, but have everlasting life. 17 For God sent not his Son into the world to condemn the world; but that the world through him might be saved. 18 He that believeth on him is not condemned: but he that believeth not is condemned already, because he hath not believed in the name of the only begotten Son of God.

Tomorrow is coming, but it is not promised to come for you. Believe this gospel of Jesus Christ and this very moment receive forgiveness of sins and everlasting life through the new birth.

Dedication

This book is dedicated to those that will read it and for the first time apply the Word of God to the interpretation of history and to their life experiences as black people.

Ezra 7.10

Other Books by Richard G. Walker

The Spiritual Gift of Tongues

Antichrist and the New World Order

Introduction

There is hope! A spiritually powerful and institutionally strong black community can begin to take root in a single generation and bear fruit in one lifetime. This book will provide a scriptural approach to reversing the effects of oppression upon black America by the systematic application of biblical concepts to individuals *via the local church*. Spiritual revival and effective discipleship will result in *nationbuilding* for any people rightly aligned to the Word of God, for then God will be on their side.

The focus of the book is the Three Nationbuilding Principles. Each principle summarizes what the scriptures have to say about an ability critical to nationbuilding:

Nationbuilding Principle One: No people have ever survived the nullification of their pastors.

Nationbuilding Principle Two: No other person's decisions about your life are more important than your own.

Nationbuilding Principle Three: In unequal power relationships, spiritual power overcomes worldly power. God reverses unequal power relations to the advantage of those who have his favor.

The following are the major themes of this book.

The Concept of Race and the Church

The idea of race is not rational, not scientific, and not biblical. Race is a concept which was created for the purpose of social engineering, to manage large groups of people for the purpose of exploitation. Race creates artificial advantages for some and depreciates the value of others. Race is one means by which Satan administers his world kingdom.

Although race is not a biblical concept, it is a real one that is the source of untold injustice and suffering. Consequently, the Word of God must be applied to this important issue. Section One[i] of this book provides definitions for terms such as *race, prejudice, discrimination, racism, diversity, whiteness, blackness, social justice, and white supremacy*. It compares the racial idea with the ways that the bible organizes humanity. The biblical method of distinguishing peoples is applied to the Jews and the Samaritans as a case study. Finally, Section One addresses how the concept of race is used to injure black people and the biblical means by which this injury may be healed.

Oppression as a Spiritual Concept

This book identifies biblical concepts that will deliver black people from racially based oppression. Section Two[ii] focuses upon Revival and Nationbuilding, the methodologies that will produce cultural revival in black America. We reject the notion that oppression was a thing of the distant past, and we reject that the current conditions of black people in America are unrelated to any systematic apparatus of race-based oppression.

Our basic position is that oppression is first[1] a spiritual concept and can only be overcome by spiritual means. Any solution or set of solutions that fails to address the spiritual expectations that God has of men and nations must fail. All solutions that do not begin with the fundamental need of men for spiritual repentance and submission to the accurate interpretation of the scriptures can only be, at best, half measures which will not create lasting improvement of the prospects of black people, like building a house upon sand.

[ii] Chapters 1-7.
[ii] Chapters 8-19.

Matthew 7:26–27 (KJV 1900)

[26] And every one that heareth these sayings of mine, and doeth them not, shall be likened unto a foolish man, which built his house upon the sand: [27] And the rain descended, and the floods came, and the winds blew, and beat upon that house; and it fell: and great was the fall of it.

Psalms 127:1 (KJV 1900)

[1] Except the Lord build the house, they labour in vain that build it: Except the Lord keep the city, the watchman waketh *but* in vain.

Many Christians have been led to believe that to seek deliverance from racial oppression is inconsistent with genuine spirituality and proper spiritual priorities.[2] Not only is this incorrect, but it is a teaching that is expressly reserved for oppressed people. The Bible teaches that the new birth through faith in Jesus Christ, by definition, changes the relation of the believer to Satan's kingdom [Colossians 1.13],[iii] including systems of oppression.[iv] Accurate and systematic Bible teaching in the local church will result in a biblical self-concept [Romans 12.1-4], which is the first casualty of racial oppression. The new birth makes the believer the object of divine protection which includes divine opposition to oppression.[v] [vi] The increase of spiritually mature individuals among a people correspondingly expands the field of divine blessing and protection to the community, these believers becoming conduits of wisdom and blessing to their own and subsequent generations. In this way even the unsaved are blessed because of the actions of the properly functioning local church.

Black Decisions Matter

It is not necessary that God change the hearts of oppressors or that He eliminate the infrastructure of oppression to deliver His people from it. The wages of racial oppression are too high to expect significant change in those profiting from it. Christendom is the most powerful institution in the establishment and maintenance of racial injustice in the United States because,

---

[iii] Matthew 12.29-30; Acts 16.18

[iv] Appendix 1-Doctrine of Oppression: God is Opposed to Oppressors

[v] 2 Chronicles 16.9; Exodus 22.21-24; Psalms 10.15-18; Proverbs 22:22–23; Isaiah 49:26; Jeremiah 6.5-7

[vi] A consistent theme of the Old Testament is God's faithfulness in applying divine judgment to oppressor nations and individuals. Israel itself was repeatedly judged due to its tendency towards oppression. See Appendix 1: The Doctrine of Oppression: God is Opposed to Oppressors.

although it claims the stewardship of the Word of God, it does not use that authority to defeat the spiritual evil of racial prejudice and discrimination *within* the local churches. [vii] Not willing to identify racism as a spiritual problem and therefore within the jurisdiction of the Church, Christendom becomes a part of the problem. As a result, the secular society has no model of proper racial relations by which to calibrate their morality. Christendom teaches the world that racial prejudice, which is the basis of racial oppression, is outside the precincts of sanctification.

Therefore, we discover in Section Two[viii] that the most important decisions are those of the Christian himself. There is no need to convince oppressors to stop practicing injustice, because God Himself responds to the believer who is rightly oriented to Him and the Scriptures. There isn't much biblical evidence of God, at a national level, changing the hearts of oppressors towards their victims. The Second Principle of Nationbuilding is "No one's decisions about your life are more important than your own decisions about your life." This means that the decisions of oppressors, the decisions of the government or any group of people in the world are less important to God than your own decisions about your life.

Your responsibility as a believer is to walk in obedience to the Scriptures, to encourage that same discipline in your family, and to model it within the institutions with which you interact. If you are a Pastor to black people, it is your responsibility to break the psychological programming of your Congregation through the application of the Word of God to the actual situations of black people [Romans 12.1-3] so that they can grow spiritually and minister to others, completing the spiritual chain reaction that will rescue the black Community.

When the local churches decide to stand against injustice, as they do other societal evils,[ix] there is a spiritual effect upon *all* of society. The revival of the local churches, the multiplication of divine blessing among mature believers creates social dynamics which can improve the character of civilization

---

[vii] All structural discrimination is the cumulative action of many individuals within a particular institution. The effective discipleship of the Church would have produced a different America had it occurred. See Chapter 2: Definition of Terms

[viii] Chapters 8-19.

[ix] Local churches that understand perfectly what it means to "stand against" homosexuality, or abortion, pretend not to know what it means to "stand against" racial injustice.

overall.[x]

No Change Without Accurate Doctrine

The entire church of the 21st century has been presented with the lie that living a godly life is not dependent upon having a correct understanding of the scriptures. Many believers have lost track of the fact that you cannot *be* something spiritually until you first *know* something biblically. This improper emphasis upon looking like a Christian while lacking a sound biblical foundation has resulted in the success-oriented Christian corporation that is devoid of actual spiritual power. Christians no longer understand that God has spoken to mankind via the Word of God and there is no fellowship with Him that does not rest upon obedience to an accurate understanding of the scriptures.[xi] The prominence today of church growth as the primary measure of ministry success necessarily results in a *doctrinal flexibility* that will attract and retain the target markets desired by today's ministries. Young Pastors and old adopt the techniques and teaching that will cultivate and maintain attendance, revenues, and reputation. These methodologies and emphases are often opposite those which produce true conversions and mature disciples. It is now possible to have multiple large churches growing and prospering in places where the surrounding communities are rampant with divorce, abortion, crime, and addiction. Because of false teaching and the and the spiritual weakness which false teaching engenders, black America finds itself helpless to counteract the forces of oppression that debilitate and threaten to destroy us. In fact, many local churches have become, because of false teaching, enablers, or sub-contractors of the racially oppressive system itself.

This book emphasizes the requirement of the *frequent, accurate and systematic teaching* [FAST] of the Word of God for the power of oppression to be eliminated in the lives of believers. It should be emphasized that oppression *requires* the saturation of the oppressed with false teachers and false teaching. Satan has consistently used false interpretations of truth to defeat generations of believers from the Garden of Eden until now.

No Change Without Proper Application of Truth

This book also addresses the way the Bible is taught to black congregations. It

---

[x] Proverbs 11.10-11; 14.34; Matthew 5.13-14
[xi] John 14.21-24; 15.14; 1 John 4.1

is emphatically asserted that the Bible is not a magic wand that can be waved over a group of people and produce results. You cannot merely wave medicine over a wound; it must be applied to it. Exciting preaching that does not systematically apply the truths of the Bible directly to the life situations of the people will not produce the quality of spiritual change that people need. Neither will *accurate* teaching that the teacher is unwilling to directly apply to the realities of being a black person in America bring about the healing the Bible can produce.

Some black preachers and Bible teachers are afraid of making direct application of biblical truths to the realities of race in America for fear of offending whites or fear of being accused of being prejudiced themselves. If we want to have the Spirit of God remove the spiritual structures in the soul that make oppression possible, then we must directly apply the Bible to the realities of systematic oppression in the world of black people and its effects upon our self-concept, our interpersonal relationships, how we are to understand and relate to government and many, many other applications of biblical truth. The proper *application* of truth is as important as the accuracy of the truth itself.[xii] The proper teaching of the Word of God results in genuine mental health: a proper orientation to God, self, and others. Spiritually healthy people are very difficult to oppress. The proper teaching of the Word of God will, by changing individuals, change civilization.

Three Nationbuilding Principles

This book identifies the Three Principles of Nationbuilding[xiii] each of which summarize biblical teaching regarding the spiritual components of national life.

The national entity is a divine institution. God established nations as a category of human organization through which spiritual effects flow. Nations are aggregations of families, another divine institution and families are aggregations of marriages, a third divine institution. Spiritual effects, both blessing and cursing, flow through these institutions from the strongest to the weakest bonds: from the individual, through marriage and then family, to the

---

[xiixii] Churches having accurate doctrinal statements can, by their faulty application of the truth, become gatekeepers of injustice, all the while claiming to stand upon biblical accuracy. This practice will be developed in Chapter 18 under "Slave Theology."

[xiii] Chapters 15-19

nation.

The Old Testament is the record of the creation of a nation, Israel: its blessing, and its eventual judgment due to spiritual failure. It is also the record of God's dealings with many Gentile nations. In these dealings, augmented by the New Testament revelation, the principles of nationbuilding are derived.

The Three Nationbuilding Principles are the *biblical* means by which black America may be stabilized and productive spiritual activity can be initiated and maintained. The nationbuilding principles are not secular strategies. Oppression is a spiritual initiative that has serious consequences in the secular realms of economics, politics, social organization, and culture. There can be no lasting progress in the secular until there is effective spiritual activity. This is why attempts by the local church to defeat oppression by secular action have proved unable to secure lasting results.

The Modification of Biblical Christianity to Serve Injustice

Under race-based slavery the *thinking* of the slave was an important component of his becoming a productive financial resource. Free thinking slaves increased the *costs of slavery* through reduced productivity, escapes, and rebellions, all caused by the slaves' consciousness that he and his heirs were living in a system designed to extort, through violence, their labor and that of their offspring forever. [3] The slave and his descendants were *never* intended to become a sharer in the perpetually compounding wealth that he was critical in producing.[4]

The evangelization of the slave made this problem worse by exposing him to the Scriptures which demonstrated the true character of slavery. The Bible teaches that slavery is opposed to God's intent for mankind in general and His intent for believers in particular. Through the Scriptures, the slave was able to learn that slavery was consistent with the spirit of the devil's administration upon the earth. The slave also became exposed to direct statements of Scripture concerning the institution of slavery. Not only this, but slave masters that were truly saved were freeing their slaves because of the conviction of Scripture, the Holy Spirit and of conscience. What was needed by the slave industry was a *version* of Christianity that would address these problems. In this book that solution is termed *Slave Theology*.[xiv]

A system biblical interpretation has been fabricated and provided to blacks that assists in their psychological programming[xv] while also providing a biblical justification for slavery and for the construction of post-slavery systems of oppression.[5]

One of the effects of accurate biblical instruction is the renewing of the mind [Romans 12.1-2]. Romans 12 teaches that one cannot render appropriate spiritual service to God unless one is in his right mind. However, systems of oppression based upon race cannot allow a healthy self-concept in the objects of oppression, much less a biblical one. Modern oppression relies, in part, upon the *self-oppression* of individuals through self-destructive patterns of thinking and behavior. Slave Theology is an important aspect of the mental programming that produces the spiritual [and therefore the psychological] malfunction of the oppressed. Thus, the oppressed individual is systematically deprived of accurate bible information and false concepts are designed that corrupt the process of spiritual development in those who are born again.

The objective of this book is to provide a framework for the deliverance of black people from oppression by the accurate teaching of the Word of God. In doing this the reader will be challenged to face hard facts that will question his own spiritual commitment and activity. For some, the costs of changing their viewpoint and their practices to align with a biblical standard will appear to be too costly. For the rest, local church implementation of the nationbuilding principles can *begin* to produce visible changes in your community in one to two decades. There is hope! Let's get started.

[xiv] Chapter 18
[xv] This programming is designed to provide black people a limited, non-biblical self-concept and to prohibit the application of biblical principles to the issue of oppression.

---

[1] See Appendix I: The Doctrine of Oppression

[2] Walker, Richard. "A Response: The Statement on Social Justice and the Gospel." A Richer Walk (blog), Accessed 04-19-2022. https://aricherwalk.com/2018/09/25/a-response-the-statement-on-social-justice-and-the-gospel/.

Also: Walker, Richard. "A Response to 'Social Injustice and the Gospel." A Richer Walk (blog), Accessed 08-31-2018. https://aricherwalk.com/2018/08/31/a-response-to-social-injustice-and-the-gospel/.

Also: McDurmon, Joel. "Response to 'The Statement on Social Justice and the Gospel (blog),'" September 7, 2018. Accessed 04-19-2022 https://www.lambsreign.com/mcdurmon/response-to-the-statement-on-social-justice-and-the-gospel.

[3] "Juneteenth — Emancipation Day, 1865 — was supposed to start a new era of black wealth creation. After 12 generations of being subject to slavery's institutionalized theft, 4 million African Americans were now free to earn incomes and degrees, hold property, weather hard times and pass down wealth to the next generation. They would surely scramble up the economic ladder, if not in one generation then in a few.

"Eight generations later, the racial wealth gap is both yawning and growing.

"The typical black family has just 1/10th the wealth of the typical white one.

"In 1863, black Americans owned one-half of 1 percent of the national wealth. Today it's just over 1.5 percent for roughly the same percentage of the overall population.

"The cause of that stagnation has largely been invisible, hidden by the assumption of progress after the end of slavery and the achievements of civil rights. But for every gain black Americans made, people in power created new bundles of discrimination, largely hidden from sight, that thwarted, again and again, the economic promise of emancipation.

"It's a common misperception that the racial wealth gap is an unfortunate legacy of a bygone era. The myth goes like this: Slavery and Jim Crow bred black poverty. In the 20th century, millions of black families moved out of the South chasing high wages in urban industry. But after a few decades the factories closed, inner cities decayed, and a "complex tangle of pathology" emerged in single-parent households and soaring incarceration rates.

"If those were the causes, then the solutions seemed evident: end job, housing and school discrimination, enforce civil rights and sprinkle the market with affirmative action. If those things failed to close the gap, then the problem was one of follow-through. If black people would just move to the suburbs, marry, finish school, train up and play by the rules, the gap would vanish.

"But that is a myth, concealed in what Ta-Nehisi Coates terms "the quiet plunder." In the grand narrative of freedom and civil rights, the disadvantages that persist are invisible precisely because people in power continuously innovated new forms of discrimination."

Calvin Schermerhorn: Why the Racial Wealth Gap Persists More than 150 Years after Emancipation – Twin Cities." Accessed 11-04-2022. https://www.twincities.com/2019/06/27/calvin-schermerhorn-why-the-racial-wealth-gap-persists-more-than-150-years-after-emancipation/.

[4] The availability of free or cheap land to English settlers was made productive by free, permanent labor provided by black slaves. This resulted in the dramatic economic growth and prosperity of America. Anderson, Claud. Black Labor, White Wealth: The Search for Power and Economic Justice. Powernomics Corporation of America, 1994. 123-127.

[5] A premise of this book is that racial oppression did not end with the abolition of American slavery. The objective of slavery: the creation through exploitation of wealth and well-being for whites from which blacks would be largely excluded in perpetuity, by necessity *required* the permanent establishment of systems of racial oppression. Therefore, although slavery was formally abolished, innovations in the methods of injustice continue to evolve in American society, embedded in its institutions and social practices and evident in the statistics that quantify the life experiences of blacks and whites. I will document this fact throughout the book in the endnotes. The oppression that continues to be conscientiously applied in American society is defended by much of the Christian church which has historically acted as an intellectual gatekeeper of the philosophy of oppression and the justifier (often through denial) of the practices that enable the achievement of its original aims.

SECTION ONE: RACE AND RACISM-DEFINITIONS AND CONCEPTS

1. As Christians, Why Discuss Race?

> "Escapism is found in the claim that no racial problems exist. The diagnosis of the race problem as being no problem suppresses doubt, guilt, concern, anxiety, and disagreement. "A common escape from feelings of guilt is to assert that there is no reason to have them" (Allport p.357)" [6]

One of the most effective stratagems for maintaining black people under categories of oppression is the control of the contexts of racial *discussion*. To suggest that racial oppression is a spiritual problem, a theological problem and a sanctification problem in the local church is to invite immediate and apparently organized responses. The statements and actions of unbelievers and theological liberals about race and justice are regularly conflated with the scriptural arguments of actual Christians and these believers are subtly equated with unbelievers without honest analysis of their statements.[7] Secular terms such as social justice, Critical Race Theory, and "wokeness" are redefined and weaponized against blacks without serious attention to their original definitions. Above all, the existence of organized systems of oppression in America are denied or minimized.[8]

The Christian who would make a spiritual issue of racial discrimination, or worse, who would identify the policies within the local church[xvi] which serve to maintain systems of oppression in America will be called, by the less polite, a sower of division, a Marxist, a troublemaker seeking to profit from "victim" status and a theological liberal.

The corruption of theology that results in a version of Christianity that does not see racial prejudice as a malfunction of sanctification also produces a defensive network of lies, evasions and aggressions that discourage the application of the scriptures to the issue. It is the responsibility of the Pastor and the Bible teacher to initiate the personal and national healing that can result from the sound teaching of the Bible.

Why then should Christians discuss race in a biblical context?

1. Christians should carefully consider *race because it influences all aspects of the black believer's life and witness.* This influence demands the daily application of spiritual solutions to achieve and maintain spiritual victory.

For the majority of black people *race* determines where you live, where you go to church, where you work, whether you work at all, whether you will advance on the job, how you are treated by the police, how you are treated in court, what school your children go to, what they are taught or not taught when they get there, what access your community will have to public services, whether you can vote and whether that vote will be counted,[9] how you are portrayed in television, films, and the news: all of these things are directly impacted by race, usually to the detriment of black people.

Your ability as a black person to live an effective Christian life will be influenced by how you process what the *Bible* says that you are compared to what the *Bible teachers* say you are. Pretending that there is no issue or accepting the judgment of society that there is simply something wrong with black people[10] leads to spiritual shipwreck, categories of mental illness, or both. In all the matters of life, the Bible must be brought to bear upon race and what it means to be a black American.

2. Christians should apply the scriptures to the issue of race because *race has been used by the devil to injure* and divide believers.

"Long before the little signs-"White Only" and "Colored" appeared in the public utilities they appeared in the church. This is not a mere figure of speech. In 1795 the John Street Methodist Episcopal Church in New York City, a mixed church including whites and both free and slave Negroes, was divided when the Negroes under a former slave Peter Williams…withdrew to form the African Methodist Episcopal Zion Church.

[xvi] In this book, references to the Church as the Body of Christ will be capitalized, while references to the local church will be rendered in lower case.

> Prior to the split, the Negro members had suffered numerous and increasing embarrassments on account of their race:.as the Negro membership grew in number, education, spirit and independence, the color line was introduced. Negroes were assigned pews in the rear marked B.M. meaning black members, and there were discriminations at communion and at the baptismal font."[11]

The racial idea originates with the devil. It is not a biblical concept. Race is not scientific or even rational.[12] Nonetheless, race is an effective tool for the management of Satan's world. It also efficiently weakens or nullifies the spiritual influence of the believer and the local church. The crippling effects of race upon society have been nurtured and amplified by the Christian churches.[13] It is there where the earliest doctrines of racial superiority were formulated and taught.[xvii] It is in the Christian churches where the segregation of the races, and especially of adolescents, has been modeled and continues even after the secular world has relaxed its position on the subject. It is the Christian church that has vacillated between silence and active support of the resurgences of virulent discrimination occurring throughout American history to this very day. It is the Christian church that built and continues to build logical strongholds to discourage the systematic biblical analysis of its crucial role in racial oppression in America and around the world.

The effect of this centuries old agenda has been the spiritual compromise of believers in every generation. The modifications to Christian doctrine which sustain racism first result in the malfunction of sanctification in the prejudiced individual, nullifying his Christian growth. These modifications then contribute to the damaged self-concept in the objects of racism that limits their own spiritual development.[xviii]

3. Christians should analyze the history of race and theology because Pastors and Bible scholars have had a great deal to say about race that has been overwhelmingly false and detrimental to black people. To the extent that today's teaching contradicts the Bible, what has been taught is not just inaccurate, *it is false teaching*. Examples of such false teaching includes the following:

> ➢ The claim that blacks have been cursed by God.[xix]
> ➢ The notion that *American* slavery was authorized by God in scripture.[xx]
> ➢ That blacks were a numerical minority in biblical times, consisting mostly of slaves and savages.

[xvii] Chapter 6 also Appendix 2
[xviii] Chapter 8
[xix] Appendix 3: The Curse of Noah
[xx] Chapter 16

> ➤ The creation and maintenance of negative racial stereotypes about blacks.[xxi]
> ➤ Cordoning off the scriptural study of race-based discrimination as a non-issue to the Church and a danger to gospel primacy.[xxii]
> ➤ Making black nations white, such as the Egyptians, Phoenicians, and Canaanites.[xxiii]
> ➤ Making God white [Jesus is God].[xxiv]

There has developed in America a version of Christianity that enabled the psychological control of blacks and the assuagement of the consciences of slaveholding society and its heirs. This modified Christianity has sound theology on its surface, the problem is in the way that theology is applied to specific issues for each group. For example, different applications, by race, for self-defense, different applications for responses to state tyranny, different applications for social justice, different applications for slavery and of course, the prohibition of systematic biblical preaching against white supremacy and racial oppression.

At least within black churches, this version of Christianity must be understood and replaced with genuine Christian doctrine. [xxv] This will not change the attitudes of whites, but the Second Principle of Nationbuilding[xxvi] indicates that the most important decisions in the life of a believer is his own decisions and not those of others. God can bless and deliver with or without the removal of prejudiced attitudes in people or of oppressive structures in society itself. The people of Israel are a notable example.

4. Christians must identify a biblical antidote to current racial thinking among black people because you cannot grow to your spiritual potential *until your mind is changed* from that of a disadvantaged and inferior minority to the mind of Christ. These two minds cannot coexist, but this is precisely what many people are grappling with spiritually. Romans 12.1-4 teaches that one must be in his "right mind" to advance spiritually and to render to God the appropriate spiritual service. Black Americans have historically been offered a self-concept which is suitable for a planned, limited participation in American life. This self-

---

[xxi] Appendix 2: Theologians on the Issue of Race
[xxii] Chapter 4
[xxiii] Chapter 18
[xxiv] Chapter 18
[xxv] Chapter 15
[xxvi] Chapter 17

concept is entirely incompatible with effective spiritual discipleship. Spiritual growth requires a biblical self-concept.

5. Christians must disinfect modern theology from its racist commitments because we have yet *to see what a generation of youth could accomplish* with an accurate perception of their role in history and in the story of redemption.

   Black young people are usually thoroughly demoralized after they have been exposed to a definition of blackness received from the media, the public school system, and the church.[14] This lack of options leads to a bleak reality: (1.) Stop searching for an identity as black men and women and accept the prefabricated, stereotype consciousness designed for them by society (There are Bible teachers that tell them that they are no longer black people in Christ) and (2.) "Live" a life unconsciously responding to a deep frustration, anger, and helplessness that they cannot comprehend. This anger produces suicides, homicides (black on black), chemical dependency and mental illness all because they cannot reconcile what they ought to be and what the world (and a part of the Church) tells them that they are.[15]

   6. Christians must recognize *a new vocabulary of race* because although God is the author of human diversity, race is a satanically inspired, man-made concept.[xxvii]

The discussion of race has been historically defined as an interaction between blacks and whites. The discussion of race that is emphasized in this book is a discussion among blacks themselves. We will show that the systematic application of accurate bible instruction to the souls of black folk is the only necessary antecedent to defeat oppression, if one believes that it is *God* who delivers the oppressed.

> Psalm 72:1–4 (KJV 1900)
> 1 Give the king thy judgments, O God, And thy righteousness unto
> the king's son. 2 He shall judge thy people with righteousness, And
> thy poor with judgment. 3 The mountains shall bring peace to the
> people, And the little hills, by righteousness. 4 He shall judge the
> poor of the people, He shall save the children of the needy, And shall break
> in pieces the oppressor.

[xxvii] Chapter 2

[6] Kelsey, George D. Racism, and the Christian Understanding of Man. Scribner, 1965. 52.

[7] "Purporting to address an alleged shift in evangelical circles away from the biblical gospel towards a false social gospel, the new Statement on Social Justice and the Gospel is driven by people I would like to believe are well-meaning but frankly not at all "getting" what those whom it primarily addresses are saying. That is at best. At worst, it represents a toxic agenda to discredit and undermine godly men and women crying out for biblical social justice, national and ecclesiastical repentance, and meaningful reconciliation. I certainly hope that this statement will not become a litmus test for orthodoxy, as if those who don't sign it should be written off as "not sound". If so the people implicated would include (barring the unlikely event one of them were to sign): Danny Akin, Thabiti Anyabwile, Matt Chandler, H. B. Charles, Charlie Dates, Ligon Duncan, Mika Edmondson, Carl and Karen Ellis, Steve Gaines, Philip and Jasmine Holmes, Eric Mason, Albert Mohler, Russell Moore, Trillia Newbell, Preston and Jackie Hill Perry, John Piper, David Platt, Kevin Smith, Robert Smith, Walter Strickland, Ralph Douglas West, and so on and so forth. These are names of people off the top of my head listed alphabetically, all of whom have spoken out on abiding racial sin in America and its churches this year and many previous years. In their number are the very people the statement erroneously has in view as in some way abandoning the gospel for a social gospel. An examination of their ministries, their sermons, writings, music, and so forth should decisively demonstrate their Christo-centric, gospel ministries and serve as the context within which, the backdrop against which, the lens through which their (in my estimation very helpful and necessary) contributions should be understood."

SBC Voices. "Why I Cannot and Will Not Sign the 'Social Justice and the Gospel Statement' (by Ryan Burton King)," September 5, 2018. https://sbcvoices.com/why-i-cannot-and-will-not-sign-the-social-justice-and-the-gospel-statement-by-ryan-burton-king/.

[8] The "Statement on Social Justice and the Gospel" demonstrates how the discussion of social justice is controlled by the conservative evangelical community. The responses take issue with the Statement and are well worth examining.

"The Statement on Social Justice & the Gospel | For The Sake of Christ & His Church." Accessed 01-17-2023. https://statementonsocialjustice.com.

Responses to the Statement:

Joel McDurmon. "Response To The Statement on Social Justice and the Gospel" September 7. 2018 (blog). Accessed 01-17-2023. https://www.lambsreign.com/mcdurmon/response-to-the-statement-on-social-justice-and-the-gospel

SBC Voices. "Why I Cannot and Will Not Sign the 'Social Justice and the Gospel Statement' (by Ryan Burton King)," September 5, 2018. https://sbcvoices.com/why-i-cannot-and-will-not-sign-the-social-justice-and-the-gospel-statement-by-ryan-burton-king/. Accessed 04-14-2023.

Richard Walker. "A Response: The Statement on Social Justice and the Gospel." A Richer Walk (blog). Accessed 04-19-2022. https://aricherwalk.com/2018/09/25/a-response-the-statement-on-social-justice-and-the-gospel/.

Carman, Molly. "How Should Christians Think About 'Wokeness'?" Accessed April 14, 2023. http://www.frcblog.com/2021/07/how-should-christians-think-about-wokeness.

Strachan, Owen. Critical Race Theory, Wokeness and Discernment Part 1. 2021 Truth in Love Conference 2 Corinthians 10.3-6. January 22, 2021. Sermon Audio. Accessed 03-25-2023.

The following is a very good summary on the background and definition of the term "social justice" and comparison with biblical concepts of justice.\.

Carter, Joe. "The FAQs: What Christians Should Know About Social Justice." The Gospel Coalition, August 17, 2018. https://www.thegospelcoalition.org/article/faqs-christians-know-social-justice/.

[9] Baker, Mike. "Rejected Mail Ballots Are Showing Racial Disparities." The New York Times, February 3, 2022, sec. U.S. Accessed 03-25-2023. https://www.nytimes.com/2022/02/02/us/mail-voting-black-latino.html.

United States Commission on Civil Rights. "Voting Irregularities in Florida During the 2000 Presidential Election, Executive Summary." Accessed 03-25-2023. https://www.usccr.gov/files/pubs/vote2000/report/exesum.htm.

Palast, Greg. "1 Million Black Votes Didn't Count in the 2000 Presidential Election / It's Not Too Hard to Get Your Vote Lost -- If Some Politicians Want It to Be Lost." SFGATE, June 20, 2004. https://www.sfgate.com/opinion/article/1-million-black-votes-didn-t-count-in-the-2000-2747895.php.

[10] White Southern Evangelicals Are Leaving the Church Daniel K. Williams August 2, 2022. Accessed 08-10-2022. https://www.christianitytoday.com/ct/2022/august-web-only/church-attendance-sbc-southern-evangelicals-now-lapsed.html

Also: It's not just Trump. Many whites view people of color as less American. Washington Post July 16, 2019, Michael Tesler. Accessed 08-10-2022. https://www.washingtonpost.com/politics/2019/07/16/its-not-just-trump-many-whites-view-people-color-less-american/

[11] Bowen, Trevor. Black Odyssey, New York: Scribner, 1948. 88. Cited in Haselden, Kyle. The Racial Problem in Christian Perspective. New York: Harper Bros, 1959. 29-30

[12] Ham, Ken, et.al. One Blood, the Biblical Answer to Racism. Green Forest: Master, 1999. 51-85

[13] Jones, Robert P. White Too Long: The Legacy of White Supremacy in American Christianity. New York: Simon and Shuster, 2020.

[14] See the online video "A Girl Like Me" http://www.youtube.com/watch?v=YWyI77Yh1Gg]

[15] Chapter 17: The Second Nationbuilding Principle

A large percentage of self-destructive and socially harmful behavior by blacks is a consequence of historically formed reactions to oppression. The consistent denial by prominent white Christian leaders of the existence of systematic racial oppression enables the conclusion that these actions must come from some deficiency that is unique to black people, rather than the effects of intergenerational spiritual, social, economic, and political violence against them.

Also: Wilson, Amos N. Black-on-Black Violence: The Psychodynamics of Black Self-Annihilation in Service of White Domination. Third edition. Brooklyn, New York: Afrikan World InfoSystems, 2020. 1-31.

Also: Kardiner A., Ovesey L., The Mark of Oppression. Cleveland: Meridian,1961. 302-6.

Also: Grier W.H., Cobbs P.M., Black Rage. New York: Basic, 1968. 1-17.

And: Fanon, Frantz. The Wretched of the Earth: Translated from the French by Richard Philcox; Introductions by Jean-Paul Sartre and Homi K. Bhabha. New York: Grove Press, 2004.

2. Definitions Of Terms

Black people have long conceded the right to formally define things to others. Even the designation of "blackness:" of who is black and who is not, we have not claimed as our own. Defining things is an act of self-determination and of dominion. Adam named things in his role as God's designated earth ruler [Genesis 1.28; 2.19-20]. Defining things is a critical part of the construction of one's worldview; and although worldview is not the same as reality, it is our point of contact with it. Optimally, we want our worldview to reflect the biblical reality, but it has never occurred to most of us that we are free to accept or reject many definitions, especially sociological definitions and those purported to be a consequence of cultural anthropology or historical analysis.

Race

Race is the arbitrary categorization of people in order to divide, conquer and maintain social and financial control over vast sections of humanity.[16]

Arbitrary in that racial distinctions are not scientifically or even rationally based. Racial distinctions are not based upon biochemical or genetic realities.

> Example: [Irrationality] Based upon the common definition of blackness of the last 4 centuries: that blackness is the possession of any degree of black ancestry, Acts 17:26 would indicate that all humanity must be black, since blacks originated in Adam.

21

Arbitrary in that racial distinctions are assigned differently depending upon the demands of the historical period and what ends are sought.

> Example: [Inconsistency] Persons considered blacks in Alabama in 1950 A.D. are considered whites in Egypt in 1950 B.C.[17]

> Example: [Inconsistency] Definitions of "blackness" in the U.S. Census periodically change.[18]

> Example: [Inconsistency] The definition of "whiteness" has changed throughout history. According to Benjamin Franklin, much of the population of Europe was *not* considered "white" by colonial America.[19]

Whiteness

Whiteness as a concept has come to mean a store of value[20] that signifies the highest degree of aesthetic, intellectual, social, and spiritual potential, and achievement.[xxviii]

Whiteness is an artificial designation that, although related to appearance (phenotype)[xxix], does not primarily signify it, as no people on earth are actually white, neither has such a designation ["white"] always existed.[21] Whiteness, like every other racial designation, is unrelated to reality. It can be bestowed or withdrawn but it cannot be truly owned.

Whiteness has monetary value.[22] It is also the symbol of the greatest human authority and privilege. Every other racial designation is to some degree less valuable than whiteness.

Blackness

Blackness is an artificial designation that, although related to appearance (phenotype), does not primarily signify it. Blackness is an identity assigned to

---

[xxviii] P. 191-192
[xxix] phenotype /ˈfiːnə(ʊ)tʌɪp/
noun Biology the observable characteristics of an individual resulting from the interaction of its genotype with the environment.

certain[xxx] sons of Ham signifying an inherent and an enforced[xxxi] limitation upon their human potential and achievement. *We choose to repurpose this term to represent both an idea and a group of people, the descendants of Ham, as the inventors of civilization,[23] the great communicators of mankind and the most pervasive cultural influence upon the earth.*

Prejudice

Prejudice is the individual human decision to prefer or not prefer someone or something.

This decision may be based on facts or opinions, experience, or the influence of others. The decision to prefer or not to prefer may be rational or irrational, beneficial, or self-destructive.

Racial prejudice is preference based upon one's beliefs about a man-made category of people.

Prejudice is internal; it is based upon a system of beliefs, attitudes, thoughts, and motivations, but not actions. Prejudice is a mental attitude.

Discrimination

Discrimination is the externalization of prejudice. It is the outworking in actions of the attitudes of the prejudiced individual.

Discrimination can be practiced by individuals or groups.

Discrimination can be organized or disorganized.

Racial discrimination manifests itself in any and all human activities, social, political, economic and spiritual, as the actions of one individual or group of individuals to deny to one group what they would not deny to others and to attach to one group what they would not attach to others.

[xxx] That only certain sons of Ham receive the designation of black is another example of the arbitrary nature of the concept of race.

[xxxi] "Enforced" by structural safeguards built into every institution. See "Racism."

Racism

Racism is the science of discrimination. Racism is the calculated introduction of discrimination into the institutions of society. Racism is a conspiracy to scientifically marginalize or destroy a specific racial group by the manipulation of the organs of society such as the family, government (including legislation, law enforcement and the courts), academia, the media, and the church.

Therefore racism, by this definition, although implemented by individuals, is *always* structural. Racism is cultural warfare, or the extension of conventional warfare to the cultural sphere.

White Supremacy

White Supremacy pertains to the *maintenance* of whiteness as the supreme store of personal value. As a store of value, whiteness cannot be allowed to depreciate relative to other racial categories. Since racial designations have no basis in reality, the relative value of whiteness and all its privileges must be sustained artificially.

White Supremacy, therefore, is the commitment to the pre-eminence of whiteness as well as a commitment to the totality of strategies (psychological, legal, political, theological, and military) deployed to maintain it.

Diversity

Diversity is the recognition of the physical differences among mankind, the linguistic differences within mankind, the ethnic or cultural distinctions that result from the expansion of mankind upon the earth, and the national divisions which have resulted from these cultural realities.

God created human diversity by placing its genetic potential within Adam. Diversity is based upon distinctions created by God, who is the Author of human diversity.

Acts 17:26 (KJV 1900)

[26] And hath made of one blood all nations of men for to dwell on all the face of the earth, and hath determined the times before appointed, and the bounds of their habitation;

Social Justice

Social Justice is the attainment of honest and equitable relations between men and between men and institutions, based upon the dictates of human consciences informed by divine revelation (general and special).

Social Justice as an ideal is powerfully advanced in society by the Church when saved people begin living [speaking and acting] like saved people in all their relationships with individuals and institutions. Christian holiness is the biblically mandatory lifestyle that models before unbelieving society the behaviors that characterize human relations under Social Justice.[24]

---

[16] "Records indicate that the word race was selected because the various European slave trading nations were in a contest, competing to profit from the mineral and human wealth of Africa. The prize for winning the race was the power to develop Western civilization, using the wealth extracted out of Africa. Black people were non-competitors in the race. They were the prizes, so they could neither play nor win. All the competing slave trading nations, religions and ethnic groups benefited and were advantaged by black slavery."

Anderson, Dr Claud. PowerNomics: The National Plan to Empower Black America. 1st edition. Bethesda, MD: PowerNomics Corp of Amer, 2001. 3

[17] "What we cannot understand however, is how it has been possible to make a white race of Kemit: Hamite, black, ebony, etc. (even in Egyptian). Obviously, according to the needs of the cause, Ham is cursed, blackened and made into the ancestor of the Negroes.

"On the other hand, he is whitened whenever one seeks the origin of civilization, because there he is inhabiting the first civilized country in the world."

Cook, Mercer (Ed). The African Origin of Civilization: Myth or Reality by Cheikh Anta Diop. Chicago: Lawrence Hill and Co, 1974. 9. Also, Chapter 3: Modern Falsification of History.

[18] "The census is conducted every decade and establishes the official population count of the country. Efforts to create a "multicultural category" in the 2000 census will most likely dilute and distort downward the number of Blacks in America. Dilution of population numbers assures that Blacks will lose status as the numerical majority minority. Government efforts to change racial definitions will

retain the White population majority [monopoly] and inflate the numbers of Hispanics in the population."

Anderson, Claud Dr. PowerNomics. 16.

"Poverty in the United States 2002 Current Population Reports: Consumer Income
Issued September 2003 P60-222

"New Racial Groups
The estimates in this report are based on the Current Population Survey (CPS) 2001, 2002, and 2003 Annual Social and Economic Supplement (MEC) and provide information for calendar years 2000, 2001, and 2002, respectively. For the first time in 2003, CPS respondents were asked to identify themselves in one or more racial groups;5 previously they had to choose one. This change complicates year-to-year
comparisons. We do not know how people who reported more than one race in 2002 previously reported their race. Therefore, there is no single way to compare changes to poverty by race. Table 1 compares last year's single-race figures with two different figures this year: one comparison is based on those who reported one race alone and the other is based on those who reported either that race only or that race and at least one other race. For example, this year's poverty report will compare the 2001 poverty figures for blacks with 2002 poverty figures for those who reported themselves as:

1. black alone, did not report any other race, and
2. black alone or in combination with some other
race(s).

The Census Bureau will provide year-to-year comparisons for each racial group, with the exception of American Indians and Alaska Natives, and Native Hawaiians and Other Pacific Islanders, who will not be examined separately (because the sample was not sufficiently large) 0MB establishes the official guidelines for the collection and classification of data for race (including the option for respondents to mark more than race) and Hispanic origin. Race and Hispanic origin are treated as separate and distinct concepts in accordance with OMB's guidelines. For further information, see

www.whitehouse.gov/omb/ombdirl5.html. Poverty in the United States 2002 Current Population Reports: Consumer Income. Issued September 2003 P60-222."

[19] Benjamin Franklin: Observations Concerning the Increasing of Mankind, Peopling of Countries [1775]

"And since Detachments of English from Britain sent to America, will have their Places at Home so soon supply'd and increase so largely here; why should the Palatine Boors [Germans] be suffered to swarm into our Settlements, and by herding together establish their Language and Manners to the Exclusion of ours? Why should Pennsylvania, founded by the English, become a Colony of Aliens, who will shortly be so numerous as to Germanize us instead of our Anglifying them, and will never adopt our Language or Customs, any more than they can acquire our Complexion.

"Which leads me to add one Remark: That the Number of purely white People in the World is proportionally very small. All Africa is black or tawny. Asia chiefly tawny. America (exclusive of the new Comers) wholly so. And in Europe, the Spaniards, Italians, French, Russians and Swedes, are generally of what we call a swarthy Complexion; as are the Germans also, the Saxons only excepted, who with the English, make the principal Body of White People on the Face of the Earth. I could wish their Numbers were increased. And while we are, as I may call it, Scouring our Planet, by clearing America of Woods, and so making this Side of our Globe reflect a brighter Light to the Eyes of Inhabitants in mars or Venus, why should we in the Sight of Superior Beings, darken its People? why increase the Sons of Africa, by Planting them in America, where we have so fair an Opportunity, by excluding all blacks and Tawneys, of increasing the lovely White and Red? But perhaps I am partial to the complexion of my Country, for such Kind of Partiality is natural to Mankind." [emphasis added]

Strom, Adam. "Benjamin Franklin and German Immigrants in Colonial America." *Re-Imagining Migration* (blog), October 3, 2019. https://reimaginingmigration.org/benjamin-franklin-and-german-immigrants-in-colonial-america/.

Also cited in: "Founders Online: Observations Concerning the Increase of Mankind, 1751." University of Virginia Press. Accessed 02-05-2023. http://founders.archives.gov/documents/Franklin/01-04-02-0080.

[20] What Is a Store Of Value? A store of value is an asset, commodity, or currency that maintains its value without depreciating. Investopedia. "What Is a Store Of Value?" Accessed 07-31-2022. https://www.investopedia.com/terms/s/storeofvalue.asp.

[21] The term "white" as a racial designation was not used in the Americas until the 1680's, and the term "Caucasian" was not coined by Blumenbach until 1795.

Time. "Facing America's History of Racism Requires Facing the Origins of 'Race' as a Concept." Accessed 02-05-2023. https://time.com/5865530/history-race-concept/.

Also: Bishop Alfred G. Dunston, "The Black Man in the Old Testament and its world" Africa World Press Trenton, 1992 pg. 6

Also: Bernal, Martin. *Black Athena: The Afroasiatic Roots of Classical Civilization*. Volume 1 First Edition. New Brunswick, N.J: Rutgers University Press, 1987. 219.

[22] Anderson, Dr. Claud. PowerNomics. Chapter 1.

Also: Shambaugh, Kriston McIntosh, Emily Moss, Ryan Nunn, and Jay. "Examining the Black-White Wealth Gap." *Brookings* (blog), February 27, 2020. https://www.brookings.edu/blog/up-front/2020/02/27/examining-the-black-white-wealth-gap/.

Also: CitiGPS. "Closing the Racial Inequality Gaps," September 22, 2020. https://www.citivelocity.com/citigps/closing-the-racial-inequality-gaps/.

[23] Bunsen, Philosophy of Ancient History 52. Cited in Houston, Drusilla D. Wonderful Ethiopians of the Ancient Cushite Empire, Book 1. Baltimore, Md.: Black Classic Press, 1985. 20.

Diop, Cheikh Anta. Civilization or Barbarism: An Authentic Anthropology. Translated by Yaa-Lengi Meema Ngemi. 1st Edition. Brooklyn, N.Y: Chicago Review Press, 1991. xx.

Cheikh Anta Diop, The African Origin of Civilization, Myth or Reality. Lawrence Hill Books 1974. 7, 9, 43.

Fausset's Bible Dictionary, Electronic Database Copyright (c)1998 by Biblesoft. Art. *Egypt*, also *Ham*.

Williams, Bruce. The Lost Pharaohs of Nubia in Van Sertima, Ivan, Editor, Egypt Revisited. Transaction, New Brunswick, 1989. 90.

[24] "The biblical conception of justice is primarily captured in two Hebrew words—mishpat and tzadeqah. As Tim Keller explains,

"The Hebrew word for "justice," mishpat, occurs in its various forms more than 200 times in the Hebrew Old Testament. Its most basic meaning is to treat people equitably. It means acquitting or punishing every person on the merits of the case, regardless of race or social status. Anyone who does the same wrong should be given the same penalty.

"But mishpat means more than just the punishment of wrongdoing. It also means giving people their rights. Deuteronomy 18 directs that the priests of the tabernacle should be supported by a certain percentage of the people's income. This support is described as "the priests' mishpat," which means their due or their right. Mishpat, then, is giving people what they are due, whether punishment or protection or care.

"But to understand the biblical idea of justice, Keller says, we must also consider tzadeqah:

"We get more insight when we consider a second Hebrew word that can be translated as "being just," though it usually translated as "being righteous." The word is tzadeqah, and it refers to a life of right relationships.

"When most modern people see the word "righteousness" in the Bible, they tend to think of it in terms of private morality, such as sexual chastity or diligence in prayer and Bible study. But in the Bible, tzadeqah refers to day-to-day living in which a person conducts all relationships in family and society with fairness, generosity and equity. It is not surprising, then, to discover that tzadeqah and mishpat are brought together scores of times in the Bible.

"These two words roughly correspond to what some have called "primary" and "rectifying justice." Rectifying justice is mishpat. It means punishing wrongdoers and caring for the victims of unjust treatment. Primary justice, or tzadeqah, is behavior that, if it was prevalent in the world, would render rectifying justice unnecessary, because everyone would be living in right relationship to everyone else. Therefore, though tzadeqah is primarily about being in a right relationship with God, the righteous life that results is profoundly social…"

"How does social justice relate to biblical justice?

"As Keller says, when the two Hebrew words tzadeqah and mishpat are tied together—as they are more than three dozen times—the English expression that best conveys the meaning is "social justice." Social justice, then, would be not only a biblical concept, but also a subset of biblical justice.

"Claiming that we need only "biblical justice" and not "social justice" is a category error (i.e., a semantic or ontological error in which things belonging to a particular category are presented as if they belong to a different category). Biblical justice includes all forms of God-ordained justice, including the rectifying justice that belongs to the government (what we'd call public or legal justice) as well as justice between individuals (what could be called inter-individual justice) and justice involving organizations and groups (what we'd call social justice)."

Carter, Joe. "The FAQs: What Christians Should Know About Social Justice." The Gospel Coalition, August 17, 2018. https://www.thegospelcoalition.org/article/faqs-christians-know-social-justice/. Accessed 04-14-2023.

3. The Bible On Race

"Scientists have found that if one were to take any two people from anywhere in the world, the basic genetic differences between these two people would typically be around 0.2 percent-even if they came from the same people group. But, these so-called "racial" characteristics that many think are major differences (skin color, eye shape etc.) account for only 6 percent of this 0.2 percent variation, which amounts to a mere 0.012 percent difference genetically…Overall, there is more variation within any group than there is between one group and another.[25]"

Race is not a scientific concept. Neither is it a biblical concept. These facts do not prevent it from being used by Satan, nor does it prevent God from addressing its effects upon mankind. God did not create murder or adultery, yet He addresses the effects of these evils upon humanity. Race as a concept is irrational, but it is an effective means of crippling the spiritual development of both blacks and whites. To the extent that the Bible is used as an instrument for the justification for racial oppression, we are dealing with an issue of false teaching or false doctrine. As such it is the obligation of the conscientious Bible teacher to address it, and especially those who teach black people.

God created the diversity of mankind, [Acts 17.26] but He did not create the concept of race. God has established categories that he uses to describe the organization of humanity.

Basic Facts of the Divine Organization of Humanity

All peoples descended from one man, ADAM.[xxxii]

> Acts 17:26 (KJV 1900)
> [26] And hath made of <u>one blood</u> all nations of men for to dwell on all the face
> of the earth, and hath determined the times before appointed, and the
> bounds of their habitation;

All races (by which we mean all varieties of physical diversity) existed in Adam
and in Eve. There were no prior or subsequent creations of other human
races (polygenesis). The existence of variation in physical appearance is not
difficult to explain if Adam and Eve were multiracial. It is only impossible to
rationalize the genetic implications of race if Adam and Eve were of one
single pure race.[26.]

The people immediately after the flood had one language [Genesis 11.1].
There is no biblical evidence of the linguistic or the physical characteristics of
humanity before the flood, although Ken Ham speculates that genetics would
support the existence of a population before the Flood that was largely mid-
brown.[27]

God divided the people after the flood due to their disobedience to the divine
command to disperse throughout the world. He did not do so to implement
racial segregation [Genesis 11.1-9]. God halted the spiritual rebellion through
the confusion of languages. The separation of the people into distinct families,
clans and ultimately, nations, ensured that uncoerced human conscience and
morality would have the opportunity to exist in sovereign nations, rather than
the world order of spiritual wickedness inaugurated at Babel. Satan will
eventually re-establish an age of worldwide demonic despotism under his
protégé the Antichrist [Revelation 13].[28]

[xxxii] Genesis 2.21-22 c.f. 3.20

Divine Categories of Social Organization

> Genesis 10:1 (KJV 1900)
> [1] Now these *are* the generations of the sons of Noah, Shem, Ham, and Japheth: and unto them were sons born after the flood. [5] By these were the isles of the Gentiles divided in their <u>lands</u>; every one after his <u>tongue</u>, after their <u>families</u>, in their <u>nations</u>.
>
> Genesis 10:20 (KJV 1900)
> [20] These *are* the sons of Ham, after their families, after their tongues, in their countries (lands), *and* in their nations.

Families:

God established the concept of family by His sanction of the reproductive union of Adam and Eve.[xxxiii] The family is a divine institution, created, sanctified, and sustained by God. Family is based upon the institution of Marriage, also established by God [Genesis 2.20-25].

Languages:

God also instituted human language in Eden[xxxiv] and then expanded the concept to separate language groups at Babel [Genesis 11.6-9]. The division of language occurred along family lines [Genesis 10.1, 5].

Lands:

The division of languages resulted in the intended geographic dispersion of humanity, according to their family/language groups [Genesis 11.9]. The concentration of the human population at Babel is remedied and the world is re-populated. This would, in time, enable the establishment of sovereign nations.

Nations:

In Acts 17.26 and other places in the New Testament, the word "nation" is translated from the Greek word "ethnos"[29] from which we get our concept of

---

[xxxiii] Genesis 1.27-28; 4.1
[xxxiv] Genesis 2:20 (names) Genesis 11.1

ethnicity. A nation[30] is people or peoples in a specific geography which share a common identity, history, and political structure. Nations are divine institutions established and sustained by God [Romans 13:1-6].

These are the categories of human organization devised and ordained by God. Race is not among them.

Language and Ethnicity

Ethnicity or nationality are words used to describe a people that share a common ancestry, language, geography, and institutions over a long period of time. Ethnicity is not static. Constant interaction between people groups through intermarriage, conquest, and migration impacts ethnic identity.

Although ethnicity and language are undoubtedly related, this relationship can be misused. Anthropologists in the distant future performing an archaeological analysis of present-day North Philadelphia should not conclude that it was a white community because the people who lived there spoke English, but it is falsely proclaimed that Phoenicia was non-black because they spoke a "Semitic" language.

Race (phenotype) and language cannot be infallibly equated. In some cases, language is used to obscure the ethnic identity of a people. The Phoenicians are an example of this. Phoenicia was a region along the Mediterranean which included city states such as Arvad[xxxv] [Syria], Berytus [Beirut], Sidon[xxxvi] and Tyre[xxxvii] [Lebanon] The Phoenicians were a mixed race consisting of both black [Hamitic] and other non-black ethnic elements, but because of their significant contributions to civilization, particularly western European civilization, they have been whitened by referring to them in terms of the language which they spoke, rather than acknowledging their lineage from Ham and Canaan.[31] Thus, the Phoenicians are called Semitic when they were Hamitic.

> "For example, the Phoenicians are "Semitic" by language, but they are by no means-either by Biblical genealogy (Genesis 10.15) or by historical cultural studies-to be ethnologically classified as Semites. The Phoenicians are Hamites, regardless of how they spoke. Language, as one constituent of culture, easily changes; ethnicity and

---

[xxxv] Genesis 10.18
[xxxvi] Genesis 10.15
[xxxvii] Matthew 15.21-22 [Greek G5478 Canaan]

heritage remains, in whatever discernible degree." [32]

The example of the Canaanites/Phoenicians is an example of one part of the multifaceted strategy to write blacks out of history. That strategy was to "whiten" any black culture which made any significant cultural contribution, and to emphasize those black cultures which were in any way degenerate or primitive. This strategy was kicked into high gear whenever that people could be shown to have contributed to European development.

Divine Judgment and Race

God does not administer judgment based upon color or race. His judgment touches.

- ➤ Individuals: [Genesis 38.7-10]
- ➤ Families: [Joshua 7:24-25]
- ➤ Nations: [Isaiah 18-20; 15-16; 47]
- ➤ Humanity as a species: [Genesis 3; 6:12-13]

Any *nation* under judgment can reverse that judgment by the repentance of a significant number of citizens within that nation. The book of Jonah illustrates how the city of Nineveh escaped the judgment of God through their response to the preaching of Jonah [Jonah 3].

Concerning divine judgment and the *family*, God does not curse children for the sins of their parents. God holds each *individual* responsible for his own sin.[xxxviii] Generational curses [Exodus 20.5] occur because the sins of the parents tend to be imitated and embraced by the children.[xxxix] Despite the circumstances of any family or nation, individuals are free to choose the solution found in the cross of Christ, as it is revealed in that generation, where every sin was judged [2 Corinthians 5:20-21]. Repentance realigns individuals, families, communities, and nations to God, bringing spiritual dynamics to bear on issues such as oppression. Oppression cannot be reversed from within the devil's system because oppression is a satanic initiative.

By necessity, there is an overlap between one of the divinely sanctioned categories of people and an ethnic group. For example, if God judges a nation, it is unavoidable that ethnic groups are impacted as well. If Egypt is

---

[xxxviii] Ezekiel 18; Deuteronomy 5:9-10
[xxxix] Exodus 20.5; Matthew 23.29-33

judged, both blacks and Semites would be affected. Similarly, if Babylon is judged by God, then Semites and the Hamitic [black] Chaldeans will be punished. God does not judge according to man-made categories and distinctions such as race. *Racial curses are the creation of those who manage the world through the maintenance of racial hierarchies.*[xl]

The examination of the plight of blacks in America and worldwide must be related to divine categories, specifically, their experiences as individuals, families, and as people who once inhabited sovereign nations. God deals with peoples based upon their own attitude and actions towards His law. Where people disregard this law long enough, God judges individuals, families, and nations based upon no other criteria than His own righteous judgment.

Nations are judged by ever increasing cycles of calamity culminating in military defeat [Leviticus 26]. Military defeat in the past was often accompanied by the uprooting and relocation of conquered people. The history of Africa and Africans is punctuated by migrations. These migrations marked significant changes in the history of Africa.

> "Elsewhere I have posed the most perplexing question: If the Blacks were among the very first builders of civilization and their land the birthplace of civilization, what has happened to them that has left them since then, at the bottom of world society, precisely what has happened? The Caucasian answer is simple and well known: The Blacks have always been at the bottom. This answer is clear even in the histories and other historical material which Whites so busily prepare for Blacks. Almost all the answers will be found in the study of the causes of the migrations and the tragic results stemming directly from those seemingly endless movements of fragmented peoples.

> "How was the art of writing lost by one of the first peoples to invent it? Study the migrations. How and why did a once great people, with a common origin, splinter off into countless little independent societies and chiefdoms from which 2000 different languages and dialects developed? Study the migrations. What caused the brother-against-brother internecine wars, hatreds, slavery and mutual suspicion among the Black societies? Again, study the migrations."[33]

Migrations are often (although not always) related to divine judgment, as in the case of Israel which because of divine judgment was deported first to Assyria (721 BC.), then to Babylon (586 BC.), and later throughout the world (70 AD.). These three migrations followed divine cycles of judgment terminating with military defeat and expulsion from the land of Israel. The

---

[xl] Appendix 3: The Curse of Noah

Bible predicts military disaster and diaspora (scattering) as one of the fates to befall the nation that forsakes God's law.[xli] For this reason, many lands of antiquity do not possess their original populations. There will yet be a great migration of Israel back to the Middle East, in that instance for ultimate [but not immediate] blessing. The rejection by Hamitic kingdoms of divine truth began in Babylon [Chaldea] [34] [xlii] and Ethiopia [Isaiah 18, 20] and continued in Egypt[xliii] and Phoenicia [Ezekiel 28]. This rebellion ultimately resulted in the military defeat and dispersion (migration) of portions of these peoples. The movements of peoples and the reasons for those migrations are remembered by God even if they're forgotten or suppressed by men. God does not forget His judicial acts of the past, however long ago.

Are the Jews a Race?

Israel is an Ethnic Group that Received an Unconditional Covenant

Genesis 17:1–8 (KJV 1900)

[1] And when Abram was ninety years old and nine, the Lord appeared to Abram, and said unto him, I *am* the Almighty God; walk before me, and be thou perfect. [2] And I will make my covenant between me and thee, and will multiply thee exceedingly. [3] And Abram fell on his face: and God talked with him, saying, [4] As for me, behold, my covenant *is* with thee, and thou shalt be a father of many nations. [5] Neither shall thy name any more be called Abram, but thy name shall be Abraham; for a father of many nations have I made thee. [6] And I will make thee exceeding fruitful, and I will make nations of thee, and kings shall come out of thee. [7] And I will establish my covenant between me and thee <u>and thy seed after thee</u> in their generations <u>for an everlasting covenant</u>, to be a God unto thee, and to thy seed after thee. [8] And I will give unto thee, and to thy seed after thee, <u>the land</u> wherein thou art a stranger, all the land of Canaan, for an everlasting possession; and I will be their God.

Genesis 17:19–22 (KJV 1900)

[19] And God said, Sarah thy wife shall bear thee a son indeed; and thou shalt call his name Isaac: and I will establish my covenant with him for an everlasting covenant, *and* with his seed after him. [20] And as for Ishmael, I have heard thee: Behold, I have blessed him, and will make him fruitful, and

---

[xli] Leviticus 26:23-33; Isaiah 20.1-4
[xlii] Isaiah 13.19 c.f. Genesis 10.6-12
[xliii] Isaiah 19, 20; Ezekiel 30:13-19

will multiply him exceedingly; twelve princes shall he beget, and I will make him a great nation. 21 But my covenant will I establish with Isaac, which Sarah shall bear unto thee at this set time in the next year. 22 And he left off talking with him, and God went up from Abraham.

God's covenant with Abraham was to be passed on to his physical seed Isaac. Isaac was born via a miracle as his father and mother were incapable of reproduction due to advanced age. So there coexists a *spiritual* promise intertwined with the miraculous creation of an *ethnic group*. This fact accounts for a great deal of the confusion regarding the identity of Israel.

Isaac also had a miracle son [Genesis 25.21] named Jacob, who was a twin. Jacob believed the divine promise [the Abrahamic Covenant] made to his father and grandfather, and his name was changed to Israel [Genesis 32.24-30]. Jacob was the father of the twelve patriarchs of Israel.

Therefore, Israel as a people were created by God through a miracle. This people will have an ethnic identity:[xliv] a common ancestry, language, religion, government, and land. Although there is no such thing as a pure ethnic group,[35] Israel, as a people is distinct because of the miracle of its genetic origin and because of the special covenant made with its founder Abraham.

Israel is a Nation, a Political Entity

> Exodus 19:3–6 (KJV 1900)
> 3 And Moses went up unto God, and the Lord called unto him out of the mountain, saying, Thus shalt thou say to the house of Jacob, and tell the children of Israel; 4 Ye have seen what I did unto the Egyptians, and *how* I bare you on eagles' wings, and brought you unto myself. 5 Now therefore, if ye will obey my voice indeed, and keep my covenant, then ye shall be a peculiar treasure unto me above all people: for all the earth *is* mine: 6 And ye shall be unto me a kingdom of priests, and an holy nation. These *are* the words which thou shalt speak unto the children of Israel.

Israel was to be a unique and private possession of God. "Special treasure" signifies "property" in the special sense of a private possession one personally acquires and carefully preserves.[36] Israel was created as God's own possession, for his own pleasure. This statement "special treasure" itself indicates that no

---

[xliv] Romans 9.1-4

other nation is meant to be like this nation.

The *nation* of Israel was inaugurated by the creation of a different covenant, the Mosaic Covenant, which was a conditional and temporary covenant. So there exists the unconditional Abrahamic Covenant and its codicils [Palestinian, Davidic and New Covenants] and the Mosaic Covenant with its three divisions [Moral Code, Ceremonial Code, Civil Code]. Israel is unique in the special legal relationship that it has with God. The Abrahamic Covenant addresses the spiritual requirements of that relationship, and the Mosaic Covenant addresses the legal aspects of the nation in its relation to God, although it also has an important spiritual function as well.

Distinguishing Spiritual Israel and Ethnic/Political Israel

Israel is an ethnic, a political and a spiritual entity.

Although the election of the *nation* Israel as God's spiritual representative upon the earth was revealed in the Abrahamic Covenant [Genesis 17.7],[xlv] the participation of every *individual* Jew in the unconditional Abrahamic Covenant was conditioned upon their personal faith. Abraham was reckoned righteous because he *believed* the promise of God [Genesis 15.6]. Each Jew became a partaker in the benefits of this covenant, not by natural birth, but by the new birth [John 3.3-4, 9-10].

> Romans 9:7–9 (KJV 1900)
> [7] Neither, because they are the seed of Abraham, *are they* all children: but, In Isaac shall thy seed be called. [8] That is, They which are the children of the flesh, these *are* not the children of God: but the children of the promise are counted for the seed. [9] For this *is* the word of promise, At this time will I come, and Sara shall have a son. [Matthew 3.7-10]

The nation was later legally incorporated under the conditional Mosaic Covenant, Israel's "Declaration of Dependence."

Mosaic Covenant, specifically the Ceremonial Code, was given to provide the gospel information upon which faith was to be exercised for the individual Jew to receive the benefit of the unconditional covenants made to Israel.

[xlv] Psalms 105.8-11; Romans 9.4

Galatians 3:24 (KJV 1900)

[24] Wherefore the law was our schoolmaster *to bring us* unto Christ, that we might be justified by faith.

The purpose of the Mosaic Law was to point the Jews to the Messiah. This Messiah was typified in their sacrifices, in their High Priest and in their festivals and solemn assemblies.[xlvi] The Law also accomplished this purpose by demonstrating to them their inability to keep God's righteous requirements.[xlvii] The realization of this inability was to drive them to the altar where propitiation was made through the animal sacrifices. However, the Jew was supposed to understand that *these sacrifices in themselves did not remove guilt* but pointed to a Savior who would be the effective Sacrifice, the anointed one [Messiah], the Lamb of God.

Hebrews 10:4 (KJV 1900)

[4] For *it is* not possible that the blood of bulls and of goats should take away sins.

Therefore, it was through an accurate understanding of the purpose of the Mosaic Law that the Jews received and believed the gospel of the coming Messiah. The Israelites knew or should have known that they were incapable of adhering to the entirety of the Law of Moses. However, they should also have known that anything less than complete obedience would result in eternal damnation.

James 2:10 (KJV 1900)

[10] For whosoever shall keep the whole law, and yet offend in one *point*, he is guilty of all.

The only solution was a sacrifice that would be condemned in their place. It was the continual blood sacrifice of unblemished animals that was the catechism of these truths.

Faith in Christ as revealed through the Mosaic Law granted the individual Jew access to the privilege of the Unconditional Covenants, which by virtue of being *everlasting* covenants, *could only be enjoyed by those who possessed eternal life*. The Jews were not saved based on adherence to the many Mosaic laws. They were

---

[xlvi] Luke 24.27 John 5:46-47
[xlvii] Joshua 24.19; Galatians 3.24

saved by faith in that to which the Law *pointed*, the coming Messiah who would fulfill the symbolism of their Levitical sacrifices. That Messiah, or Christ, was Jesus.

> John 1:35–36 (KJV 1900)
> 35 Again the next day after John stood, and two of his disciples; 36 And looking upon Jesus as he walked, he saith, Behold the Lamb of God!

Here we can begin to see the biblical distinction between ethnic/political Israel and spiritual Israel.

Throughout the Old Testament Israel was unfaithful in its obedience to the Mosaic Covenant. The following passage was taken from the book of Jeremiah and was written in the 6th century BC not long before the destruction of Jerusalem by the Babylonians and the exile and enslavement of the Jews.

> Jeremiah 11:6–8 (KJV 1900)
> 6 Then the Lord said unto me, Proclaim all these words in the cities of Judah, and in the streets of Jerusalem, saying, Hear ye the words of this covenant, and do them. 7 For I earnestly protested unto your fathers in the day *that* I brought them up out of the land of Egypt, *even* unto this day, rising early and protesting, saying, Obey my voice. 8 Yet they obeyed not, nor inclined their ear, but walked every one in the imagination of their evil heart: therefore I will bring upon them all the words of this covenant, which I commanded *them* to do; but they did *them* not.

Although the *nation* remained the chosen and elect treasure of God, *individual Jews* who failed believe the gospel as revealed in the Mosaic Covenant were judged and suffered eternal punishment as unbelievers. Just as you cannot be saved by joining a church, you cannot be saved by being born an Israelite. This is a part of the complexity in defining the Jews. They are an ethnic group, they were made into a nation and tied to God by various legal and spiritual covenants, yet there is within political Israel a spiritual remnant, a nation within a nation, consisting of redeemed individuals, a special treasure [Romans 9:4-11].

Fast forward to the time of John the Baptist. Fifteen hundred years have passed since the establishment of the nation of Israel under the Mosaic Covenant. Two thousand years have passed since the time of Abraham. John the Baptist came to administer the Baptism of Repentance unto Israel in preparation for the establishment of the Kingdom promised in the unconditional covenants made to the nation of Israel through Abraham, David, Jeremiah, and others.

> Matthew 3:1–12 (KJV 1900)
> [1] In those days came John the Baptist, preaching in the wilderness of Judaea, [2] And saying, Repent ye: for the kingdom of heaven is at hand. [3] For this is he that was spoken of by the prophet Esaias, saying, The voice of one crying in the wilderness, Prepare ye the way of the Lord, make his paths straight. [4] And the same John had his raiment of camel's hair, and a leathern girdle about his loins; and his meat was locusts and wild honey. [5] Then went out to him Jerusalem, and all Judaea, and all the region round about Jordan, [6] And were baptized of him in Jordan, confessing their sins.
>
> [7] But when he saw many of the Pharisees and Sadducees come to his baptism, he said unto them, O generation of vipers, who hath warned you to flee from the wrath to come? [8] Bring forth therefore fruits meet for repentance: [9] And think not to say within yourselves, We have Abraham to *our* father: for I say unto you, that God is able of these stones to raise up children unto Abraham. [10] And now also the axe is laid unto the root of the trees: therefore every tree which bringeth not forth good fruit is hewn down, and cast into the fire. [11] I indeed baptize you with water unto repentance: but he that cometh after me is mightier than I, whose shoes I am not worthy to bear: he shall baptize you with the Holy Ghost, and *with* fire: [12] Whose fan *is* in his hand, and he will throughly purge his floor, and gather his wheat into the garner; but he will burn up the chaff with unquenchable fire.

John reminded the Jews that *genetic descent* was insufficient to inherit eternal life ("And think not to say within yourselves, We have Abraham to our father:"). Nor was their political status as citizens of the nation Israel sufficient to inherit the unconditional promises that were to be delivered in the coming Kingdom. To inherit eternal blessings, it was necessary to have eternal life! The choice was faith in the gospel as revealed in the Law of Moses [called by John, Repentance[37]] or the Unquenchable Fire of Hell itself.

The Land of Israel

> Genesis 17:8 (KJV 1900)
> 8 And I will give unto thee, and to thy seed after thee, the land wherein thou art a stranger, all the land of Canaan, for an everlasting possession; and I will be their God.

Israel is a geographic entity or *land* as well as a political entity or *nation*.[xlviii] The land of Canaan was bequeathed to the *seed [redeemed individuals Genesis 17.7]* of Abraham through the Abrahamic Covenant.

> Galatians 3:16 (KJV 1900)
> 16 Now to Abraham and his seed were the promises made. He saith not, And to seeds, as of many; but as of one, And to thy seed, which is Christ.

Obedience to the *Mosaic* Covenant was the condition for any specific generation of Israelites (believer or unbeliever) to remain in the land [Leviticus 18.22-30]. The Land of Canaan was *eternally* promised to *redeemed* Israel alone. Political Israel was allowed to live in the land on the condition of obedience to the Law of Moses. The Law was to the redeemed Jew the basis of true worship, but to the unbelieving Jew a civil responsibility. The Mosaic Law was repeatedly broken resulting in expulsions from the land, demonstrating both principles [Jeremiah 11.1-11].

Israel's rejection of the Messiah, Jesus Christ, led to the *temporary* suspension of God's dealings with the Jews as the covenant nation.

> Matthew 27:21–25 (KJV 1900)
> 21 The governor answered and said unto them, Whether of the twain will ye that I release unto you? They said, Barabbas. 22 Pilate saith unto them, What shall I do then with Jesus which is called Christ? *They* all say unto him, Let him be crucified. 23 And the governor said, Why, what evil hath he done? But they cried out the more, saying, Let him be crucified. 24 When Pilate saw that he could prevail nothing, but *that* rather a tumult was made, he took water, and washed *his* hands before the multitude, saying, I am innocent of the blood of this just person: see ye *to it*. 25 Then answered all the people, and said, His blood *be* on us, and on our children.

> Romans 11:25 (NASB95)
> 25 For I do not want you, brethren, to be uninformed of this mystery—so that you will not be wise in your own estimation—that a partial hardening has happened to Israel until the fullness of the Gentiles has come in;

Since that time, the first phase of the New Covenant and the overlapping Church Age have temporarily changed the status of the land of Israel as a Jewish possession. Upon the crucifixion of Christ, the Law of Moses was

---

[xlviii] Genesis 15:8-21; 17:8; Exodus 19.3-6

replaced by the New Covenant, a paragraph of the Abrahamic Covenant.[xlix] The Church was created on the first Pentecost following the resurrection of Christ [Acts 2.47]. From that point to the yet future resurrection of the Church [Rapture] every person who is born again, Jew or Gentile, becomes a member of the Body of Christ and an heir to the inheritance associated with *that* spiritual body.

> Galatians 3:28–29 (KJV 1900)
> [28] There is neither Jew nor Greek, there is neither bond nor free, there is neither male nor female: for ye are all one in Christ Jesus.

The Jew who becomes a Christian *does not* receive the inheritance of the Kingdom promised to Israel, but the inheritance promised to the Church. Likewise, the Gentile Christian is *not* an heir to the promises made to redeemed Israel. The Christian of Jewish ethnicity is not an heir to the land of Israel now or in the future. The *unbelieving* ethnic Jew has *never* been promised the land of Israel.

> Galatians 3:16 (KJV 1900)
> 16 Now to Abraham and his seed were the promises made. He saith not, And to seeds, as of many; but as of one, And to thy seed, which is Christ.

God continues to preserve the *ethnic* Jews, physical descendants of Abraham, and the destiny of *redeemed* Israel remains as predicted in the Old and New Testaments. Today, ethnic Israel largely rejects Christ, faith in whom is mandatory to inherit eternal life.

Today, during the Times of the Gentiles,[38] the Land of Israel remains dominated by the Gentiles, until the return of Christ. The Jewish people have been periodically evacuated and returned to the land since the times of the apostles. These returns to the land are not the fulfillment of the Abrahamic Covenant, which is made only to *redeemed* Israel. The land of Israel was never promised to unredeemed Israel.

At the second coming of Christ, the land of Israel will be restored to the Old Testament believers, who will be resurrected[l] and those Israelites who believed during the Tribulation period, after the Church has been removed from the earth via the Rapture. The Kingdom promised to Old Testament Israel, the same Kingdom that was rejected at Christ's first advent, will

---

[xlix] Matthew 26.28; Hebrews 8.7-13
[l] Deuteronomy 30.3-6; Jeremiah 23.6-8; Ezekiel 37.21-28; Daniel 12.2; Micah 4.6-9

commence at this point, with Christ as its sovereign [Revelation 20.1-6].[li]

The very name of the "Land of Israel" points to the conversion of Jacob when he received this new name from God. Spiritual blessings must be spiritually apprehended. Even in the unique case of the nation of Israel, a supernaturally created ethnic group, neither salvation nor residence in the land is promised because of genetic lineage or ethnicity.

Jewish Ethnicity and Race

The Jews are not depicted as a racial group (as defined in Chapter 2) in scripture. In fact, just about any ethnic group could become Jews (proselytes) by a right relation to Jehovah and to His Law.[lii] Because ethnicity is not static, the appearance (phenotype) of the Jews has not remained constant.

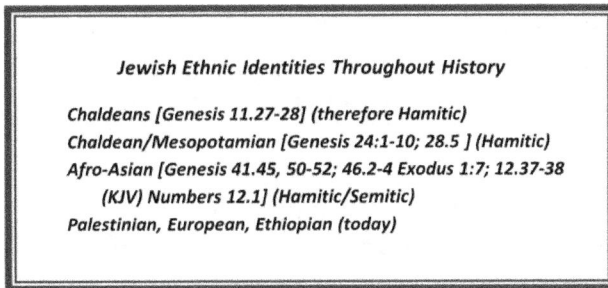

Jewish Ethnic Identities Throughout History

Chaldeans [Genesis 11.27-28] (therefore Hamitic)
Chaldean/Mesopotamian [Genesis 24:1-10; 28.5] (Hamitic)
Afro-Asian [Genesis 41.45, 50-52; 46.2-4 Exodus 1:7; 12.37-38
(KJV) Numbers 12.1] (Hamitic/Semitic)
Palestinian, European, Ethiopian (today)

Figure 1: Changing Ethnicity of the Israelites

Ethnic intermarriage occurred among the Jews as it does among all peoples. Non-Jews converted to the Jewish faith, and Jews persisted in marrying those prohibited from marriage due to their religious practices.[liii]

Of all the nations of the world, the Jews were given an accurate and comprehensive revelation of God and his worship. They were forbidden to marry those who did not worship Jehovah or even Jews who did not obey the

---

[li] It should be noted that the present age is not the Kingdom, as many Christians appear to believe. The Kingdom focus is Israel, with promises and blessings directed to the redeemed (born again) Jews. The spiritual principles which will prevail in the Kingdom are presented in the Sermon on the Mount [Matthew 5-7]. The Kingdom will be physically ruled by Jesus who will reign from the throne of David [Luke 1.32-33; Acts 2.25-35; Revelation 19.1-6].
[lii] Esther 8:17; Deuteronomy 23:7-8
[liii] Deuteronomy 21.10-14; 23.7; Ezra 9; Deuteronomy 7.1-4 c.f. Joshua 23.12-13; 1 Kings 11.1-4

Law of Moses.[liv] Throughout American history, false teachers deliberately mistaught this principle to support by scripture the doctrines of segregation and white supremacy.[39]

There were legitimate opportunities to marry outside the 12 tribes of Israel:

> Non-Canaanite captives [Deuteronomy 20.14; 21:10-14]
> Egyptians (therefore blacks) [Deuteronomy 23:7]
> Converts to the Mosaic faith of *any* racial or ethnic identity except the Ammonites and Moabites [Deuteronomy 23.3-6]

Thus, the Jews are an ethnic group, a political entity, and a spiritual remnant, but they are not a race. Race is the arbitrary categorization of people to divide, conquer and maintain social and financial control over vast sections of humanity. The concept of race is a mechanism of control, which is why the oppressed are not allowed to define it or its boundaries, except in a narrow range permitted by those who oppress. Although genetic differences [Diversity] are a manifestation of the creative purpose of God, race as a means of categorizing humanity is a human concept with a satanic origin. God has established and communicated to us in scripture the categories by which he has organized humanity.

We deal with race because race is a strategy by which Satan administers his world kingdom. Racial oppression is first and foremost a spiritual initiative. Racism is empowered by the sin nature, but it is also energized by demonic spirits. Racism is built into the operation of Satan's world system and is administered at the highest levels by Mystery Babylon [Revelation 17] as one of many projects under the Mystery of Iniquity [2 Thessalonians 2.7] which is Satan's prehistoric plan to overthrow God and to establish himself and his "son" as rulers of the heavens and the earth [Isaiah 14.12-17].[40]

Therefore, racism can be most effectively addressed by spiritual means. Prejudice, discrimination, and racism are not solved by changing the oppressors, but by changing the thinking of the oppressed. For example, the attitude of Israel's enemies towards them has never changed, the critical factor has been whether Israel had God as an ally or an enemy. Spiritual power directed towards the minds of the oppressed is the key to their spiritual health and the amelioration of their situation under oppression. As an added benefit,

---

[liv] Exodus 34.14-16; Deuteronomy 7.1-4; Joshua 23.12-13; Ezra 9:1-2, 12; Nehemiah 9.2; 1 Kings 11.1-4

when God delivers the oppressed, the entire nation benefits.[lv]

It is imperative that we deal with race. The issue of race is a part of the spiritual conflict that prevents the spiritual growth of the oppressed and the oppressor. The theological justification of racial discrimination by churches, actively or by silent consent, makes gospel proclamation absurd once unbelievers perceive their hypocrisy. Racial oppression causes untold personal suffering; it is also an enormous waste of national resources that are first used to enforce white supremacy and then to manage its effects upon those oppressed. We must shine cleansing light of scripture upon the issue and administer the means of healing to those afflicted with pathologies associated with oppression. Pretending that the problem does not exist, or that God has no solution, is a part of the pathology caused by the syndrome of racism.

An Example Of Biblical Racism-The Samaritans

I have defined *racism* as the deliberate and scientific application of discrimination to the institutions of society for the purpose of the marginalization or destruction of a people. The case of the Jews and the Samaritans is an accurate illustration of this principle in action.

The Samaritans were a people that came about because of the expulsion of the Jews from the Northern Kingdom of Israel in 721 BC. [2 Kings 17.1-7]. Shalmaneser the king of Assyria repopulated the northern part of Israel with peoples from several nations:

> 2 Kings 17:24 (KJV 1900)
> [24] And the king of Assyria brought *men* from Babylon, and from Cuthah, and from Ava, and from Hamath, and from Sepharvaim, and placed *them* in the cities of Samaria instead of the children of Israel: and they possessed Samaria, and dwelt in the cities thereof.

Samaria was the capital Northern Kingdom of Israel. It was established by the Israelite king Omri who the Bible says surpassed all the kings of Israel before him in wickedness and idolatry.

> 1 Kings 16:25–26 (KJV 1900)
> 25 But Omri wrought evil in the eyes of the Lord, and did worse than all that were before him. 26 For he walked in all the way of Jeroboam the son

---

[lv] Proverbs 11.10; 14.34

of Nebat, and in his sin wherewith he made Israel to sin, to provoke the Lord God of Israel to anger with their vanities.

This was quite an accomplishment, for Jeroboam caused the departure of all the Northern Kingdom of Israel from the Law of Moses when he established a new religion: a new system of worship based on idolatry, with a new altar, liturgical calendar, and priesthood [1 Kings 12].

As bad as he was, Omri was outdone by his son, Ahab, who went him one better, marrying an idol worshipping Sidonian named Jezebel [Hamite] and replacing bad with worse as Israel became a nation of Baal worshippers.

It was only appropriate that God, after centuries of patience, replaced the Jews of the Northern Kingdom with idolaters from amongst the Gentiles. These idol worshippers intermarried with the Jewish idol worshippers that remained in the land, producing the Samaritans.

The hated Samarians were a people created as a direct result of the sin of their oppressors, the Israelites of the Northern Kingdom. The Samarians were an ethnically mixed people, created by the Assyrian practice of relocating conquered peoples to prevent uprisings. These displaced people intermarried with the few remaining Jewish peasants to become the Samaritans of the New Testament era.

The Samaritans were an idolatrous people; they did not worship the God of Israel.[lvi] Yet here they were in the promised land, amidst the chosen people. The Law of Moses demanded physical separation from the people and practices that were contrary to that Law. The purpose of these restrictions was the sanctification of the Jews who lived in the presence of God, whose glory rested between the cherubim of the Temple, above the mercy seat. God's purpose was not to suggest or to justify Jewish racial prejudice towards Gentiles. The Jews were to be God's evangelistic agency to the world. God went to lengths to teach Israel to treat others with kindness, generosity, and respect, for they too were once strangers in Egypt [Exodus 22.21; 23.9].

God also made provisions in the Law for strangers in their midst who were willing to obey the Law of Moses [Exodus 12.48-49].

God absolutely prohibited that Israel become an oppressor nation, using

---

[lvi] Ezra 4.2; 2 Kings 17.24-41

scripture and secular laws to marginalize and destroy non-Jewish peoples, regardless of their religious beliefs.[lvii]

Jesus created a permanent scriptural record of how the Jews should have treated the Samaritans in John 4. John 4.9 states that the Jews had absolutely no dealing with the Samaritans, which made the actions of Jesus in that passage so remarkable. Unger states:

> "The Samaritans were publicly cursed in their (the Jews) synagogues-could not be adduced as witnesses in the Jewish courts- could not be admitted to any sort of proselytism, and was thus, so far as the Jew could affect his position, excluded from eternal life."[41] [emphasis added]

Unger reveals that the Samaritans experienced not only racial *discrimination* at the hands of the Jews, but also *racism*. Racial discrimination is the externalization of racial prejudice by individuals or groups, it may be organized or disorganized. By contrast, *racism* is the calculated introduction of discrimination into the institutions of society for the purpose of marginalizing or destroying a people. Racism is the *science* of discrimination. The Jews deliberately organized their society to marginalize the Samaritans. Two institutions of society, the synagogue (theological) and the courts (legal) were formally aligned against the best interests of the Samaritans. Since the mere act of speaking to the Samaritan woman was considered noteworthy [John 4.9, 27] we may safely assume that intermarriage with these people, regardless of their religious orientation, was also out of the question, implicating a *third* institution [marriage]. The Jews would not even convert the Samaritans to Judaism. Certainly, this relationship was not sanctioned by scripture. Exodus 12.44, 48, 49 indicates that a purchased slave, a stranger or a native of the land could participate in the Passover if he submitted to the circumcision and thus identified himself with the people of God.

Racial oppression depends upon the corruption of truth for its continued function. The morality, common law and Bible doctrine of a nation are compromised to sustain the environment of oppression. Therefore, it may be clearly seen that *oppression is a destroyer of civilization*, first of the oppressor and inevitably, of the oppressed themselves.

In John 8:48 the Jews were using the strongest language to insult Jesus. After accusing Him of having been born of sexual sin in v 41, they then called him

---

[lvii] Ezekiel 22.1-7; Malachi 3.5

demon possessed and worse yet, a Samaritan! Racial prejudice elevates one race at the expense of other races who are deprived of virtue and worth to sustain the artificial valuation of the oppressor race. We don't know much about the character of the Samaritans from the Bible, except that they were gross idolaters, who mixed elements of the Mosaic faith with the worst excesses of pagan religion. However, we do know that these objects of racism and ethnic bigotry returned the favor to the Jews with their own form of retaliatory prejudice. Luke 9.52-54 says that the Samaritans would not allow Jesus to pass through their territory, because His ultimate destination was Jerusalem. The satanic genius of prejudice is found in its ability to nullify the spirituality of both the oppressor and the oppressed. Like the perpetrator of discrimination (albeit for different reasons), the person experiencing racism *feels morally justified* in hating his persecutor, with the effect that he becomes capable of equally heinous thinking and behavior. These negative feelings on the part of the oppressed do not lead to constructive action, but to psychological disability that increases their oppression. When functioning at its greatest efficiency, oppression can cause a mental disorder in its victim that results in self-oppression.[42]

The attitude of God towards the Samaritans is declared by the actions of Jesus, the Second Member of the Godhead, God in the flesh.

> ➤ In John 4, He saved the woman of Samaria, using water in a well as an object lesson that revealed His divine Person and the means of salvation. In Luke 10:25 Jesus uses a Samaritan to demonstrate the principles of the Kingdom of God and the fruit of true salvation.

> ➤ In Luke 17.16 Jesus heals a Samaritan leper who among ten others was the only one to return and thank Him.

> ➤ Christ sent Philip to evangelize the Samaritans in Acts 8. Later Peter and John joined Philip there, and the Samaritans received the Holy Spirit. Acts 8.31 notes that God granted the church in Samaria both peace and growth.

> ➤ Paul and Barnabas travel through Samaria in Acts 15 encouraging the brethren there.

The Samaritans were great sinners, and the policies of the Jews worsened this spiritual condition. The *religion of race* blocked both the Jews and the Samaritans from the benefits of fellowship with God. Nonetheless, God demonstrated that His love, though more discriminating than the most prejudiced human, is made inclusive because of the cross of Christ. The solution to oppression is again revealed to be spiritual. There is no evidence in scripture that the attitude of the Jews towards the Samaritans ever changed. Nonetheless, through the transformation of the new birth, the Samaritans was blessed and healed.

---

[25] Ham, Ken, Wieland, Carl, Batten, Don. One Blood, The Biblical Answer to Racism. Master Books, 2000. 54

[26] Ibid. 57-70

[27] Ibid.

Rev. Finis Dake provides an alternate explanation:
"All colors and types of men Came into existence after the flood. All men where white up to this point, (before the flood rw) for there was only one family line, that of Noah, who was white…" Finis Jennings Dake, "Dake's Annotated Reference Bible", Dake Bible Sales Inc, Lawrenceville Ga., 1963. 8, 40 (Old Testament notes)

[28] Walker, Richard G., Antichrist and the New World Order. A Richer Walk Ministries, 2022.

[29] **Nation:** 1484 ἔθνος [ethnos /eth·nos/] n n. Probably from 1486; TDNT 2:364; TDNTA 201; GK 1620; 164 occurrences; AV translates as "Gentiles" 93 times, "nation" 64 times, "heathen" five times, and "people" twice. **1** a multitude (whether of men or of beasts) associated or living together. 1a a company, troop, swarm. **2** a multitude of individuals of the same nature or genus. 2a the human race. **3** a race, nation, people group. **4** in the OT, foreign nations not worshipping the true God, pagans, Gentiles **5** Paul uses the term for Gentile Christians. Strong, James. *Enhanced Strong's Lexicon.* Woodside Bible Fellowship, 1995.

Nation: 11.55 ἔθνος, ους *n*; λαός[a], **οῦ** *m*: the largest unit into which the people of the world are divided on the basis of their constituting a socio-political community—'nation, people. Louw, Johannes P., and Eugene Albert Nida. Greek-English Lexicon of the New Testament: Based on Semantic Domains. New York: United Bible Societies, 1996.

[30] **Nation,** *noun* [to be born]
1. A body of people inhabiting the same country, or united under the same sovereign or government; as the English nation; the French *nation* It often happens that many nations are subject to one government; in which case, the word *nation* usually denotes a body of people speaking the same language, or a body that has formerly been under a distinct government, but has been conquered, or incorporated with a larger *nation* Thus the empire of Russia comprehends many nations, as did formerly the Roman and Persian empires. *nation* as its etymology imports, originally denoted a family or race of men descended from a common progenitor, like tribe, but by emigration, conquest and intermixture of men of different families, this distinction is in most countries lost.
Webster, Noah, *An American Dictionary of the English Language,* Accessed 11-17-2022.
https://webstersdictionary1828.com/Dictionary/Nation

[31] **Canaan:** 3667 כְּנַעַן, כְּנַעַן [Kâna'an /ken·ah·an/] n pr m loc. From 3665; TWOT 1002, 1002b; GK 4046 and 4047; 94 occurrences; AV translates as "Canaan" 89 times, "merchant" three times, "traffick" once, and "traffickers" once. **1** the 4th son of Ham and the progenitor of the Phoenicians and of the various nations who peopled the seacoast of Palestine. **2** the land west of the Jordan peopled by the descendants of Canaan and subsequently conquered by the Israelites under Joshua. **3** merchant, trader. *Additional Information:* Canaan = "lowland".[31]

Ezekiel 17:4 "He plucked off the topmost of its young twigs and brought it to a land of merchants (H3667-Kenaan); he set it in a city of traders. NAS

Isaiah 23:8 Who has planned this against Tyre, the bestower of crowns, Whose merchants were princes, whose traders (H3669-Kenaan-iy) were the honored of the earth? NAS

Hosea 12:7 A merchant (H3667-Kenaan), in whose hands are false balances, He loves to oppress. NAS

These scriptures indicate that the Phoenicians and the Canaanites were one and the same people-the Phoenicians were sons of Ham and members of the Black Alliance of nations descended from the sons of Ham.

"The Phoenicians most likely considered themselves Canaanites (Kuhrt, *The Ancient Near East*, 403), probably because the Phoenician cities that survived the Bronze Age collapse ca. 1200 BC carried on the Canaanite society that was destroyed elsewhere (Van De Mieroop, *A History of the Ancient Near East*, 198). The main Phoenician religion was also Canaanite, although the form varied from city to city. "Hamilton, Matthew. "Phoenicia, Geography and Demographics of." In *The Lexham Bible Dictionary*, edited by John D. Barry, David Bomar, Derek R. Brown, Rachel Klippenstein, Douglas Mangum, Carrie Sinclair Wolcott, Lazarus Wentz, Elliot Ritzema, and Wendy Widder. Bellingham, WA: Lexham Press, 2016.

[32] McCray, Rev W.A. The Black Presence in the Bible and the Table of Nations. Black Light Fellowship, 1990. 4.

[33] Williams, Chancellor. The Destruction of Black Civilization: Great Issues of a Race from 4500 B.C. to 2000 A.D. 3rd. ed. Chicago: Third World Press, 1987.

[34] It is difficult to get a straight answer from biblical scholars about the ethnic origins of the Chaldean, but the following are a couple of attempts as doing so. You will find that although the original inhabitants, the founder of the nation, their original and sacred language, their religion, and the surrounding nations were all Hamitic, the biblical historians insist upon identifying them by their language, thereby disassociating them (the Chaldeans, who did not disappear into the mists of history) from who they were, which was black people.

"Chaldea, Chaldeans.
Ancient region in Mesopotamia and its inhabitants. The name comes from the Chaldean (or Kaldu) tribes which shared Babylonia in southeastern Mesopotamia with several other peoples, especially the Sumerians and Akkadians. After the Old Babylonian empire was absorbed by the Assyrians, the Chaldeans under Nebuchadnezzar's leadership took control and built a Neo-Babylonian empire that dominated the Middle East for nearly a century. The region called Chaldea is also associated with the patriarch Abraham, whose Mesopotamian home was "Ur of the Chaldeans" (Gn 11:28).Walter A. Elwell and Barry J. Beitzel, Baker Encyclopedia of the Bible. Grand Rapids, MI: Baker Book House, 1988. 422.

Fausset tends to be somewhat more honest [but not necessarily less prejudiced] in his treatment of issues pertaining to the Hamite than other biblical historians.

"CHALDEA
In another sense the "CHALDAEANS" are a priest caste, with a peculiar tongue and learning, skilled in divination. In the ethnic sense we saw it was applied first to a particular Cushite tribe, then to the whole nation from the time of Nabopolassar. The Semitic language prevailed over the Cushite in Assyrian and later Babylonian times, and was used for all civil purposes; but for sacred and mystic lore the Cushite language was retained as a learned language. This is "the learning and the tongue of the Chaldaeans" (Dan 1:4), in which the four Jewish youths were instructed, and which is quite distinct from the Aramaean, or Chaldee so-called (allied to Hebrew), of those parts of the book of Daniel which are not Hebrew, as not being so connected with the Jews as with the Babylonians. The Cushite Chaldee had

become a dead language to the mass of the people who had become Semitized by the Assyrians. All who studied it were called "Chaldaeans," whatever might be their nation; so Daniel is called "master of the Chaldaeans" (Dan 5:11). Their seats of learning were Borsippa, Ur, Babylon, and Sepharvaim. The serene sky and clear atmosphere favored their astronomical studies; Cahisthenes sent Aristotle from Babylon their observations for 1903 years. Afterward their name became synonymous with diviners and fortunetellers. They wore a peculiar dress, like that seen on the gods and deified men in Assyrian sculptures. At the time of the Arab invasion the Chaldaeans chiefly still preserved the learning of the East. We owe to them the preservation of many fragments of Greek learning, as the Greeks had previously owed much of their eastern learning to the Chaldees." (from Fausset's Bible Dictionary, Electronic Database Copyright © 1998, 2003, 2006 by Biblesoft, Inc. All rights reserved.)

[35] Abram himself was from Ur of the Chaldees. If he was a native of that land, then it is likely that he was a son of Ham.

[36] **Special treasure:** 6035 סְגֻלָּה (sᵉḡŭl·lā(h)): n.fem.; ≡ Str 5459; TWOT 1460a—**1.** LN 57.1–57.21 treasured possession, i.e., valued personal property, what is owned by someone, which the owner has special affection or holds special value (Ex 19:5; Dt 7:6; 14:2; 26:18; Psalms 135:4; Mal 3:17+); **2.** LN 57.25–57.35 **personal wealth**, i.e., a personal accumulation of values, as contrasted with a governmental treasury (1Ch 29:3; Ecc 2:8+) Swanson, James. *Dictionary of Biblical Languages with Semantic Domains : Hebrew (Old Testament)*. Oak Harbor: Logos Research Systems, Inc., 1997. #6035

[37] In the time of John the Baptist, the only gospel available was that expressed through the Ceremonial Code of the Mosaic Law, which illustrated the necessity of a blood sacrifice for sins. Jesus would not begin his public ministry until the death of John, and he would preach the same message as John. Jesus was born, lived, died, and rose again under the Mosaic economy [Galatians 4.4]. John called for repentance, that is, a return to faithful adherence to the Law of Moses, based upon faith in the coming Messiah, who would make an end to sins. In the event of national repentance, the Kingdom promised to the faithful would be immediately inaugurated, as it was already "at hand."

[38] (Luke) 21:20–24. Jesus then returned to the disciples' original question about when the temple would be destroyed. In these five verses He noted that Gentile domination included the destruction of **Jerusalem** which would come about when the city was **surrounded by armies**. Gentile domination would continue **until the times of the Gentiles are fulfilled** (v. 24). The times of the Gentiles' domination over Jerusalem actually began when the Babylonians took the city and the nation into Captivity in 586 BC. Jerusalem will again fall under Gentile domination in the Tribulation (Zech. 14:1–2) just before the Messiah returns to restore Jerusalem. It is that restoration of which Jesus spoke next (Luke 21:25–28). [emphasis in original] Walvoord, John F., and Roy B. Zuck, Dallas Theological Seminary. The Bible Knowledge Commentary: An Exposition of the Scriptures. Wheaton, IL: Victor Books, 1985.

[39] "4. "Miscegenation means the mixture of races, especially the black and white races, or those of outstanding type or color. The Bible goes ever further than opposing this. It is against different branches of the same stock intermarrying such as Jews marrying other descendants of Abraham…" "30 reasons for the segregation of races" Dake, Finis Jennings. "Dakes' Annotated Reference Bible" Lawrenceville Ga.: Dake Bible Sales Inc. 1963.) 159 [New Testament].

[40] For the development of the concepts of Satan's world system, Mystery Babylon, the Mystery of Iniquity and Satan's "son" see: Walker, Richard G. Antichrist and the New World Order. A Richer Walk Ministries, 2022.

[41] Unger, Merrill. Unger's Bible Dictionary. Chicago: Moody Press, 1966. 960.

[42] Fanon, Frantz. The Wretched of the Earth: Translated from the French by Richard Philcox; Introductions by Jean-Paul Sartre and Homi K. Bhabha. New York: Grove Press, 2004.

Also: Grier, William H., and Price M. Cobbs. Black Rage. New York: BasicBooks, 1992.

Also: Kardiner, Abram, and Lionel Ovesey. The Mark of Oppression Explorations in the Personality of the American Negro. Meridian, 1951.

And: Wilson, Amos N. The Falsification of Afrikan Consciousness: Eurocentric History, Psychiatry and the Politics of White Supremacy. Second Edition. New York: Afrikan World InfoSystems, 2014.

4. How Christians Perpetuate Racial Sin

"Numerous incidents have been recorded which show that the so-called spontaneous and voluntary withdrawal of the Negroes to form their own churches was actually compelled by the discriminations and the subordinations which the Negroes suffered from white Christians in integrated churches. The case of Richard Allen, pulled from his knees during prayer and bodily expelled from the St. George Church in Philadelphia; the special partitions and galleries for worshippers of the Negro race; segregation in the time of worship for the different races where the same building had to be used by both...such acts and incidents which were many times duplicated, are proof enough that segregation and discrimination against the Negro had been established as patterns within the Christian churches before the Negro and white churches became separate bodies and long before segregation was adopted and applied as a specific and legalized form in society."[43]

Throughout the history of America, the descendants of Africans brought here to be slaves have sought to achieve full participation in the American way of life as citizens and as human beings. They have sought participation and protection under the founding documents of the nation to enable their pursuit of life, liberty, and happiness.

History clearly shows that the aspirations of black people have been consistently met with the steadfast resistance of many, if not most Americans. This resistance has been political and legal, as demonstrated by the laws and court decisions designed to maintain black people in a separate and unequal class. It has been social, as illustrated in the many social conventions designed to separate black people from the best of housing, education, and public facilities. It has been enforced economically by the "walling off" of black people from equal participation in the workplace in hiring, compensation, and promotions. The resistance to black enjoyment of the prerogatives of liberty has often been enforced by violence: many blacks and some whites have died in the effort to exercise their own legal rights or to secure these rights for others.

It must be added that while economic, social, political, and legal means have been marshalled to deprive black people of equality and justice, these means have always been justified by use of the Bible.[44] It is Christendom which has supplied and still supplies the moral and biblical justification for injustice towards black people. From the slave trade to the Redemption and Jim Crow, to the civil rights movement of the 1950's and 1960's to the current retrenchment of racism as a tool of modern social control, there have been Christian Pastors, theologians and Bible teachers supporting the regressive social order through the Scriptures. By their use of the Bible, they have attempted to identify Jesus Christ as the ultimate Author of injustice against black Americans.[45]

Princeton theologian and slaveholder[46] Charles Hodge exclaimed in his paper, "The Bible Argument for Slavery (1860), "If the present course of the abolitionists is right, then the course of Christ and the apostles were wrong."[47]

Dake's Study Bible offers "30 Reasons for the Segregation of Races"[48]

Keil and Delitzsch in their Commentary of the Old Testament taught that the Hamitic race was characterized by sexual sin.[49]

C. I. Scofield taught that from Ham descended an "inferior and servile people."

Dr Tony Evans observed that even some of the best-known religious leaders of early America justified slavery by theology, indirectly assisting the efforts of secular intellectuals devising a scientific doctrine of race. These religious men cited by Dr. Evans included Jonathan Edwards, George Whitefield, John Davenport, and Evera Stiles, President of Yale.[50]

When asked about the racial issues represented by the Charlottesville Va. march[51] and the Black Lives Matter movement Dr. John MacArthur stated that, in the church, it is "in a sense a non-issue, it doesn't exist as an issue."[52]

These statements provide a succinct but profound summary of the spectrum of arguments that have inadvertently or otherwise perpetuated white supremacy by creating a new definition of sanctification and of holiness that excludes all issues that might jeopardize it.

White Supremacy

"White Supremacy pertains to the maintenance of "whiteness" [see definition] as the supreme store of personal value. As a store of value, whiteness cannot be allowed to depreciate relative to other racial groups. Since racial designations have no basis in reality, the relative value of whiteness and all its privileges must be sustained artificially. White Supremacy therefore is the commitment to the pre-eminence of whiteness as well as a commitment to the totality of strategies [psychological, legal, political, theological, and military] deployed to maintain it."[lviii]

The doctrines identified in the quotations above[lix] are found throughout the literature used by Bible students, seminarians and Pastors and influence the preaching, teaching, and witness of countless local churches throughout America. At the same time there is the strong denial of the existence of the religious doctrines and social strategies of white supremacy among Christians.

"Across a range of questions, the overall pattern that emerges is abundantly clear. On the one hand, white Christians explicitly profess warm attitudes toward African Americans. At the same time, however, they strongly support the continued existence of Confederate monuments to white supremacy and consistently deny the existence not only of historical structural barriers to black achievement but also of existing structural injustices in the way African Americans are treated by police, the courts, workplaces, and other institutions in the country." [53]

Furthermore, any attempt by believers to refute these claims with Scripture or to effect changes in society that will remove the discriminatory apparatus is condemned as a departure from the gospel and evidence of worldly priorities.

By comparison, many thousands of churches see no conflict between the primacy of the gospel and the establishment of a national ultra-conservative political movement that vigorously supports positions on a variety of social

---

[lviii] See Chapter 2: Definitions of Terms
[lix] Appendix 2: Theologians on the Issue of Race

issues.[ix] A close examination of this conservative Christian political movement will disclose that the sum of its positions reveal an attitude towards racial justice that suggests that is indeed a serious issue to them.

For example, one of the catalysts for the emergence of a modern, politically significant Christian Right movement has long been believed to have been the Supreme Court decision legalizing abortion: Roe vs. Wade. The actual motivation for its formation was to be found in the prospect of losing the right to maintain segregated schools. Tax exempt status was removed from Bob Jones University by the IRS because the University forbade interracial dating or marriage of its students. The government argued that any organization with practices of this kind could not claim to be a charity. This action precipitated a reaction in the Christian community which had established thousands of Christian Academies organized to circumvent court ordered busing for the integration of public schools. Randall Balmer, Professor at Dartmouth College, relates the following firsthand experience:

> "The Religious Right's self-portrayal as mobilizing in response to the Roe decision was so pervasive among evangelicals that few questioned it. But my attendance at an unusual gathering in Washington, D.C., finally alerted me to the abortion myth. In November 1990, for reasons that I still don't entirely understand, I was invited to attend a conference in Washington sponsored by the Ethics and Public Policy Center, a Religious Right organization (though I didn't realize it at the time). I soon found myself in a conference room with a couple of dozen people, including Ralph Reed, then head of the Christian Coalition; Carl F. H. Henry, an evangelical theologian; Tom Minnery of Focus on the Family; Donald Wildmon, head of the American Family Association; Richard Land of the Southern Baptist Convention; and Edward G. Dobson, Pastor of an evangelical church in Grand Rapids, Michigan, and formerly one of Jerry Falwell's acolytes at Moral Majority. Paul M. Weyrich, a longtime conservative activist, head of what is now called the Free Congress Foundation, and one of the architects of the Religious Right in the late 1970s, was also there. In the course of one of the sessions, Weyrich tried to make a point to his Religious Right brethren (no women attended the conference, as I recall). Let's remember, he said animatedly, that the Religious Right did not come together in response to the Roe

---

[ix] These issues include abortion, homosexuality, human trafficking, limiting the voting franchise, and gun ownership. A subset of these Christian and churches support Dominionist positions that seek Christian control of government and the imposition of Christian standards by law. So, these people are not against social action in principle, they are simply against its use in directing the application of Christian sanctification towards race relations. This, they claim, is outside the scope of the gospel and a non-issue to the local church.

decision. No, Weyrich insisted, what got us going as a political movement was the attempt on the part of the Internal Revenue Service (IRS) to rescind the tax-exempt status of Bob Jones University because of its racially discriminatory policies. Bob Jones University was one target of a broader attempt by the federal government to enforce the provisions of the Civil Rights Act of 1964. Several agencies, including the Equal Employment Opportunity Commission, had sought to penalize schools for failure to abide by anti-segregation provisions. A court case in 1971, Green v. Connally, produced a ruling that any institution that practiced segregation was not, by definition, a charitable institution and, therefore, no longer qualified for tax-exempt standing. The IRS sought to revoke the tax-exempt status of Bob Jones University in 1975 because the school's regulations forbade interracial dating; African Americans, in fact, had been denied admission altogether until 1971, and it took another four years before unmarried African Americans were allowed to enroll. The university filed suit to retain its tax-exempt status, although that suit would not reach the Supreme Court until 1983 (at which time, the Reagan administration argued in favor of Bob Jones University). Initially, I found Weyrich's admission jarring. He declared, in effect, that the origins of the Religious Right lay in Green v. Connally rather than Roe v. Wade."[54]

As this firsthand account shows, the modern iteration of the religious right was given critical early momentum by the strong desire to maintain the right to segregate blacks and whites, especially young black and white people. It also shows that the movement was heavily endorsed by white, theologically conservative Christians.

The religious defenders of the status quo of racial injustice start from the social order that they wish to maintain and argue backwards to the Scriptures. In other words, they have a certain social order in mind, and they are looking for a scriptural justification for it. Once they have locked in that unjust system, proclaiming it to be the will of God, they throw away the key and argue that any attempt to change the unjust social order is unscriptural and that people ought to "just stick with the gospel." After using the Bible to justify social injustice, they then affirm that any attempt to educate the church on the impact of the gospel and conversion upon one's racial attitudes and actions [i.e., sanctification] is a departure from the priorities of the spiritual life and that those people must be unbelievers, theological liberals or carnally minded.

At many crucial points in the history of the last four hundred or so years, *apparently* theologically orthodox Christians have utilized biblical arguments to avoid confronting oppression in their times. In so doing, they have used a variety of arguments, but mostly, they have relied upon an artificial *truncation*[lxi] of the gospel. Truncated in its power to change the life of the one who is born again and thereby rendered impotent in its ability, through saved individuals, to provide salt and light to those in their periphery [Matthew 5.13-16]. Through loud proclamations of their commitment to defend the gospel, they hope to drown out the demands of Christian sanctification, when those demands for sanctification are connected to the social or political issues that they wish to avoid. However, it is the practical outworking of the new birth in the decisions and actions of the believer [i.e., sanctification] that are the true issue when one speaks of the categories of impact that the Christian may have upon the world. These decisions and actions of saved individuals complement and fortify gospel proclamation.

The scriptures teach expressly that the new birth results in Christian attitudes and actions which have direct social effects. The Bible uses explicit language to show that it is the intent of God that believers, in their pursuit of holiness, will become influencers of this fallen world for good.

> Ephesians 5:8–11 (KJV 1900) 8 For ye were sometimes darkness, but now are ye light in the Lord: walk as children of light: 9 (For the fruit of the Spirit is in all goodness and righteousness and truth;) 10 Proving what is acceptable unto the Lord. 11 And have no fellowship with the unfruitful works of darkness, but rather reprove[55] them.

> James 1:27 (KJV 1900)
> 27 Pure religion and undefiled before God and the Father is this, To visit the fatherless and widows in their affliction,[56] and to keep himself unspotted from the world. [James 2.14-17]

> Isaiah 1:16-17 (NKJV)
> 16 "Wash yourselves, make yourselves clean; Put away the evil of your doings from before My eyes. Cease to do evil, 17 Learn to do good; Seek justice, Rebuke the oppressor; Defend the fatherless, Plead for the widow.

The central problem of those who oppose a Christian social justice

---

[lxi] Truncate: "to shorten by or as if by cutting off"
Merriam-Webster.com Dictionary, s.v. "truncate," accessed January 2, 2023, https://www.merriam-webster.com/dictionary/truncate.

movement[lxii] is that they themselves misrepresent the Gospel. This is the reason that they do not provide a systematic biblical treatment on why they believe that the pursuit of justice for people in the community, workforce and elsewhere is such a negative influence upon gospel primacy. To attempt to do so would throw open the floodgates to host of scriptures[lxiii] which describe God as concerned about the oppressed in this world and this life, and who directs the righteous to their support. Instead, they create the false issue of an alleged manipulation of the gospel by a conspiracy of unidentified, misguided Christians. They then "defend" the gospel by cutting it off from that portion of scripture that teaches what the gospel actually accomplishes in the world through a person who is born again. These arguments are advanced to absolve the church from its responsibility to oppose certain categories of evil that white conservative Christians have traditionally avoided confronting biblically.

In view of these realities, it would be appropriate for Pastors to confront the issue of race and to use the scriptures to short-circuit the intergenerational transfer of prejudiced racial attitudes and behaviors in their Congregations. However, to preach about the sin of racial prejudice and racial discrimination could lead to congregational unrest and a loss of members or, at worse, the calling of a new Pastor!

Thus, racial sin is perpetuated by ignoring the issue altogether or by limiting the discussion to a bi-annual statement that "racism is bad," with no definition of what it is that is bad or preaching regarding what should be done about it.

The consequence of this inaction by white Pastors is a powerful *negative* spiritual chain reaction. The unrepentant Pastors extinguish their own spiritual lives by failing to preach against this sin in their own churches, communities, and nation. This results quickly in the cessation of spiritual growth in many of their congregation who harbor and pass on racial prejudice and practice discrimination in the church, workplace, and community. Even worse, these unchallenged attitudes and doctrines are passed on to the next generation who will one day, like their parents, see no contradiction between these attitudes

---

[lxii] When I write, "Christian social justice movement" I do not refer to a movement to change unbelievers and their institutions, but a movement *to get Christians to live like Christians* when it comes to issues pertaining to race in their personal lives and in their lives as members of various institutions such as schools, workplaces, and as citizens of communities and nations.
[lxiii] Exodus 22.21; Leviticus 25.17; Deuteronomy 24.14; Judges 2.18; Job 36.15; Psalms 9.9; 10.18; 62.10; 103.6; 146.7; Proverbs 22.22; Isaiah 1.17; 5:7; 33.15; Jeremiah 7.6; Zechariah 7.8-12; Malachi 3.5; Acts 7.24

and Christian holiness. The final link in the chain reaction is when the secular community witnesses the inconsistency of these attitudes with even common morality and become insensible to the evangelistic efforts of the church.

In this way a *reverse evangelism* is initiated where the racially prejudiced Christian is an advertisement for a version of Christianity that is entirely comfortable with racial prejudice, racial discrimination, and the systematic undermining of citizens of other races from equal participation in the American system. The church becomes ground zero of a negative spiritual chain reaction by which the entire nation is eventually brought under divine judgment.

> Zephaniah 3:1–7 (KJV 1900)
>
> 1 Woe to her that is filthy and polluted, <u>to the oppressing city!</u> 2 She obeyed not the voice; she received not correction; She trusted not in the LORD; she drew not near to her God. 3 Her princes within her are roaring lions; Her judges are evening wolves; They gnaw not the bones till the morrow. 4 <u>Her prophets are light and treacherous persons: Her priests have polluted the sanctuary, they have done violence to the law.</u> 5 The just LORD is in the midst thereof; he will not do iniquity: Every morning doth he bring his judgment to light, he faileth not; But the unjust knoweth no shame. 6 I have cut off the nations: their towers are desolate; I made their streets waste, that none passeth by: Their cities are destroyed, so that there is no man, that there is none inhabitant. 7 I said, Surely thou wilt fear me, thou wilt receive instruction; So their dwelling should not be cut off, howsoever I punished them: But they rose early, and corrupted all their doings.[57]

---

[43] Haselden, Kyle. The Racial Problem in Christian Perspective. New York: Harper Bros, 1959. 30.

[44] Appendix 2. Also: Jones, Robert P. White Too Long: The Legacy of White Supremacy in American Christianity. New York: Simon and Shuster, 2020. Chapters 1-2, 5.

[45] "30 Reasons for Segregation of Races"

"#1. God wills all races to be as He made them. Any violation of God's original purpose manifests insubordination to Him Acts (17.26; Rom 9.19-24)
#21. All nations will be segregated from one another in their own parts of the earth forever (Acts 17.26; Genesis 10.5, 32; 11.8-9; Dt 32.8; Dan 7.13-14; Zech 14; Rev 11.15; 21.24
#23. Even in heaven certain groups will not be allowed to worship together...
#30. Christians and certain other people of like race should be segregated..."

Dake, Finis Jennings. Dake's Annotated Reference Bible. Lawrenceville Ga.: Dake Bible Sales Inc. 1963. 159 [New Testament notes].

[46] "Charles Hodge (1797-1878), a native of Philadelphia and after 1820 the third person to join the Seminary faculty, likewise employed slave labor. In 1828, as his family was growing, he purchased Henrietta and a few years later acquired Lena, perhaps through his mother's estate."

Princeton Seminary and Slavery. "Princeton Seminary and Slavery." Accessed 03-28-2023. https://slavery.ptsem.edu/the-report/seminary-founders/.

[47] The Bible Argument On Slavery. By Charles Hodge, D.D., of Princeton, N. J. cited in Elliott, E.N. LL.D. Cotton is King and Pro-Slavery Arguments, Comprising the Writings of Hammond, Harper, Christy, Stringfellow, Hodge, Bledsoe, And Cartwright, on this Important Subject. Augusta, Ga: Pritchard, Abbott & Loomis. 1860.

[48] Dake. Finis. Dakes' Study Bible

[49] Keil, Karl Freidrich Delitzsch, Franz. *Commentary On The Old Testament, New Updated Edition, Electronic Database.* Peabody: Hendrickson Publishers, 1996. 134

[Note that when the subject is one of pathology or cursing, the Hamites are identified by scholars as black. When these same descendants of Ham are supplying the basis for Western civilization in the arts and sciences, they are whitened, or ethnic identification is largely absent. rw]

[50] Evans, Dr. Anthony. Are Blacks Spiritually Inferior to Whites. Renaissance Productions Inc., 1992. 26. Citing Sweet, William W. The Story of Religion in America. 170, 285.

[51] TIME.com. "Scenes From the Deadly Unrest in Charlottesville." Accessed April 30, 2023. https://time.com/charlottesville-white-nationalist-rally-clashes/.
[52] John MacArthur, The Gospel and Black Lives Matter https://www.youtube.com/watch?v=s3QZcVEDEPI

[53] Jones, Robert P. White Too Long: The Legacy of White Supremacy in American Christianity (p. 162). Simon & Schuster. Kindle Edition.

[54] Balmer, Randall. Thy Kingdom Come (pp. 13-14). Basic Books. Kindle Edition.

[55] **Reprove**: 33.417 ἐλέγχω; ἔλεγξις, εως *f*; ἐλεγμός, οῦ *m*: to state that someone has done wrong, with the implication that there is adequate proof of such wrongdoing—'to rebuke, to reproach, rebuke, reproach.'

[56] **Affliction**: G2347 45 occurrences; AV translates as "tribulation" 21 times, "affliction" 17 times, "trouble" three times, "anguish" once, "persecution" once, "burdened" once, and "to be afflicted + 1519" once. 1 a pressing, pressing together, pressure. 2 metaph. oppression, affliction, tribulation, distress, straits. [emphasis added]

[57] "3:1–2. The prophet made a general statement about Jerusalem's wickedness: she had sunk to the level of the heathen nations (cf. Hab. 1:2–4). Though Jerusalem is not named in Zephaniah 3:1, verse 2 shows that it was meant. Woe was a pronouncement of an indictment, an indictment that was here threefold: a city of oppressors (cf. Nineveh, which Nahum called "the city of blood," Nahum 3:1), rebellious and defiled. This general threefold indictment was then elaborated in Zephaniah 3:2–5: they oppressed their own people (v. 3), were rebellious against God (v. 2), and were defiled religiously (v. 4)."

John D. Hannah, "Zephaniah," in The Bible Knowledge Commentary: An Exposition of the Scriptures, ed. J. F. Walvoord and R. B. Zuck, vol. 1. Wheaton, IL: Victor Books, 1985. 1532.

The Scriptures provides a complete picture of the development of institutional, national oppression as a characteristic of the nation that has departed from the authority of the Word of God and the laws of morality. As individuals from every strata of society embrace oppression in their personal relationships, a culture of oppression develops which the Bible identifies as 1. the affliction of the weakest members of the society, 2. the subverting of the system of justice, 3. the proliferation of illegal and immoral schemes to acquire wealth and power at the expense of others and 4. systematic discrimination against the righteous.

5. Uses For The Concept Of Race

"Racism is the science of discrimination. Racism is the calculated introduction of discrimination into the institutions of society. Racism is a conspiracy to scientifically marginalize or destroy a specific racial group by the manipulation of the organs of society such as the family, government (including legislation, law enforcement and the courts), academia, the media, and the church."[lxiv]

The title of this Book is Revival and Nationbuilding. Its primary audience is the black local church.[58] Its objective is to explain how spiritual revival results in concrete positive changes to nations and peoples. These biblical truths must be applied to the hard realities of life as a black person in the United States. It is not practical to wave biblical generalities over these issues and hope that they go away. The scriptures provide definite answers to the problems faced by oppressed people. The scriptures expressly teach that Lucifer is the author of oppression in all its forms and that God is concerned about oppression and oppressed people.

> Luke 4:18–19 (KJV 1900)
> 18 The Spirit of the Lord is upon me, because he hath anointed me to preach the gospel to the poor; he hath sent me to heal the brokenhearted, to preach deliverance to the captives, and recovering

---

[lxiv] Chapter 2

63

of sight to the blind, to set at liberty them that are <u>bruised</u>, 19 To preach the acceptable year of the Lord.

> **Bruised** 22.22 θραύω; καταδυναστεύω; συμπνίγως (a figurative extension of meaning employing the base πνίγωα 'to choke,' 19.53): to cause serious trouble to, with the implication of dire consequences and probably a weakened state—'<u>to cause severe hardship, to oppress</u>, to overwhelm.[59] [emphasis added]

Although oppression is most often considered in its physical aspects, the most powerful effects of oppression are psychological and spiritual. Oppression is sustained by spiritual victories over the oppressed that result in psychological outcomes.[lxv] We must now address the *mind* of the black Christian. Until a believer has a self-concept that is consistent with what the Bible says about them, even correct Bible teaching will not have the effect it should have.

The man-made concept of race serves many useful functions consistent with its purpose as a means of consolidating and retaining power:

- ➢ Creating unearned self-esteem for the privileged groups.
- ➢ Justifying wars to gain geography, raw materials, and markets.
- ➢ Justifying slavery, the theft of labor.[60]
- ➢ Insulating and protecting wealth within privileged groups.
- ➢ Placing the most unattractive aspects of the curse of Adam upon others.

Biblical scholars have systematically taught a view of black people that is inconsistent with the Bible and with sound biblical interpretation [e.g., The Curse of Ham].[lxvi] The scholars quoted above and many others like them have been relied upon by preachers, teachers, and theologians throughout the history of this country. This is one reason why the church is still segregated and why social conservatism is still so closely identified with racial prejudice. People have been taught that God is racially prejudiced.

You, as a black person, cannot be in your right mind until proper Bible teaching has reversed the mental programming designed to enable your use under oppression. In Chapter 14 entitled, "Why there are so many churches" we establish that Satan has a plan for the church. Satan's plan for the church and for the nations includes a hefty dose of racism. Racism weakens nations and robs the church of its power. The strength of racism is magnified when it

---

[lxv] Isaiah 14.16-17; Romans 12.1-3
[lxvi] Chapter 4; Appendix 2; Appendix 3

is justified by scripture and incorporated into the practical theology of local churches.

---

[58] Some will take issue with the concept of a "black church." They will argue that a black church is not a biblical concept. To clarify, we must distinguish between the *Church spiritual* [which I will capitalize], the universal Body of Christ which spans all the Church age and all redeemed persons and the *local church*, which exists in some place and at some point in history. The universal Body of Christ knows no specific ethnicity but is of every tribe and tongue. The local church, on the other hand is almost always of some dominant ethnicity depending upon its location, point in history and other factors.

In the case of the black local church in America, it was created in large part by white churches who wanted no part of black members in their assemblies. The very persons who object to the term "black church" would depart their own congregations if the black population in the church exceeded the tipping point at which they began to feel personally threatened. They would leave even sooner if the black membership consisted of a significant number of black adolescent males. White Christians in America are also unwilling to sit under the authority of a black senior Pastor, another fact that ensures the continuation of the black local church.

White Christians essentially created the black church due to racial prejudice and ensures its continuation by policies that limit black and white engagement as equals in majority-white churches.

Also: Weems, Jr, Lovett H. "Challenge and Opportunity for Predominantly White Churches." Accessed 11-21-22 Lewis Center for Church Leadership (blog), January 18, 2022. https://www.churchleadership.com/leading-ideas/challenge-and-opportunity-for-predominantly-white-churches/.

Also: Craig, Maureen A., Julian M. Rucker, and Jennifer A. Richeson. "The Pitfalls and Promise of Increasing Racial Diversity: Threat, Contact, and Race Relations in the 21st Century." Accessed 11-21-22 Current Directions in Psychological Science 27, no. 3 (June 1, 2018): 188–93. https://doi.org/10.1177/0963721417727860.

Also: Mitchell, Travis. "Faith Among Black Americans." *Pew Research Center's Religion & Public Life Project* (blog), February 16, 2021. https://www.pewresearch.org/religion/2021/02/16/faith-among-black-americans/.

And: Lipka, Michael. "The Most and Least Racially Diverse U.S. Religious Groups." Pew Research Center (blog). Accessed November 21, 2022. https://www.pewresearch.org/fact-tank/2015/07/27/the-most-and-least-racially-diverse-u-s-religious-groups/.

[59] Johannes P. Louw and Eugene Albert Nida, Greek-English Lexicon of the New Testament: Based on Semantic Domains. New York: United Bible Societies, 1996. 244.

[60] The scriptures distinguish between slavery as the consequences of warfare, financial extremity, crime, or a permanent employment contract and slavery as an outright theft of labor. The former instances were regulated by God, the fourth was punishable by the death penalty by Scripture. In American history, Abraham Lincoln recognized slavery as nothing less than the theft of labor.

> "To read carefully the Lincoln economic parable of the ant (reprinted here) suggests a lost truth about our sixteenth president: during most of Abraham Lincoln's political career he focused not on anti-slavery but on economic policy. Yet anti-slavery and economic policy,

in his worldview, were tightly linked. As Lincoln explained, slavery was grounded in coercion. It was, and is, an involuntary economic exchange of labor. In commercial terms, slavery is theft: "The ant, who has toiled and dragged a crumb to his nest, will furiously defend the fruit of his labor, against whatever robber assails him. .&nsp;"

"'To Give All a Chance': Lincoln, Abolition, and Economic Freedom | Gilder Lehrman Institute of American History." Accessed November 21, 2022. https://www.gilderlehrman.org/history-resources/essays/give-all-chance-lincoln-abolition-and-economic-freedom.

Also, from President Lincoln himself:

"I have always thought that all men should be free; but if any should be slaves it should be first those who desire it for *themselves*, and secondly, those who *desire* it for *others*. Whenever [I] hear any one arguing for slavery I feel a strong impulse to see it tried on him personally," President Lincoln told an Indiana Regiment passing through Washington less than a month before his murder.1

"Indeed, work was as essentiala (sic) value as freedom, argued Mr. Lincoln. In 1854, Mr. Lincoln wrote: "The ant, who has toiled and dragged a crumb to his nest, will furiously defend the fruit of his labor, against whatever robber assails him. So plain, that the most dumb and stupid slave that ever toiled for a master, does constantly know that he is wronged. So plain that no one, high or low, ever does mistake it, except in a plainly selfish way; for although volume upon volume is written to prove slavery a very good thing, we never hear of the man who wishes to take the good of it, by being a slave himself."9"

Lehman, Lewis E. "Mr. Lincoln and Freedom." Accessed 04-09-2023. https://abrahamlincoln.org/features/essays/mr-lincoln-and-freedom/.

6. What Racism Does To Black People

"The Political Economic Necessity of Madness"

"If an effort is made to get to the roots of mental problems and other kinds of problems that exist within the Afrikan American individual and community, it must begin with an analysis of the political context in which they exist.

"It must start with the recognition of the fact that juvenile delinquency, criminality, mental problems, family problems, and other kinds of problems which are prevalent in our community **are social necessities**...that in order for us as a people to be in the situation we are in, and not be in concentration camps and not have guns pointed at our heads throughout the day, we must be maintained in a particular state of mind. In a sense then, we literally must be out of our minds--and we must be kept out of our minds."[61] [emphasis added]

In Chapter 1, reasons were provided as to why it is imperative to discuss race *biblically*. One reason was because you cannot grow to your spiritual potential until your mind is changed from that of a disadvantaged and inferior minority to the mind of Christ. These two minds (inferior minority vs. mind of Christ) cannot profitably coexist, but this is precisely what many people are grappling with spiritually.

These spiritual realities have effects in every other realm: social, economic, political, and psychological. Oppression, from its spiritual base of operations within the *world system*,[62] launches attacks within each of these spheres.

The black American lives in a world where race determines nearly everything:

Race determines for many black people where they will live, where they go to church, where they work, whether they can work at all, whether they will advance on the job, how they are treated by the police, how they are treated in court, what school their children go to, what they are taught or not taught when they get there, what access their community will have to public services, whether they can vote and whether that vote will be counted, [63] what kind of medical treatment they receive,[64] how they are portrayed in television, films, and the news: all of these things are directly impacted by race and more often than not the black individual is the recipient of the short end in each of these situations.

On the other hand, a black person is told that she is in the situation she is in because her people, black people, have the tendency to make bad decisions. She is loudly told that there is no racial conspiracy (while books and curricula that accurately portray American history are banned from libraries and schools)[65] and anyone who claims that there is anything systematic about discrimination is a whiner, a democrat, subject to paranoia and is playing the race card to extort some benefit or advantage.

This same black person goes to church where a well-meaning Pastor tells her that now that she's a Christian, she isn't black anymore (in other words, that cultural identity is no longer a factor in life) and that she shouldn't see color. Now, this Christian knows that everybody sees color, and especially Christians. She also notes that other groups get to retain their ethnic and cultural identity after salvation. No one must stop being Korean, Ukrainian, or Jewish because they have been born again. No one except her. She reads Galatians where Paul confronts Peter on making the saved Gentiles live like Jews [Galatians 2.11-21]. Meanwhile every time she listens to conservative Christian radio, she feels uneasy, as if there is a problem in America and she is that problem.

If this woman does not have an emotional problem, then it is a miracle. She may have what W.E.B. DuBois called a "double consciousness:"[66] as a black citizen she is a part of America, but she is also the enemy of her country, the source of her country's problems.

Many therapists, psychologists and psychiatrists have shown that individual and structural racism creates an undercurrent of rage in black people.[67] This rage is harshly punished by society if it is expressed towards[68] or even in the presence of white people. This rage results in many self-destructive behaviors[lxvii] and even in physical illness. Happy, humble black people are complimented, while a serious and possibly angry countenance is questioned and discouraged.

The effect of this double consciousness and the rage which is beneath it may come out in her attitude towards her husband, or in the way she disciplines her children, or perhaps, at work one day after 15 years she will tell off her white manager over some mistreatment she had put up with without complaint all that time. She may develop a dependency that, unknown to her, she is using to address the pain caused by having an identity, a self-concept, that she cannot live with.

The situation is very painful for young people who are bombarded with negative black concepts on television, in the music specifically produced for their consumption, in the depressed nature of their communities, in the education that informed them that they had no history before slavery and that the institution of slavery was the means by which they heard the gospel, the brainwashing that slavery was a civilizing and sanctifying event for Africans.

These young black people are forming a self-image that is conflicted between the miserable model of blackness provided by our American institutions and what every young person innately believes should be their potential and birthright. The really sad part is that they cannot go to the typical black church and receive an accurate picture of who they are, what their people have accomplished and what their personal destiny might be in Christ, because the acquisition an accurate self-concept is outside the precincts of the gospel, according to their Pastors, if it touches race in any way and if it offends white people in any way.

Black young people are usually thoroughly demoralized after they have been exposed to a definition of blackness received from the media, the public school system, and the church. They have been told that they and their parents are the *sole* reason for their situation and if they would only make decisions like white people do, then they could live like white people live. The fact that there is a massive intergenerational system devoted to their disadvantage, if it is mentioned at all, is labeled as a conspiracy theory that is an excuse for irresponsibility.

[lxvii] Chapter 18-See Chart: Psychosocial Effects of Racism

Romans 12 teaches that a person who is not thinking rationally about themselves, a person that is out of touch with reality when it comes to their self-concept, cannot properly advance spiritually, or serve God as they should.[lxviii] Wrong thinking regarding race and one's identity as a black American can and does result in spiritual disaster. The attempt to layer a theology of the spiritual life upon this psychological wreckage, without addressing its existence, is Pastoral malpractice of the first order.

[lxviii] Chapter 7

[61] Wilson, Amos N. The Falsification of Afrikan Consciousness: Eurocentric History, Psychiatry, and the Politics of White Supremacy. Second Edition. New York: Afrikan World InfoSystems, 2014. 65, 66.

[62] Referring to the word "world" in 1John 2.15-17 Wuest notes the following:

"(2:15–17) The word "world" here is kosmos (κοσμος) which in its use here is defined by Vincent as follows: "The sum-total of human life in the ordered world, considered apart from, alienated from, and hostile to God, and of the earthly things which seduce from God (John 7:7; 15:18; 17:9, 14; I Cor. 1:20, 21; II Cor. 7:10; James 4:4)." Kosmos (Κοσμος) refers to an ordered system. Here it is the ordered system of which Satan is the head, his fallen angels and demons are his emissaries, and the unsaved of the human race are his subjects, together with those purposes, pursuits, pleasures, practices, and places where God is not wanted. Much in this world-system is religious, cultured, refined, and intellectual. But it is anti-God and anti-Christ.

"Trench quotes Bengel as saying that this world of unsaved humanity is inspired by "the spirit of the age," the Zeitgeist, which Trench defines as follows: "All that floating mass of thoughts, opinions, maxims, speculations, hopes, impulses, aims, aspirations, at any time current in the world, which it may be impossible to seize and accurately define, but which constitutes a most real and effective power, being the moral, or immoral atmosphere which at every moment of our lives we inhale, again inevitably to exhale." This is the world-system to which John refers." (Emphasis added) Kenneth S. Wuest, Wuest's Word Studies from the Greek New Testament: For the English Reader, vol. 13 (Grand Rapids: Eerdmans, 1997), 125–126.

[63] Baker, Mike. "Rejected Mail Ballots Are Showing Racial Disparities." The New York Times, February 3, 2022, sec. U.S. Accessed 03-25-2023 https://www.nytimes.com/2022/02/02/us/mail-voting-black-latino.html.

United States Commission on Civil Rights. "Voting Irregularities in Florida During the 2000 Presidential Election, Executive Summary." Accessed 03-25-2023. https://www.usccr.gov/files/pubs/vote2000/report/exesum.htm.

Palast, Greg. "1 Million Black Votes Didn't Count in the 2000 Presidential Election / It's Not Too Hard to Get Your Vote Lost -- If Some Politicians Want It to Be Lost." SFGATE, June 20, 2004. https://www.sfgate.com/opinion/article/1-million-black-votes-didn-t-count-in-the-2000-2747895.php.

[64] "Why Do Some Americans Live Longer Than Others? | Time." Accessed April 15, 2023. https://time.com/6270808/americas-life-expectancy-divide/

AAMC. "How We Fail Black Patients in Pain." Accessed April 15, 2023. https://www.aamc.org/news-insights/how-we-fail-black-patients-pain.

[65] Heim, Joe, and Lori Rozsa. "African Americans Say the Teaching of Black History Is under Threat." Accessed 11-21-2022 Washington Post, February 26, 2022. https://www.washingtonpost.com/education/2022/02/23/schools-black-history-month-crt/.

Also: Meckler, Laura, and Hannah Natanson. "New Critical Race Theory Laws Have Teachers Scared, Confused and Self-Censoring." Accessed 11-21-2022 Washington Post, February 15, 2022. https://www.washingtonpost.com/education/2022/02/14/critical-race-theory-teachers-fear-laws/.

[66] DuBois, W. E. B. "Strivings of the Negro People." The Atlantic, August 1, 1897. https://www.theatlantic.com/magazine/archive/1897/08/strivings-of-the-negro-people/305446/.

[67] Op. Cit., Fanon, Frantz. The Wretched of the Earth.

Also: Wilson, Amos N. Understanding Black Adolescent Male Violence: Its Prevention and Remediation. 1st ed. AWIS Lecture Series. New York: Afrikan World InfoSystems, 1992. 1-20.

Also: Kardiner, Abram, Ovesey, Lionel. The Mark of Oppression, Explorations in the Personality of the American Negro. Cleveland: World 1951. 303-307.

And: Grier W.H., Cobbs P.M., Black Rage. New York: Basic, 1968. 1-17.

[68] Kennedy, Randall. Race, Crime, and the Law. 1st ed. New York: Pantheon Books, 1997. 71, 74

7. A New Frame Of Mind

The Road to Real Mental Health through the Word of God

"For oppression begins as a psychological fact and is in good part a psychological state. If oppression is to operate with maximum efficiency, it must become and remain a psychological condition achieving self-perpetuating motion by its own internal dynamics and by its own inertial momentum."[69]

Romans 12:3 (KJV 1900)
3 For I say, through the grace given unto me, to every man that is among you, not to think of himself more highly than he ought to think; but to think soberly [NT4998], according as God hath dealt to every man the measure of faith.

NT:4998 sophron (so'-frone); from the base of NT:4982 and that of NT:5424; safe (sound) in mind, i.e. self-controlled (moderate as to opinion or passion):[70]

A.T. Robertson translates, "to be in ones right mind"[71]

Paul tells the Romans that they need to be in their right minds. He informs them that having an improper estimation of oneself will interfere in the objective given in verse one of chapter 12.

Romans 12:1 (KJV 1900)
1 I beseech you therefore, brethren, by the mercies of God, that ye present

your bodies a living sacrifice, holy, acceptable unto God, which is your
reasonable service.

Not being in one's right mind will result in the malfunction of the spiritual
life, limiting sanctification ("present your bodies…") and thus limiting one's
ability to serve and to glorify God.

What does the concept of race accomplish but to put one group in the
position of having unearned self-esteem ("to think of himself more highly
than he ought") while others are made symbols of inferiority? Racism
manufactures a corrupted self-concept in both its beneficiaries and its victims.

Therefore, the race concept destroys spiritual capacity in the one who "thinks
more highly of himself than he ought to think" as well as the one trained to
accept his permanent inferior status to others.

*When you harbor incorrect attitudes about who you are, you are out of touch with reality
and not in your right mind. The person in this condition is hampered in their ability provide
God reasonable spiritual service.*

The Scriptures are supernatural, but they are not magic. The Word of God
must be directly applied to the issue of race to counteract its disastrous mental
and spiritual effects in both blacks and whites. The lack of accurate Bible
teaching and preaching in this area is part of the satanic strategy against the
Church. Oppression *requires* the suppression of accurate Bible teaching,
especially to the objects of oppression.

> Romans 12:3 (KJV 1900)
> 3 For I say, through the grace given unto me, to every man that is among
> you, not to think of himself more highly than he ought to think; but to think
> soberly, according as God hath dealt to every man the measure of faith.

The context of verse three is that believers should not be inflated in pride by
an inaccurate self-assessment based upon who has what spiritual gift. An
inaccurate self-concept based upon spiritual gifts *or anything else* cripple's one's
capacity to serve God. An accurate self-concept based upon the Word of God
and faith is necessary to provide reasonable service to God. It is precisely this
capacity that is damaged by racism. I use the term "racism' here because the
operation that corrupts the self-image is the product of an organized,
premeditated strategy that is designed to perpetuate oppression. This
psychological and spiritual damage can be reversed by the Word of God, but

it just so happens that sound Bible teaching is the one thing that is always lacking among people who are under oppression.

Romans 12.1-3 commands the believer to present himself to God, which is his "reasonable service." The sense is that we are at God's disposal, always ready to execute his commands, whatever they may be.

> Romans 12:2 (KJV 1900)
> 2 And be not conformed to this world: but be ye transformed <u>by</u> the renewing of your <u>mind</u>, that ye may prove what is that good, and acceptable, and perfect, will of God.

> **Mind: 3563 νοῦς** [*nous*/nooce/] n.m. Probably from the base of 1097; TDNT 4:951; TDNTA 636; GK 3808; 24 occurrences; AV translates as "mind" 21 times, and "understanding" three times. **1** the mind, comprising alike the faculties of perceiving and understanding and those of feeling, judging, determining. **1a** the intellectual faculty, the understanding. **1b** reason in the narrower sense, as the capacity for spiritual truth, the higher powers of the soul, the faculty of perceiving divine things, of recognising goodness and of hating evil. **1c** the power of considering and judging soberly, calmly and impartially. **2** a particular mode of thinking and judging, i.e thoughts, feelings, purposes, desires[lxix]

That mental attitude spoken of in verse three is to be acquired in verse two by the renewing of the *mind*. If you are not in your right mind by means of this renewal,[lxx] then you cannot consistently be at God's disposal; you will experience greater than normal difficulty in serving him because of your cognitive issues. This applies to the mentally oppressed as well as the one with artificial self-esteem because of the race concept. To perform the spiritual service of Romans 12.1 we must have the cognitive renewal of Romans 12.2 resulting in the biblical self-concept of Romans 12.3.

The proper understanding of the Word and its application to the actual problems we face as black people results in a renewal that gives you an accurate [biblical] self-concept. You are responsible for your life [thoughts, motivations, decisions, and actions], but you are not responsible for the spiritual and social strategies of discrimination and racism. It is the denial of the existence of *racism as a system*, often by Christians, that makes the only explanation of your situation personal irresponsibility, ethnic inferiority, or both. Despite the claims of the world around you, you are not imagining

---

[lxix] James Strong, Enhanced Strong's Lexicon (Woodside Bible Fellowship, 1995).
[lxx] By "renewal" is meant the process of mental rehabilitation that occurs when one receives sound biblical teaching under the power of the Holy Spirit.

things: Satan sponsors racism as a key tactic to weaken nations and to destroy the spiritual power of the Church. You are not crazy, someone has been lying to you: but if you are systematically learning and applying the Word to your entire life, including your experience as a black person in America, you are in your right mind, or you will be soon.

A Word to Black Pastors

A word to black Pastors. Black people have been speaking in code[72] when around white people since the days of slavery. This was necessary to communicate without incurring the certain retaliation that resistance to oppression would bring. That retaliation still occurs today, usually in non-violent ways. Often the only thing that prevents us from saying to our congregations the things that need to be said is *an internal alarm* that warns you to resort to coded language or avoid the topic altogether. Add to this the accusation by both whites and some black people that by teaching your people directly about these things you are sowing division in the church and drawing focus away from Christ. These are effective internal and external safeguards that prevent important teaching that black believers must hear.

Others among you are convinced that there may be racism embedded in our society, but it is a spiritual problem for the whites who participate in the system, not us. You should see by now that this is false. The only audience that you have any reasonable chance to rescue from the spiritual effects of racism is your own congregation.

Still others do not want to be stigmatized: you see issues like these as many white Pastors like to see them: as side issues, peripheral concerns that do not pertain to the gospel or the kingdom of God. Racism as a spiritual strategy of Satan and its role as an organizing principle of western society depends upon your retaining these positions. On the other hand, the spiritual health of your congregation and the spiritual revival of your community depend upon the overthrow of these false concepts. No nation or people has ever overcome the nullification of their pulpits (First Principle of Nationbuilding). You must understand the issues and the stakes and then speak plainly to your Congregation so that they will be equipped for effective spiritual ministry to the Community. The purpose of this book is to assist you in accomplishing this end.

A Word to White Pastors

A word to white Pastors. If you had a problem in your congregation with adultery; if there was an epidemic of fornication, divorce, and remarriage among your people, how would you address it? Would you continue your series on Colossians and pray that the Lord handles it? What if one Sunday you attempted to directly address the issue in your sermon and after the service, members approached you saying, "Pastor, just stick to the gospel?" It is likely that you have a racial prejudice problem[73] with more than a few members of your church. If you do, it is destroying the spiritual lives of your flock just as any besetting sin would, with cascading effects to the surrounding community. Denial doesn't mean it is not there. God holds the watchman responsible regardless [Ezekiel 3.18].

Secondly, it is impossible to limit oppression to its intended victims forever. The oppression practiced by biblical Israel ultimately was practiced upon them by other nations. In America the scientific oppression beta-tested and perfected upon black people over the centuries, is now being unleashed upon the white population. *You* are now experiencing the loss of legal rights, an increase in police power, and many encroachments upon personal freedom that are being blamed upon other races but originate in your own cherished systems of privilege. Without divine intervention, it will get worse.[lxxi] The closing of churches from coast-to-coast during the COVID outbreak is emblematic of this judgment. God can provide revival and refreshing to the nation, but not without repentance. If you are not a direct participant in the justification of oppression, then you must become a voice against it in the pulpit and in the Sunday school. Or you can do nothing and maybe it will go away on its own.

[lxxi] Leviticus 26.14-40; Romans 1.21-32

SECTION TWO: REVIVIAL AND NATIONBUILDING

8. Why Isn't the Church More Effective?

Important Questions for the Church

> ➤ Do you ever wonder why we have churches on every corner, but we live in a world where it often appears that the Bible is having no impact? Why isn't the church more effective?
> ➤ Do you ever wonder why there are so many preachers and so many different and conflicting interpretations of the Bible?
> ➤ Do you believe that the Bible should teach a people how to lift themselves up, to elevate their families and communities and to secure a better destiny on earth as well as heaven?
> ➤ Do you believe that the Bible should equip people to rise above problems like racism?

All of these questions have biblical answers and Pastors, churches and individuals can implement them to bring about spiritual Revival and Nationbuilding.

Quick Answers

➤ The local church cannot be effective unless Pastors and elders [**Clergy**] are spiritually fit.

➤ The local church will not positively and powerfully impact the **Community** until it is committed to making disciples of Christ among the **Congregation**.

➤ The local church will not change the destiny of black America for the better if false teaching is tolerated, embraced and financially rewarded.

➤ The local church will not bring about spiritual revival and national blessing if believers (the Congregation, not Pastors) are not *spiritually* impacting the Community themselves in a direct way.

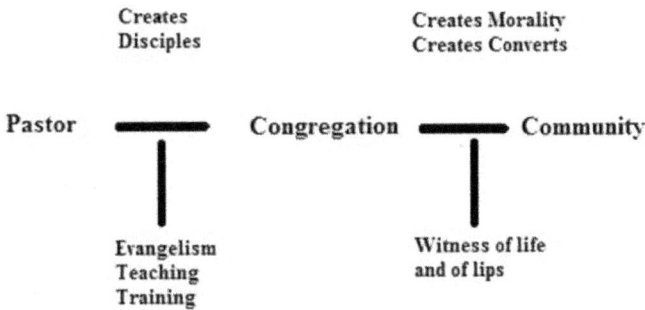

	Creates Disciples			Creates Morality Creates Converts

Pastor ━━━━▶ **Congregation** ━━━▶ **Community**

	Evangelism Teaching Training			Witness of life and of lips

Figure 2: Overview of Positive Spiritual Chain Reaction

Overview-Pastors to Congregation to Community: The Spiritual Chain Reaction

When the Pastor/Elder (Clergy)[lxxii] is spiritually revived, when he becomes committed to a biblical lifestyle and the frequent, accurate, systematic teaching (FAST) of the Word of God then *disciples* of Jesus Christ are created within the Congregation.

[lxxii] From this point forward, the three major constituencies of our study will be capitalized: Clergy, Congregation and Community [meaning the secular Community]

Disciples effectively wage spiritual warfare in order to live as God requires	Disciples know their bibles and love the Word of God
Disciples hear, read, study, memorize and meditate upon the Word for themselves	Disciples know how to pray and how to witness
Disciples use their spiritual gifts to minister to others	Disciples teach others to be disciples.

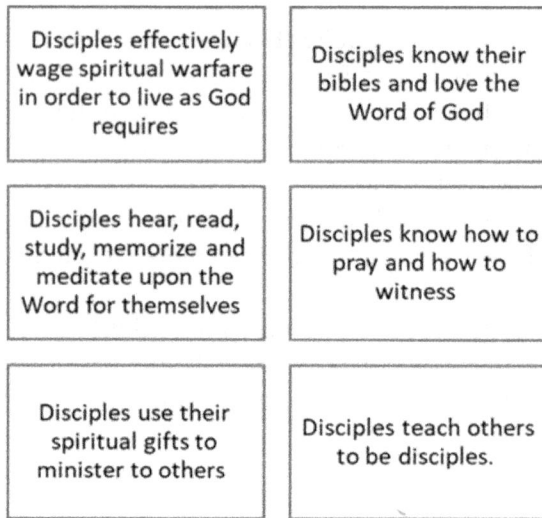

Figure 3: What Disciples Do

The Congregation that is spiritually mature can apply its own spiritual gifts in ministry both within and outside of the church. The Congregation realizes its dual responsibility to impact the Community through the witness of its Life (through sanctification) and its Lips (through gospel proclamation). The Congregation understands that they are the Church, and it is their responsibility to minister to the Community.

This ministry of the Congregation to the Community has profound consequences. First, the Community sees the example (or model) of the Congregation in their marriages, their families, in the workplace and in citizenship. These models demonstrate God's design for these institutions to the unbeliever. Secondly, some members of the Community become Christians themselves, ultimately becoming agents of God in the Community. Eventually, through evangelism and through the modeling of mature believers, the marriages, and families of *unbelievers* are strengthened and the Community is restored to healthy function. The repair and strengthening of Marriage and Family is the first stage of nationbuilding and cultural rebirth. These benefits cascade to impact Community economics and political power. Cultural expression through the arts and education is purified and advanced by this same spiritual process.

Culture   Economics   Community   Spiritual Life   Political
                         Dynamics   Power

Family

Marriage

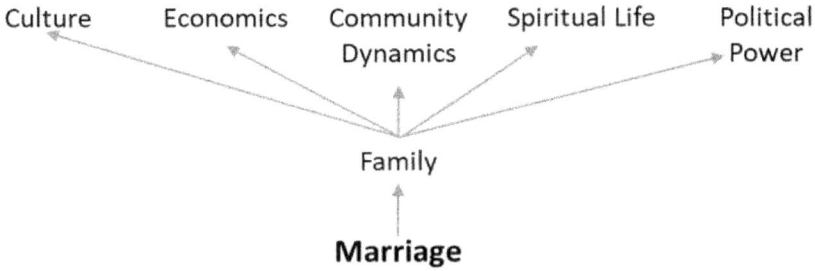

Figure 4: The Power of Family Dynamics

---

[69] Wilson, Amos N. The Falsification of Afrikan Consciousness: Eurocentric History, Psychiatry, and the Politics of White Supremacy. Second Edition. New York: Afrikan World InfoSystems, 2014. 3.

[70] Strong, James. A Concise Dictionary of the Words in the Greek Testament and The Hebrew Bible. Bellingham, WA: Logos Bible Software, 2009.

[71] "[Not to think of himself more highly than he ought to think (μη ὑπερφρονειν παρ' ὁ δει φρονειν [mē huperphronein par' ho dei phronein]). Indirect negative command after λεγω [legō] (I say). Play on the two infinitives φρονειν [phronein], to think, and ὑπερφρονειν [huperphronein] (old verb from ὑπερφρων [huperphrōn], over-proud, here only in N. T.) to "over-think" with παρ' ὁ [par' ho] (beyond what) added. Then another play on φρονειν [phronein] and σωφρονειν [sōphronein] (old verb from σωφρων [sōphrōn], sober-minded), to be in one's right mind (Mark 5:15; 2 Corinthians. 5:13). Self-conceit is here treated as a species of insanity. A measure of faith (μετρον πιστεως [metron pisteōs]). Accusative case, the object of the verb ἐμερισεν [emerisen]. Each has his gift from God (1 Corinthians. 3:5; 4:7). There is no occasion for undue pride. To each man (ἑκαστῳ [hekastōi]). Emphatic position before ὡς [hōs] (as) and emphasizes the diversity." [emphasis added] Robertson, A.T. Word Pictures in the New Testament Nashville, TN: Broadman Press, 1933. Romans 12:3.

[72] "Broadly, code-switching involves adjusting one's style of speech, appearance, behavior, and expression in ways that will optimize the comfort of others in exchange for fair treatment, quality service, and employment opportunities. Research suggests that code-switching often occurs in spaces where negative stereotypes of black people run counter to what are considered "appropriate" behaviors and norms for a specific environment." McCluney, Courtney L., Kathrina Robotham, Serenity Lee, Richard Smith, and Myles Durkee. "The Costs of Code-Switching." *Harvard Business Review*, November 15, 2019. https://hbr.org/2019/11/the-costs-of-codeswitching.

[73] From Chapter 2: Definition of Terms

"Prejudice is the individual human decision to prefer or not prefer someone or something."

This decision may be based on facts or opinions, experience, or the influence of others. The decision to prefer or not to prefer may be rational or irrational, beneficial, or self-destructive.

Racial prejudice is prejudice based upon one's beliefs about a man-made category of people.

Prejudice is internal; it is a system of beliefs, attitudes, thoughts, and motivations, but not actions. Prejudice is a mental attitude.

9. The Spiritual Chain Reaction-Pastors and Elders (Clergy)

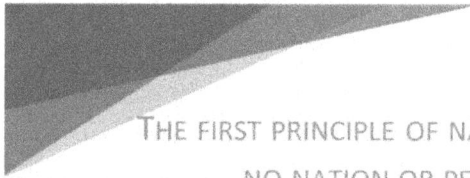

THE FIRST PRINCIPLE OF NATION BUILDING:
NO NATION OR PEOPLE HAVE EVER
SURVIVED THE NULLIFICATION OF THEIR
PASTORS.

Richard Walker

Figure 5: First Nationbuilding Principle

Spiritual Instruction Through Pastors and Elders

There is no real Nationbuilding without spiritual power.

The *accurate* teaching of the Word of God is the prerequisite for the exercise of spiritual power. This teaching is the primary job of the Pastors and Elders [1 Timothy 5.17].

Either you are building with God's power or with the power of this world, which is Satan's power.[lxxiii] For there to be dynamic spiritual impact upon any Community we must unleash God's power.[lxxiv] God is not going to spend power on behalf of half-committed Christians [Ephesians 4.30]. This is especially true if the Pastor is the half-committed individual. For the kind of power to be brought to bear that will make lasting changes in the Community, the leadership of the local church must be spiritually revived.

God has ordained the Clergy (Pastors and Elders) as the means of the spiritual instruction, training, and protection of the Congregation. He is the key human actor in the healthy function of the local church. The first principle of Nationbuilding is that "No nation or people have ever survived the nullification of their Pastors." The Pastors and Elders protect the local church through the accurate teaching of the Word of God, and the identification of spiritual error.

> Ephesians 4:11–14 (KJV 1900)
> 11 And he gave some, apostles; and some, prophets; and some, evangelists; and some, Pastors and teachers; 12 For the perfecting of the saints, for the work of the ministry, for the edifying of the body of Christ: 13 Till we all come in the unity of the faith, and of the knowledge of the Son of God, unto a perfect man, unto the measure of the stature of the fulness of Christ: 14 That we henceforth be no more children, tossed to

---

[lxxiii] John 12.31; 2 Corinthians 4.4
[lxxiv] Matthew 28.19-20; Acts 1.8

and fro, and carried about with every wind of doctrine, by the
sleight of men, and cunning craftiness, whereby they lie in wait
to deceive;

Acts 20:28 (KJV 1900)
28 Take heed therefore unto yourselves, and to all the flock,
over the which the Holy Ghost hath made you overseers, to feed
the church of God, which he hath purchased with his own
blood.

Spiritual Protection Through Pastors and Elders

While God himself ensures there is always a remnant of sound and
faithful teachers in the Community, the 21st century has been a
time of doctrinal retrogression for the black local church, as it has
been for all churches.

Many churches in the black community today have issues with
erroneous teaching.[74] False biblical teaching cripples the local
church by disrupting the process of discipleship. Disciples are
made by accurate teaching and training from the Word of God.
The lack of mature disciples entering the Community eventually
results in a negative spiritual chain reaction which undermines
primary institutions of marriage and family. This is because the
malfunctioning local church is no longer performing its role as the
immune system of the Community, which is now subject to spiritual
disease systems originating from both unrestrained humanity and
demonic principalities.

Acts 20:29-30 (KJV 1900)
29 For I know this, that after my departing shall grievous wolves
enter in among you, not sparing the flock. 30 Also of your own
selves shall men arise, speaking perverse things, to draw away
disciples after them.

Jeremiah 2:8 (KJV 1900)
8 The priests said not, Where is the LORD? and they that handle
the law knew me not: the Pastors also transgressed against me,

and the prophets prophesied by Baal, and walked after things that do not profit.

Figure 6: How the Local Church Protects the Community

False teaching is always prevalent and in good supply among oppressed people: it is a key factor in keeping them oppressed.[lxxv] Spiritual actions always precede effects in the world [Psalms 127.1]. The reason for this is the inherent weakness of humanity. There are a great many things that men can do, but they cannot do these things except under the auspices and power of a spiritual authority.[lxxvi]

The practitioners of the science of discrimination know this fact

---

[lxxv] Jeremiah 2.8; Hosea 4.6; 1 Timothy 1.3; Titus 1.9
[lxxvi] Psalms 127.1; Ephesians 2.1-3

well and liberally support the sowing of exploited communities with false teachers and false Christian doctrine. The nullification of the local church means that the oppressed Community will suffer from every category of human exploitation and spiritual deception. This is how you can have 100 churches in your Community and yet lose your institutions of marriage and family.

Many sound Pastors who should know better have sacrificed sound teaching to grow their Congregations and to retain church members.[lxxvii] The world wants religion without submission to God through the Scriptures. It wants a spiritual experience that does not get in the way of the beliefs and preferences of the churchgoer. God's method of church ministry is counterintuitive to men. God convicts the Community of sin, directs them to a single, exclusive way of salvation and promotes the spiritual development of the believer by denial of self and the rigorous study and application of the Word of God. By contrast, the methods that will rapidly grow churches are usually the same practices that will *obstruct* evangelism and disciple making. In fact, the most effective church growth techniques cause the destruction of spiritual lives by teaching people that the Bible is not to be taken seriously.

The Bible does not instruct the Elders to grow the church, but to evangelize and make disciples. Growing the church is God's own business. It is not the responsibility of the Clergy to manage outcomes, not even spiritual ones. Only God has the power to cause spiritual success. The job of the believer, regardless of his gift, is to faithfully execute what God has commanded.

The truly called and spiritually effective Pastor is not attempting to please man but God. It is in this way that God provides all that is

---

[lxxvii] There is a popular church growth formula that includes the acceptance of charismatic doctrine as well as the ordination of women [1 Timothy 2.9-14]. This methodology has spread throughout the black church and with it, elements of the equally false Word of Faith teaching. You cannot advance the Will of God by violating the Word of God.

needed for the growth and well-being of the local church. *There are no celebrity Pastors in the Bible.* From John the Baptist preaching in the wilderness of Judea to John the apostle on the isle of Patmos, true gospel preaching brought not fame but persecution and death.

Even worse, many Pastors have become friends with the spiritual exploiters and the false teachers. They share their pulpits and do not warn their people about their preacher friends' teachings and lifestyles. These otherwise sound Pastors want to be a part of the "Honorarium Club" and can only remain if they keep their mouths shut.

Other Pitfalls of Modern Pastors

Still other Pastors and Elders are wedded to dead traditions which do not edify the church. They are committed to rituals and practices that were meaningful in the agricultural era but had lost their meaning even in our grandparents' time. These churches have sound doctrinal statements but unsound preaching, they demand adherence to the church covenant but not to the Bible. The church building is pointing east, and upstairs is the Masonic Lodge.

There are other good men who have lost their way into sin and have thereby killed the effectiveness of their preaching and teaching by grieving the Spirit.[lxxviii] Their lifestyle, marriages and family have become liabilities in the gospel ministry, but they will not correct the situation and they will not leave the church.

Yet there is every reason for hope. God does not need the many to rescue the black nation. The few sound men who are faithfully discharging their ministry are sufficient to catalyze the revival necessary for nationbuilding. They need encouragement, support, and divine direction for this specific task of nationbuilding, but they already possess the main things God demands of the man of

---

[lxxviii] Ephesians 4.30; 1Timothy 3.2-7

God.

> Colossians 1:25–29 (KJV 1900)
> [25] Whereof I am made a minister, according to the dispensation
> of God which is given to me for you, to fulfil the word of God;
> [26] *Even* the mystery which hath been hid from ages and from
> generations, but now is made manifest to his saints: [27] To whom
> God would make known what *is* the riches of the glory of this
> mystery among the Gentiles; which is Christ in you, the hope of
> glory: [28] Whom we preach, warning every man, and teaching
> every man in all wisdom; that we may present every man perfect
> in Christ Jesus: [29] Whereunto I also labour, striving according to
> his working, which worketh in me mightily.

This means that for those Pastors who are not erroneous teachers
and who have not disqualified themselves from the gospel ministry,
a change of motivation may need to occur. It may be a change
from a financial motivation; a change from a church growth
motivation; perhaps a change from a self-preservation motivation
to a motivation to glorify God by winning the lost and making
disciples. For other men of God there must be a change of lifestyle:
repentance, prayer, a new commitment to the Word of God and
victory over sin.

This kind of fundamental change in the life and ministry of the
Pastor/Elder comes from repentance which always precedes
revival. *Repentance must start with leadership or there will be no revival.*
Spiritually compromised leadership kills revival. It is repentance
among the leadership of the church that starts the change that will
result in the renovation of a Community though God's power.

The Pastor is the key human actor in the spiritual warfare who, if
he performs his duty, will make possible the transformation of our
Community through the Congregation.

---

[74] Major erroneous systems include Charismatic and Word of faith teaching, ecumenical associations of Pastors and congregations, and local churches given over to politics.

A Pew Study indicates that one half of church services attended by blacks include speaking in tongues.

Mitchell, Travis. "Faith Among Black Americans." Accessed 11-22-2022 Pew Research Center's Religion & Public Life Project (blog), February 16, 2021. https://www.pewresearch.org/religion/2021/02/16/faith-among-black-americans/.

This does not include churches that believe in tongues but do not practice it in their services. The charismatic and Word of Faith teachings have become so intertwined. as to become indistinguishable.

MacArthur, John. Strange Fire: The Danger of Offending the Holy Spirit with Counterfeit Worship. Nashville, Tennessee: Thomas Nelson, 2013. 8-9; 14-1

10. The Spiritual Chain Reaction: The Congregation

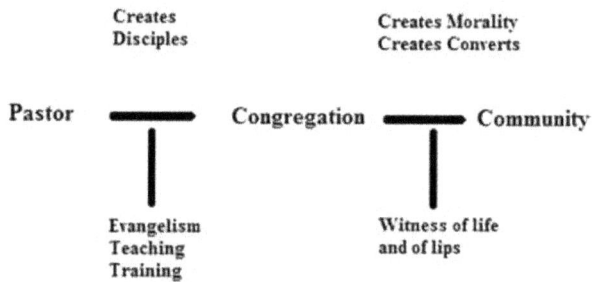

		Creates Morality
Creates		Creates Converts
Disciples		

Pastor ■━━━▶ Congregation ■━━━▶ Community

Evangelism	Witness of life
Teaching	and of lips
Training	

Figure 7: The Spiritual Chain Reaction-Pastor to Congregation

Once the Pastor has dealt with his own spiritual issues, he can now focus upon his ministry. The second stage of the spiritual process that will result in the transformation of the Community is the Pastor's single-minded focus upon creating disciples of Christ in the Congregation. The emphasis moves from the *heart* of the Pastor to his *ministry* to the Congregation. Through discipleship, the

Congregation becomes spiritually mature and able to apply its gifts in ministry within and outside of the church.

> **Discipleship** is the process of teaching and training Christians to become followers of Christ who can spiritually reproduce themselves through evangelism and the training of new believers. [Matthew 28.18-20]

God calls and ordains the leadership, and they disciple and develop God's representatives, the Congregation, who are believers in every generation. These believers provide a witness to the secular society which informs the population regarding the plan of God and God's order for mankind. God's people are supposed to provide the moral compass by which every individual conscience is calibrated. If the Pastor malfunctions, eventually society malfunctions, leading to divine judgment. This is the First Principle of Nationbuilding.

God has not left mankind without spiritual leadership. God loves the unsaved. Christ died for the unsaved. God cares for the nations, and he provides for their spiritual well-being by placing his people in their midst. God uses the Body of Christ, the Church today, but as long as there have been people there has been God's people among them.

The job of the spiritual leader today is to enable the spiritual growth of believers as outlined in Ephesians 4. But the discipleship of the people of God was the job of Moses in the wilderness. We see Samuel and Jehoshaphat, Elijah and Jeremiah, Nehemiah and Ezra, Peter and John, Paul, and Barnabas, all attending to the spiritual development of the people of God with the spiritual tools provided for their age.

What is misunderstood is that the Pastor's ministry to the spiritual needs of believers is also critical to the health of *civilization as a whole*. The peace and happiness of every nation is related to the spiritual function of God's people in that land and that generation.

Therefore, as goes the Pastors, so goes the nation.

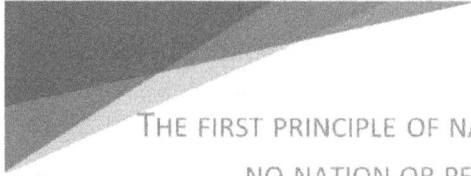

THE FIRST PRINCIPLE OF NATION BUILDING:
NO NATION OR PEOPLE HAVE EVER
SURVIVED THE NULLIFICATION OF THEIR
PASTORS.

Richard Walker

Figure 7: First Nationbuilding Principle

God has provided his representatives terrific spiritual leverage in every nation. The devil knows this and devotes himself to the undermining of Pastors everywhere.

Discipleship of Believers Changes Civilization

Discipleship is the teaching and the training of the Congregation by the Pastor/Elder resulting in spiritual maturity, when the convert becomes self-sustaining and able *themselves* to spiritually reproduce a new generation of disciples of Christ.

Disciples effectively wage spiritual warfare in order to live as God requires	Disciples know their bibles and love the Word of God
Disciples hear, read, study, memorize and meditate upon the Word for themselves	Disciples know how to pray and how to witness
Disciples use their spiritual gifts to minister to others	Disciples teach others to be disciples.

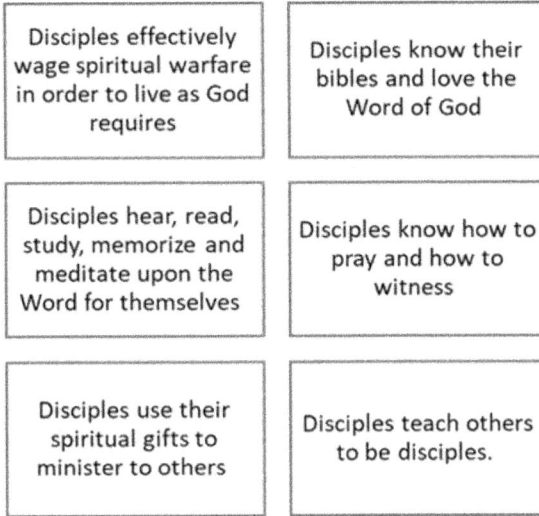

Figure 8: What Disciples Do

True disciples, when they are mature, do not merely *know* how to do these things, they *do* them, and they teach others to do them. There are people who can pass a test about discipleship, what is needed is actual disciples.

Until the Elders are producing disciples then the local church may be a great social services center, a great political action organization, a great place to meet people and even a great place to talk about God and the Bible, but it will not have the impact upon the Community that will bring about the changes that we want and need.

> Matthew 28:18–20 (KJV 1900)
> 18 And Jesus came and spake unto them, saying, All power is given unto me in heaven and in earth. 19 Go ye therefore, and teach [G3100 make disciples] all nations, baptizing them in the name of the Father, and of the Son, and of the Holy Ghost: 20 Teaching [G1321 to teach] them to observe all things whatsoever I have commanded you: and, lo, I am with you alway, even unto the end of the world. Amen.

Jesus Himself discipled the twelve and others. Likewise, the Pastors and Elders must themselves make disciples who will be capable of winning the lost and making them disciples of Jesus [2 Timothy 2.2-3]. The Pastor cannot divest himself of this responsibility without failing to fulfill his ministry.

The gospel itself commands discipleship. A young minister questioned my commitment to the gospel because I was unwilling to unite with people who teach false doctrine to do what he called evangelism. He asked me "Don't you believe in the Great Commission?"[lxxix] I answered that yes, I believe in the Great Commission, but I believe in all three verses. The Great Commission sends the followers of Jesus into the world to make disciples and to accomplish this you must evangelize the lost. Then, when they are converted you must teach them to observe "all things whatsoever I have commanded you:" This is the goal of discipleship, and this is why you cannot make disciples alongside of people that do not have sound doctrine.

This is a critical point. There is a unity in which nationbuilding can thrive, but it is not the unity that most people think important. Spiritual power for nationbuilding can only exist if there is unity concerning the truth of the Word of God.

> Ephesians 4:11–13 (KJV 1900)
> [11] And he gave some, apostles; and some, prophets; and some, evangelists; and some, Pastors and teachers; [12] For the perfecting of the saints, for the work of the ministry, for the edifying of the body of Christ: [13] Till we all come in the unity of the faith, and of the knowledge of the Son of God, unto a perfect man, unto the measure of the stature of the fulness of Christ:

Black people need to be unified around the *truth* of the Word of God. Unity that is based upon secular objectives alone, upon ethnicity alone, or upon false biblical teaching all fail to enlist the

---

[lxxix] Matthew 28.18-20

support of God, without whom there will be no nationbuilding. Throughout the biblical record, nations are destroyed for the rejection of the Word of God provided them by the prophets. Israel's insistence upon following false prophets and false teachers has resulted in their defeat and diaspora.

As long as holding on to popular but false Christian doctrine is a non-negotiable deal breaker for black people, oppression will continue and increase.

There will be no disciples unless the Bible is taught frequently, accurately, and systematically. The devil realizes that haphazard teaching, infrequent teaching, inaccurate teaching will never produce a proper disciple of Christ. The false church that has been injected into society by the devil like a virus, looks like and sounds like a real church, but its teaching is carefully crafted by Satan to appear doctrinally correct while it is, in reality, impotent to create real disciples of Christ [Matthew 13.24-30, 36-43]. It could not be otherwise.

> 2 Corinthians 11:13–15 (KJV 1900)
> 13 For such are false apostles, deceitful workers, transforming themselves into the apostles of Christ. 14 And no marvel; for Satan himself is transformed into an angel of light. 15 Therefore it is no great thing if his ministers also be transformed as the ministers of righteousness; whose end shall be according to their works.

Unfortunately, many have disconnected Christian living from the scriptures. They believe that one is possible without the other. They may be heard saying, "People would rather see a sermon than hear one," and "We need deeds rather than creeds!" Crowds go to church mostly to attend the hour-long praise service. In these places it is the Pastors job to keep the praise going by a brief and entertaining message. However, you can only *be* something spiritually until you first *know* something scripturally.

Disciple making also involves training. The disciple must be trained how to share his testimony [witness] how to pray, how to read and study his Bible. The disciple needs to be taught how to make disciples, because he is expected to reproduce himself spiritually and not merely invite people to church. The entire point of the Great Commission is spiritual reproduction. It is through consistent and persistent spiritual reproduction accompanied, as it must be, by personal holiness that the Congregation transforms the Community.

> 2 Timothy 2:2 (KJV 1900)
> [2] And the things that thou hast heard of me among many witnesses, the same commit thou to faithful men, who shall be able to teach others also.

The Congregation Engages the Community

It is the Congregation who engages the Community, not the Pastor. This is a critically important point. It was never meant that the Elder[lxxx] be the single point of contact with the Community. Today the Pastor is a Community organizer, political activist, entrepreneur, and travelling speaker while his church is ravaged by jack-leg preachers, unqualified novices, and false teachers. It is the Elder's calling to minister to his own Congregation. It is the Congregation's job to engage the Community, to evangelize, to hold Bible studies and prayer groups, to enter political contests, to start businesses, to support their local schools, to provide to those in need, etc. Unfortunately, many church goers are merely religious consumers who pick a church like they pick a flat-screen television, then sit down and wait to be entertained on Sunday. It is through the thousands of members [disciples] of biblically sound churches that the work is done in impacting the Community and not through a small handful of faithful Pastors. Pastors equip the Congregation who then impact the Community.

[lxxx] Elder and Pastor are used interchangeably.

If we want to radically impact the Community, then it is the Congregations that are going to get it done.

11. The Spiritual Chain Reaction: The Community

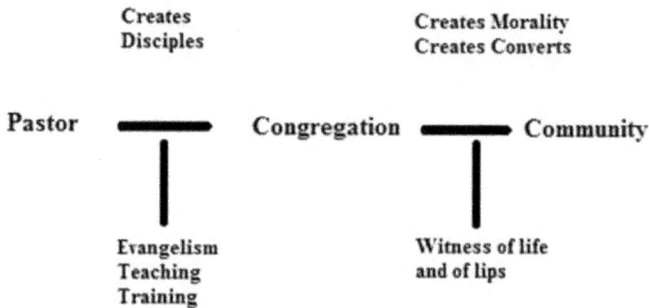

Creates
Disciples

Creates Morality
Creates Converts

Pastor ■■■■■► Congregation ■■■■■► Community

Evangelism
Teaching
Training

Witness of life
and of lips

Figure 10: Spiritual Chain Reaction-Congregation to Community

As the Congregation becomes more mature, it realizes that *it* is the Body of Christ in the world with a mission to evangelize and to make disciples of unbelievers. They also become aware that their ministry to their own spouses, children and extended family is a part of this witness: it is the witness of their Lives: a lifestyle that models the plan of God to the unbelieving world, sustaining human morality. Unbelievers will see the many benefits of this model of divine order and, in time, will emulate the example of strong marriages and families among Christians to the betterment of the entire

Community.

How the Church Influences Unbelievers

John 8:7–9 (KJV 1900)

7 So when they continued asking him, he lifted up himself, and said unto them, He that is without sin among you, let him first cast a stone at her. 8 And again he stooped down, and wrote on the ground. 9 And they which heard it, <u>being convicted by their own conscience</u>, went out one by one, beginning at the eldest, even unto the last: and Jesus was left alone, and the woman standing in the midst.

God has hardwired every person with a conscience[75] whereby they may understand concepts of right and wrong. Conscience is the possession of every person regardless of their spiritual status. The conscience is a witness to every man that there is a God and that He is righteous. The outworking of the conscience in society is called morality.

"**MORAL'ITY**, *noun* The doctrine or system of moral duties, or the duties of men in their social character; ethics.

"The system of *morality* to be gathered from the writings of ancient sages, falls very short of that delivered in the gospel.

1. The practice of the moral duties; virtue. We often admire the politeness of men whose *morality* we question.

2. The quality of an action which renders it good; the conformity of an act to the divine law, or to the principles of rectitude. This conformity implies that the act must be performed by a free agent, and from a motive of obedience to the divine will. This is the strict theological and scriptural sense of *morality* But we often apply the word to actions which accord with justice and human laws, without reference to the motives form (sic) which they proceed."[76]

The conscience is an imperfect means of self-regulation. It can be manipulated or even damaged [1 Timothy 4.2]. God has built into civilization several means by which the human conscience can be recalibrated.

➢ The creation[lxxxi]
➢ The written law of God
➢ The living witness of God's elect.[lxxxii]

[lxxxi] Romans 2.19-20
[lxxxii] Jeremiah 5.1-5; Romans 1.19-21; 2.14-15; 1 Peter 2.12

Through these means the human conscience is refreshed and mankind is preserved from the expression of all the depravity of which it is capable.

In this way the Church has an invisible impact on civilization through the witness of a sanctified lifestyle. When believers illustrate the plan of God for living in marriage, the family, the church, the workplace, and Community, it calibrates the consciences of unbelievers in their periphery.

> Matthew 5.16 (KJV)
> Let your light shine before men, <u>that they may see your good works,</u> and glorify your Father which is in heaven.

When Christians live like Christians society is stabilized and is changed for the better.[lxxxiii] Before a single person receives Christ as Savior, the local church has a powerful invisible effect upon the Community by its righteousness.

The reverse is also true. The powerful influence of the believer can become the beginning of a *negative spiritual chain reaction* which accelerates the moral decay of the Community and strips it of all spiritual protection. When the local church is carnal[lxxxiv], when its members share the same values as the unbelieving Community, whatever evils were already present in the Community are magnified and demonic activity increased.

> Proverbs 14:34 (KJV 1900)
> 34 Righteousness exalteth a nation: But sin *is* a reproach to any people.

> Psalms 9.17 (KJV 1900)
> And the wicked shall be turned into hell, And all the nations that forget God.

The other witness of the Congregation is the witness of their Lips or the

---

[lxxxiii] Christian sanctification is also the basis for social justice impact upon the Community. There are Christians who deliberately confuse social justice with the social gospel. The *social gospel* is a theologically liberal movement designed to supplant true Christianity. *Social justice* is what begins to occur when saved people live like saved people in all settings. When holiness is demonstrated Christian's dealings with individuals and institutions [family, workplace, local church, Community] the unsaved world can see social justice in practice. Those who seek to confuse the issue have an interest, an investment in social *injustice*, to whatever degree.

[lxxxiv] Carnal (sarkinos) "Literally, "made of flesh." A very strong expression. "This unspiritual, material, phenomenal nature" so dominates the unrenewed man that he is described as "consisting of flesh." Others read sarkikos "having the nature of flesh." (from Vincent's Word Studies in the New Testament, Electronic Database. Copyright © 1997, 2003, 2005, 2006 by Biblesoft, Inc. All rights reserved.)

verbal witness of the gospel of Jesus Christ. Mature believers are unashamed of the gospel because they are growing in sanctification. Believers that live like Christians do not have to be afraid of unbelievers or ashamed to tell others how to be born again. God will save many through the witness of the gospel in the Community by the Congregation. The growth of the local churches by the addition of new converts, rather than by swapping half-saved and unsaved religious consumers, produces invisible spiritual benefits to the entire Community.

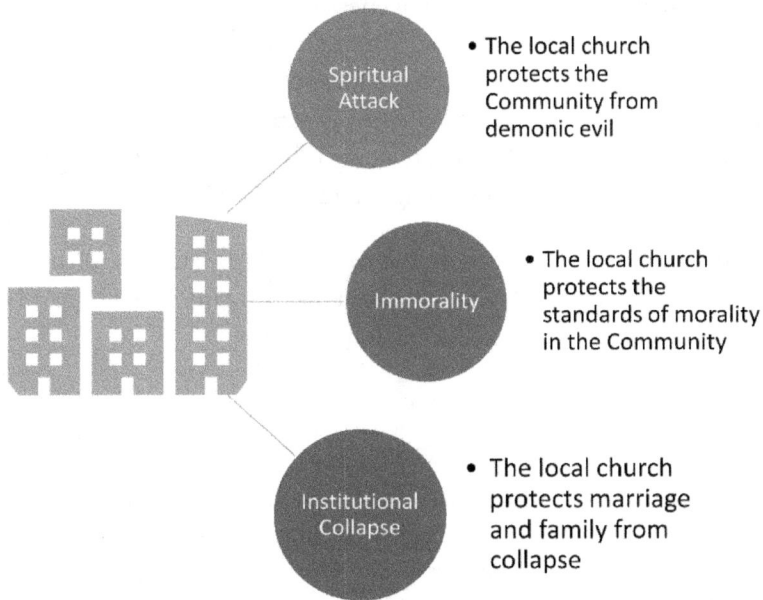

Figure 9: How the Local Church Protects the Community

It is important to understand that it is not the Pastor who transforms the Community directly through his actions. The Pastor prepares the Congregation through discipleship to minister to the Community. It is the Congregation which impacts the Community though their influence in the workplace, their influence in the neighborhoods, their influence as citizens and as members of families. When the believer is obedient to God in his own marriage and family life, then unbelievers see the biblical model for the family and can apply the principles to their own families. When the believer models good citizenship then others can see it and model it themselves. The instability of conscience means that *there is often no way for people to learn these things unless believers are an example.* These two witnesses of evangelism and personal holiness are how the Congregation can bring about dramatic change in their Community through spiritual means.

Marriage and Family

When a believer is spiritually mature, it can be seen in his own personal holiness, but it can also be seen in the strength of his marriage and family. This is an effective test of the effectiveness of a local church: not how big it is, but how stable are its marriages and families? After the gospel conversions, the second most powerful effect of the local church upon the Community in its impact upon marriages and families. It is extremely difficult to oppress strong families, especially if there are many of them. Oppressors are heavily invested in preventing strong marriages and families.[77]

Marriage is the *basis* of civilization, the *backdrop* of the story of salvation and the *blueprint* of the mystical relation between Christ and the Church. Marriage is the critical institution of nationbuilding.

Marriage is the Basis of Civilization

> Genesis 1:26–28 (KJV 1900)
> [26] And God said, Let us make man in our image, after our likeness: and let them have dominion over the fish of the sea, and over the fowl of the air, and over the cattle, and over all the earth, and over every creeping thing that creepeth upon the earth. [27] So God created man in his *own* image, in the image of God created he him; male and female created he them. [28] And God blessed them, and God said unto them, Be fruitful, and multiply, and replenish the earth, and subdue it: and have dominion over the fish of the sea, and over the fowl of the air, and over every living thing that moveth upon the earth.[lxxxv]

God delegated dominion over the earth to Adam and Eve, a marriage. The

---

[lxxxv] The image of God in this passage consists of what mankind was to *be*: one entity consisting of two persons of the same nature, just as the Godhead is one entity, subsisting in three Persons of the same nature or essence. The Godhead *is* one, whereas the man and the woman are *to strive* to become one. The image of God also consists in what mankind was to *do*, which was to exercise dominion over the earth, just as God rules over all things, seen and unseen. In the fall of mankind Lucifer *divided* the man and woman to conquer them both, seizing their *dominion* in the process.

earth fell largely because of the failure of this marriage. Eve was deceived by the serpent because she circumvented the authority of her husband, who could have informed her that the devil's arguments were lies [1 Timothy 2.14]. Adam deliberately rebelled against God, in full knowledge of what he was doing he failed to exert his authority, because he placed his relationship with Eve above his submission to God. If sinning was ok with Eve, then it was ok with him. If the first marriage had succeeded, then there would have been an entirely different destiny for mankind.

Marriage is the Backdrop for the Story of Salvation

> Matthew 1:18–21 (KJV 1900) [18] Now the birth of Jesus Christ was on this wise: When as his mother Mary was espoused to Joseph, before they came together, she was found with child of the Holy Ghost. [19] Then Joseph her husband, being a just *man*, and not willing to make her a publick example, was minded to put her away privily. [20] But while he thought on these things, behold, the angel of the Lord appeared unto him in a dream, saying, Joseph, thou son of David, fear not to take unto thee Mary thy wife: for that which is conceived in her is of the Holy Ghost. [21] And she shall bring forth a son, and thou shalt call his name JESUS: for he shall save his people from their sins.

Joseph's decision to marry Mary despite her situation was a triumph of marriage that led to the salvation of mankind through Christ's sacrifice. Jesus was raised under a successful marriage where he learned discipline and grew in stature with God and man [Luke 2.52]. Married people need to realize that this thing (marriage) is bigger than the both of you.

Marriage is a blueprint of the mystical relations between Christ and the Church.

> Ephesians 5:28–32 (KJV 1900)
> [28] So ought men to love their wives as their own bodies. He that loveth his wife loveth himself. [29] For no man ever yet hated his own flesh; but nourisheth and cherisheth it, even as the Lord the church: [30] For we are members of his body, of his flesh, and of his bones. [31] For this cause shall a man leave his father and mother, and shall be joined unto his wife, and they two shall be one flesh. [32] This is a great mystery: but I speak concerning Christ and the church.

Marriage is so significant to God and is so important to his design of the universe, he makes it an illustration of the Church, the reciprocal indwelling of

God in man and man in God, the Body of Christ.

Having already secured for the believer all the benefits of the blood of Christ in the imputation of His righteousness to us, God goes infinitely further by making man spiritually one with Himself through the baptism of the Holy Spirit. Thus, the believer in the Church Age has a marvelous expansion of his spiritual potential in time and eternity. The intimacy of the Godhead and of the Body of Christ is simulated in marriage where two persons are to realize the oneness that the creation mandates. The whole of the marital union is far greater than the individual parts. "One flesh" is a reality which suggests the eventual coalescence of two souls and two wills. God did not use two handfuls of dust to make man and woman, but one: "He that loveth his wife loveth himself."

When disciples are made, the first relational impact is on our rapport with God; the second strongest relational impact is upon marriage because *marriage is the strongest human bond*. When the Congregation begins to understand this truth, their discipleship results in stronger marriages and stronger marriages change *everything*.

The Congregation will impact the Community when the marriages and families within the local church are strong *and not before*. Big prosperous churches in themselves do not change the Community for the better, celebrity Pastors will not strengthen the institutions of the Community, the resurrection of defunct spiritual gifts will not increase the spiritual protection of the Community, making your ministry "Church Growth Headquarters" will not prepare the next generation of youth, and the ordination of female ministers will not make the church more attractive, but rather, will attract divine judgment [Isaiah 3.12].

Although it is God who provides the power for the transformation of society, it is the family that provides the foundation from which this strength operates. In turn, the basis of the family is marriage. *A people or a nation are no stronger than the marriages and families that make it up.*

American Evangelicals are divorcing at the same rate as non-believers.

> "In fact, when evangelicals and non-evangelical born again Christians are combined into an aggregate class of born-again adults, their divorce figure is statistically identical to that of non-born-again adults: 32% versus 33%, respectively."[78]

Marriage failure is a fundamental problem in the local church since it creates intergenerational problems for both the church and the Community in which it resides. The first marriage on earth failed resulting in the fall of humanity. Marriage from then until now has been a critical field of spiritual warfare and a significant witness to the unsaved world: for bad or for good. Until black marriages become strong, there will be no successful generation of young people to pass on *human capital*: the beliefs, aptitudes, knowledge, and skills upon which a people or nation relies. Marriage failure results in each new generation of black people starting out in a deficit position where they are no match for a system designed to keep them there.

When strong families produce a generation of successful young people, the Community will see crime diminish. A reduction in crime leads to better Community dynamics[lxxxvi] and a better quality of life. A successful generation of young people will achieve careers or establish businesses and increase prosperity in the Community. Economic strength leads to political strength. The witness of Christian lifestyles ultimately contributes to the purification and excellence of cultural expression in the Community.

All of this is based on the foundation of strong disciples producing strong families. *If your church is not producing strong families, then you can be sure that you are not producing disciples either.* That bears repeating: if your church is producing more divorces and unwed mothers than disciples then your church is malfunctioning. There is a priority somewhere in the leadership of the church that is greater than the Great Commission [Matthew 28.18-20].

The Consequences of Strong Marriages

- ➤ A model for young people
- ➤ Greater social stability in the Community
- ➤ More affluent families
- ➤ Well balanced, mentally healthier children
- ➤ Stronger Community networks
- ➤ Reduction in crime
- ➤ Stronger churches
- ➤ More disciples of Christ
- ➤ Longer life spans
- ➤ Care for the aged

[lxxxvi] **Community dynamics**: the positive or negative interaction of individuals, marriages, families, and institutions that contribute to or detract from Community life.

- ➤ Increased home values
- ➤ Economic development of the black Community
- ➤ Political power in the black Community

---

[75] **Conscience**: 26.13 συνείδησις[b], εως f: (contrast συνείδησις[a] 'knowledge about something,' 28.4) the psychological faculty which can distinguish between right and wrong—'moral sensitivity, conscience. Louw, Johannes P., and Eugene Albert Nida. *Greek-English Lexicon of the New Testament: Based on Semantic Domains*. New York: United Bible Societies, 1996.

[76] Webster, Noah American Dictionary of the English Language
https://webstersdictionary1828.com/Dictionary/Morality

[77] Rockefeller Commission Report: Population and the American Future 1972. "Rockefeller Commission on Population and the American Future - Intro and Chapter 1." Accessed February 8, 2023. https://www.population-security.org/rockefeller/001_population_growth_and_the_american_future.htm#Chapter%201.

Also: Hare, Nathan, and Hare, Julia. The Endangered Black Family: Coping with the Unisexualization and Coming Extinction of the Black Race. A Black Male/Female Relationships Book, no. 1. San Francisco, CA: Black Think Tank, 1984. 44-50.

This book discusses the early plans to disrupt the family by making women more masculine and men more feminine, which the Hare's call "unisexualization." It traces the roots of the movement and its development throughout the 20th century. It also traces the role of the feminist movement upon the black marriages and families.

[78] New Marriage and Divorce Statistics Released, March 31, 2008, The Barna Group, Accessed 10-09-2022. https://www.barna.com/research/new-marriage-and-divorce-statistics-released/

12. Definitions Related to Nationbuilding

What is Nationbuilding?

Nationbuilding is the national, structural consequence of spiritual revival. Nationbuilding is the environmental outcome of breaking our psychological programming, of being in our right minds. Nationbuilding is what happens to the Community when people respond to the accurate teaching of the Word of God. Nationbuilding is the irresistible result of a people living in obedience to the accurate teaching of the Word of God.

When Israel was delivered from 400 years of slavery in Egypt, it was for the purpose of establishing them as a nation. It was necessary to transform them from a nation of slaves into a people that could operate under freedom. The first thing that God did was to get them spiritually oriented. The first of the Ten Commandments was that the Jews were to have no other god before Jehovah. The Commandments summarized the principles that would enable right relations with God and between themselves, the principles that would perpetuate freedom. There was no way that the nation of Israel could succeed without first freeing themselves from the false religion they had practiced in Egypt, which was a mixture of the worship of the true God with the false religion of the Egyptians.

An entire generation of Israelites had to die in the wilderness before this point was made to the next generation. The Law of Moses established the priority of faithfulness to God and His Word. It also established the proper function of marriage and the family. *The entire nation was organized around twelve families.* Israel would be no stronger than the marriages and families that comprised it.

Therefore, the final product of Nationbuilding is the re-establishment of the institutions which comprise the nation: the marriages, families, businesses, and governmental structures that promote the advancement of human life rather than the maintenance of oppression.

Nationbuilding occurs on three levels: the last level is the physical comprised of institutions, the second level is psychological, consisting of genuine mental health, largely free from the mental structures designed to maintain oppression. The first level of nationbuilding is spiritual, consisting of the edification of the soul by sound teaching of the Word of God, the Bible.

What is Pulpit Revival?

Pulpit Revival is the re-commitment of the Pastors/Elders and teachers to devotion to God and personal sanctification. If God cannot revive a Pastor, how can He revive a people? Pulpit Revival is a re-commitment to the frequent, accurate and systematic teaching of the Word of God to the Congregation for the purpose of developing strong disciples. Pulpit Revival is the renewal of a vision of God's purpose for the Church in the world in its full significance: the application of the power of God to the real problems of people via the categories of ministry available to the Church.

What is the Spiritual Chain Reaction?

Figure 10: Another Look at the Spiritual Chain Reaction

The Spiritual Chain Reaction is the process whereby the local church blesses, transforms, and protects the surrounding Community by its spiritual influence. The Pastors/Elders and Teachers are the first link in the chain. It is by their commitment to God and to the development of spiritual maturity in the Congregation that the chain reaction is begun.

The spiritually mature Congregation understands its mission to the Community and willingly models the Christian lifestyle and proclaims the gospel message.

The Community experiences the witness of the Congregation and discovers the benefit of God's design for marriage and the family. They also see the power of the Christian life in the workplace, school and elsewhere. Most importantly, the faithful gospel proclamation of the Congregation in the Community results in the salvation of many unbelievers, completing the positive spiritual chain reaction. The Community, influenced by the Congregation is, over time, healed and transformed in its institutions resulting in cultural rebirth.

It should be noted that *every* local church in a Community need *not* operate properly for these forces to take effect. The properly functioning churches are constantly alerting believers to false teaching and false teachers in their midst. This is a key function of the approved shepherds, who are not looking to form an association with false teachers but to expose them. Furthermore, the frequent, accurate and systematic teaching and preaching of the Word of God is an antiseptic that cleanses the local church and Community from the influences of these malfunctioning churches and apostate bodies.

What is a Negative Spiritual Chain Reaction?

A **Negative Spiritual Chain Reaction** is what happens when the local church fails in its spiritual function. This failure magnifies the normal problems in the Community, accelerating the decay of its institutions and intensifying the effects of oppression. Marriage and family are corrupted, poverty and crime increase, political power is non-existent, and the people become victims of every category of exploitation, including demonic activity.

The negative spiritual chain reaction normally begins with church leadership that is committed to false doctrine, personal sin, dangerous alliances or all three. Churches in this condition may be prosperous and growing, they may be small and poor and everything in between. Satan goes to significant effort to seed oppressed Communities with this kind of Pastor and church because their existence is critical to the continuation of oppression. Spiritually strong people are difficult to oppress, which is why Satan has had to resort to killing such Christians.

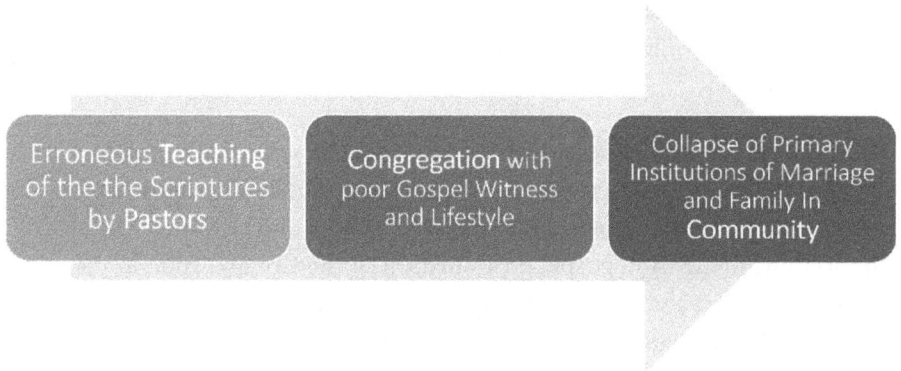

Erroneous Teaching of the the Scriptures by Pastors → Congregation with poor Gospel Witness and Lifestyle → Collapse of Primary Institutions of Marriage and Family In Community

Figure 11: The Negative Spiritual Chain Reaction

What is "FAST"

"FAST" Stands for Frequent, Accurate, Systematic Teaching. The church needs frequent teaching, not just once a week; it needs accurate teaching because *false teaching does not produce spiritual growth or spiritual blessing*; systematic teaching reaches the entire Bible and reaches the entire life of the believer. Teaching is needed rather than entertainment.

Why are Marriage and Family Important to Nationbuilding?

Because no nation is any stronger than the marriages that comprise it. Families are the human engines of national function and marriages are the backbone of the family. A local church that cannot positively impact the family must weaken them, hastening the destruction of the nation by a negative spiritual chain reaction.

What is Community Economics?

Community Economics pertains to the production, consumption, and transfer of wealth within the black Community.

Community economics begins with marriages. Strong marriages create strong families. Strong families create safer, healthier Communities. This is because strong families produce mentally strong, productive children. These children grow up to become contributors to the Community rather than a danger to it. Strong families pass on "human capital" (knowledge, skills, aptitudes, beliefs) to the next generation which ultimately produces a talent pool within the Community and a network outside of it.

The following are the stages leading to strong Community Economics:

1. The abolition of the oppressed mindset through the accurate teaching of the Word of God.
2. Strengthening marriages and families through spiritual discipleship.
3. The creation of a generation of talented and motivated young people.
4. The passing of human capital to that and successive generations.

These factors will lead to Community Economics that will produce businesses, jobs and a tax base that supports the Community, managed by local people who will increase the circulation of dollars *within* the Community.

What is Cultural Renaissance?

Cultural Renaissance is the purifying and life-giving effect that the Word of God has upon the culture [the arts, education, sciences, theology, media, entertainment, etc.] that has been impacted by spiritual revival in the local church. Every category of human interaction is influenced by the impact of the properly functioning local church. This is the blessing to humanity that God intended the Body of Christ to be.

What are the Three Nationbuilding Principles?

There are three spiritual principles that, if observed by *believers*, will perpetuate the momentum created in their pulpits towards Revival and Nationbuilding.

The believer must first maintain their own spiritual fellowship with God through the study of the Word of God, prayer, and obedience to the scriptures. Even then, opposition in the spiritual and human realms, as well as the lack of immediate results may possibly frustrate the Christian and tempt him to believe that there will be no revival, or that spiritual revival cannot transform the Community. The mechanisms described *will take at least a decade before results can begin to be seen and then an entire generation to take hold.* These three principles, if internalized and followed, will keep the believer motivated and focused on the right things during this time.

1. No nation can survive the nullification of their Pastors
2. No other person's [or group's] decisions about you are more important than your own decisions about your life.
3. In unequal power relationships, spiritual power overcomes worldly power. God can and does overcome the advantage of the powerful on behalf of those who have his favor.

We will return to these three concepts with biblical examples in coming chapters.

Our first question to begin this study of Revival and Nationbuilding was "Why aren't the local churches more effective in impacting the Community." These questions have now been answered.

Quick Answers

- ➢ Revival must begin in the pulpit among the Pastors/Elders, and teachers.
- ➢ The local church will not positively impact the Community in a powerful way until it is committed to making disciples of Christ.
- ➢ The church will not change the destiny of black America for the better if false teaching is tolerated and financially rewarded by those who know better.
- ➢ You know that you are in revival if marriages and families within the church are strengthened.
- ➢ The Community is blessed by the Congregation taking the gospel and their witness of a righteous lifestyle into the Community and its institutions. This responsibility should not be passed off to the Pastoral staff, it is the job of the Congregation.

13. Why Are There So Many Churches And Conflicting Interpretations Of The Bible?

God Has a Plan. Satan has a Plan.

God left instructions for the Church to make disciples. The work of the local church is to win the lost, but not to stop there, but to teach them the full spectrum of Christian doctrine so that they become followers of Christ. This process of teaching and training leads to spiritual maturity, which is the goal of discipleship, that believers become followers of Christ.

> Matthew 28:18–20 (KJV 1900)
> [18] And Jesus came and spake unto them, saying, All power is given unto me in heaven and in earth. [19] Go ye therefore, and teach all nations, baptizing them in the name of the Father, and of the Son, and of the Holy Ghost: [20] Teaching them to observe all things whatsoever I have commanded you: and, lo, I am with you alway, *even* unto the end of the world. Amen.

> 2 Timothy 2:1–2 (KJV 1900)
> [1] Thou therefore, my son, be strong in the grace that is in Christ Jesus. [2] And the things that thou hast heard of me among many witnesses, the same commit thou to faithful men, who shall be able to teach others also.

God has also provided gifted individuals for the execution of His plan:

> Ephesians 4:11–15 (KJV 1900)
> [11] And he gave some, apostles; and some, prophets; and some, evangelists; and some, Pastors and teachers; [12] For the perfecting of the saints, for the work of the ministry, for the edifying of the body of Christ: [13] Till we all come in the unity of the faith, and of the knowledge of the Son of God, unto a perfect man, unto the measure of the stature of the fulness of Christ: [14] That we *henceforth* be no more children, tossed to and fro, and carried about with every wind of doctrine, by the sleight of men, *and* cunning craftiness, whereby they

lie in wait to deceive; [15] But speaking the truth in love, may grow up into him in all things, which is the head, *even* Christ:

Ephesians 4.13-14 describes the outcome of discipleship:

13a Till we all come in the unity of the faith:

God has devised a system of spiritual instruction that results in agreement regarding the truth of scripture. One Bible interpreted by one Spirit to every generation. Significant disagreement regarding essential aspects[lxxxvii] of bible teaching is not to be the status quo of the Church but is evidence of satanic tampering.

13b and of the knowledge of the Son of God:

One of the chief areas of our doctrinal agreement should be about the Son of God: who He is, what He did, what He is doing now and what He is going to do in the future.

13c unto a _perfect_ man, unto the measure of the stature of the fullness of Christ:

Here again is the clear statement that the end of the ministry of these gifted individuals is the production of spiritually mature believers.

> **Perfect** 5046 τέλειος [teleios /tel·i·os/] adj. From 5056; TDNT 8:67; TDNTA 1161; GK 5455; 19 occurrences; AV translates as "perfect" 17 times, "man" once, and "of full age" once. 1 brought to its end, finished. 2 wanting nothing necessary to completeness. 3 perfect. 4 that which is perfect. 4A consummate human integrity and virtue. 4B of men. 4B1 full grown, adult, of full age, mature.[79]

A tactical objective of God's plan for the Church is the creation of transformed individuals who partake of the motivation and character of Christ. The disciple is a "perfect man:" a man or woman who has learned by practice to achieve consistent victory over the old nature, walking by the Spirit.

[lxxxvii] Exactly what constitutes "essential elements of bible teaching" has been reduced to "Jesus died to save sinners." However, Jesus expects unity on a lot more than this. This abbreviating of the essentials of the faith exists to create an "on-ramp" to a variety of false religious beliefs and practices. The nature of the Father, Christ, and the Spirit, the work of Christ and its fruit in the believer, the Church Age ministry of the Spirit, the authority and perspicacity of the scriptures, and the way in which believers grow into maturity are all aspects of biblical essentials.

14 That we henceforth be no more children, tossed to and fro, and carried about with every wind of doctrine, by the sleight of men, and cunning craftiness, whereby they lie in wait to deceive;

This verse shows clearly that it was not God's intent that people be bamboozled into following false teachers, or erroneous teachers, or to be deceived, robbed of their money, and waste their lives in churches that will never produce mature believers. On the contrary, Ephesians 4.14 says that the Church has been provided gifted individuals to produce, through discipleship, believers who cannot be tricked like this because they are no longer spiritual children but self-sustaining spiritual adults.

Verse 14 is also saying that there is *a deliberate conspiracy to spiritually neuter believers through false teaching that looks like spiritual truth.* There are men and women who "lie in wait to deceive" believers, manipulating spiritual truth to exploit them by the "sleight[lxxxviii] of men, [and] cunning[lxxxix] craftiness." Oppression is one of the programs of Mystery Babylon that uses this very method to keep the objects of oppression under that system.

While Ephesians 4.13-14 describes the immediate product of the effort of the gifted individuals listed, it is verse 12 that tells us what these finished products are to accomplish.

> Ephesians 4:12 (KJV 1900)
> 12 <u>For the perfecting of the saints, for the work of the ministry,</u>[80] for the edifying of the body of Christ:

The end for which the Congregation is being prepared is the work of the ministry. This group of disciples will themselves possess ministry gifts which will be made productive by their spiritual growth. Their work, the work of the ministry, like that of those who prepared them, will occur both within the

---

[lxxxviii] **"Sleight"** 2940 κυβεία [kubeia /koo·bi·ah/] n f. From kubos (a "cube", i.e. die for playing); GK 3235; AV translates as "sleight" once. 1 dice playing. 2 metaph. the deception of men, because dice players sometimes cheated and defrauded their fellow players. James Strong, Enhanced Strong's Lexicon (Woodside Bible Fellowship, 1995).

[lxxxix] **"Cunning craftiness"** 3834 πανουργία [panourgia /pan·oorg·ee·ah/] n f. From 3835; TDNT 5:722; TDNTA 770; GK 4111; Five occurrences; AV translates as "craftiness" three times, "subtlety" once, and "cunning craftiness" once. 1 craftiness, cunning. 2 a specious or false wisdom. 3 in a good sense, prudence, skill, in undertaking and carrying on affairs. James Strong, Enhanced Strong's Lexicon (Woodside Bible Fellowship, 1995).

local church, but also outside of it in the Community. It is the job of the Congregation to minister to the Community and this is the work for which gifted individuals in the local church are preparing them.

So, we can stop right here and introduce several reasons for the many competing and conflicting doctrines and the proliferation of churches in our Communities. First, there is an entire apparatus of spiritual deception in all Communities that exist to deceive both unbeliever and believer alike, consisting of false teachers and others who create local churches and apparently Christian ministries.

These uncalled ministers, their churches and ministries fulfill a demand for organizations that provide spiritual comfort while leaving sin unchallenged. People want uplifting preaching, programs for their children and a stimulating worship experience. All these things can be provided without the gospel, without systematic teaching and without disciple making. In fact, the gospel and discipleship might slow the growth of such a church.

To please this large mass of religious consumers it is necessary to reinterpret the Bible, to align its teaching to correspond with the worldly orientation of unsaved and half-saved people who crowd their pews. Some of the people want justifications for their racial prejudices, some want political religion, others want feminism, still others want preaching that promises the satisfaction of their felt needs today. Apparently, quite a few people want a religion that promises spiritual power without submission to the Bible. These uncalled, spurious churches and ministries operate much like Jeroboam of the Old Testament, who changed the entire Law of Moses to accommodate the desires of the people who wanted a different ritual, a different priesthood, and a different gospel [1 Kings 12].

There are other reasons for the many churches in the Community: men [and women] start churches because they have chosen the ministry as a profession to earn a living. These are not deliberately seeking to deceive people, but an uncalled Pastor is a spiritual danger to everyone in the Community. Some have seen the fame of celebrity Pastors and want some of that shine on themselves. Still others have been told by someone that they have the call to Pastoral ministry when they do not. Some might argue, "How do *you* know that God did not call most or all of these people?" Because if God called them, and they were obedient to his plan, then their Communities would be quite different places than they are today. Either God is a liar or man is.

Either the new birth followed by proper instruction changes the way people think and act or it does not.

> Jeremiah 23:21–22 (KJV 1900)
> 21 I have not sent these prophets, yet they ran: I have not spoken to them, yet they prophesied. 22 But if they had stood in my counsel, and had caused my people to hear my words, then they should have turned them from their evil way, and from the evil of their doings.

We can see that God has a plan. His plan is not secret but is disclosed throughout the Scriptures to all who will take the time to learn them. But Satan also has a plan for the church. His plan is a part of his ultimate objective of demonstrating his equality to God and establishing his own kingdom upon the earth and in the heavens. Just as God has supplied his Word, spiritually gifted individuals, and the local church to accomplish his purposes in this age; Satan also has his own doctrine, his own spiritually gifted individuals, and his own churches within which his disciples are manufactured. The devil has managed to do this in such a way that it is difficult for the average person to tell the difference between the two systems.

Satan Has a Plan for the Church

Satan attempts to confuse people by devising a system of counterfeits that render his churches nearly indistinguishable from the true Church to the unbeliever and the carnal believer. His church looks like the real church, his people look like real Christians, his Pastors look like real Pastors with teaching that sounds a lot like real Christian teaching.

> Matthew 13:24–30 (KJV 1900)
> 24 Another parable put he forth unto them, saying, The kingdom of heaven is likened unto a man which sowed good seed in his field: 25 But while men slept, his enemy came and sowed tares among the wheat, and went his way. 26 But when the blade was sprung up, and brought forth fruit, then appeared the tares also. 27 So the servants of the householder came and said unto him, Sir, didst not thou sow good seed in thy field? from whence then hath it tares? 28 He said unto them, An enemy hath done this. The servants said unto him, Wilt thou then that we go and gather them up? 29 But he said, Nay; lest while ye gather up the tares, ye root up also the wheat with them. 30 Let both grow together until the harvest: and in the time of harvest I will say to the reapers, Gather ye together first the tares, and bind them in bundles to burn them: but gather the wheat into my barn.[81]

Two Kinds of Religious Consumer

It is difficult to impossible to tell the difference between *religious unbelievers* and *deceived believers*. They act alike. The deceived believers are not growing spiritually, so they do not have lives which demonstrate the power of the Spirit and the Word of God. They may be very religious, but their esteem for the Word of God as the sole authority for faith and practice is absent. Consequently, they perceive God as existing solely for their own benefit and understand the meaning of life to be the achievement of their personal needs and aspirations. Their preoccupation with themselves makes them subject to spiritual movements that focus upon *experience* of the spiritual life and the *appearance* of religion. They are also subject to political movements that offer benefits to their faction or tribe while professing ostensibly Christian objectives. What they will not tolerate for long is the plain and practical study and *application* of the full counsel of the scriptures without dilution by modern evasions and denials of unpopular biblical truths.

These two groups, *religious unbelievers and deceived believers create a tremendous demand for Pastors* who can thrill and mystify, who can argue philosophies and satisfy the desire that many have for religion without Christ, spirituality without transformation, Christian entertainment rather than genuine worship of God. Satan has provided for this large demand for a consumer-driven church by a careful manipulation of Bible teaching, the spawning of an army of attractive and skilled false teachers, a powerful church growth marketing strategy and the provision of a false spirit who imitates the Holy Spirit.

> 1 John 4:1 (KJV 1900)
> [1] Beloved, believe not every spirit, but try the spirits whether they are of God: because <u>many</u> false prophets are gone out into the world.

> 2 Peter 2:1 (KJV 1900)
> [1] But there were false prophets also among the people, even as <u>there shall be false teachers among you</u>, who privily[xc] shall bring in damnable heresies, even denying the Lord that bought them, and bring upon themselves swift

---

[xc] **"Privily bring in:"** 3919 παρεισάγω [pareisago /par·ice·ag·o/] v. From 3844 and 1521; TDNT 5:824; TDNTA 786; GK 4206; AV translates as "privily bring in" once. 1 to introduce or bring in secretly or craftily. James Strong, Enhanced Strong's Lexicon (Woodside Bible Fellowship, 1995).

destruction.

Two Kinds of Dangerous Teachers

There are two major categories of dangerous teachers that occupy the pulpits and lecterns of the local church today.

False Teachers

These may be Pastors, Bible teachers, evangelists or fall under any number of legitimate or illegitimate titles. They are in every denomination including non-denominational churches. These individuals *deliberately teach false doctrine.*[xci] They mix false doctrine with true doctrine, often their accurate teaching is helpful, but it is bait, their accurate teaching only serves to set up the deadly doctrines that they wish to convey.

False teachers also mislead people by the doctrines that they omit. They omit some key doctrines that are necessary to salvation or to spiritual growth. False teachers do not produce disciples of Christ, because they are working, consciously or through self-deception, for the other side. They may be moral people, they are good teachers and speakers, sometimes excellent teachers; they are often fascinating and likeable people. However as false teachers, they mislead people *on purpose* from a variety of motivations.

Erroneous Teachers:

These also may be Pastors, Bible teachers, evangelists or fall under any number of legitimate or illegitimate titles. They are also in every denomination including non-denominational churches. They are probably more numerous than false teachers. They are a big reason for the number of churches and conflicting doctrines, and they have the same deadly spiritual effects as false teachers. Erroneous teachers are of significant use to Satan, even though *they have no knowledge of how useful they are to the devil.*

Erroneous teachers teach false doctrine, *but not on purpose.* They mix false and true doctrines, but not to deceive people. Erroneous teachers are not Pastors who have biblical topics that they may not fully understand, nor are these teachers those who have the same occasional errors that all Bible teachers experience. *The erroneous teacher is wrong in entire doctrinal systems or significant*

[xci] See 1 Timothy 4.1-2; 2 Timothy 4.3-4 and Acts 20.29-30 below.

subcategories of doctrine. For example, wrong about how to be saved, or wrong about the ministry of the Holy Spirit to the Church; or wrong about how to grow up as a believer; or wrong about the nature of God; or wrong about the purpose and function of the local church.

There are many reasons why erroneous teachers are erroneous: a big reason is an unwillingness to be properly instructed in the Word of God. Laziness and arrogance result in many Pastors and teachers feeding their congregations slop, rather than the Word of God rightly divided. Many erroneous teachers are not called to the ministry: they have no teaching gift from the Holy Spirit. Many erroneous teachers are in ministry to earn a living and therefore are not interested in getting any education in the Bible. Others realize that most churchgoers are far more impressed with exciting speakers than in effective teachers, so they justify that they are just "giving the people what they want." Still others want to gain a following or create a large organization: there are people who have great organizational ability who become Pastors with no interest in making disciples at all.

Erroneous teachers are just as dangerous as false teachers. The fact that someone accidentally shoots you with a gun leaves you just as shot as had the person fired on purpose.

Two Kinds of Christian Doctrine

Satan has a Plan for the church; and that plan includes an organized system of doctrine which is designed to resemble true Bible doctrine but will never produce mature believers.

We all know that there is food, "fast food" to be exact, that has all the *appearance* of food but little to no nutritional value. In fact, the more you eat this kind of food, the unhealthier you will become. This food tastes good to us, we enjoy it and buy so much of it that we have made it a multi-billion-dollar industry. Yet that food which we buy, consume, and enjoy is *anti-life*. The same is true with the doctrinal systems of Lucifer; they are appealing, they *resemble* valid Christian teaching, they may temporarily satisfy our emotional and intellectual desires, but that teaching is anti-life.

True Christian doctrine is the opposite of satanic doctrine in that true doctrine brings life, eternal life through the gospel of Jesus Christ. False doctrine often[xcii] provides a corrupted gospel because the devil is not trying to get folks saved. True Christian doctrine also gives life to the believer by removing carnality and increasing knowledge, faith, and true worship of God. False doctrine can deliver an intense religious experience that brings one no closer to God than the priests of Baal in Elijah's days [1 Kings 18].

> 2 Timothy 4:3–4 (KJV 1900)
> [3] For the time will come when they will not endure sound doctrine; but after their own lusts shall they heap to themselves teachers, having itching ears; [4] And they shall turn away *their* ears from the truth, and shall be turned unto fables.

> 1 Timothy 4:1–2 (KJV 1900)
> [1] Now the Spirit speaketh expressly, that in the latter times some shall depart from the faith, giving heed to seducing spirits, and doctrines of devils; [2] Speaking lies in hypocrisy; having their conscience seared with a hot iron;

> Acts 20:29–30 (KJV 1900)
> [29] For I know this, that after my departing shall grievous wolves enter in among you, not sparing the flock. [30] Also of your own selves shall men arise, speaking perverse things, to draw away disciples after them.

Basic Principles of Spiritual Deception

The specific kinds of satanically inspired doctrines masquerading as orthodox Christianity change based upon the times and the people being seduced. However, several basic principles of demonic deception are found in the original temptation of mankind in the Garden of Eden.

Principle of Deception

> Genesis 3:1a (KJV 1900)
> [1] Now the serpent was more subtil[xciii] than any beast of the field which the

---

[xcii] "Often" By this we mean many *erroneous* Pastors will provide the true gospel. However, it is not uncommon to find the gospel corrupted by the requirement of human works, emotional experiences, promises to God, etc. In more extreme cases there may be the omission of Christ' substitutionary sacrifice, (i.e., the blood), or the omission of faith itself.

[xciii] **"Subtil"** 6874 עָרוּם ('ā·rûm): adj.; ≡ Str 6175; TWOT 1698c—1. LN 32.24–32.41 prudent, shrewd, crafty, discerning, sensible, i.e., pertaining to wisdom and shrewdness in the management of affairs, showing a capacity for understanding (Pr 12:16, 23; 13:16; 14:8, 15, 18; 22:3; 27:12+), note: often referring to prudent, wise persons; 2. LN 88.262–88.270 crafty, clever, i.e., pertaining to being tricky and cunning, with a focus on evil treachery (Ge 3:1; Job 5:12; 15:5+) James Swanson, Dictionary of Biblical Languages with Semantic Domains : Hebrew (Old Testament) (Oak Harbor: Logos Research Systems, Inc., 1997).

Lord God had made.

Here we see the **Principle of Deception**. Lucifer did not come as himself, but in the form of something familiar to the woman, the serpent. Those who will mislead the church and mislead unbelievers will come in the form of legitimate spiritual leaders in apparently legitimate churches. Even the Antichrist will pass himself off, not as a tool of Lucifer, but at first as a beneficent and brilliant statesman, and then later as the Messiah of Israel, as Jesus. It is important to understand that *false teachers do not look like false teachers, they look like an acceptable version of what people expect to see.*

> 2 Corinthians 11:13–15 (KJV 1900)
> 13 For such are false apostles, deceitful workers, transforming themselves into the apostles of Christ. 14 And no marvel; for Satan himself is transformed into an angel of light. 15 Therefore it is no great thing if his ministers also be transformed as the ministers of righteousness; whose end shall be according to their works.

Principle of the Bible Test

> Genesis 3:1b (KJV 1900)
> And he said unto the woman, Yea, hath God said, Ye shall not eat of every tree of the garden?

This is the **Principle of the Bible Test**. The devil will test your knowledge of the Bible, your understanding of what God has said. He will use your ignorance or doubt of the Word of God against you in powerful but subtle ways.

Satan is constantly at work dumbing down the religious population. The emphasis upon church growth has made sound Bible teaching churches hard to find. Solid, uncompromising teaching and preaching is the key to strong Christians, but it is *not* the key to rapid church growth. Rapid church growth and revenue growth does not come from demanding that people deny themselves, or by telling them that they are going to Hell. Consequently many Christians are not taught to even *read* the Bible, much less memorize it. False and erroneous teachers can represent any nonsense as scriptural, and most believers have no idea whether these preachers are right or wrong. Satan will use the Bible Test to trap the believer in their own ignorant misperceptions about the Scriptures.

In the Garden of Eden, Eve's repetition of the Lord's command regarding the

Tree of the Knowledge of Good and Evil betrayed her feelings about the prohibition. She added to God's instruction "neither shall ye touch it" [Genesis 3.3b]. She also changed the *certainty* of death into the *possibility* of death from partaking of the tree "lest ye die" [Genesis 3.3b]

Satan used this resentment and uncertainty about God's command to draw her into his trap. The reason the devil can so easily question the Word of God is because, so few people know it and so many others resent its demands upon them. The devil was rebuked in Matthew 4 when he tried the same tactic with Jesus, who, of course, knew His own Word. False and erroneous teachers today can teach the most ridiculous doctrines regarding the Holy Spirit, or giving, or eternal life or prayer because so many Christians have failed the Bible Test, never having even read through the New Testament.

Principle of the Lie

> Genesis 3:4 (KJV 1900)
> 4 And the serpent said unto the woman, Ye shall not surely die:

This is the **Principle of the Lie.** Eve had walked and talked with God but did not know him with the intimacy she should have. Satan exploited this by openly questioning the character of God by calling Him a liar. Eve had already performed poorly on the Bible Test; now, by accepting the possibility that God had lied to her, she made herself available to *the* Lie. The devil cannot acknowledge God to be who Scriptures says that He is without jeopardizing his own claims [Isaiah 14.14-16]. Therefore, Lucifer is the author of *the* Lie. Satan advances the idea that God is a liar and Jesus is not the Christ [1 John 2.22].[xciv]

Many Pastors today approximate Satan's attitude by ascribing to God teachings that, when followed to their logical conclusions, compromise His character. Some teach that God is subject to cosmic principles that He must obey at our command, they teach that God does not know the future perfectly, that God is obligated to heal or to prosper all that meet certain conditions, that God will say yes to our praise after he has said no to our prayers, that God contradicts himself and so on and so on. This is the

---

[xciv] This is not necessarily what the devil truly believes, but it is what he represents to the world as his position, by a variety of subtle arguments.

misrepresentation of the character of God.

Principle of Occult Religion

> Genesis 3:5 (KJV 1900)
> 5 For God doth know that in the day ye eat thereof, then your eyes shall be opened, and ye shall be as gods, knowing good and evil.

This is the ***Principle of Occult Religion***. How did Satan acquire this information about what God knew? Where did he get this data regarding the effects of the Tree of Knowledge? Satan convinced Eve that he had access to hidden [occult] knowledge about God and God's plan that was unavailable to her.

The Substructure of Luciferian Doctrine
Principle of Deception: Genesis 3.1 If you ever encounter Lucifer, you will not recognize him. Lucifer modifies his appearance and manner to deceive men.
Principle of The Lie: Genesis 3.4-5 Matthew 4.3a Lucifer denies that Jehovah is who He claims to be in scripture. He denies that Jesus is Christ. He claims that God lied to Adam and Eve to prevent their spiritual progress.
Principle of Occult Religion: Genesis 3.4-5 Lucifer represents himself as the benefactor of man, the champion of freedom and the conductor of souls to spiritual evolution and godhood.
Principle of Human Non-Culpability: Genesis 3.4 Lucifer claims that disobedience to God leads not to death but to spiritual evolution.
Principle of Scriptural Misuse: Gen 3.1 Matthew 4.1-10 Satan uses his mastery of the scriptures to deceive man by their misuse. Satan attempted to use God's own words to control Him.
Principle of the Superhero: Matt 4.3-10 Lucifer represents spiritual power, spiritual gifts and spiritual ministry as ours to use as we please.
Principle of Prosperity: Job 1.1-11; 2.3-7 Lucifer argues to God that man serves Him because it is in his best interests to do so. Man serves God to receive blessings and protection alone. The inverse of this argument is that man is entitled to prosperity [health, wealth, and protection] at all times as a servant of God. [Job 2.7-10].
Principle of Pragmatism: Genesis 3.4-5 Matthew 4.8-10 Satan deceives men by the claim that God's plan can be advanced by the violation of His Word. Man is the judge of scripture. His ends justify his means.

Figure 12: The Substructure of Luciferian Doctrine

We live in a day when Pastors and teachers are claiming to have spiritual truth that supersedes the Bible. The origin of this secret information is said to be "God," or the "Holy Ghost." The typical church member believes that he can accept or reject what the Bible says on a subject without a biblical justification, simply because he doesn't like what the scriptures say about that subject. What is the origin of this authority to overrule the plain statements of scripture? There are words of knowledge and words of wisdom, there are prophets and prophetesses, there are senior prophets and apostles and seers, all claiming to provide direct revelation. Anyone can walk up to you during church and give you a "word" that "the Lord has for you."

Eve responded to the serpent's claims like many Christians today, she accepted it without question. She accepted that the serpent had occult or hidden knowledge and changed her interpretation of God's command. We can see how unfortunate this is, she didn't even know that it was Satan who was talking, but she accepted his authority as an expert on God and his plan.

Under the Principle of Occult Religion, the individual is promised spiritual evolution and actualization that is outside the promises of Scripture. Eve was told that both God and the serpent knew that partaking of the fruit of the Tree of Knowledge would result in spiritual transformation and a form of godhood. Today, both false and erroneous teachers offer spiritual power and spiritual victory through means that are constructed from improper biblical interpretation.

Just as God has a plan for the Church, the devil has a plan as well and his plan involves the multiplication of Pastors, teachers and churches that look like the real thing but are designed to be religious factories that deliberately manufacture spiritual losers.

Contrasting the Two Plans

- ➢ God created the local church to make disciples of Christ.
- ➢ Satan plants local churches to prevent the making of disciples of Christ.
- ➢ God calls people to whom he gives spiritual gifts to equip believers so they cannot be deceived.
- ➢ Satan calls and equips his own ministers in the art of spiritual deception.
- ➢ God uses disciples to spread the gospel and to provide moral light to unbelievers.
- ➢ Satan weakens nations [Isaiah 14.12b] by short-circuiting the spiritual process by which institutions [marriages and families] are strengthened.

The devil weakens the nations by the multiplication of his churches throughout the world. There are also many erroneous teachers who inadvertently advance his program by teaching what is wrong. This is why there are so many churches and conflicting doctrines.

The long-term effect of Satan's plan for the churches is the breakdown of the institutions in the Community. Marriages and families collapse because they are maintained and strengthened by properly functioning local churches which serve as *the immune system* of the Community. The local church led by false or erroneous teachers cannot produce spiritually mature believers and their churches produce a negative spiritual chain reaction. As a result, Communities are destroyed by Satan's plan for the local church. There can be no nationbuilding without positive spiritual dynamics.

How A Believer Can Avoid Deception

➢ Pray to God for guidance regarding a good church. The problem with Christians is not that God is not leading them, but that they are resisting His guidance so that they can stay somewhere they have no business being.

Psalms 25:12 (KJV 1900)
12 What man *is* he that feareth the Lord? Him shall he teach in the way *that* he shall choose.

James 1:5 (KJV 1900)
5 If any of you lack wisdom, let him ask of God, that giveth to all *men* liberally, and upbraideth not; and it shall be given him.

➢ Support your church. If you are blessed to belong to a church with a faithful, Bible teaching Pastor or Elders, then give it your full support. Pray for your church. Commit yourself to grow spiritually. Get involved. Give generously to that church. Encourage your Pastors. Make disciples.

➢ Do the work to know your Bible. Hear, read, study, memorize and meditate upon the scriptures daily. God is committed to guiding and teaching every Christian through his Word.

➢ Obey the Bible that you know. There is no spiritual progress without obedience to the Word of God. Personal transformation to Christlikeness is the goal of discipleship and the ultimate spiritual power.

Prelude to Revival

We have covered the issues of why the black Community is largely not transformed, and why there are so many churches and Pastors. Although we plan to continue answering still more legitimate questions that Christians and unbelievers have about the local church and its role in the black Community, it is an appropriate place to consider a biblical example of revival in spiritual leadership.

The key to the transformation of any people is the spiritual revival of their leadership, specifically their Pastors. The Christian Community in America is fixated upon politics as the method that God will use to establish his will in our nation. Nothing could be further from the truth. God didn't establish the Church and provide it with unlimited spiritual power, so that we could manipulate the government into establishing some sort of Christian nation.[xcv]

Instead of the Christians converting the people in government, politicians [and Pastors] have converted the churches whose members will now lie to protect their political interests, embrace, and practice racial politics, ignore abominations sanctioned by their favorite political party, and generally tread underfoot the scriptures to justify the amalgamation of Satan's kingdom with the Church in the name of a theonomic world order.[82]

The bottom line is that Jesus is not returning for our political party, he is returning for the Church [1 Thessalonians 4.17-18]. It was a political system that was used to crucify Jesus and it will be a political system through which the Antichrist will establish his leadership and control of the earth. Government is a legitimate institution which is ordained by God to restrain evil [Romans 13.1-4]. The laws by which nations are governed should be informed by consciences calibrated by the witness of the Word of God manifested in the lives of true believers. The biblical nation of Israel (and not the Israel of today) is the only true theocratic state in history. In the final analysis, the character of government is, at its best, influenced by the spiritual power of the Body of Christ in a nation. Human government has no charter or spiritual resources to address any spiritual issue. Therefore, we are not looking to any government administration, liberal or conservative, to bring about the Kingdom of God. We must begin with spiritual revival and that

---

[xcv] It is the thesis of that book that the obedience of Christians to accurate bible instruction results in spiritual maturity, which has many beneficial effects upon society. These *spiritual* effects can improve society. But they are *spiritual* effects and *do not require any direct changes to how or by whom society is ruled or operated for their effectiveness*. The Bible does not require the takeover of human institutions by the Church to achieve the Kingdom or any prophetic outcome. In fact, the takeover of human institutions such as government will be the modus operandi of the Antichrist in his effort to establish his Kingdom, his own New World Order.

revival must begin in the pulpit.

14. Ahaz and Hezekiah: A Revival In Leadership

2 Chronicles 29:1–11 (KJV 1900)

1 Hezekiah began to reign when he was five and twenty years old, and he reigned nine and twenty years in Jerusalem. And his mother's name was Abijah, the daughter of Zechariah. 2 And he did that which was right in the sight of the LORD, according to all that David his father had done. 3 He in the first year of his reign, in the first month, opened the doors of the house of the LORD, and repaired them. 4 And he brought in the priests and the Levites, and gathered them together into the east street, 5 And said unto them, Hear me, ye Levites, sanctify now yourselves, and sanctify the house of the LORD God of your fathers, and carry forth the filthiness out of the holy place. 6 For our fathers have trespassed, and done that which was evil in the eyes of the LORD our God, and have forsaken him, and have turned away their faces from the habitation of the LORD, and turned their backs. 7 Also they have shut up the doors of the porch, and put out the lamps, and have not burned incense nor offered burnt offerings in the holy place unto the God of Israel. 8 Wherefore the wrath of the LORD was upon Judah and Jerusalem, and he hath delivered them to trouble, to astonishment, and to hissing, as ye see with your eyes. 9 For, lo, our fathers have fallen by the sword, and our sons and our daughters and our wives are in captivity for this. 10 Now it is in mine heart to make a covenant with the LORD God of Israel, that his fierce wrath may turn away from us. 11 My sons, be not now negligent: for the LORD hath chosen you to stand before him, to

serve him, and that ye should minister unto him, and burn incense. [See also 2 Kings 18.1-7]

The Essentials of the Case

Ahaz was the father of Hezekiah and King of the Southern Kingdom of Judah from 732 to 717 BC. He sacrificed several of his children to false gods [2 Chronicles 28.3]. He debased the Temple worship by setting up a pagan altar in the Temple grounds; by giving the gold in the Temple to a foreign nation to negotiate a war treaty; by destroying the Temple furniture, eventually shutting the doors of the Temple, and setting up pagan altars "in every corner of Jerusalem" [2 Chronicles 28.24].

> 2 Chronicles 28:24 (KJV 1900)
> 24 And Ahaz gathered together the vessels of the house of God, and cut in pieces the vessels of the house of God, and shut up the doors of the house of the LORD, and he made him altars in every corner of Jerusalem.

The true beginning of revival is not a *process* but a decision to turn away from sin and to do what is right.

Figure 13: Principle of Revival One

Ahaz bankrupted Judah through foreign treaties that did not make the nation secure from her enemies [2 Chronicles 28]. As judgment for his sins God allowed Israel [Northern Kingdom] and Syria to kill 120,000 of the soldiers of Judah in one day. Judah was also oppressed by Assyria, her "ally."

Hezekiah rose to power as co-regent with his father in 727 and became the sole authority in 717. His first actions as sole regent were directly opposite to those of his father Ahaz and demonstrate the principles of Revival and Nationbuilding. The scriptures do not describe why Hezekiah was so different than his father. Nor does the Bible describe a process that led to revival in his case. I believe that this is *because the true beginning of revival is <u>not a process but a decision</u> to turn away from sin and to do what is right.*

Revival in Leadership

> 2 Kings 18:3–6 (KJV 1900)
> 3 And he [Hezekiah] did that which was right in the sight of the LORD, according to all that David his father did. 4 He removed the high places, and brake the images, and cut down the groves, and brake in pieces the brasen serpent that Moses had made: for unto those days the children of Israel did burn incense to it: and he called it Nehushtan. 5 He trusted in the LORD God of Israel; so that after him was none like him among all the kings of Judah, nor any that were before him. 6 For he clave to the LORD, and departed not from following him, but kept his commandments, which the LORD commanded Moses.

Revival is a change in thinking that results in a change in behavior. The values of this new king were different than those of his father; we know this because his behavior was different.

Some want to claim that they hold to sound teaching while running their churches in the same way as those who have no respect for the Bible. Revival will not occur until we change our behavior. Hezekiah put his value system into action, He trusted the Lord and therefore he did not fear the people, or the false prophets, or the devil.

Hezekiah did not esteem his father more than the Lord. He demolished the concepts and the works of his father. Hezekiah did not esteem tradition over the Word of God. The reason that Pastors do not overturn harmful traditions is because they fear the people. The great danger of filling an existing pulpit is that the pulpit committee is often looking to preserve something rather than to move forward by faith. The existing pulpit offers the Pastoral candidate financial security and administrative continuity but often at a dear price. Hezekiah was not trying to fill his father Ahaz's shoes.

The people had turned the brazen serpent of Moses [Numbers 21] into an idol and therefore Hezekiah destroyed it. I am sure that there were many people who were angry over the elimination of an 800-year-old relic and tradition handed down by Moses himself, but Hezekiah trusted God to protect him and did what needed to be done to restore the Lord's favor. *The heart of revival is a life changing commitment the truth of the Word of God.*

> John 14:15 (KJV 1900)
> 15 If ye love me, keep my commandments.

> Daniel 9:4 (KJV 1900)
> 4 And I prayed unto the Lord my God, and made my confession, and said, O Lord, the great and dreadful God, keeping the covenant and mercy to them that love him, and to them that keep his commandments;

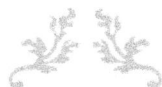

Revival is a change in thinking that results in a change in behavior.

Figure 14: Principle of Revival Two

Regarding King Hezekiah:

> 2 Kings 18.6 For he clave to the LORD, and departed not from following him, but kept his commandments, <u>which the LORD commanded Moses</u>

The words, "which the Lord commanded Moses" [v6] indicate that he followed the Word *accurately*, not "as the Lord commanded Abram" or "as the Lord commanded Adam," because God had given in the Mosaic law as a later revelation designed for these people at this time. In the time of Hezekiah there were many false religious practices in Israel; some from the surrounding nations, others from the misapplication of the Bible. His own father was an idolater who shut up the Temple itself and prevented the worship of the Lord.

Hezekiah returned the nation to the worship of God based upon the law of Moses. He did not seek out teaching from a bygone age, he did not create his own religion, nor did he seek to find fellowship with those who followed other religious practices, but he adhered to the words which the Lord had commanded Moses. Hezekiah was not looking to achieve the appearance of unity with the Northern Kingdom or with heretical elements within his own nation by compromising the Word of God.

In the same way, we today cannot embrace practices suited for the apostolic age simply because they are in the Bible. We all must "rightly divide the word of truth." God is not going to help us merely because we say our new practices and beliefs come from the Bible.

> 2 Chronicles 29:3–5 (KJV 1900)
> 3 He in the first year of his reign, in the first month, opened the doors of the house of the LORD, and repaired them. 4 And he brought in the priests and the Levites, and gathered them together into the east street, 5 And said unto them, Hear me, ye Levites, sanctify now yourselves, and sanctify the house of the LORD God of your fathers, and carry forth the filthiness out of the holy place.

We know that the Word of God changed Hezekiah's life because it changed his ministry.

The first thing that Hezekiah did was to address the *spiritual* problems of his nation. In the first year and the first month of his reign over Judah he set his hand to the spiritual work that would enable the success of every other endeavor that he would undertake as King.[xcvi] The most serious and pressing problems of a nation, any nation, are *not* political or military, economic or social. Therefore, the Pastor or Elder who would immerse himself in politics or entrepreneurship has misunderstood what the Bible has said about the engines which drive national life. He has devalued his calling and has neglected the one thing that no politician, general, scholar or businessman can provide to the nation, which is the preparation of soldiers for the spiritual conflict which determines the outcome of every other conflict in the world.

[xcvi] Hezekiah ruled a theocracy. For the secular nation, it is God's expectation that it prioritize ethical behavior which aligns with the conscience which God has bestowed upon every human being. The basis of just laws is this God given moral capacity, which is one reason why laws around the world largely coincide with divine revelation [the Bible]: both human conscience and the Scriptures share the same origin.

Psalms 127:1 (KJV 1900)
1 Except the Lord build the house, they labour in vain that build it: Except the Lord keep the city, the watchman waketh *but* in vain.

First, Hezekiah opened the doors of the Temple, which had been closed. He also repaired or strengthened them. We need to open the doors of the church for evangelism and then close the doors to make disciples of believers. Evangelism must be a high priority in the local church. The Congregation must be taught that they have a responsibility to share the gospel and to make disciples. Contrary to tradition, it is the Congregation that evangelizes the Community.

The Elders need to close the doors of the church for the teaching of the Word of God. The gospel is for the unbeliever, Bible doctrine is for the believer. Churches are not evangelizing the Community because Congregations are full of spiritual children and religious consumers. Some Pastors spend all their time in evangelism and their disciples are hungry for more advanced teaching. Even when we have accurate teaching, we are starving the people by not feeding them often enough (Frequent, Accurate, Systematic, Teaching). Therefore, our people are out foraging and scavenging for spiritual food on television, YouTube and the radio where they are mostly getting junk food, if not out and out poison.

Hezekiah Preaches to the Pastors

2 Chronicles 29:4–5 (KJV 1900)
4 And he brought in the priests and the Levites, and gathered them together into the east street, 5 And said unto them, Hear me, ye Levites, sanctify now yourselves, and sanctify the house of the LORD God of your fathers, and carry forth the filthiness out of the holy place.

We know that the Word of God changed Hezekiah's life because it changed his ministry. *Hezekiah did not ask the priests and Levites to think or pray about revival, but to sanctify themselves. We are not revived because we do not want to be revived.*

 Hezekiah commanded the preachers to sanctify themselves and the Temple: to carry out the filthiness first from their own lives and then from the place of worship. This command *should* have come from the Levites themselves and been directed towards the administration of Ahaz. It is the job of the preacher and the teacher to speak truth to power as God's representative. Instead, the

Hezekiah did not ask the priests and
Levites to think or pray about revival, but
to sanctify themselves. We are not revived
because we do not want to be revived.

Figure 15: Principle of Revival Three

spiritual leaders of Israel needed to be commanded by the secular authority to do their jobs. Hezekiah demanded that they sanctify themselves, and then the

Temple. Once the Pastor has eliminated the sin out of his own life, he must then eliminate high handed sin from the local church. He must exercise church discipline; he must cease from encouraging sinful behavior though church traditions and policies. For example, he must remove unqualified men from the deaconate and from Eldership. Rather than operating from a motive of self-preservation, he must operate from a faith motive. This is what Hezekiah did. It is not guaranteed that the man who does these things will keep his job. However, he will be fired by God if he does not do them.

The alternative to revival is divine discipline, because not to be revived is to be stiff-necked and disobedient. There can be no revival of the people without a revival of the pulpit, for if God cannot revive a Bible teacher, how can he revive an entire nation?

Naming the Sin

2 Chronicles 29:6 (KJV 1900)
6 For our fathers have trespassed, and done that which was evil in the eyes of the LORD our God, and have forsaken him, and have turned away their faces from the habitation of the LORD, and turned their backs.

Hezekiah bravely identified the cause of their current condition as his father and his father's generation. Biblical preaching requires courage. Pastors have stopped preaching about adultery, divorce and addiction and these things have increased in the church. Many Pastors have steadfastly refused to teach *comprehensively* about racial prejudice and today the world ridicules the gospel because of the hypocrisy of Christians. We have decreased church discipline and the wicked have increased. Many preach for numerical growth and with that growth has come a harvest of disobedience and its fruits. Effective preaching requires faith in God, because the preacher must at the very least be willing to risk his *job* weekly to properly prepare his people for their roles in the Plan of God for their generation. A sin-infested church will not be used

The alternative to revival is divine discipline, because not to be revived is to be stiff-necked and disobedient.

Figure 16: Principle of Revival Four

by God, except as an object lesson in divine judgment. This is precisely what

happened to Jerusalem and Judea.

The Spiritual Roots of National Crisis

> 2 Chronicles 29:8 (KJV 1900)
> 8 Wherefore the wrath of the LORD was upon Judah and Jerusalem, and he hath delivered them to trouble, to astonishment, and to hissing, as ye see with your eyes.

Hezekiah connected the social and political crisis: *trouble* (or maltreatment), *astonishment* (ruin), *hissing* (derision) that the nation was experiencing, to spiritual causes. He recognized the connection between the spiritual world and the physical world [Psalms 127.1].[83] The Scripture says that God "delivered them to trouble..." God will use many agencies to punish the disobedient state. The Bible relates his use of medical, economic, political, military, and natural disasters to punish the nation that commits itself to sin and injustice. It is God who determines the rise and fall of kingdoms and nations.

> Daniel 4:17 (NKJV)[84]
> 17 'This decision is by the decree of the watchers, And the sentence by the word of the holy ones, In order that the living may know That the Most High rules in the kingdom of men, Gives it to whomever He will, And sets over it the lowest of men.'

It is the job of God's representatives to draw the clear connection between the overall condition of the nation and the status of its relationship to God. Because *believers* have separated the national well-being from God's legitimate expectations from men, both saved and unsaved, *we have allowed ourselves to be caught up into the fiction that our exertions in politics can rescue us from the consequences of rebellion against God.*

> 2 Chronicles 29:9 (KJV 1900)
> 9 For, lo, our fathers have fallen by the sword, and our sons and our daughters and our wives are in captivity for this.

Hezekiah identified the spiritual origin of the national security crisis. Even though the people were fighting Syrians and their brothers the Israelites, Hezekiah calls for a surrender to God and a cessation of hostilities with the Most High as the first step to resolving their national security crisis.

This verse also demonstrates that oppression itself can be used to discipline the disobedient nation. Israel had become an oppressive nation who after a prolonged period of divine forbearance, was itself made subject to cruel oppression by others [Jeremiah 6.6; Zephaniah 3.1-7].

After Sanctification, Biblical Praise

When the Preachers and teachers (Clergy) were sanctified, they then ministered to the people (Congregation) with accurate biblical worship (sin offerings, burnt offerings) and with praise (voluntary offerings).

> 2 Chronicles 29:23 (KJV 1900)
> 23 And they brought forth the he goats for the sin offering before the king and the congregation; and they laid their hands upon them: 27 And Hezekiah commanded to offer the burnt offering upon the altar. And when

> the burnt offering began, the song of the LORD began also with the
> trumpets, and with the instruments ordained by David king of Israel.

The burnt offering and praise followed the sin offerings and preceded the
voluntary offerings from the people. Confession ("they laid their hands upon
them") and repentance (the burnt offering as entire submission) precede
fellowship and worship. A big problem in the church today is worship without
a true adjustment to the justice of God, worship without a proper
relationship, praise without repentance.

Christian worship in our time is too often man-centered, experience oriented
and entertainment focused. What God has done for me, should do for me,
will do for me is the character of much of today's worship. The worship
described in our passage begins with the Cross (the sin offering-2 Corinthians
5.21). Worship proceeds with the burnt offering, signifying fellowship based
upon the Sacrifice who was wholly consumed by the wrath of God that we
might have peace with God. Only then does the praise begin which includes
the element of giving in freewill offerings.

Ministry to the Community!

> 2 Chronicles 30:1 (KJV 1900)
> 1 And Hezekiah sent to all Israel and Judah, and wrote letters also to
> Ephraim and Manasseh, that they should come to the house of the
> LORD at Jerusalem, to keep the passover unto the LORD God of
> Israel.

Finally, when the Congregation was back into fellowship and revived,
Hezekiah moved to the Community to bring the benefits of revival to the
Israelite population in the Transjordan and the Northern Kingdom. What
could not be accomplished by diplomacy or by war was made possible by the
restoration of cordial relations with God.

Nationbuilding is the institutional consequence of a spiritual movement. It is the invisible
bringing the visible into existence. The Kingdom of God itself will be the
global product of universal submission to the will of God.[xcvii]

[xcvii] The Kingdom will be brought about by the return of Christ to the earth. His return will bring about
what did not occur at his first advent, acknowledgement of his divine authority and Person by Israel
and by the Gentiles.

---

[79] **Perfect:** G5046 Strong, James. Enhanced Strong's Lexicon. Woodside Bible Fellowship, 1995.

[80] In other translations, [ex. NKJV, NASB], there is no comma after the word "saints."

[81] The Parable of the Wheat and Tares is comprehensive instruction in how false Christians, Pastors and churches come into being. This same technique is used to cripple the Communities of persons designated for domination. Tares [darnel] intoxicate when consumed in small quantiles and can kill in larger ones. They are planted deliberately as are false teachers and churches. They are often indistinguishable to any but those trained to discern them.

See: Laskow, Sarah. "Wheat's Evil Twin Has Been Intoxicating Humans For Centuries." Atlas Obscura, 55:00 400AD. http://www.atlasobscura.com/articles/wheats-evil-twin-has-been-intoxicating-humans-for-centuries.

[82] "In the 1970s and 1980s postmillennialism was revived in the Reconstructionist Movement led by Rousas J. Rushdoony, Greg Bahnsen and Gary North. Unlike previous American postmillennialists, who tended to view the coming kingdom as compatible with democratic values and institutions, the Reconstructionists envision a more authoritarian world run according to biblical law (theonomy), which includes an expanded use of capital punishment and a "Christian economics," which includes the re-establishment of so-called biblical slavery."

Daniel G. Reid et al., Dictionary of Christianity in America (Downers Grove, IL: InterVarsity Press, 1990).

"reconstructionism — A movement that seeks to make biblical law the foundation of all government and society; effectively attempting to bring about the explicit rule of God on earth and exercise the dominion that God delegated to Adam by reconstructing all society into something that conforms with God's law."

Douglas Mangum, The Lexham Glossary of Theology (Bellingham, WA: Lexham Press, 2014).

[83] The architects of oppression recognize that the spiritual and the physical worlds are one fabric of reality, created and orchestrated ultimately by God.

> Hebrews 11:3 (KJV 1900)
> 3 Through faith we understand that the worlds were framed by the Word of God, so that things which are seen were not made of things which do appear.

They use this knowledge to enslave the world. The oppressed usually have no knowledge of the spiritual means that secure their subjugation, even as they practice a version of Christianity designed to maintain their status as oppressed people. This is because the first casualties of this spiritual warfare are the pulpits in the Communities of the oppressed. (First Principle of Nationbuilding).

[84] The New King James Version. Nashville: Thomas Nelson, 1982.

15. The First Nationbuilding Principle

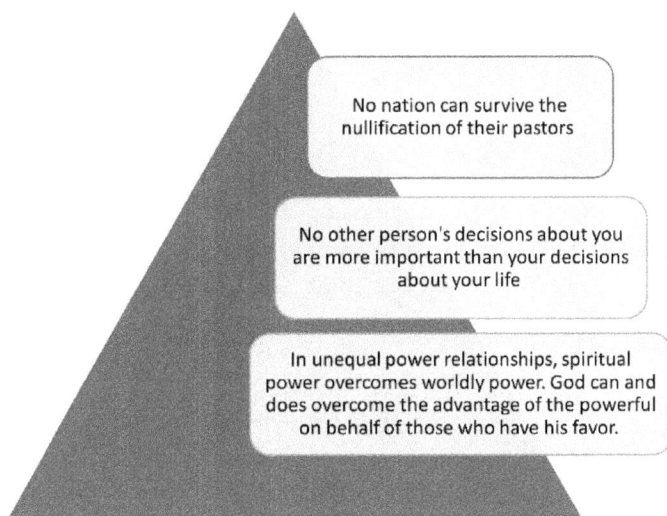

Figure 17: Three Nation Building Principles

First Nationbuilding Principle:

"No nation can survive the nullification of their Pastors."

The three components of Revival and Nationbuilding are the Pastor/Elders (Clergy), the Congregation, and the Community. The Pastor is responsible for the teaching and training [discipleship] of the Congregation. The Congregation is responsible for their dual witness of their lives and lips: that is, they are to live according to the Word of God and they are to proclaim the gospel. Finally, this witness of the Congregation impacts the Community, some of whom become Christians and some of whom learn to practice morality, creating an environment where national transformation may proceed, beginning with the healing of the institutions of Marriage and Family.

The First Nationbuilding Principle highlights the critical importance of spiritual leadership to the preservation of the nation. The believer is the invisible factor in history, whose obedience or disobedience to the Word of God invisibly but powerfully impacts the destiny of nations.

The engines of national destiny have always been spiritual. Leadership, economics, and military power are the *effects* of spiritual developments.

The principle that God's people determine the fortunes of nations is found throughout the scriptures. Abraham and Sodom and Gomorrah [Genesis 18], Joseph in Egypt [Genesis 41] and the ministry of Daniel and his friends in the government of both Babylon and Persia [Book of Daniel] all show that the presence of mature believers drive positive historical trends in the nations they inhabit. Jesus provides commentary on the principle of believers as the crucial factor in history:

> Matthew 5:13–14 (KJV 1900)
> 13 Ye are the salt of the earth: but if the salt have lost his savour, wherewith shall it be salted? it is thenceforth good for nothing, but to be cast out, and to be trodden under foot of men. 14 Ye are the light of the world. A city that is set on an hill cannot be hid.

Since the Pentecost that followed the resurrection of Jesus, the Church, the Body of Christ, is the instrument by which God dispenses spiritual blessing to nations and the world. The Elders of the local churches are the spiritually gifted and divinely sent men who provide the human leadership factor which makes the local church function. Today, in the Church age, God has specifically provided Pastors/Elders to equip the saints [Congregation] to minister to others [Community], igniting the forces that will bring about nationbuilding [Ephesians 4.11-15].

> Ephesians 4:11–15 (KJV 1900)
> 11 And he gave some, apostles; and some, prophets; and some, evangelists; and some, Pastors and teachers; 12 For the perfecting of the saints, for the work of the ministry, for the edifying of the body of Christ: 13 Till we all

come in the unity of the faith, and of the knowledge of the Son of God, unto a perfect man, unto the measure of the stature of the fulness of Christ: 14 That we henceforth be no more children, tossed to and fro, and carried about with every wind of doctrine, by the sleight of men, and cunning craftiness, whereby they lie in wait to deceive; 15 But speaking the truth in love, may grow up into him in all things, which is the head, even Christ:

The Purpose of the Pastor/Elder

According to this passage, the Pastor/Elder, is given to the church for the following purposes:

1. For the perfecting (equipping) of the saints, for the work of the ministry. The Pastor is to train believers. This involves preaching but also teaching and training. Today the Pastoral ministry has become primarily a sermonizing profession. Preaching is critical to the Pastoral ministry, but Christians do not know how to study their Bibles, they do not know how to share the gospel, they do not know how to engage in private prayer, and they do not know how to disciple a new believer. The word translated "perfecting" means "to make someone completely adequate or sufficient for something—'to make adequate, to furnish completely, to cause to be fully qualified, adequacy"[85]

2. For the systematic teaching of the entire Bible to disciples. The word "edifying" means: "the construction of something, with focus on the event of building up or on the result of such an event—'to build up, to construct, construction"[86] It conveys the idea of building something from a foundation to completion. The ministry of the Elder is not just to motivate the believer through exhortation but to impart to him a complete understanding of God's revelation in the scripture. This implies verse by verse exposition covering every book in the Bible. Systematic instruction approaches *all* the scriptures, but it also makes the proper applications to *all* aspects of the believer's experience: as a husband or wife, as a parent, as an employee or a citizen, or as a black man or woman[xcviii] living in the United States in

---

[xcviii] The idea that the Scriptures need not be directly applied to the life experience of black people *as* black people in America is clear evidence of spiritual warfare and what we will call Slave Theology later in this work.

the 21st century.

3. One outcome of this training and teaching is that a local church will achieve a "unity of the faith," that is agreement regarding what constitutes the truth of the Word of God. It may appear that unity of the faith is impossible. However, the new birth will result in such a unity of belief when believers [and not unbelievers pretending to be saints] are properly taught by men who are genuinely called, gifted and obedient to God. The "unity of the faith" is a work of the Spirit effectually operating through the Church. It is an objective entrusted to every generation of the Church and part of the Great Commission mandate:

> Matthew 28:19–20 (KJV 1900)
> [19] Go ye therefore, and teach all nations, baptizing them in the name of the Father, and of the Son, and of the Holy Ghost: [20] Teaching them to observe all things whatsoever I have commanded you: and, lo, I am with you alway, *even* unto the end of the world. Amen.

> 1 Corinthians 1:10 (KJV 1900)
> 10 Now I beseech you, brethren, by the name of our Lord Jesus Christ, that ye all speak the same thing, and that there be no divisions among you; but that ye be perfectly joined together in the same mind and in the same judgment.

4. The end of this unity is the "knowledge of the Son of God." Intimacy with God is the superpower of the believer whereby the potential of the new birth is realized in sanctification and ministry. The teaching and training by the Elders and teachers produce believers who know from personal experience that the Christian life is lived by means of an ever-growing fellowship with the living Christ. All Christian power, biblical understanding, and ministry effectiveness flow from abiding with Christ.

5. Another outcome of Pastoral ministry is when believers acquire the character of Christ: "unto a perfect man, unto the measure of the stature of the fulness of Christ." The Pastor *is not commanded to grow the church*, or to build a ministry empire, or to implement a political agenda. He is called to promote the spiritual transformation of his flock by means of the Word of God. This, along with his own

sanctification, is the basis of the Pastor's evaluation before God.[xcix]

6. The Pastoral ministry is truly effective when the Congregation becomes *spiritually self-sustaining*. They have learned how to feed themselves from the Word of God. Their prayer lives are self-motivated and illustrate an intimacy with Christ. They know enough and have experienced enough that they become largely impervious to the trickery of the devil through false prophets and false teachers. The clearest evidence of a deficiency in the leadership of any church is the gullibility of the people, a willingness to follow just about anyone who claims to have a Word from God. The properly taught Congregation is no longer able to be deceived for they are "no longer... children."[c]

7. Finally, the completed disciples can "speak the truth" [v. 15] to the benefit of others. They are equipped for the work of ministry. They possess both the truth and love, the two evidences of spiritual maturity. They are unwilling to place the Second Great Commandment before the First, therefore they speak truth to man *because* they love God. They can speak to their spouses and their children: their marriages and families are characterized by truth and love. They are qualified to speak, to go out into the Community and to evangelize the lost. They are effective ambassadors in the workplace and effective citizens unafraid to speak out against evil.[ci]

The Congregation, Mature Disciples and Social Justice

These facts are the solution to the dreaded Social Justice controversy that so many churches avoid. When believers are spiritually mature, their righteousness accompanies them into every relationship with individuals and interaction with institutions. The mature disciple's ability to apply the Word of

---

[xcix] 1 Corinthians 9.27; Colossians 1.28

[c] The unwillingness of Pastors to clearly identify error is one of the prominent failures of the local church in the 21st century. It is the very opposite of what the term "Pastor" signifies. The outcome is the spiritual malfunction of the local church: the onset of a negative spiritual chain reaction, the decay of the Community institutions, and exposure of the Community to demonic infiltration.

[ci] There is little reason to expect the Congregation to be any more courageous than their Pastors to speak the truth in love concerning the issues of good and evil in the world around them [Luke 6.40]. If the Pastor is unwilling to extend beyond evangelism into the realm of being salt and light, why would his people do so? In this way the Community is again deprived of the complete benefits of genuine Christian sanctification.

God to all situations, his personal holiness and fear of the Lord will not allow him to be silent in the face of injustice, nor will it allow him to be used as an instrument of injustice (by his actions or inactions) by any institution. Thus, by their commitment to personal righteousness and justice (or holiness) mature believers calibrate the consciences of their Community and refresh standards of morality. This is how responsible behavior by Pastors could have produced a very different America.

Social Justice is the application of true principles of equity and righteousness to every person and institution. When it comes to defining Social Justice, people like to pretend as if they do not know what it is or assign foolish descriptions in the attempt to ridicule the concept. These same people know precisely what Social Justice is when they are deprived of it.

> *Social Justice is the attainment of honest and equitable relations between men <u>and</u> between men and institutions, based upon the dictates of human consciences informed by divine revelation.*[cii]

> *Social Justice as an ideal is powerfully advanced in society by the Church when saved people begin living (speaking and acting) like saved people in all their relationships with individuals and institutions. Christian holiness is the biblically mandatory lifestyle that models before unbelieving society the behaviors that characterize human relations under Social Justice.*

> *Social Justice is an ideal of human relations which will be perfectly achieved when Christ reigns in his Kingdom, when he will personally enforce righteousness and justice among men.*[ciii]

The Congregation leaves the church building as a powerful, invisible transforming agent in society because their Pastors and Elders did their jobs.

[cii] Psalms 146.7-9; Isaiah 1.16-17; 33.15-16; Jeremiah 7.6-7; Philippians 2.15; Zechariah 7.8-12; 1 John 3.10.
Human conscience may be calibrated both by general and special revelation. When believers proclaim or model biblical righteousness, special revelation becomes accessible to unbelievers.
[ciii] Psalms 98.9; Isaiah 11.4, 9; Zechariah 14.9

The Fall of the Local Church

The Church will eventually triumph [Matthew 16.18]. Jesus will accomplish

---

First Nationbuilding Principle: *"No nation can survive the nullification of their Pastors"*

Figure 19: The First Nationbuilding Principle

every objective in his program for the Church. This, however, does not mean that *your* local church or *your* nation will triumph or continue to exist. This depends upon spiritual factors that we have begun to outline.

When God adds a vanguard of biblically oriented, effective Pastors to a nation, that nation *will* be blessed [2 Chronicles 16.9; Proverbs 11.10].

> Proverbs 14:34 (KJV 1900)
> 34 Righteousness exalteth a nation [H1471][87]: But sin is a reproach to any people [H3816].[88]

On the other hand, when the Pastors fail through various categories of sin, the number of properly equipped disciples' plummets and the nation is crippled. God has designated the Church as the most powerful source of spiritual light available to the nation. When that light is dimmed, the nation is overwhelmed by a vast darkness that weakens every human institution. God is forced to judge both disobedient believers and their nation which now disregards the dictates of morality and sponsors oppression and degeneracy.

When the man of God falls into sin and abuses his calling, a vacuum is created into which false teaching and false teachers are drawn. The neglect of the Word of God by legitimate Pastors creates an opportunity for smooth imitators[civ] who get rich and make a name for themselves off the flock. Paul, in his last address to the Elders in Ephesus warns them of this degenerative process whereby the people of God become merchandise for Satan's

---

[civ] Romans 16.17-18; 2 Corinthians 11.15

ministers.

> Acts 20:26–32 (KJV 1900)
>
> 26 Wherefore I take you to record this day, that I am pure from the blood of all men. 27 For I have not shunned to declare unto you all the counsel of God. 28 Take heed therefore unto yourselves, and to all the flock, over the which the Holy Ghost hath made you overseers, to feed the church of God, which he hath purchased with his own blood. 29 For I know this, that after my departing shall grievous wolves enter in among you, not sparing the flock. 30 Also of your own selves shall men arise, speaking perverse things, to draw away disciples after them. 31 Therefore watch, and remember, that by the space of three years I ceased not to warn every one night and day with tears. 32 And now, brethren, I commend you to God, and to the word of his grace, which is able to build you up, and to give you an inheritance among all them which are sanctified.

The nullification of the man of God is a perpetual objective of the devil, and can be caused by many means, such as the legal actions of the State [1 Kings 18.3-5] as it is in some countries; but nullification is often inflicted by Pastors upon themselves. Men are tempted to depart from God's pattern for the ministry because of attraction to what false teachers have achieved. They can embrace false doctrine in an effort to please their congregations and to retain membership. They might *confuse church growth with evangelism*, embracing church growth as if it is a spiritual initiative commanded by God.[cv] They may remain faithful to the Word in preaching but violate the scriptures by their lifestyle, disqualifying themselves from the ministry [1 Corinthians 9.24-27].

Paul declares that he has been a model of the Pastoral care[cvi] that these Elders must now provide. He is "innocent of the blood of all men." This implies that the man who exercises Pastoral authority will be held responsible for the lives [blood] of the people that God has given to his charge. These souls belong to God, He purchased their souls with the life of His Son. God has the right to hold the man of God responsible for the people He sends him.

[cv] God has not commanded Pastors to grow the local church. He has commanded them to proclaim the gospel and to teach the local church [make disciples], presenting every person complete in Christ [Colossians 1.28]. It is God's responsibility to save the lost and to thereby grow the local church ["I will build my church" Matthew 16.18b]. God has never called a man to the ministry without also providing a flock for him to lead. If a man is truly called of God, Pastoral faithfulness in what God has commanded him to do will result in God providing souls.

[cvi] Although Paul did Pastoral work, he himself was not a Pastor.

Ezekiel 3:18 (KJV 1900)
18 When I say unto the wicked, Thou shalt surely die; and thou givest him
not warning, nor speakest to warn the wicked from his wicked way, to save
his life; the same wicked man shall die in his iniquity; but his blood will I
require at thine hand.

The reason that Paul was innocent of this blood was because he had declared
to them "the whole counsel of God." We saw this same concept in Ephesians
4.12-14. The whole counsel of God is instruction in all the Scriptures, but it is
also the application of all the Scriptures to the entire person in all his relations:
to God, to himself, to the family, to the Community and to the State. The end
of his teaching was not the memorization of theology, but the sanctification
of the entire person. Paul was not in the Christian entertainment business, nor
was he attempting to create a comfortable church atmosphere for unbelievers
and sinning Christians. His preaching was comprehensive and severe. It was
so effective that while he was in charge, the church in Ephesus was relatively
free of the influence of the false teachers who prey upon the flock like wolves.

He now charges the Elders and reminds them of their solemn responsibility to
"take heed to yourselves and to all the flock...to shepherd the flock of God
which He purchased with His own blood." The man of God must himself be
in the faith and walking with the Lord before he can minister to God's people.
Once he has accepted the responsibility to Pastor, he must also make the
flock of God his priority rather than fame, or wealth or a ministry empire. The
shepherding ministry must become the focus of his professional life and
second to no other consideration except his own spiritual life and his family.

With the departure of the Apostle, the ministers of Satan would descend upon
the Ephesian congregation. " For I know this, that after my departing shall
grievous wolves [false teachers] enter in among you, not sparing the flock.
Also of your own selves shall men [erroneous teachers] arise, speaking
perverse things, to draw away disciples after them." The objective of the true
shepherd is to minister, the objective of the minister of Satan is to serve
himself at the expense of the flock.

➢ The *priority* of the shepherd is discipleship, the priority of the wolf is
the growth and retention of the flock.
➢ The *policy* of the shepherd is grace, the policy of the wolf is control.
➢ The *motivation* of the shepherd is the glory of God, the motivation of
the wolf is his appetite.

➤ The *objective* of the shepherd is the maturity of the flock, the objective of the wolf is the consumption of the flock.

The fact that the wolf cannot eat *all* the sheep at one time does not mean that he is not consuming them. The fact that he keeps the sheep entertained and happy is only smart husbandry, his objective is still to eat them. Many of today's apparently successful Christian churches are cattle factories which acquire, house, and fatten sheep for fleecing and consumption by professional [but uncalled] Clergy.

> Ezekiel 34:1–6 (KJV 1900)
> 1 And the word of the LORD came unto me, saying, 2 Son of man, prophesy against the shepherds of Israel, prophesy, and say unto them, Thus saith the Lord GOD unto the shepherds; Woe be to the shepherds of Israel that do feed themselves! should not the shepherds feed the flocks? 3 Ye eat the fat, and ye clothe you with the wool, ye kill them that are fed: but ye feed not the flock. 4 The diseased have ye not strengthened, neither have ye healed that which was sick, neither have ye bound up that which was broken, neither have ye brought again that which was driven away, neither have ye sought that which was lost; but with force and with cruelty have ye ruled them. 5 And they were scattered, because there is no shepherd: and they became meat to all the beasts of the field, when they were scattered. 6 My sheep wandered through all the mountains, and upon every high hill: yea, my flock was scattered upon all the face of the earth, and none did search or seek after them. [Matthew 9.36-38]

> 2 Corinthians 11:13–15 (KJV 1900)
> 13 For such are false apostles, deceitful workers, transforming themselves into the apostles of Christ. 14 And no marvel; for Satan himself is transformed into an angel of light. 15 Therefore it is no great thing if his ministers also be transformed as the ministers of righteousness; whose end shall be according to their works.

The First Nationbuilding Principle holds that the nation that has too many such shepherds is on its way to destruction via divine judgment.[cvii] As a consequence of the nullification of their pulpits, the very power source by which the nation is lighted and heated, the local church, has been stopped. No matter how many earnest leaders and grassroots efforts there are in the secular world working for the rescue of the black Community, their efforts cannot produce nationbuilding, once the light of the gospel and the ancillary light of

---

[cvii] Leviticus 26; Deuteronomy 28; Psalms 9.17; Romans 3.29

morality have been dimmed. This is because it is through the spiritual operations of the local church that the institutions of marriage and family are restored. *You cannot build a black national economic and political infrastructure upon the ruins of marriage and family.* You can temporarily alleviate suffering, but you cannot build lasting national well-being without these institutions.

The defection of the local churches from the Lord through sin and the rejection of the Word of God leads to God forsaking that Community. Due to the holiness of God, it could not be otherwise. Human effort cannot succeed when God is not on our side [Hosea 4.6-9].[cviii]

[cviii] The inevitable objection here is why this principle does not apply to oppressors? It *does* apply to oppressors when their time comes. The bible repeatedly shows God raising up oppressors against His chosen people Israel because of their long term and steadfast rejection of the Word of God. From Moab and Midian, Ammon, and Philistia, to Assyria and Babylon, each oppressing nation executed divine judgment upon Israel, and *each eventually fell under divine judgment themselves.* God's judgment is righteous judgment. He will not adjust to us; we must adjust to Him. See Appendix I-Section: God is Opposed to Oppressors

---

[85] **Equipping**: Johannes P. Louw and Eugene Albert Nida, Greek-English Lexicon of the New Testament: Based on Semantic Domains (New York: United Bible Societies, 1996), 679.

[86] **Edifying**: Johannes P. Louw and Eugene Albert Nida, Greek-English Lexicon of the New Testament: Based on Semantic Domains (New York: United Bible Societies, 1996), 513.

[87] **Nation**: 1471 גּוֹיִם, גּוֹי [gowy, rarely, goy /go·ee/] n pr m. Apparently from the same root as 1465; TWOT 326e; GK 1580 and 1582; 558 occurrences; AV translates as "nation" 374 times, "heathen" 143 times, "Gentiles" 30 times, and "people" 11 times. 1 nation, people. 1A nation, people. 1A1 <u>usually of non-Hebrew people</u>. 1A2 of descendants of Abraham. 1A3 of Israel. 1B of swarm of locusts, other animals (fig.). 1C Goyim? = "nations" [emphasis added].

James Strong, Enhanced Strong's Lexicon (Woodside Bible Fellowship, 1995).

[88] **People**: 3816 לְאֹם [lâom, lâ'owm /leh·ome/] n m. From an unused root meaning to gather; TWOT 1069a; GK 4211; 35 occurrences; AV translates as "people" 24 times, "nation" 10 times, and "folk" once. 1 <u>a people, nation</u> [emphasis added].

James Strong, Enhanced Strong's Lexicon (Woodside Bible Fellowship, 1995).

16. The Second Nationbuilding Principle: Definition and Case Study

Second Nationbuilding Principle:
"No other person's decisions about you are more important than your decisions about your life."

Figure 20: The Second Nationbuilding Principle

Are your decisions more important than your *environment* in the determination of your destiny?

Are the decisions of *powerful people* more important than your own decisions in the determination of your destiny?

If the *environment* is more important, then we should focus our attentions upon changing the environment to determine our destiny:

➢ Social Environment
➢ Economic Environment
➢ Political Environment

If the decisions of *powerful people* are more important than our own, then we should focus our actions upon changing the thoughts and behaviors of powerful individuals and groups to work out our destiny.

➢ Influential members of privileged classes
➢ Powerful non-governmental organizations
➢ The government itself

These are two important questions that go to the heart of how man must live his life upon the earth. Do my decisions count in creating my destiny and how much do they count? Am I a slave to the decisions of others and the situation of my birth? Or does God provide greater weight to my own decisions as determining factors of my future and well-being?

Must I throw my energies into manipulating and influencing my environment and improving my life from the outside in; or can I achieve more satisfactory results by identifying the system of truth which, by adhering to it, I change myself and my life from the inside out?

The Book of Job: Decision or Environment

Was Job's faith the result of his own decisions about truth or the result of God's manipulation of his environment?

> Job 1:8 (KJV 1900)
> 8 And the LORD said unto Satan, Hast thou considered my servant Job, that there is none like him in the earth, a perfect and an upright man, one that feareth God, and escheweth evil?

Satan is not yet cast out of God's presence. His eviction from heaven is yet future [Revelation 12.7-9]. He continues to have access to heaven, presenting himself with the sons of God according to the divine schedule [Job 1.6]. As God is working his will among men, He also has a plan for the angelic creation. In the Book of Job, we are granted insight into the interrelationship between these two strands of the divine purpose.

It is God who presents Job to Satan for his evaluation, knowing what this act would precipitate. Every *mature* believer will be tested to demonstrate his faithfulness to God, to accelerate his spiritual development, and to illustrate to the angels the character and intention of God in His dealings with the heavenly hosts.

> 1 Peter 1:6–7 (KJV 1900)
> 6 Wherein ye greatly rejoice, though now for a season, if need be, ye are in heaviness through manifold <u>temptations</u> [G3986]:[89] 7 That the trial of your faith, being much more precious than of gold that perisheth, though it be tried with fire, might be found unto praise and honour and glory at the appearing of Jesus Christ:

> James 1:12 (KJV 1900)
> 12 Blessed is the man that endureth temptation [G3986]: for when he is tried [or approved], he shall receive the crown of life, which the Lord hath promised to them that love him.

Why engage Satan in the testing of Job? Why involve him in the temptation of the first humans [Genesis 3]? Why send Jesus into the wilderness specifically to be tempted by the devil [Matthew 4.1]?

We do not know fully the divine motivation for the creation of humanity. However, we do know that one motive for the creation of man was to resolve the prehistoric conflict between God and the fallen angels, led by Lucifer. The angelic world is intimately involved in the administration of the plan of God for humanity. From Eden to the giving of the Law, to their supernatural interventions on behalf of Israel, to their ministry to Mary and Joseph, to their Church Age ministry to the saints, to their pivotal role in the unfolding of judgments of the seven seals of Revelation, the angels have been involved, for bad or for good, in the fortunes of mankind.

The creation, fall and redemption of mankind illustrate to the angels the character God towards to morally culpable beings. The Bible teaches that the Church itself is an object lesson to the angelic hosts.

Ephesians 3:9–11 (KJV 1900)
9 And to make all men see what is the fellowship of the mystery,
which from the beginning of the world hath been hid in God, who
created all things by Jesus Christ: 10 To the intent that now <u>unto the</u>
<u>principalities and powers in heavenly places might be known by the</u>
<u>church the manifold wisdom of God</u>, 11 According to the eternal
purpose which he purposed in Christ Jesus our Lord:

A key question of human history is how man will use his volition when given
a similar set of circumstances as the angels, a portion of whom fell in eternity
past [Hebrews 2.5-7?]. God is testing man under a variety of combinations of
divine economies [dispensations] and historical circumstances that
demonstrate His righteousness and justice. From one perspective, human
history may be seen as an experiment to demonstrate the "manifold wisdom
of God' in his actions in response to the angelic revolt of prehistory.

Satan used his free will to disobey and rebel against God. The existence of
other fallen angels testifies to the fact that other beings joined him in his
rebellion.

Ezekiel 28:14–18 (KJV 1900)
14 Thou art the anointed cherub that covereth; and I have set thee so: thou
wast upon the holy mountain of God; thou hast walked up and down in the
midst of the stones of fire. 15 Thou wast perfect in thy ways from the day
that thou wast created, till iniquity was found in thee. 16 By the multitude of
thy merchandise they have filled the midst of thee with violence, and thou
hast sinned: therefore I will cast thee as profane out of the mountain of
God: and I will destroy thee, O covering cherub, from the midst of the
stones of fire. 17 Thine heart was lifted up because of thy beauty, thou hast
corrupted thy wisdom by reason of thy brightness: I will cast thee to the
ground, I will lay thee before kings, that they may behold thee. 18 Thou hast
defiled thy sanctuaries by the multitude of thine iniquities, by the iniquity of
thy traffick; therefore will I bring forth a fire from the midst of thee, it shall
devour thee, and I will bring thee to ashes upon the earth in the sight of all
them that behold thee.

Because of the experiment of humanity, God's sentence upon Satan and the
fallen angels has not been fully executed, as it is under appeal. This may be
seen by their presence throughout human history as enemies of God and man.
In every generation God is raising up human witnesses to demonstrate the
culpability of created beings for their own decisions and ratifying his own

design and plan for the created universe. The Book of Job is an extended treatment of this subject. The devil introduces arguments (through Job's friends) and temptations (through circumstances) designed to undermine Job's thought processes so that he might condemn God and rebel against Him as did the angels who followed Lucifer in the beginning.

Through every combination of biblical economy and historical circumstance [environment], God is demonstrating that human decisions matter and that our decisions create our destiny.

God is also demonstrating that His plan for His creation has been and continues to be better than any human or satanically derived plan for the universe.

These truths are particularly relevant to nationbuilding. The point of human life is to find God and his truth and to direct your attention to it with the objective of obtaining and maintaining a relationship with Him [Matthew 16.26]. It is through this relationship with God through Jesus Christ[cix] that one achieves his personal destiny on the earth and in eternity [John 10.10]. This way of life is simultaneously the means which produces the best outcomes for civilization, as will be seen.

God is personally concerned with earthly outcomes, as both man and earth belong to Him. It is a devilish subterfuge that forces the believer to choose between heavenly or earthly impact, that the spiritual believer should not expect his faith to have earthly impact for the better. This is an argument designed to provide spiritual justification for the oppressive status quo and is a foundational principle of Slave Theology.

The application of this truth for black America is profound. *Nationbuilding is achieved by means of spiritual transformation and not by direct actions upon the organs of society, or upon powerful individuals or groups.*[cx] Every time a Pastor forsakes ministry to the Congregation to get involved in politics or entrepreneurship or some other diversion, he proves the First Nationbuilding Principle by precipitating the decline of his Community. Societal transformation[cxi] is a by-

---

[cix] John 14.6; Romans 10.9; Acts 16.31
[cx] Therefore, the Nationbuilding Principles cannot be conflated with Reconstructionism, Theonomy or Dominionism.
[cxi] Societal transformation is not universal salvation, nor any form of Postmillennial optimism. The Church, the Body of Christ, by its existence and proper function restrains both Satan and the human sin nature from the full potential of demonic and human depravity [2 Thessalonians 2.6,8]. The

product of spiritual revival through the proper spiritual function of the local church.

Case Study: The Civil Rights Movement

The civil rights movement of the 1950's and 1960's was honorable in its motivation and its objective to lift the mass of black Americans to a greater participation in American life through a full enjoyment of our rights as citizens. Many men and women, black and white, sacrificed or died to relieve the suffering of our people and to create opportunity for future generations. Today, in the 21st century, we can see that the very rights achieved in that era are being rapidly reversed.[90] There is a spirit of change in America that seeks to restore the way of life that existed prior to the modern civil rights era. This spirit has found a home in many Congregations, producing a negative spiritual chain reaction that has resulted in actions such as the January 6th revolt in Washington D.C. where the symbol of the cross was lifted in proximity to the symbol of the lynching noose.[91]

Perhaps more disappointing is the realization that although the civil rights movement alleviated much black suffering, it had little impact upon the institutions upon which every Community relies. Marriage statistics have been in decline for black people since the 1940's.[92] The increase in divorces and decrease in marriage rates increases the likelihood that female headed households will slide into poverty [31% of female headed black families lived below the poverty line in 2021].[93]

The fragility of the legal victories of the civil rights movement and its inability to produce institutional strength in the black Community is *because although the movement was largely led by the Clergy, it was not primarily a spiritual movement.* Its success was based upon its ability to impact critical government institutions, powerful individuals, and groups.

To be clear, the civil rights movement was necessary: it was not the pursuit of redress for the unconstitutional denial of rights to blacks which was at fault for the fragility of the progress achieved. Nor was the use of legal means such as economic boycotts or lawsuits improper. What was improper was the large group of *Pastors* who sought political means over spiritual means to change

---

Nationbuilding Principles refocus the Church upon the priorities that can optimize this effect for any Christians who are willing to obey the Scriptures.

the destiny of black people. Men who should have known better exchanged short-term success for long-term defeat. They achieved real progress that they could not defend or secure because that progress was not founded upon the spiritual mechanisms that create long-term institutional strength. It might have been better to allow the Congregation to engage in the struggle for civil rights as Christian citizens, not forsaking their gospel witness, while the Clergy maintained a single-minded focus upon the spiritual development [discipleship] of the Congregation.

The most important decisions are our own decisions, *and those decisions must engage God in our defense.*

This is not an argument to neglect the pursuit of justice as if it is mutually exclusive from spiritual priorities. The Christian that tells black people, "just stick with the gospel" is not representing good theology but simply wishes to exclude racial justice from the influence of Christianity. The point is that a secular movement, by itself, cannot initiate or sustain the spiritual processes necessary to deliver the oppressed. It does not cease to be a secular movement because the Clergy are leading it. Oppression is first and foremost a spiritual initiative and must be fought primarily by spiritual means. If the Pastors do not realize this, then there is no hope for the rest of us (First Principle of Nationbuilding).

Book of Job: God's Argument

God argues that Job's decisions to be blameless and upright, his decisions to fear God and his decisions to shun evil have made him unique in the earth and a special servant of the Lord.

> Job 1:8 (KJV 1900)
> 8 And the LORD said unto Satan, Hast thou considered my servant Job, that there is none like him in the earth, a perfect and an upright man, one that feareth God, and escheweth evil?

God is directing the devil to consider, to examine ["put his heart upon"-Adam Clarke] a person who is the exact opposite of himself. Job's character and blessings are not a consequence of a better *environment* than the devil, they are a consequence of better *decisions*.

Servant [OT:5650]: God refers to Job as a *Servant* of God. Lucifer was also once the servant of God, the *anointed cherub that covereth*, the antitype to the golden cherubs which covered the ark of the covenant, upon which rested the glory of God in Jerusalem.[cxii] Lucifer *made a decision* to elevate himself[cxiii] and became the *adversary*[cxiv] of God. He was in heaven what Judas was on earth. Thus, Satan's attack upon Job is revealed to be an attack upon God, an attempt to invalidate the rule of God over the heavens and the earth by proving His judgment of the rebellious angels to have been capricious and arbitrary.

Perfect [OT: 8535]: means complete, perfect, undefiled. Although Lucifer was created blameless, and every day gazed upon the unshielded glory of God, he averted his eyes to look upon himself and fell through pride [Ezekiel 28.17; 1Timothy 3.6]. Satan hoped that by cross-examining Job with pain, he would cause him to look away from God and unto himself and his circumstances.

Upright [OT:3477]: straight, level, just, upright. The term *devil* means slanderer, false accuser and therefore a deceiver. The devil is not "on the level" [John 8.44]. Even during the temptation of Job, Satan will change the conditions that he had boasted would surely cause him to sin. God is not only drawing attention to Job, but he is also using Job's testimony to highlight the ugliness of Lucifer's character. In this context, Job is a weapon against Satan. We must ask ourselves, are we a weapon for God or against Him?

Escheweth evil [OT: 5493/7451] to turn aside from evil. Job may encounter an evil, but seeing it, he will turn from it. Lucifer places evil in men's paths with the objective of tempting them to engage and cooperate with evil.

Feareth God [OT: 3373]: fears God with the result that he is ethically reverent. One thing that is clear from this conversation with God is that Satan does not fear Him. Like a murderer who has already received the death penalty [Matthew 25.41], Lucifer boldly defies God.

None like him on the earth: Here we have a similarity between Job and Lucifer. There is none like Job in his generation and there is none like Satan either. There are many fallen angels, but Lucifer is unique among them in rank and in the fact that he was not tempted by any external force.

It is noteworthy that there are so few believers of Job's caliber upon the earth.

[cxii] Exodus 25.20
[cxiii] Ezekiel 28.11-19
[cxiv] Satan: Adversary H7854

160

He was unique in his generation.

> Noah was unique in his generation.

Genesis 7:1 (KJV 1900)
1 And the LORD said unto Noah, Come thou and all thy house into the ark;
for thee have I seen righteous before me in this generation.

> Daniel was unique in his generation.

Ezekiel 14:19–20 (KJV 1900)
[19] Or *if* I send a pestilence into that land, and pour out my fury upon it in
blood, to cut off from it man and beast: [20] Though Noah, Daniel, and Job,
were in it, *as* I live, saith the Lord God, they shall deliver neither son nor
daughter; they shall *but* deliver their own souls by their righteousness.

> John the Baptist was unique in his generation.

Matthew 11:11 (KJV 1900)
11 Verily I say unto you, Among them that are born of women there hath
not risen a greater than John the Baptist: notwithstanding he that is least in
the kingdom of heaven is greater than he.

It is apparent that among believers, genuine sustained spiritual maturity is not
a commonplace thing. This must have something to do with Satan's
effectiveness.

Before the test begins God clearly establishes that *the difference between Job and
Lucifer is based upon the decisions that each have made*: the one, who rejected truth
and its Author, and the other, by living according to truth in submission to
God. If anything, Satan had been given far better circumstances than Job.

Job was not merely in philosophical agreement with truth in principle. He
acquired a practical righteousness which glorified God in the world. This
uprightness is an attribute born of fear of the Lord and results in God's
willingness to bless the believer in time. In other words, the decisions of the
upright literally create his environment. His decisions create his destiny.[cxv] The
same holds true for the ungodly.

[cxv] This is not the same as the heresy that one's words create his environment. Proper decisions are
those which are in obedience to the Word of God, not man's words. God is on record that he will
honor obedience to His Word [John 14.21].

Psalms 37:37–38 (NKJV)
37 Mark the blameless man, and observe the upright; For the <u>future</u> of that man is peace. 38 But the transgressors shall be destroyed together; The <u>future</u> of the wicked shall be cut off.

In all the spiritual tests of individuals throughout history, it is the devil that is manipulating the environment to change human decisions. The mature believer realizes that spiritual power must be directed not at the world, but at himself, resulting in a life through which God can change the world.

The Impact of External Decisions

What about the bad cards that many people are dealt in every generation of mankind? People suffer under bad parents, negative historical circumstances, racial discrimination, wicked leaders, etc. We are all impacted by the decisions of others. Are these decisions more important than our own?

Job's troubles: the loss of his wealth, his children, and his health, although originating outside of his own decisions, are still demanding that he make new choices regarding what God has said in revelation. Although we are not responsible for the cards dealt to us in life, we are responsible for how we play those cards. Do we believe that God holds the destiny of every individual in his hands and that He has the wisdom and power to control the future? Do we affirm that He is a God who is disposed towards the well-being of man because of His own goodness, righteousness, and love? Do we acknowledge that God will bless the upright? If we do, then we must also believe that the cumulative good decisions of many righteous people have an even greater impact.

Proverbs 14:34 (KJV 1900)
34 Righteousness exalteth a nation: But sin is a reproach to any people.

We should also recognize that a good environment does not necessarily result in better decisions. The perfect environment of the Garden did not prevent Adam and Eve from sinning. Prosperity and peace did not prevent the fall of Solomon into gross sin. The absolute perfection of Lucifer and the angelic order did not prevent the fall of a portion of their number.

The decisions of others do impact us in good. bad, and even tragic ways.

However, the quality of our life is ultimately determined by *the decisions that we make about truth* while within these circumstances. What we believe about God and His Word is still more important than our immediate situation. This is the meaning of faith.

> Psalms 23.4a [KJV 1900]
> Yea, though I walk through the valley of the shadow of death, I will fear no evil: for thou art with me;

The Book of Job: Satan's Argument

> Job 1:9–11 (KJV 1900)
> 9 Then Satan answered the LORD, and said, Doth Job fear God for nought? 10 Hast not thou made an hedge about him, and about his house, and about all that he hath on every side? thou hast blessed the work of his hands, and his substance is increased in the land. [this is environment-rw] 11 But put forth thine hand now, and touch all that he hath, and he will curse thee to thy face.

After Satan destroyed the wealth, servants, and children of Job, yet failed to elicit sin from the mouth of Job, but rather praise to God, there was the following exchange:

> Job 2:3–5 (KJV 1900)
> 3 And the LORD said unto Satan, Hast thou considered my servant Job, that there is none like him in the earth, a perfect and an upright man, one that feareth God, and escheweth evil? and still he holdeth fast his integrity, although thou movedst me against him, to destroy him without cause. 4 And Satan answered the LORD, and said, Skin for skin, yea, all that a man hath will he give for his life. 5 But put forth thine hand now, and touch his bone and his flesh, and he will curse thee to thy face.

Satan's argument is that Job fears God due to the Lord's provision of prosperity and blessing. In other words, Job serves God because God pays him to do so with positive environment.[cxvi] He accused God of misrepresenting Job's true motivation: Job's integrity was situational, change Job's environment and you will change Job. Remove those benefits and Job is

---

[cxvi] The "Health and Wealth Gospel" is this same argument when presented to man. It holds that because of the atonement, a Christian is entitled to health and wealth, immediately and at all times. When the "promise" of this ill-defined prosperity inevitably fails due to the sovereign will of God in dispensing blessing to believers, Satan will be there to incite rebellion against the Lord.

no different than those condemned in the angelic Fall.

Satan misrepresented God to Eve in the Garden [Genesis 3.4-5]. The devil implied that God was arbitrary and not entirely honest in his denial of access to the Tree of Knowledge. Satan even tries to persuade Jesus that Godhood is about power alone: God is right because God has might, and that he [Satan] as the prince of this world [John 12.31] can give Jesus the kingdom, power, and glory [Luke 4.5-7] without reference to righteousness at all.

Satan uses the power of ideas [doctrines, philosophies] to convince, to induce or to coerce men into abandoning God and His truth in exchange for the promise of better circumstances in this life. When directed at believers, Satan's temptations require that the Christian reject [true] faith and thereby reject the Word of God.

The Application to Nationbuilding

The futile efforts of the local church to effect nationbuilding exclusively through economics and politics plays directly into the hands of Satan by bypassing the Word of God, unwittingly sidestepping God in the process. Christians are historically guilty of attempting to take control of government and make it serve the interests of the Church. Inevitably they find themselves justifying the corruption and usurpations of government when the administration in power shares their interests. However, the government never completely delivers on its promises to believers, it simply solicits them to exchange spiritual strategies for partial and temporary secular remedies. It could not do otherwise, since human government lacks a spiritual mandate, spiritual power, or submission to the Word of God.

This does not mean that believers should avoid government involvement or that they should sit still for illegal treatment. Mature believers have a dramatic impact upon the moral climate, extending even to the function of government. Furthermore, mature believers should be excellent citizens who take responsibility for their part in governing their towns, states, and nation. Some believers [Congregation, not Pastors][cxvii] will even hold office.

[cxvii] Any qualified man or woman can hold elective office in government. Almost no one, comparatively speaking, is qualified to be a Pastor, because such a one must be called and gifted by God alone. Furthermore, the calling of the Man of God is infinitely higher in importance and impact than any

The primary and effective means of executing societal change is the exertion of spiritual power upon the Congregation, resulting in spiritual ministry to the Community.

> 2 Corinthians 10:3–5 (KJV 1900)
> 3 For though we walk in the flesh, we do not war after the flesh: 4 (For the weapons of our warfare are not carnal, but mighty through God to the pulling down of strong holds;) 5 Casting down imaginations, and every high thing that exalteth itself against the knowledge of God, and bringing into captivity every thought to the obedience of Christ;

The "strong holds," "imaginations," and "high thing(s)" are the spiritual structures of the soul which create and sustain oppression [and many other things] in the world. The visible policies, laws and even the violence that is essential to oppression are the physical *consequences* of these spiritual antecedents. Satan's followers can find the spiritual power *in him* to overthrow each other, it has happened throughout history. It is a fact that Satan's kingdom is divided [Daniel 11.40; Matthew 12.22-27]. However, *Christians* have zero chance of eliminating the effects of oppression without God's help and that means submission to an accurate understanding of the Word of God.

It is the right and privilege of the Congregation to engage in political life, to start businesses and to use every legal means to advocate for what is right in society, so long as they are not deceived into believing that such action is any more than the necessary but temporary alleviation of human suffering, and the maintenance activity necessary for the upkeep of the State. The State will founder and collapse into tyranny without the involvement of individuals properly oriented to truth and morality. However, lasting spiritual impact upon civilization can only occur as the gospel is proclaimed and obedient soldiers for Christ are created and sent into the world to manifest righteousness [sanctification] in *every* human institution and in every human relationship. The believer who forgets this truth unknowingly serves the interests of Satan who is committed to enticing the Christian into rearranging

---

elective office or hereditary title. The man of God deals every day with matters of life, death, and eternity. He is intimate [or should be] with the Most High God who has commissioned him to influence his generation via the Word of God. The Pastor who becomes a political representative and does that job properly, must become a poor Pastor.

the deck chairs on this Titanic of a world.[cxviii]

Therefore, we must take responsibility for our decisions, which God has decreed will have consequences in time and eternity. But good decisions are based on truth and not error. God does not honor sincerity about false teaching. Our most important decisions are responses to the accurate teaching of the Word of God, these are the decisions which have positive impact upon our lives and the lives of those around us.

The True Doctrine of Prosperity

When the believer makes consistently good decisions, God is free to bless that believer in accordance with Scripture. Job was blessed because he was righteous [see below], because he had faith in God. In other words, because of his decisions [James 2.17-18]. The true doctrine of prosperity is not the doctrine which Satan has foisted upon Christendom today. God is not obligated to make believers rich or healthy. In grace God provides certain blessings to all believers; mature believers who have been tested and approved will receive additional, multifaceted blessings in this life and the next because of genuine spiritual growth.

The most important decision a person can make is the one to believe the gospel, resulting in the forgiveness of sins and eternal life. This decision leads to the imputation of Christ's righteousness to the one who believes the gospel. This imputation is the source of many grace operations which will benefit the believer on earth and in heaven.

First, there is a basic provision of grace provided to every believer. Because it is grace it is not dependent upon his obedience or disobedience but is a product of his new relation to God through Christ. This grace is referred to many times in the scriptures. This grace provides for the *basic physical needs* of the Christian and includes the *spiritual resources* that he will need to advance to spiritual maturity.

[cxviii] There is a difference between the effort to *correct* the world through *social action* and the effort to be used of the Spirit to *convict* the world through standing up for what is right. *Social action* is first aid: necessary to save lives, and able to be administered by most people. *Spiritual action* is surgery, necessary for the long-term viability of the Community, and can only be administered by the local church. *Social action*, seeking to change people and institutions for the better, is not a bad thing until it becomes the *main thing* that occupies the people of God. *Spiritual action*, standing up for righteousness in all situations, is the responsibility of every believer.

Psalms 37:25–26 (KJV 1900)
25 I have been young, and now am old; Yet have I not seen the righteous forsaken, Nor his seed begging bread. 26 He is ever merciful, and lendeth; And his seed is blessed.

Matthew 6:31–33 (KJV 1900)
31 Therefore take no thought, saying, What shall we eat? or, What shall we drink? or, Wherewithal shall we be clothed? 32 (For after all these things do the Gentile seek:) for your heavenly Father knoweth that ye have need of all these things. 33 But seek ye first the kingdom of God, and his righteousness; and all these things shall be added unto you.

Philippians 4:19 (KJV 1900)
19 But my God shall supply all your need according to his riches in glory by Christ Jesus.

These provisions are "by Christ Jesus" that is, they are consequences of the forgiveness of sins and the adoption of the believer by God.[cxix] Therefore, these *logistical* blessings are made even to disobedient believers, although they may also be squandered by them.

Nehemiah 9:18–21 (KJV 1900)
18 Yea, when they had made them a molten calf, and said, This is thy God that brought thee up out of Egypt, and had wrought great provocations; 19 Yet thou in thy manifold mercies forsookest them not in the wilderness: the pillar of the cloud departed not from them by day, to lead them in the way; neither the pillar of fire by night, to shew them light, and the way wherein they should go. 20 Thou gavest also thy good spirit to instruct them, and withheldest not thy manna from their mouth, and gavest them water for their thirst. 21 Yea, forty years didst thou sustain them in the wilderness, so that they lacked nothing; their clothes waxed not old, and their feet swelled not.

The foundation of this basic level of grace is not our obedience, but the integrity, the character of God towards the believer.[cxx] This grace is the response of the justice of God to His own righteousness imputed to you at salvation [Romans 4.20-5.1]. This grace is also His recognition of your

---

[cxix] Salvation produces the same fundamental benefits in the Old and New Testaments, because salvation is the same, regardless of the biblical economy in view. Dispensational distinctives, such as the ministry of the Holy Spirit to the Church, are in addition to the spiritual transactions in salvation. The Jews of the Old Testament were expected to understand the mechanism of the new birth [John 3.1-10].

[cxx] In Nehemiah 9 above, that grace was expressed towards the covenant *nation* of Israel.

adoption by Him as sons and daughters [Galatians 4.4-7].

There are also *greater* gifts of grace available to believers. These gifts of grace are related to the spiritual maturity of the believer. It is wrong to think of these later blessings as *earned* by obedience. Rather, obedience to the Word of God over time creates the spiritual *capacity* to glorify God through greater blessing.

> 2 Peter 3:18 (KJV 1900)
> 18 But grow in grace, and in the knowledge of our Lord and Saviour Jesus Christ. To him be glory both now and for ever. Amen.

Similarly, rewards in heaven are not earned, there is nothing that man can do in himself to meet God's righteous requirements. Eternal rewards are given according to the spiritual capacity acquired by spiritual growth.

> Luke 17:7–10 (KJV 1900)
> 7 But which of you, having a servant plowing or feeding cattle, will say unto him by and by, when he is come from the field, Go and sit down to meat? 8 And will not rather say unto him, Make ready wherewith I may sup, and gird thyself, and serve me, till I have eaten and drunken; and afterward thou shalt eat and drink? 9 Doth he thank that servant because he did the things that were commanded him? I trow not. 10 So likewise ye, when ye shall have done all those things which are commanded you, say, We are unprofitable servants: we have done that which was our duty to do.

> Ephesians 2:10 (KJV)
> 10 For we are his workmanship, created in Christ Jesus unto good works, which God hath before ordained that we should walk in them.

As the believer grows spiritually, God is free to greatly bless the believer without compromise to his holiness. For example, a parent may be financially able to provide his teenage child with an automobile, but a parent with integrity would not provide such a blessing to an immature child; to do so would not be a blessing to the child, but a curse both to him and to the Community. In like manner, there are many blessings available to the mature believer with the capacity to appreciate them without worshipping them.

> James 4:5–6 (KJV 1900)
> 5 Do ye think that the scripture saith in vain, The spirit that dwelleth in us lusteth to envy? 6 But he giveth more grace. Wherefore he saith, God resisteth the proud, but giveth grace unto the humble.

Revelation 4:10–11 (KJV 1900)
10 The four and twenty elders fall down before him that sat on the throne, and worship him that liveth for ever and ever, <u>and cast their crowns before the throne, saying</u>, 11 Thou art worthy, O Lord, to receive glory and honour and power: for thou hast created all things, and for thy pleasure they are and were created.

Some Categories of Temporal Prosperity

> - Ministry Prosperity: prosperity related to the skillful use and productivity of one's spiritual gift and ministry [Paul].
> - Relationship Prosperity: prosperity related to the quality of one's relationships: friends, relatives, others.
> - Professional Prosperity- prosperity related to one's skill and effectiveness in the workplace [Daniel].
> - Health Prosperity-prosperity related to good health [Caleb, Hezekiah].
> - Financial Prosperity-prosperity related to finances and possessions [Job, Solomon]. This, like all other prosperity, varies by individual, even under spiritual maturity.
> - Marital Prosperity-prosperity related to marriage, including sexual, reproductive, and relationship prosperity [Abraham and Sarah]
> - Mental Prosperity: Prosperity related to mental function, intellect, and wisdom [Solomon, Paul]
> - Historical Impact: Prosperity related to unusual positive spiritual impact upon history [Moses, Samuel, Mordecai, Esther, Ezra, Nehemiah, Daniel]

There are other categories of prosperity available to the one that grows into spiritual maturity [e.g., Longevity (Methuselah, John the Apostle), Leadership Dynamics (Joshua, David)]. God expresses infinite variety in his bestowal of categories of blessings upon spiritually mature believers upon the earth and in heaven.

1 Corinthians 2:9 (KJV 1900)
9 But as it is written, Eye hath not seen, nor ear heard, neither have entered into the heart of man, the things which God hath prepared for them that love him.

You will, as a tested and proven Christian, receive some subset of the categories of prosperity and each different in expression and degree. Some graces may come early and some after longer time spent as a mature Christian. Growth should never stop for the believer and there is no limit to God's creativity in assigning spiritual blessing to the spiritual adult.[94]

The believer that receives the blessings of maturity will also receive rewards in eternity.

> 1 Corinthians 3:10–15 (KJV 1900)
> 10 According to the grace of God which is given unto me, as a wise masterbuilder, I have laid the foundation, and another buildeth thereon. But let every man take heed how he buildeth thereupon. 11 For other foundation can no man lay than that is laid, which is Jesus Christ. 12 Now if any man build upon this foundation gold, silver, precious stones, wood, hay, stubble; 13 Every man's work shall be made manifest: for the day shall declare it, because it shall be revealed by fire; and the fire shall try every man's work of what sort it is. 14 If any man's work abide which he hath built thereupon, he shall receive a reward. 15 If any man's work shall be burned, he shall suffer loss: but he himself shall be saved; yet so as by fire.

The analogy of the foundation of the Church, built upon by apostles, prophets, pastors, and teachers is, for the individual believer, his own construction upon the foundation of the new birth in his own life by means of spiritual growth through discipleship [Luke 6.48; 14.28-30, 33]. The *quality* ["of what sort it is"] of that edifice built in his soul is demonstrated by the transformed life of the Christian. This transformed life indicates his spiritual capacity for further divine blessing, greater grace, in this life and rewards in the life to come: the crowns of life [James 1.12], righteousness [2 Timothy 4.8] and glory [1 Peter 5.4], which symbolize honors, decorations, and privileges in eternity.

Blessing By Association

When God is free to bless the obedient believer, this blessing logically impacts those around him. The spiritually mature mother might receive longevity and wisdom from God which benefit both she and her family; spiritually mature employees could receive professional, leadership and health capacities that overflow to their company perhaps as greater worker productivity, increased profitability, or lower costs because of God's blessing upon these Christians.

➤ Blessings accrue to the believer who is obedient to the Word of God and fulfills the plan of God by achieving spiritual maturity.[cxxi]

➤ Blessings to the mature believer impact friends, relatives and associates who live and work in his periphery. The mature believer has tremendous invisible impact because individuals and organizations receive blessing by their association with him [cxxii]

➤ God is glorified by blessing mature believers. He directs history for their advantage.[cxxiii] These believers are the basis of the prosperity of the families, Communities, and nations to which they belong. Although not perceived by the unsaved, God blesses humanity through His people, which in the Old Testament was Israel, but in this age is the Church.

➤ Christ disciplines believers and judges unbelievers who reject truth and violate his plan. This leads to *cursing by association* in the same way that blessing travels along relational lines. Cursing by association expands to become collective divine discipline against the nation which, without the spiritual influence of obedient believers, slips into spiritual degeneracy.[cxxiv] Had Sodom ten residents who served the Lord, the entire region would have been spared. Instead, the spiritual ineffectiveness of believers there[cxxv] aided its decline into degeneracy and ultimate judgment.

Blessing by Association is a principle whereby discipleship of the Congregation changes history by creating categories of blessing that flow along relational bonds.[cxxvi] This blessing can be dramatically expanded

---

[cxxi] Deuteronomy 15.4-5; 28:1-14; Psalms 1; 128; Isaiah 3:10; Luke 11:28; John 14:21; 15:9-10; 2 Chronicles 31:21

[cxxii] Genesis 39:2-3,21-23; 50:20; Proverbs 11.10-11; 13:20-22 Psalms 25:12-13; 37:25; 112:1-4a (v1-H1755 generation); Matthew 5:13-14

[cxxiii] Genesis 18.20-26; 20.1-4; Psalms 33.12-18; Proverbs 14.34; Isaiah 30.18; Matthew 5.13-16; Acts 10:34-35; Romans 8:28; 2 Thessalonians 2:3-8;

[cxxiv] Proverbs 11.10-11; 13.34; 28.12, 28; 29.2

[cxxv] Genesis 19.1-8; 12-14; 15-26; 30-38

[cxxvi] Spiritual blessings flow from the strongest to the weakest human bonds: from the individual soul, to marriage, then family, Community, nation.

> *Second Nationbuilding Principle:* "No other person's decisions about you are more important than your decisions about your life."

Figure 21: Second Nationbuilding Principle

when a significant number of believers are involved. The efforts of faithful Pastors to make disciples of their Congregations have national and historical impact for the good. *Blessing by Association is another reason why the greatest contribution of the believer to his nation is via spiritual action.* It is also a clear demonstration of the Second Principle of Nationbuilding.

Viewed from this perspective, the following scripture is infused with new meaning.

> Matthew 5:13–16 (KJV 1900)
> 13 Ye are the salt of the earth: but if the salt have lost his savour, wherewith shall it be salted? it is thenceforth good for nothing, but to be cast out, and to be trodden under foot of men. 14 Ye are the light of the world. A city that is set on an hill cannot be hid. 15 Neither do men light a candle, and put it under a bushel, but on a candlestick; and it giveth light unto all that are in the house. 16 Let your light so shine before men, that they may see your good works, and glorify your Father which is in heaven.

---

[89] **Temptation** 3986 πειρασμός [peirasmos /pi·ras·mos/] n m. From 3985; TDNT 6:23; TDNTA 822; GK 4280; 21 occurrences; AV translates as "temptation" 19 times, "temptations" once, and "try" once. 1 an experiment, attempt, trial, proving. 1A trial, proving: the trial made of you by my bodily condition, since condition served as to test the love of the Galatians toward Paul (Gal. 4:14). 1B the trial of man's fidelity, integrity, virtue, constancy. 1B1 an enticement to sin, temptation, whether arising from the desires or from the outward circumstances. 1B2 an internal temptation to sin. 1B2A of the temptation by which the devil sought to divert Jesus the Messiah from his divine errand.

James Strong, Enhanced Strong's Lexicon (Woodside Bible Fellowship, 1995).

[90] Smith, David. "Half-Century of US Civil Rights Gains Have Stalled or Reversed, Report Finds." The Guardian, February 27, 2018, sec. US news. https://www.theguardian.com/us-news/2018/feb/27/us-civil-rights-report-kerner commission.

Also: "7 Years of Gutting Voting Rights | Brennan Center for Justice," June 3, 2020. https://www.brennancenter.org/our-work/analysis-opinion/7-years-gutting-voting-rights.

Also: Riley, Charmaine. "U.S. Supreme Court Rolls Back Historic Civil Rights Protections In Comcast Ruling." The Leadership Conference on Civil and Human Rights, March 23, 2020. https://civilrights.org/2020/03/23/u-s-supreme-court-rolls-back-historic-civil-rights-protections-in-comcast-ruling/.

And: "Research Shows Reversal of Civil Rights Era Gains in Southern Schools — The Civil Rights Project at UCLA." Accessed 02-15-2023. https://www.civilrightsproject.ucla.edu/news/press-releases/2017-press-releases/southern-schools-83-press-release.

[91] https://www.cnn.com/2022/01/03/politics/gallery/january-6-capitol-insurrection/index.html Also: https://cdn2.opendemocracy.net/media/images/Cross_outside_Capitol_building_6_January.max-760x504.jpg

[92] "Marriage to Divorce Ratio by Race-Ethnicity

- All racial-ethnic groups had more marriages than divorces. 'Other' race women (including Asian, American Indian, Alaska Native, and multiracial women) had the highest marriage to divorce ratio (3.0)—meaning three women married in 2018 for every one woman who divorced. The second highest ratio was found among Hispanic women (2.5) followed by White women (2.1) and Black women (1.6).
- Black women were the only group that had a higher divorce rate than marriage rate, with nearly 31 divorces per 1,000 married women aged 15 and older and only 17.3 marriages per 1,000 unmarried women."

Schweizer, V. (2019). Marriage to divorce ratio in the U.S.: Demographic variation, 2018. *Family Profiles, FP-19-27*. Bowling Green, OH: National Center for Family & Marriage Research. Accessed 11-26-2022. https://doi.org/10.25035/ncfmr/fp-19-27.

"Variation in Percentage Currently Separated/Divorced According to Race and Ethnicity, 1940-2018

- Among ever-married women in 1940, about 2% were currently separated/divorced regardless of race/ethnicity, except for Asians (0.9%).
- In 2018, Other and Hispanic ever-married women had similar shares who were separated/divorced, at 24% and 22%, respectively [White-Non Hispanic 19% rw].
- The percentage of Black ever-married women who were separated/divorced diverged from the other groups early in the period, rising to 33% by 2018.
- Asian ever-married women have had the lowest percentage separated/divorced at every decade since 1940, with only 11% currently separated or divorced in 2018."

Schweizer, V. J. (2020). Divorce: More than a century of change, 1900-2018. *Family Profiles, FP-20-22*. Bowling Green, OH: National Center for Family & Marriage Research. Accessed 11-26-2022. https://doi.org/10.25035/ncfmr/fp-20-22

"Variation in Percentage Currently Married According to Race and Ethnicity, 1940-2018

- In 1940, about 60% of women were married regardless of race or ethnicity.

- By 2018, the percentage of women who were currently married had declined among all racial and ethnic groups except Asian women.
- The percentage of Asian women who were married has remained the most stable since 1940. In 2018, 58% were currently married compared to 57% in 1940.
- The most dramatic drop in the share currently married was observed among Black women. In 2018, only about one-quarter (26%) of Black women reported being currently married.
- In 2018, the percentage of Hispanic and Other women who were married dropped to their lowest levels, at 43% and 38%, respectively.
- Since 1940, the percentage of White women who were married dropped ten percentage points to 51%.

Schweizer, V. J. (2020). Marriage: More than a century of change. *Family Profiles, FP-20-21.* Bowling Green, OH: National Center for Family & Marriage Research. Accessed 11-26-2022. https://doi.org/10.25035/ncfmr/fp-20-21

[93] Historical Poverty Tables: People and Families - 1959 to 2021
https://www.census.gov/data/tables/time-series/demo/income-poverty/historical-poverty-people.html
Accessed 11-26-2022.

[94] Categories of prosperity including "blessing by association" concept: Thieme, Robert B. Jr., The Integrity of God, Houston: Thieme, 2005. 142-149.

17. The Second Nationbuilding Principle: Implications

Implications of the Second Nationbuilding Principle

> "No other person's decisions about you are more important than your decisions about your life."

The decisions that matter most for the Christian are his own decisions, not the decisions of institutions or other individuals. Accordingly, the believer should not waste time and emotional energy trying to change their circumstances by convincing others to change their thinking or behavior. The biblically approved method for improving one's circumstances is to align oneself to God through obedience to His Word. This is also the quickest and most effective path. This is because Jesus Christ controls history. Your best possible destiny depends upon what you do, not what others do.

The intergenerational apparatus of racism and the effects of organized and unorganized racial discrimination have created an environment of oppression that no amount of effort in the flesh will correct. Oppression is an initiative of Satan and is primarily a spiritual problem. Racism and discrimination are historical constants and black people are not the only group in history to experience systematic discrimination. The implementation of the Nationbuilding Principles set into motion biblically prescribed processes that

175

result in the spiritual transformation of the individual, followed by the renovation of every relationship that touches that individual. Spiritual revival must precede cultural rebirth.

The following concepts will be helpful as the reader moves through the rest of this book.

Is Black America a Nation?

> **"NATION**, *noun* [to be born]
>
> **1.** A body of people inhabiting the same country, or united under the same sovereign or government; as the English nation; the French *nation* It often happens that many nations are subject to one government; in which case, the word *nation* usually denotes a body of people speaking the same language, or a body that has formerly been under a distinct government, but has been conquered, or incorporated with a larger *nation* Thus the empire of Russia comprehends many nations, as did formerly the Roman and Persian empires. *nation* as its etymology imports, originally denoted a family or race of men descended from a common progenitor, like tribe, but by emigration, conquest and intermixture of men of different families, this distinction is in most countries lost."[95] [emphasis added]

The United States is a national entity which consists of many sub-nations each of which share a distinct identity and history. All these groups, to the degree permitted at any point in history, share the same political system. African Americans are one of the earliest and largest of these distinct peoples.

Black America is distinct ethnically, culturally and has a distinct history and identity within the United States. Through various methods of segregation, a sizable portion of the black population is isolated within specific areas of the nation. Although not a nation politically, black America has many of the characteristics of nation. Because of its distinctive history and treatment under the law,[cxxvii] black America has a distinct identity in American jurisprudence.

[cxxvii] An important part of African American history is the story of centuries of theft of black labor and the effort to separate blacks *in perpetuity* from the benefits created by their forced labor. These efforts include the limit of the voting franchise, the denial of equal access to education, housing and employment and the denial of equal treatment under the law. These efforts continue to this very day. The evidence of the *continuity* of these inequities is found in the many legal actions taken [up to this very year-2022] to *reverse* structural racism by the enactment of special laws such as the Thirteenth, Fourteenth and Fifteenth Amendments to the Constitution, the First, Second, and Third Enforcement Acts, the Civil Rights Acts [1875, 1957, 1960, 1968] the Voting Rights Act [1965], the Equal Employment Opportunity Act [1972] and the Emmitt Till Antilynching Act [2022], which were designed to provide rights to black people that were already provided every other citizen. This list does not

Consequently, black America has specific national interests. Every statewide and national election is at least in part a debate and referendum on what rights black America will continue to enjoy. Black America is a nation within a nation in every sense that the dictionary conveys.

What is Culture?

1. A : the customary beliefs, social forms, and material traits of a racial, religious, or social group

B : the set of shared attitudes, values, goals, and practices that characterizes an institution or organization

C : the set of values, conventions, or social practices associated with a particular field, activity, or societal characteristic

D : the integrated pattern of human knowledge, belief, and behavior that depends upon the capacity for learning and transmitting knowledge to succeeding generations[96]

What personality is to the individual, culture is to the nation. Culture is the identity of a people that is influenced by history, language, and spirituality and produces beliefs, values, skills, aptitudes, and aesthetic sensibilities. Culture is a product of the human condition; culture is of God as the creator of humanity.

Culture, all culture, is marred by the Fall and the inherent depravity of all men. Culture can be influenced by the new birth and the Word of God. A spiritual chain reaction [Clergy-Congregation-Community] may improve or degenerate the quality of a culture. The individual can positively influence culture by his or her progressive sanctification. The new birth and achievement of spiritual maturity does not eradicate culture but improves it.

Despite the claims of evangelicalism,[97] there is no single culture or group of cultures that are the model for all others. Racism as the science of discrimination establishes a cultural hierarchy, related to race, conformity to which it rewards. Ultimately, America is the beneficiary of many cultural influences, of which black culture[cxxviii] is a major contributor. It would be impossible to extricate these influences due to the intimate relations of blacks and the majority European culture, and of blacks and the Native American culture, both beginning long before the founding of the Republic. It is in this

---

include the extensions and the laws enacted to strengthen these Acts in the last 40 years. Despite this there are still people who claim that systemic discrimination exists only in the distant past, or the imaginations of black people.

cxxviii Black people in America are not monolithic. *Black culture here refers to the descendants of American slaves.* Of course, there are many black immigrants from all over the world who live in the United States and have their own distinct cultural heritages.

cultural sense that America is truly a melting pot.

Because of this intimate history and cultural identification, it takes huge sums of money and energy to *prevent* the amalgamation of black and white America. There are real dollar costs to maintain inequality in every key area of life and to fight those, both white and black, who wish to change that system. This is a heavy tax upon every generation of Americans of all races. There is also the opportunity cost of not being able to direct these enormous sums of money and effort towards building the nation. This is the opportunity cost of racism, and it is truly staggering, not even considering events like the Civil War that killed a generation of the nation's men. Finally, there are the spiritual costs incurred by the nation and the Church. The mistaken assumption that the Lord shares the racial views of those who work to preserve existing systems of inequality by theology, by preaching or by not teaching what ought to be taught, cost their Congregations dearly in this life and in the life to come, and have subjected the nation to a minimum of 160 years of divine judgment.

> "We [Citigroup-rw] discover that closing racial gaps is a pareto improvement to both the U.S. economy and society. If racial gaps for Blacks had been closed 20 years ago, U.S. GDP could have benefitted by an estimated $16 trillion. If we close gaps today, the equivalent add to the U.S. economy over the next five years could be $5 trillion of additional GDP, or an average add of 0.35 percentage points to U.S. GDP growth per year and 0.09 percentage points to global GDP growth per year."[98]

What is an Institution?

> INSTITU'TION, noun [Latin institutio.]
>
> 1. The act of establishing.
>
> 2. Establishment; that which is appointed, prescribed or founded by authority, and intended to be permanent. Thus we speak of the institutions of Moses or Lycurgus. We apply the word institution to laws, rites, and ceremonies, which are enjoined by authority as permanent rules of conduct or of government.
>
> 3. A system, plan or society established, either by law or by the authority of individuals for promoting any object, public or social. We call a college or an academy, a literary institution; a Bible society, a benevolent or charitable institution; a banking company and an insurance company are commercial institutions.[99]

There are institutions that are *established* by the *authority* of God. These include Marriage [Genesis 2.20-25], the Family [Genesis 1.28; 4.1] the State [Romans 13.1-7] and the local church as an assembly of born-again individuals [Matthew 16.18].

The divine institutions are important to mankind because they enable the orderly function of civilization. These institutions exercise control over the fallen human nature which, left to its own devices, would destroy civilization. These institutions are also how the blessings of God are conveyed to mankind.

Consequently, the divine institutions are under constant spiritual attack by the devil and his demonic and human servants. God uses the Church to *sustain* these institutions by the gospel and by the positive spiritual chain reaction initiated by the Church. It is also through the Holy Spirit operating in and through the Church that the Lord *restrains* Satan from his agenda to weaken the nations.

> 2 Thessalonians 2:7 (NASB95)
> 7 For the mystery of lawlessness is already at work; only he who now restrains *will do so* until he is taken out of the way.

Application of the Second Nationbuilding Principle

> Acts 17:26 (KJV 1900)
> 26 And hath made of one blood all nations of men for to dwell on all the face of the earth, and hath determined the times before appointed, and the bounds of their habitation;

> Genesis 10:6–7 (KJV 1900)
> 6 And the sons of Ham; Cush, and Mizraim, and Phut, and Canaan. 7 And the sons of Cush; Seba, and Havilah, and Sabtah, and Raamah, and Sabtecha: and the sons of Raamah; Sheba, and Dedan. 20 These are the sons of Ham, after their families, after their tongues, in their countries, and in their nations.

The only decisions that can help you are decisions based upon truth. No amount of sincerity and hard work will overcome decisions made based on bad information. A significant obstacle in the way of black nationbuilding is the fact that we sometimes do not have correct Bible information and the accurate information we possess is not directly applied to our actual situation in America.

When limited to our religious *expression*, black ethnic identity and its cultural elements are allowed and even celebrated by society. Our music, preaching and general approach to worship are authentically African American. It is when we transition from worship styles to theology and doctrine that we are discouraged from making factual *application* of the truth to our real situation as Americans.

The application of the Word of God to a cultural context cannot be limited solely to the style of worship.[100] The scriptures must also be applied directly to the real-life circumstance of the people. If a local church suffered under rampant adultery, the Pastor is not serving the people by general, non-specific preaching upon holiness [Ezra 9-10]. If the marriages, families, and general mental health of your black Congregation is being disrupted by the effects of intergenerational racism [and it is], preaching that fails to address the issue is ministerial malpractice.

Ministerial Malpractice

Systemic racism begins with the corruption of the self-concept of black people.[101] From childhood this negative self-image is reinforced through the institutions of society: media,[102] school[103] and even in religious instruction. To make these deficits permanent, black education and participation in the workforce are strictly controlled.[104] These limitations promote segregation or social quarantine[105] of the lower classes. Drugs and violence are then imported into these black Communities by the same system.[106] The social structure that manufactures these effects punishes the crimes that result from them earlier in life, more frequently and more harshly among black people, creating felons who are essentially excluded from the rights of citizenship, often unjustly.[107] These psychological, economic, and social deficits greatly exacerbate pressures that are on all American marriages resulting in divorce rates and single parent poverty that are highest among black Americans. I have defined the word *racism* as the science of discrimination, the scientific marginalization of a people by the systematic introduction of discrimination into the organs [institutions] of society. The process described above is racism in action.

There are some black Pastors who will not even acknowledge these facts, let alone apply the scriptures to them. How can a Pastor address the self-image problems of black people when he believes that race is no longer an issue to the Christian? How can he address the respect problem between black men and women, when he does not perceive that society degrades the black male from birth? How does the black Pastor prepare black children for the day when, in elementary school, they are made to realize that they are not as good as white children or Asian children or East Indian children?[108] How does the black Pastor reconcile the promise of provision in scripture with the last hired, first fired, unequal pay, glass ceiling reality of many black people?

Christ spat in the dirt and spread it upon the blind man's eyes because he was blind [John 9.1-7]. Jesus did not put it in the man's ears because the man's problem was blindness, not deafness. The Word of God must be applied to the problems that the people face if it is to heal them.

> Ezekiel 34:1–10 (KJV 1900)
> 1 And the word of the Lord came unto me, saying, 2 Son of man, <u>prophesy against the shepherds of Israel</u>, prophesy, and say unto them, Thus saith the Lord God unto the shepherds; Woe be to the shepherds of Israel that do feed themselves! should not the shepherds feed the flocks? 3 Ye eat the fat, and ye clothe you with the wool, ye kill them that are fed: but ye feed not the flock. 4 <u>The diseased have ye not strengthened, neither have ye healed that which was sick, neither have ye bound up that which was broken, neither have ye brought again that which was driven away, neither have ye sought that which was lost</u>; but with force and with cruelty have ye ruled them. 5 And they were scattered, because there is no shepherd: and they became meat to all the beasts of the field, when they were scattered. 6 My sheep wandered through all the mountains, and upon every high hill: yea, my flock was scattered upon all the face of the earth, and none did search or seek after them. 7 <u>Therefore, ye shepherds, hear the word of the Lord; 8 As I live, saith the Lord God, surely because my flock became a prey, and my flock became meat to every beast of the field</u>, because there was no shepherd, neither did my shepherds search for my flock, but the shepherds fed themselves, and fed not my flock; 9 Therefore, O ye shepherds, hear the word of the Lord; 10 Thus saith the Lord God; Behold, I am against the shepherds; and I will require my flock at their hand, and cause them to cease from feeding the flock; neither shall the shepherds feed themselves any more; for I will deliver my flock from their mouth, that they may not be meat for them.

A proper understanding of and response to the Word of God is essential to nationbuilding. The rise and fall of nations in the Bible are directly attributed to their response to divine revelation [general and special]. Men interact with God and the Word from within a cultural context.[cxxix] The very languages into which the scriptures are translated imply the existence of such a context. The Spirit of God works within and through these cultural distinctives to convey

---

[cxxix] John 4.22-23; Romans 9.1-3; Galatians 4.4

the unchanging truth of the Word to every culture.

> 2 Corinthians 4:7 (KJV 1900)
> [7] But we have this treasure in earthen vessels, that the excellency of the power may be of God, and not of us.

This means that just as individuals have human personality from which they must approach and relate to God and the scriptures, so also the personality of a *nation* is its culture which is a framework from which it relates to God and scripture. If that cultural context is labeled evil or if it is denied altogether that nation is stripped of its capacity to relate properly to God. Just as a person without a personality cannot have a spiritual life (by virtue of not actually being a person), a nation of people denied a cultural context cannot experience healthy relations with God. Therefore, if a nation is prevented from making a correct cultural *application* of what the scripture teaches, that nation is stunted in its spiritual development. *This is a key operational objective of racial oppression as a spiritual initiative.*

No Such Thing as Black Theology

When I speak of the "application of doctrine to culture" I do not mean that culture interprets the Bible or that the Bible must be changed in some way to accommodate culture. The concept called "Black Theology" is a negation of biblical theology. The Word of God is sufficient to address the problems of race and oppression. No racially constructed theology is needed for this task. "Black Theology" is thrown up as a rhetorical device to confuse the true issue of how the Bible must be applied to reality and not to unreality. This is the same technique that is used with Social Justice vs. the Social Gospel. What is meant is that the Bible must be applied to the *reality* of a people if it is to be of maximum benefit to that people. People raised from childhood to believe in the inferiority of black people and who are informed that their position in society is the evidence of that inferiority cannot simply be told that they are a new creation in Christ without any attention given to the reality of their corrupted self-concept. The scriptures are supernatural, but they are not magical incantations that transform the soul without the hard work of responsible teachers and preachers who understand the people. Even worse are the black Pastors who deny the existence of systematic racial oppression or deny its serious effects upon the lives upon their people, which is the same thing. There can be no application of scripture to a situation that the Congregation is told doesn't exist. This ignorance is itself a manifestation of the slave theology designed to provide a version of Christianity that will maintain the unjust status quo. *Today, the cultural context to which the Bible is applied for black folks is that of unreality, if it is relevant to a cultural context at all.*

---

[95] Webster, Noah, An American Dictionary of the English Language. Accessed 11-17-2022. https://webstersdictionary1828.com/Dictionary/Nation

[96] Merriam-Webster.com Dictionary, s.v. "culture," Accessed 01-06-2023. https://www.merriam-webster.com/dictionary/culture.

[97] **WE AFFIRM** that some cultures operate on assumptions that are inherently better than those of other cultures because of the biblical truths that inform those worldviews that have produced these distinct assumptions. Those elements of a given culture that reflect divine revelation should be celebrated and promoted." The Statement on Social Justice. Accessed 01-06-2023 https://statementonsocialjustice.com/Affirmations and Denials-Culture

" This is perhaps the most frightening and dangerous section of the entire document. The first sentence is the heart of the problem. "WE AFFIRM that some cultures operate on assumptions that are inherently better than those of other cultures because of the biblical truths that inform those worldviews that have produced these distinct assumptions."

"The word "operate" like many of the other key words in the document remains undefined. The entire issue of social justice and the Church rests upon the assertion by many that neither Christians or their Pastors are "operating" on the basis of the alleged Christian assumptions that they lay claim to. The idea of cultural superiority itself implies a willful and systematic blindness to the moral, social, political, and military excesses of the very cultures who are implied to have these superior values. A casual perusal of history affirms this with finality. The fact that they did not decide to eliminate this section altogether shows that there is a great deal to fear in the thinking, the actual thinking, that lies behind this Statement."

"A Response: The Statement on Social Justice and the Gospel – A Richer Walk (blog)." Accessed 10-22-2022. https://aricherwalk.com/2018/09/25/a-response-the-statement-on-social-justice-and-the-gospel/.

[98] Closing the Racial Inequality Gaps, The Economic Cost of Black Inequality in the U.S., Citi GPS: Global Perspectives & Solutions. September 2020. 7 Accessed 12-07-2022. https://ir.citi.com/NvIUklHPilz14Hwd3oxqZBLMn1_XPqo5FrxsZD0x6hhil84ZxaxEuJUWmak51UHvYk75VKeHCMl%3D

[99] Webster, Noah. *Institution*

Thus, under definition #3. Racism as a *system* is a *social institution*, *established* to achieve a permanent social *end*, which is the perpetual separation of blacks from the wealth created by their labor which has been stolen, to one degree or another, since slavery began until this very day.

[100] MacArthur John, A Biblical Response to the Church-Growth Movement Accessed 11-28-2022. https://www.gty.org/library/sermons-library/GTY114/a-biblical-response-to-the-churchgrowth-movement

I have included this citation to show how the way in which scripture is *interpreted* might be confused with how it is to be *applied*. Please see the entire sermon for, forgive the expression, the context.

It is important to distinguish between the contextualization that belongs to Christian Liberalism which seeks to establish a "New Christianity" incorrectly based on a shift of the demographic, geographic and cultural center of the visible church, and what it is I am talking about, which is entirely different. It is the same kind of confusion that confounds social justice, with the Social Gospel.

The message of the Word of God is unchanging, as are its specific doctrines. The Bible is the inspired Word of God, both in its entirety and its very words and is not subject to change. However, the issues to which scripture must be *applied* differ by Community, by the cultural context of the audience. Scriptural *interpretation* is based upon the intent of the author of and his context [e.g., Paul and the local Roman churches], scriptural *application* is based upon the context of the hearer. The mighty acts of healing performed by Jesus were specific to the individual, divine power was put to a use applicable to the problem of the person being healed. In the same way, the unchanging Word of God must be applied to the specific ailments of the people being served. In each of his epistles, Paul addressed some of the specific problems that his audience were experiencing, some were individual problems and other encompassed an entire class of people [Acts 6.1-3; Galatians 3.1; Colossians 2; Titus 1.5, 10-14;]. Proper ministry to black people in America must address the elephant in the room, which is the presence of intergenerational, structural racism which can disfigure the soul of those subjected to it. The Word must be specifically [but not solely, anticipating another objection] applied to this context, which includes the systems that produce the damage: the damage to the soul itself and the sinful actions which may result from this damage.

[101] Video "A Girl Like Me" Accessed 12-02-2022. https://www.youtube.com/watch?v=

Also: Kardiner, Abram, Ovesey, Lionel. The Mark of Oppression, Explorations in the Personality of the American Negro. Cleveland: World, 1951. 377-387.

[102] Entman, Robert M., and Andrew Rojecki. The Black Image in the White Mind: Media and Race in America. Repr. Studies in Communication, Media, and Public Opinion. Chicago, Ill.: University of Chicago Press, 2007.

[103] Romero, Simon. "Texas Pushes to Obscure the State's History of Slavery and Racism." *The New York Times*, May 20, 2021, sec. U.S. https://www.nytimes.com/2021/05/20/us/texas-history-1836-project.html.

Also: Gross, Terry. "From Slavery to Socialism, New Legislation Restricts What Teachers Can Discuss." *NPR*, February 3, 2022, sec. Education. https://www.npr.org/2022/02/03/1077878538/legislation-restricts-what-teachers-can-discuss.

[104] Holzer, Harry J. "Why Are Employment Rates so Low among Black Men?" *Brookings* (blog), March 1, 2021. https://www.brookings.edu/research/why-are-employment-rates-so-low-among-black-men/.

[105] Example Northeast Ohio:

"V. RACIAL AND ETHNIC SEGREGATION IN NORTHEAST OHIO

"A. Racial Dissimilarity Indices Due to a long history of housing discrimination, the Cleveland-Lorain-Elyria Metropolitan Statistical Area (Cuyahoga, Geauga, Lake, Lorain, and Medina Counties) is ranked as one of the most racially and ethnically segregated areas in the United States. Segregation has a damaging effect on all members of a community. It polarizes regions on the bases of race and income. It prevents access to wealth and educational opportunities, which has the effect of limiting job access and depressing housing values.126 [emphasis added] The Racial Dissimilarity Index is a measure of the distribution of individuals of one race compared to another race (usually the majority). Using the dissimilarity index, a score of 0 would represent a completely integrated distribution of individuals, while a score of 100 represents a completely segregated region where every member of the minority group would have to move in order to achieve complete integration. For 2010, the Racial Dissimilarity Index score, for African Americans (20.7% of the total population of the MSA) to white people for the MSA is 74.1 (above 60 is considered very high; the MSA is ranked 5th most segregated in the United

States); meaning 74.1% of all African Americans would have to change residence to achieve equal distribution in the region. Using the dissimilarity index for African Americans and whites, the Cleveland-Elyria MSA has had little change in the past twenty years, moving from the fifth most-segregated area in the country in 1990, to the sixth in 2000, and back to the fifth most-segregated area in 2010 (Table 6 and Figure 11). During this period, the MSA's ranking on the dissimilarity index has improved slightly from a score of 82.8 in 1990 to 78.2 in 2000 to 74.1 in 2010. 127

Table 7: Residential Segregation for African Americans in Large Metropolitan Areas Ranked by Dissimilarity Index

	1990	2000	2010
Rank	MSA Name	MSA Name	MSA Name
1	Detroit	Detroit	Milwaukee-Waukesha
2	Chicago	Milwaukee-Waukesha	New York
3	Milwaukee-Waukesha	New York	Chicago
4	Newark	Newark	Detroit
5	Cleveland-Lorain-Elyria	Chicago	Cleveland-Lorain-Elyria
6	New York	Cleveland-Lorain-Elyria	Buffalo-Niagara Falls
7	Buffalo-Niagara Falls	Buffalo-Niagara Falls	St. Louis
8	St. Louis	Cincinnati	Cincinnati
9	Bergen-Passaic	St. Louis	Philadelphia
10	Philadelphia	Nassau-Suffolk	Los Angeles

Source: Population Studies Center/University of Michigan

Figure 6: African American Population of the Region by Census Tract, 2010

Lepley, Michael, and Lenore Mangiarelli. *"The State of Fair Housing in Northeast Ohio,"* 2019, 46-48.

[106] "The time I spent investigating the allegations of the "Dark Alliance" series led me to the undeniable conclusion that the CIA, DEA, DIA and FBI knew about drug trafficking in South Central Los Angeles. They were either part of the trafficking or turned a blind eye to it, in an effort to fund the Contra war." (Cong. Maxine Waters, Foreword) Dark Alliance. Webb, Gary. Dark Alliance: The CIA, the Contras, and the Crack Cocaine Explosion. Seven Stories Press 1st ed. New York: Seven Stories Press, 1998. X. See also 14, 189-190.

Also: "ATLANTA - — Wang Jun, who sipped coffee with President Clinton at the White House, heads a company that had been the subject of a federal sting investigation into its alleged scheme to sell 2,000 AK-47 assault rifles destined for gang members in California." "Arms Dealer Was Subject of Sting Operation – Sun Sentinel." Accessed 02-02-2023. https://www.sun-sentinel.com/news/fl-xpm-1997-01-05-9701040227-story.html

Also: "Sting's 18 Months of Cloak and Dagger." Reynolds Holding, Chronicle Legal Affairs Writer. Accessed 02-02-2023. https://www.sfgate.com/crime/article/Sting-s-18-Months-of-Cloak-and-Dagger-2981324.php.

There is a reason that you have violence in the Community, and it is not due to racial inferiority.

[107] "Every respectable, half-way competent social scientist who has paid attention at all to all the issues of crime and delinquency knows that crime is endemic in all social classes : that the administration of justice is grossly biased against the Negro and the lower class defendant; that arrest and imprisonment is a process reserved almost exclusively for the black and the poor; and that the major function of the police is the preservation, not only of the public order, but of the social order-that is, of inequality between man and man."

185

Parenti, Michael. Democracy for the Few. 5th ed. New York: St. Martins Press, 1987. 129. Cited in Wilson, Amos N. Black on Black Violence, The Psychodynamics of Black Annihilation in Service to White Domination. New York: African Word Infosystems, 1990. 21

"To sum up, poor and working-class persons, the uneducated and the racial minorities are more likely to be arrested, less likely to be released on bail, more likely to be induced to plead guilty, more likely to go without a pretrial hearing even though entitled to one, less likely to have a jury trial if tried, more likely to be convicted and receive a harsh sentence, less likely to receive probation or a suspended sentence *than are mobsters*, businesspeople and upper- and middle-class whites in general." [emphasis added]

Parenti, Michael. Democracy for the Few. 5th ed., 133 cited in Wilson, Amos N. Black on Black Violence. 22.

"Far from fading away, it appears that prisons are here to stay. And despite the unprecedented levels of incarceration in the African American community, the civil rights community is oddly quiet. One in three young African American men will serve time in prison if current trends continue, and in some cities more than half of all young adult black men are currently under correctional control—in prison or jail, on probation or parole.20 Yet mass incarceration tends to be categorized as a criminal justice issue as opposed to a racial justice or civil rights issue (or crisis)."

Alexander, Michelle. The New Jim Crow (p. 9). The New Press. Kindle Edition.

"Despite claims that these radical policy changes were driven by fiscal conservatism—i.e., the desire to end big government and slash budget deficits—the reality is that government was not reducing the amount of money devoted to the management of the urban poor. It was radically altering what the funds would be used for. The dramatic shift toward punitiveness resulted in a massive reallocation of public resources. By 1996, the penal budget doubled the amount that had been allocated to AFDC or food stamps.100 Similarly, funding that had once been used for public housing was being redirected to prison construction. During Clinton's tenure, Washington slashed funding for public housing by $17 billion (a reduction of 61 percent) and boosted corrections by $19 billion (an increase of 171 percent), "effectively making the construction of prisons the nation's main housing program for the urban poor."101 Clinton did not stop there. Determined to prove how "tough" he could be on "them," Clinton also made it easier for federally assisted public housing projects to exclude anyone with a criminal history—an extraordinarily harsh step in the midst of a drug war aimed at racial and ethnic minorities. In his announcement of the "One Strike and You're Out" Initiative, Clinton explained: "From now on, the rule for residents who commit crime and peddle drugs should be one strike and you're out."102 The new rule promised to be "the toughest admission and eviction policy that HUD has implemented." 103 Thus, for countless poor people, particularly racial minorities targeted by the drug war, public housing was no longer available, leaving many of them homeless—locked out not only of mainstream society, but their own homes.

Alexander, Michelle. The New Jim Crow. 57.

Also: "Handcuffs in Hallways: Hundreds of Elementary Students Arrested at U.S. Schools." Accessed December 3, 2022. https://www.cbsnews.com/news/hundreds-of-elementary-students-arrested-at-us-schools/.

Also: The Exoneration Project. Accessed 0316-2023. https://www.exonerationproject.org/issues/

[108] Kunjufu, Jawanza. Countering the Conspiracy to Destroy Black Boys. 1st ed. Chicago: Afro-Am Pub. Co, 1983. 7-31.

18. The Second Nationbuilding Principle: Slave Theology

Slave Theology: A Synthetic Christianity for Blacks

"One of the first acts of the U.S. Congress following the ratification of the Constitution was the enactment of the nations first naturalization and immigration law in 1790. This law declared America to be a "White nation" and set a zero quota on Black immigrants, except as slaves. A quota of approximately zero remained in effect until 1965 when it was increased to its current level of one half of one percent."[109]

"SECTION 1. Be it enacted by the Senate and House of Representatives of the United States of America in Congress assembled, That any alien, being a free white person, who shall have resided within the limits and under the jurisdiction of the United States for the term of two years, may be admitted to become a citizen thereof, on application to any common law court of record, in any one of the states wherein he shall have resided for the term of one year at least, and making proof to the satisfaction of such court, that he is a person of good character..." [First Congress Session Two Chapter Three. Approved March 26, 1790][110]

Because of its commitment to the maintenance of white supremacy in a white nation, Christian America, from the beginning, has denied African Americans the benefit of biblically consistent applications of doctrine and theology. There are predictable negative effects resulting from this denial, including the loss of the institutional and cultural benefits which result from an accurate application of biblical truth to African American culture. We will identify six cultural imperatives which should be points of emphasis for the local church as it promotes the spiritual growth of black believers. *The overall message is that the agenda of oppression creates unique spiritual challenges for black Christians in the United States.* Therefore, biblical black decisions are the answer to these uniquely black problems. Your decisions, not your ability to get others to change their behavior, but your decisions about the church you will attend, how you will respond to the demands of scripture, how Pastors and Elders will lead the black churches, these decisions by black people will determine black destiny.

The Old Testament demonstrates through the nation of Israel that spiritual slavery precedes physical slavery. God warned the Jews that their disobedience to the Law of Moses would result in their defeat and humiliation by their enemies. The maintenance of black Americans under oppression would not be possible without the short-circuiting of the spiritual processes that inoculate a people against it. By this means, black people assist in the work of their own debasement.

As we are emphasizing reality, we will begin with the reality that black people, Africans, were brought to America for the express purpose of creating wealth and wellbeing for others.[111] The African slaves *and their descendants* were never meant to enjoy the product of their labor, ever. To secure the permanent status of servitude, the doctrine of racial inferiority was created, by theologians initially, [112] later to be "scientifically" systematized by historians, anthropologists, and sociologists, codified into law by government and reinforced by ministers, educators, and media.

A theological doctrine of inferiority assuaged the guilt of Christian America which claimed to believe the Bible and its teachings regarding the genetic equality of men in Adam [Acts 17.26], equality of spiritual status through faith in Christ [Galatians 3.28] equality of divine judgment without respect of persons [Romans 2.11], and equality of rights by their own founding documents. It did so *by removing American slavery and its ancillary evils from the category of sin.* The theft, violence and injustice that formed the essential nature of racial coexistence both during and after slavery was made exempt from the demands of Christian sanctification by making the black man a lower level of creation, cursed by God to be the slaves of others forever. It is still argued that in view of this cursed condition, slavery was an improvement in the fortunes of the black man, exposing him, in America, to the gospel that had already been in Africa for over 1300 years.[113]

This false doctrine justified the creation of a permanent underclass based upon race and continues to be a part of the education of every generation of Americans. The idea that poverty, crime, and institutional weakness in the black Community is overwhelmingly a result of an intergenerational flaw in the race is the predominant view among white Christians today.[114]

The *psychological* product of this doctrine of inferiority served as a cost-effective control upon the black man. It was perhaps the first major mind control experiment in American history. Every aspect of the life of the slave: his family life, his social interactions with whites, his education, and his religion were adjusted to promote a mental attitude of inferiority, fear and servitude, while reinforcing an equally false and opposite self-evaluation in the minds of white Americans.

Even today, the terrible inertia of these forces set into motion centuries ago, aided and abetted by the descendants of these same individuals and institutions, continue to foist the onerous elements of the Curse of Adam upon those they still claim to be cursed by Noah. While the descendants of the architects of this system enjoy the fruits of the slave system with interest compounded over centuries, that wealth and privilege remains insulated within a continuing caste system of race. In every significant measure of social life, political life, medical life, actuarial life, economic life, black people remain distant from the majority,[115] and as in colonial days these undeniable facts are attributed to the "inherent inferiority or unfitness of blacks for freedom." Whether by nature or nurture, this unfitness is never associated with a now ancient system of church and state sanctioned inequality and its effects but are asserted to be due to modern manifestations of the deficiencies of African American people *because* they are African American people.

Black Complicity

An honest evaluation of these forces demands an explanation of the decisions and actions of black people that consistently contribute to our own disadvantage. What are the factors that motivate black impulses to self-destruction? Rather than recoiling in blind rejection of these facts, we must examine the spiritual factors that underlie the social reality. *It is upon this very analysis to which we must put theology to work.*

In the first half of this book, we demonstrated that it is the activity of the local church in civilization that is critical to the proper function of morality. Men left to their own devices will be crushed under the weight of their own depravity without the gravity defying influence of the Body of Christ functioning in the world. This is true for all nations and peoples. "Righteousness exalts a nation and sin is a reproach to any people."[cxxx]

Unfortunately, when natural human depravity is intensified by oppression and the powerful spiritual influence of accurate biblical teaching is limited, the necessary outcome is what we see. It is indeed black decisions that are influenced by these pressures, and we must bear responsibility for these decisions, but we must acknowledge these other factors as well. Absent a highly unlikely repentance in white Pulpits and Congregations, the oppressive systems and the attitudes that maintain the pressure will not change. This is no reason, however, to despair. Black decisions can make all the difference under the Second Principle of Nationbuilding, but we need better information than we have been getting to make those decisions. When you know better, you can do better.

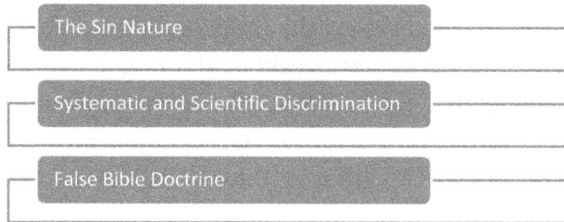

Figure 22: Negative Factors in Black Decision Making

Something has happened to the spiritual truth that is taught to Americans in general and to black people in particular.

The Tenets of Slave Theology

The slave was initially denied the benefit of evangelism and Bible teaching on many plantations. It was the legitimate fear of the slave industry, many participants of which were professed Christians, that Bible teaching would

---

[cxxx] Proverbs 14.34

render slavery unacceptable to a man.[116] There was also the fear that Christian baptism would legally entitle a slave to freedom. The investors in slavery were eventually convinced that baptism would not entitle the slave to freedom and that *the proper version of Christianity* would not make the slave resentful of servitude, but more compliant and industrious in his role as wealth producer for his owner.

> "Christianity became an intolerable doctrine unless translated into Southern Christianity, and in the 1840's, Southern Baptist and Methodist congregations seceded from the national groups and formed Southern denominations whose ministers and teachings would not question the rightness of the Southern course and would call God and the Bible to the defense of human slavery"[117] (emphasis added)

Thus began the ingenious development of two theologies: one for the slave and another for the free.

One orthodox formulation of doctrine was *applied* in two different ways depending upon the race of the hearer. In this way two systems of theology were created. One theology taught the inherent supremacy of whites and their right not only to heaven, but to inherit the earth *today*. The necessary obverse of this doctrine inculcated the natural inferiority of the black and his need of a sponsor, the slave master, to live under limited freedom and limited manhood. The inheritance of the slave was reserved for the heavenly future exclusively, only if he adhered to the modified Christianity provided him.

Under the civil law, the inalienable rights of one race[cxxxi] did not extend to the other. The constitutional rights of the slave owners and whites in general were inalienable because the rights of life, liberty and happiness were provided by God to *mankind* in the Ten Commandments. The slave was said to be not quite a man and therefore not a citizen. In denying these same rights to the African, the black slave was placed in a different relation to *humanity*, to the Bible and to God. Those natural rights that belonged to all men *because* they were men did not apply to blacks.

This is the basis of slave theology: the truths of the Bible are orthodox in their theological formulation, but inconsistently *applied* to blacks versus other groups. *This is why both Christianity and white dominance have always been essential*

[cxxxi] The concept of race was the *necessary* antecedent to Slave Theology. It was essential that men be distinguished by the artificial and arbitrary distinctions of race to enable the stratification of human value and the *permanent* separation of the slave and his descendants from the profit of their labor. Unlike slavery in ancient history, American slavery was theft of labor based upon race alone.

elements of the American identity, while the use of Christianity to condemn American racism and to seek its correction is called a departure from the gospel.[cxxxii] It is indeed a departure from the *modified* gospel of slave theology. This version of Christianity is designed to protect the social system from tampering by those seeking to apply the scriptures to it.

John MacArthur argues Jesus did not attempt to upset the social order, and neither should we: that believers are to submit.[118] Princeton theologian Charles Hodge exclaimed in his paper, "The Bible Argument for Slavery (1860), "If the present course of the abolitionists is right, then the course of Christ and the apostles were wrong."[119]

This is also why the concept of black nationbuilding is difficult for many black believers to accept. The building of any nation other than the one in which they are second class citizens seems vaguely sacrilegious.[cxxxiii] This foreboding is immediately ratified by the retaliation heaped upon Pastors [especially white Pastors] that violate their historical role as the gatekeepers of the American version of Christianity.

Slave theology is a system of false religion. A false religion nullifies some significant portion of its genuine counterpart, but not necessarily all. Baal worship was made more powerful by allowing the conjoining of Judaism with the abominable excesses of the Canaanites. Nebuchadnezzar did not condemn Shadrach and his two friends for worshipping Jehovah, but for being unwilling to subsume Him under the Babylonian pantheon. In like manner, slave theology retains the theological content of the scriptures but empties them of meaning when it comes to issues of race and power. Therefore, this version of Christianity encourages intergenerational sin by believers against black people by teaching them that it *is not sin.* Slave religion, by its sanction of racial oppression, destroys the spiritual life of the oppressor even before it damages the oppressed.

[cxxxii] The *gospel* is here understood as not limited to the death, burial, and resurrection of Jesus Christ, but also the act of faith in this truth and the subsequent transformation of the person and destiny of the one possessed of this faith. The *modified* gospel seeks to separate the gospel from the effects of the new birth in the life of the believer whenever that life is examined in the context of race relations.
[cxxxiii] Some would argue that second class citizenship in the United States is better than first class citizenship in the rest of the world. Such persons are affirming that blacks are indeed second-class citizens and should be grateful for it. The fact is, however, that black Americans are not illegal aliens, but citizens who built this country for free. As American citizens, for black people to live without the benefits of equality under the law and to suffer affirmative discrimination in the institutions of the nation is both illegal and immoral.

The following are some elements of slave theology:

American Slavery as the Will of God:[cxxxiv]

This doctrine involves at least three errors: first the conflating of the forms of ancient and biblically regulated slavery with American slavery, secondly, deliberately confusing the permissive will of God with His directive will in scripture,[120] and thirdly, the irresponsible interpretation of Genesis 9.18-28.

In Appendix 1, the biblical doctrine of oppression is presented, and slavery is examined more completely. The following is a quotation from the Appendix:

> "Slavery was entirely incompatible with the divine ownership of His people. Israelites could not be made slaves by fellow Jews because they were already the slaves of God. They were not even to be referred to as slaves, but as hired servants. Therefore, because of their relation to God, the status of the Jewish slave was different from the Gentile slave. He was not considered property, his service was temporary, he was not to be treated with the cruelty that characterized their treatment in Egypt. Even the Gentiles residing in Israel did not have the right to permanently hold a Jewish slave if the slave himself or another Jew could redeem him [Exodus 25.39-55].

> "In the Church Age, this same principle is in force. Although the new birth does not eliminate the institutions of this world, such as slavery, it does modify them to believers. Christians are not allowed to make slaves of their brethren in Christ for the same reason that the Jews of the Old Testament were not allowed to do so. Slaves in Israel did not possess a greater privilege under salvation than the members of the Body of Christ who were slaves to believers. The failure to make this distinction under American slavery is yet another artifact of Slave Theology."[cxxxv]

Briefly then, the three primary elements of *American* slavery: theft of persons[cxxxvi] and their labor,[121] general violence, and the specific violence of rape, are all prohibited in the Old and New Testaments. These prohibitions especially [but not only] applied to believers who were slaves. Practitioners of American slavery would be subject to the *death penalty* in biblical Israel regardless of the ethnic or spiritual status of their slaves.[cxxxvii]

[cxxxiv] A more complete treatment of this subject may be found in Appendix I: The Doctrine of Oppression-Oppression and Slavery

[cxxxv] Ibid.

[cxxxvi] It will be argued by some that, in the case of American slavery, often the original kidnappers were Africans. This argument is biblically and legally irrelevant. The receipt of stolen property is not justified by the ethnicity of the original thief. European and American slavery created a large demand for black slaves. We have learned through the immoralities and illegalities [including illegal wars] stimulated by the oil markets what people and governments will do to profit off what we know as "black gold." Long before the discovery of oil, black bodies were the original "black gold" and I do not doubt that Africans exploited one another to profit from this market. Again, the theft of labor is theft regardless from whom the person was originally purchased. It is the purchase of stolen property and therefore theft in scripture [Exodus 21.16; 1 Timothy 1.9-10] and a felony under State law [N.C. G.S. 14-72].

[cxxxvii] Appendix 1: The Doctrine of Oppression-Oppression and Slavery

Preachers and theologians deliberately confuse the permissive will of God [that some Africans be enslaved] with his directive will by claiming that He assigned the degradations of American slavery to persons according to their *color*. They teach that God intended that people of a particular color, irrespective of their connection to a nation, in the absence of any of the causes of slavery in ancient times [war, debt or crime] to be *perpetually* oppressed. After a very few generations, children of the slaves brought from Africa were no longer Africans, but Americans of African descent. Nonetheless, because of their color alone, were qualified for racial oppression from cradle to grave and their children after them. By this justification, systems of racial oppression are devised where many of the benefits of oppression may continue for whites even after the institution of slavery has been *partially* abolished.

Slavery is partially abolished in that criminals may be legally imprisoned and enslaved.[122] Thus, through the strategy of mass incarceration, first enacted in 1865 under the Black Codes and updated and made much worse in the 1980's and 1990's,[123] blacks are introduced to the penal system at a very early age[124] and in grossly disproportionate numbers. By incarceration, many rights are taken from the inmate[125] and from the person who has a criminal record, even though released from prison. In this way, race-based slavery is perpetuated through the mass incarceration of black people.

> "While these individuals have often completely exited criminal supervision (for example, through a prison sentence or probation), individuals with criminal records still face potentially thousands of collateral consequences upon reentering society. These collateral consequences are sanctions, restrictions, or disqualifications that attach to a person because of the person's criminal history. For example, individuals with criminal histories can face barriers to voting, jury service, holding public office, securing employment, obtaining housing, receiving public assistance, owning a firearm, getting a driver's license, qualifying for financial aid and college admission, qualifying for military service, and maintaining legal status as an immigrant. The reach of each collateral consequence extends past people with criminal records to affect families and communities."[126] (emphasis added)

Before the existence of scientific theories of racial inferiority and "color-blind" methods of enforcing racial discrimination, Pastors, and theologians biblically justified color-based oppression by the false doctrine of the Curse of Ham [Genesis 9.18-28].[cxxxviii] This doctrine taught that black people descended from Ham who was cursed because of an alleged disrespect to his father Noah. (Interestingly, while Ham is acknowledged as black by theologians in Genesis 9,[cxxxix] his family is not considered black in Genesis 10, when his descendants are shown to be creators of the science, art, philosophy, government, and

---

[cxxxviii] See Appendix 2 for an analysis of this passage in Genesis.
[cxxxix] See Appendix 3

civilization after the flood.) The doctrine of the Curse of Ham is not supported by any legitimate exegesis of the biblical text.

Although the doctrine of the Curse of Ham is still openly held by some today, it is largely transformed and transferred into new symbols and language in an age when the science of discrimination has advanced to the place where racism no longer needs to be justified by blatantly false theology. Slave theology protects injustice with conservative, biblically sound theology that is misapplied. Just as the Jews of Jesus day used the concept of "Corban" to deprive their parents of financial support, slave theology uses the gospel as an excuse to perpetuate systems of exploitation.

> Mark 7:10-13 (NASU)[127]
> 10 "For Moses said, 'HONOR YOUR FATHER AND YOUR MOTHER'; and, 'HE WHO SPEAKS EVIL OF FATHER OR MOTHER, IS TO BE PUT TO DEATH'; 11 but you say, 'If a man says to his father or his mother, whatever I have that would help you is Corban (that is to say, given to God),' 12 you no longer permit him to do anything for his father or his mother; 13 thus invalidating the word of God by your tradition which you have handed down; and you do many things such as that."

Racism today is structural, infused into every institution in race-neutral language. The doctrine of the inherent inferiority of blacks is programmed into every person by Hollywood, mass communications, religious imagery, and the educational system. Systematic, intergenerational exclusion from opportunity places many [but certainly not all] blacks in a situation that cannot but produce the breakdown of marriage and family, and crime which is the inevitable consequence of this institutional decay.[128] These effects are deliberately intensified by outside forces,[129] which supply the black Community with wholesale drugs and weapons, thereby funding gangs, addiction, and urban violence.[130] This situation is then broadcast over media in such a way as to convince the public of black inferiority.[cxl] The Curse of Ham is no longer needed; we now have news editors to do the job.[131] Today's Pastors need only prevent the association of racial prejudice with the demands of Christian sanctification, and to discourage those that do.

[cxl] The media has taken the *effects* of poverty and oppression, effects that have been documented around the world in all peoples, and convinced America that they are the characteristics of a *race*, that is, black people.

Black Self Defense Unbiblical:[cxli]

The systematic crippling of black marriage and family by the prohibition of black self-defense as an un-Christian violation of the Sermon on the Mount (Luke 6:29), while self-defense up to and including revolution and civil war,[132] was and is considered the Christian responsibility of whites.[133] This principle has its origins in slavery, when it was illegal for blacks to defend themselves or their families.[134]

> "South Carolina's code reflected the white obsession with controlling the former slaves. It banned black people from possessing most firearms, making or selling liquor, and coming into the state without first posting a bond for "good behavior.""[135]

This tenet of slave theology enabled the unhindered rape, beating and murder of blacks throughout American history.[cxlii] The relation of the black man to his wife and family was damaged by his inability to protect their lives without risking the loss of at least his own [their primary provider] freedom or his life, and perhaps the loss of all their lives due to the lack of legal protections for self-defense. The same doctrine is the invisible basis for the non-punishment of police who illegally beat and kill black men, women, and children and the lack of outrage by white Pastors and their Congregations.

An illustration of this doctrine is seen in the attitudes towards the American slave rebellions as compared to attitudes regarding the American rebellion against England.[136] Although tyranny was the basis of both and Christians were involved in both, the first were savagely repressed, then vilified, and finally wiped from history, while the other is celebrated annually with patriotic events and barbeque. There is a great deal of difference between the white or the black Christian uttering the phrase, "Give me liberty or give me death." The first is a patriot, the second a criminal.

Scores of laws were established throughout American history to the present day to prevent black people from possessing weapons or defending themselves[137] while prosperous black towns and districts were repeatedly destroyed by white mobs[138] the record of which is also cleansed from history

---

[cxli] If the slave attempted to protect his wife and family and provide for their welfare, he was forcefully and violently reminded that they were not his family but the masters' family. The slave woman was granted the authority in the home (and even the masters' home) and the man was at best a companion and at worse a breeder. His interests and the interests of the woman/mother did not coincide in the eyes of the master; they could not align because the family is the basis of a people's strength and independence.

[cxlii] An employee would be free to defend himself against crimes by his employer, not so the slave.

and banned from discussion in public schools.[139] *Black people have been taught by Christians that raw power is better than moral consistency, if you are victorious.* The evangelical church is generally pro-war irrespective of the justification for the conflict and regularly proclaims the latest armed interventions abroad as the will of God and consistent with the usually unidentified interests of our country. The only Christians required to be passive in the face of violence are black Christians.

God is White:

The continual, over the top representation of God (Jesus Christ is God) as an Anglo Saxon violates the express command of God (Exodus 20:4) and has significant psychological effects upon the spiritual development of both blacks and whites [Romans 12.3].

> Exodus 20:3–5 (KJV 1900)
> [3] Thou shalt have no other gods before me. [4] Thou shalt not make unto thee any graven image, or any likeness *of any thing* that *is* in heaven above, or that *is* in the earth beneath, or that *is* in the water under the earth: [5] Thou shalt not bow down thyself to them, nor serve them: for I the Lord thy God *am* a jealous God, visiting the iniquity of the fathers upon the children unto the third and fourth *generation* of them that hate me;

This representation of The Father [Sistine Chapel[140]], the Son,[141] the apostles, the fathers of the church, and the biblical world as Europeans, in art and in educational tools has convinced whites that God is in their image, and they therefore have the "divine right" to subjugate and to rule all the non-white nations.[142]

> **"WE AFFIRM** that some cultures operate on assumptions that are inherently better than those of other cultures because of the biblical truths that inform those worldviews that have produced these distinct assumptions. Those elements of a given culture that reflect divine revelation should be celebrated and promoted."[143] (The Statement on Social Justice and the Gospel-2019) (emphasis in the original)

On the other hand, blacks are from their earliest years inculcated that God is not like them, that God is white, setting into motion psychological programming that inevitably assists in the process of self-limitation and passivity in the face of racial oppression.

> "In Judeo-Christian imagery, the Caucasian bows down and worships himself, and the African-American worships the Caucasian as god as well…The first psychological

necessity of making someone into a slave is to make the person believe *he or she ought to be a slave.*" (emphasis in the original).[144]

This practice is especially effective upon children who are most susceptible to racial programming. Biblical teaching tools for children represent the entire biblical world as white, which is the almost the exact opposite of the truth and clear evidence of cultural warfare.

It is appropriate here to review our definition of racism:

> *"Racism is the science of discrimination. Racism is the calculated introduction of discrimination into the institutions of society. Racism is a conspiracy to scientifically marginalize or destroy a specific racial group by the manipulation of the organs of society such as the family, government (including legislation, law enforcement and the courts), academia, the media, and the church."*

Racism is cultural warfare, or the extension of conventional warfare to the cultural sphere.

Segregation as Biblically Justified

The creation of the false doctrine of segregation maintains the insulation of wealth and privilege in perpetuity through a "biblically endorsed" racial caste[cxliii] system, while also avoiding the dilution of the value of "whiteness."[cxliv]

> "Residential integration and segregation studies continually show that the degree of segregation between blacks and non-blacks is far greater than between any other two racial groups in the United States.23 Further, outside the South, the greater the percentage of African Americans in an area, the greater the level of segregation.24 In other words, because limited contact with African Americans is preferred by most other Americans,25 increasingly higher levels of segregation are needed as the proportion of African Americans increases. What is more, unlike other groups, whose level of segregation declines with increased socioeconomic status, no strong pattern emerges for African Americans.26 Segregation is not merely separation but, in the contemporary United States, is hierarchical. Residential segregation by race, researchers show us, isolates African Americans, and concentrates poverty and social problems in their neighborhoods. This is more evidence of a black-white racialized

---

[cxliii] Caste: 1. one of the hereditary social classes in Hinduism that restrict the occupation of their members and their association with the members of other castes
2a: a division of society based on differences of wealth, inherited rank or privilege, profession, occupation, or race
b: the position conferred by caste standing : PRESTIGE
3: a system of rigid social stratification characterized by hereditary status, endogamy, and social barriers sanctioned by custom, law, or religion
"Caste." Merriam-Webster.com Dictionary, Merriam-Webster, https://www.merriam-webster.com/dictionary/caste. Accessed 9 Jan. 2023.
[cxliv] Chapter 2

society."[145]

One of the two main reasons for widespread segregation in the Christian church in America (including churches that reject segregation in principle) is the strong desire to separate black and white adolescents. The other is the near universal unwillingness for American whites to submit to a black senior Pastor. We revealed earlier[cxlv] that the original motivation for the formation of the new Christian Right was not Roe vs Wade but Green vs. Connally, whereby the government withdrew tax-exempt status from Bob Jones University because of its practice of segregation.

One of the original justifications for this tenet of slave religion was the interpretation of biblical commands for *spiritual* separation to mean racial or ethnic separation. Thus, the Jews were to separate from the Canaanites because they were *Canaanites*, rather than because they were *idolaters* that God had placed under terminal judgment. Although segregation is alive and well in evangelical churches, this reasoning for the practice of segregation has been largely discarded. The old justification is not needed, since slave theology allows for the orthodox *formulation* of doctrine that is *applied* in separate ways to blacks and to whites. By strictly controlling the racial makeup of senior church leadership, by the elimination of systematic teaching on the subjects of racial prejudice and discrimination not only from discussion, but from the catalogue of sins and from the influence of sanctification, and by excluding black adolescent males [and therefore their families] from the life of the congregation, modern church segregation is about as effective as the days when blacks were confined to the balconies of white churches, all the while giving the appearance of integration. All of this is usually accomplished while maintaining an air of courtesy and even kindness towards every black person who supports this fragile arrangement.

No Jew or Greek or Black:

This tenet of slave theology involves the forbidding of the conception by black Christians of a black national identity in the United States as "woke," CRT,[cxlvi] a violation of the concept of the oneness of the Body of Christ and a distraction from the Great Commission.

[cxlv] Pgs. 56-57
[cxlvi] CRT: Critical Race Theory. However, the term has been co-opted and redefined by some to mean the whole spectrum of beliefs and plans concerning racial justice originating from uppity blacks.

This limitation does not apply to European, Jewish, Asian or any other body of believers except blacks. The cooperative function of other ethnic groups as ethnic groups to promote group advancement within America is considered a cherished right. Thus, the same Bible that has been used to justify racial and ethnic *separation* is also used to forbid racial *unity* as militancy, if practiced by black Americans.

It should be noted that the unity of black Christians for the purpose of addressing black *pathology* is not included in this limitation. If the reason for black Christian unity is the application of solutions to the *symptoms* of oppression (crime, single pregnancy, drug addition, family counseling, mental health) there is no difficulty. It is when this unity begins to address the systems, policies and philosophies that *cause* many of these pathologies, and when the search for solutions is beyond the confines of slave theology, this is when the alarm bells ring and the theological gatekeepers spring to their battle stations.

This tenet of slave theology prevents the deprogramming [Romans 12.1-3] of the oppressed by making ethnic consciousness *in blacks* a sin.

The Whiteout of Biblical History

This subtle practice eliminates the large black presence in scripture by *ignoring* ethnicity, *denying* ethnicity or by *changing* the ethnicity of the biblical nations. Biblical scholars are aware of the ethnicities of Bible nations and peoples. The truth is available, but the student must work for it because it is deliberately made obscure. The accurate representation of the Egyptians, Ethiopians, Chaldeans, Canaanites/Phoenicians, Arabians, and others as descendants of the four sons/families of Ham, in other words, as black peoples[cxlvii] would have an undesirable effect upon the self-esteem of those taught that black people possess a congenital inability to produce a great civilization.

[cxlvii] When one describes *biblical peoples* in terms of black ethnicity, some claim to no longer know what race is or how it is assigned. These same people choose neighborhoods, schools, and churches based upon their racial makeup. The same racial definitions that we use today must be used to define the ethnicity of ancient peoples. If one of your parents were black, then so are you, regardless of your language, geography, or historical context. Under scientific racism, definitions of race change because race is a tool of social management, not of scientific identification. Consequently, we must deprive the social managers the power of defining race, or discarding it, based upon the needs of oppressive systems.

Consequently, the ethnicity of these people is ignored, or their race is confused with the language they spoke, or their race is denied outright as in the case of the Egyptians. Thus, in an area of the world dominated by black people for thousands of years, Americans are taught that blacks in scripture are limited to a few slaves, the "third" wise man and a man with a title that originally described castration. This misrepresentation cannot be accidental, or unintentional. The power of this deception to influence history is undeniable.

This is an adequate, but probably not exhaustive summary of the key elements of Slave Theology in the United States. Not one of these doctrines has gone away and you will not hear television or radio Pastors refute these as heretical, which they are. In fact, the more biblically conservative a preacher is, the more he will tend to agree with these positions.[146]

The Second Nationbuilding Principle is that no one's decisions about you are more important than your own decisions regarding your life. Slave Theology exists to circumscribe the decisions that can be made by manipulating Bible information. Slave Theology places its adherents in unreality where Christian maturity is made more difficult and nationbuilding impossible. Slave Theology is false doctrine, and false doctrine is no basis for making sound decisions about your life. Slave Theology must be replaced by true Christianity so that the mind of believers may be renewed, and Christian victory achieved.

Black Responsibility

Slave Theology does not eliminate black responsibility for self-destructive attitudes and actions. The Bible and the nationbuilding principles drawn from it make all responsible for their decisions. All of humanity is fallen and depraved. Left to our own devices, our thoughts tend towards unrighteousness. Oppression is an external influence which exacerbates what is already wrong with humanity. False biblical information from the local church, however well-meaning, closes every exit to the nightmare created by oppression and the indwelling sin nature.

The denial of opportunity, childhood racial psychological programming, and race-based and income-based segregation, produce in some, a maladjusted manhood that is a threat rather than a support to marriage, the family, and the black Community as a whole. This subset of black men are themselves unwitting agents of oppression, producing embittered black women and neglected children. These decisions are indeed black decisions subject to divine evaluation, but they are made by men who are deliberately manufactured by oppressive racial science.[147]

For the many black men who are *not* severely malformed by oppression, scientific discrimination still has effects.

> "...the failure of "mature" Afrikan American males to assume full responsibility for educating and training Afrikan American boys and adolescents for productive manhood-their failure to take economic and political control of their national communities...their apparent inability, lack of will or courage to form a nation within a nation... glaringly reveal their inadequate preparation for assuming the responsibilities of Afrikan manhood, whether they may be classified as prosocial or antisocial, responsible or irresponsible."[148]

The Destroyer of Civilization

Because Satan is the implacable enemy of all mankind, the perpetrators of evil are destined to become its victims. The Pastors and Congregations which actively or passively enforce slave theology share the same incorrect assessment of themselves as do the psychologically programmed blacks, but in the opposite direction. The consequences of this belief system must lead to spiritual disaster in both the oppressed and oppressor. As a bonus, slave theology, by corrupting the interpretation and application of the scriptures for both blacks and whites, creates a vacuum drawing in both false doctrines and the religious parasites ['antichrists' 1 John 2.18-19] which now overrun the church. Therefore, the theology of race[cxlviii] is a destroyer of civilization for all people, both through its direct effects and the divine discipline that is visited upon the oppressor and his victims.[cxlix]

[cxlviii] Some will object saying that any connection of race to bible doctrine is a "Theology of Race." This is an example of slave theology which prohibits the application of the Scriptures to the issue of structural racism. The Theology of Race is the use of the Scriptures to perpetuate structural racism. It should also be noted that the strengthening of institutional discrimination eventually leads to the open sanction of personal discrimination, as we can see today.

[cxlix] One might ask, "Why are the victims of oppression subject to diving discipline?" The Second Principle of Nationbuilding dictates that all human decisions count, that is, they all have consequences. God holds all men responsible for their decisions. All humanity have been provided with an inward guide, the conscience, to determine good and evil [Romans 2.15]. God holds both individuals and nations responsible for their response to this internal witness. The weight He places upon the victim versus his oppressor is governed by His perfect and immutable righteousness. All will give an account to God, many in this life, but all in the life to come. True saints who overcome will judge the world, many who are last shall be first [1 Corinthians 6.2-3; Matthew 19.30].

The Reversal of Slave Theology

Black nationbuilding depends upon black decision making. This is the Second Principle of Nationbuilding. Just as oppression cannot be eliminated by secular actions alone, a commitment to changing the thinking of the *beneficiaries* of oppression will be equally futile. In view of this, what are the doctrinal principles that must be elevated in the black local church to powerfully refute this evil theology? The following doctrinal imperatives may at first fail to resemble doctrines at all because of our centuries of programming with false Christianity. Nevertheless, they are doctrinal and essential to the reversal of the spiritual problems that prevent nationbuilding and the nullification of oppression.

Christ First!

If historical trends are activated by spiritual factors, if the people of God are the key actors in initiating the spiritual processes by which nations advance or retrogress, if the Word of God, the Bible, is the standard of truth by which the people of God must operate,[cl] then the first principle that must be restored is "Christ First."

The religious gatekeepers of oppression say "Christ First" in the way that the religious leaders of Jesus' time purported to put "Jehovah [Yahweh] First" as they transgressed the Law of Moses and crucified Christ [Matthew 15.8-9]. They claim spiritual orthodoxy while relying upon every secular means to maintain the status quo of worldwide injustice. If the local church places any method or philosophy before Christ and his teaching,[cli] it must fail in nationbuilding. Nationbuilding has failed because of the lack of application of sound biblical principles. It is important to note that nationbuilding has not failed due to a lack of black unity, or because of insufficient resources. Nationbuilding requires *spiritual power* in addition to human effort. Therefore, a people need either God [Psalms 127.1-2] or the devil [Luke 4.6-7] to accomplish nationbuilding.

To enlist the aid of God, one must serve Him [2 Chronicles 16.9]. The instrumentality of this service is the Scriptures, the Word of God [2 Timothy 3.16-17]. Israel was not united when they separated from Egypt under the

---

[cl] Deuteronomy 28.1-2; 2Ch 7.14-15; Proverbs 11.10-11; 14.34; Matthew 5.13-16; Acts 10 34-36
[cli] By "his teaching" is meant the whole realm of biblical doctrine.

leadership of Moses [Exodus 12.38; Numbers 14.22]. Neither did they have resources, until God caused the Egyptians [Exodus 12.35-36] to enrich them. It was God's purpose to free them and make them a nation because He heard their cries unto Him.[clii]

Erroneous teaching cannot produce spiritual achievement. False teaching is no basis for the proper worship of God. The Old Testament worship demonstrates that God must be served according to His own protocol, or not at all. *Nationbuilding is the irresistible result in living in submission to accurate teaching.* Christ First requires that the Word of God be obeyed. Sound doctrine elevates Christ because it produces believers who are conformed to His image in holiness and who operate within the sphere of His power in ministry. When the black local church says "Christ First" it must mean it.

Christ First means the following:

> ➤ The primary *objective* of the believer and the local church is to *glorify Christ.*[cliii] There is no ethnic agenda that can supersede this purpose. Nationbuilding is a product of serving Christ according to the scriptures. We glorify Christ to the maximum degree when we are spiritually transformed thereby manifesting His character in our homes, churches, Communities, and the world at large.
> ➤ The *methodology* of the local church is *discipleship*. It is the responsibility of the Congregation to win the lost and to teach and train them to become disciples of Christ themselves. This is not a job that we can pass off to the Elders of the church. It is their job to prepare you. It is your job [the Congregation] to make disciples. Christian discipleship is the foundation of nationbuilding. It trains Christians to be spiritually self-sustaining and therefore better spouses, better family members, better employees and better citizens who influence the Community through their verbal witness and their righteous lifestyles.
> ➤ Our *policy* is grace. All our ability and our resources are from God according to His grace. It is because of divine grace directed towards believers that a people who are without strength can initiate and achieve nationbuilding. This is another reason that the Church is the primary agent of nationbuilding.

[clii] Exodus 3.9; 2 Corinthians 9.8
[cliii] Matthew 22.36-38; Romans 15.5-6

Our attitude towards all is grace. We acknowledge the reality of oppression and seek to eliminate its effects upon our families and Communities, but *the Christian is not focused upon oppression or his feelings about it or its perpetrators*. The Christian is preoccupied with Christ. Contrary to the claims of slave theology, consciousness of oppression can coexist with the joy of the Lord. It is in this way that we demonstrate to God that our trust is in Him and his power. Although we are single-minded in our pursuit of healing for our people, we are without malice or revenge motivation. Deliverance is not of man but of God.

> Christ First requires that we place *doctrine* first. Our doctrine is found exclusively in the systematic study and proper interpretation of the Bible. We do not overturn truth for the benefit of our people. Neither do not neglect the full implications of scripture to spare the feelings of the disobedient, be they black, or white. The one who misrepresents doctrine is an enemy: we must love him, but we must not follow him.[cliv] We must protect the local church both from false teachers and from well-meaning but erroneous teachers.[clv]

It is critical that the movement of black people towards nationbuilding not be sidetracked by a fixation upon opposition to whites or upon the systemic injustices of this world. *Nationbuilding is not the removal of oppressive structures in society.*[clvi] Nationbuilding is making decisions about our sanctification, how we will function as husband and wives and how we will minister to our families and Communities. It is through proper relation to God that a people attain the highest and truest expression of its personhood and national destiny. Nationbuilding is the sociopolitical outcome of putting Christ first.

Because a healthy ethnic self-concept is consistent with God's design for any people (Acts 17:27; Romans 12:3), the proper alignment of a people to God ensures the development of a sanctified self-concept, freed from the need to dominate, or devalue other cultures. Likewise, a psychological fixation upon what has been done to us defeats spiritual growth and is a part of the oppressive mental paradigm. A healthy and righteous cultural identity is consistent with God's creative purpose for mankind. This is because all

---

[cliv] Acts 20.28-31; Romans 16.17-18; Colossians 2.8-9; Titus 1.6-11; 1 John 2.22-26
[clv] Chapter 12: Two Kinds of Dangerous Teachers
[clvi] Nationbuilding is not opposed to the removal of these structures, and it is not wrong to use legal means to do so. The priority of nationbuilding is the *spiritual* function of the believer and the local church. Under this concept, the oppressive system and its instrumentalities will be made impotent, even if they remain in place.

ethnicity, including blackness, originates from God [Acts 17.26]. It is the false doctrines of slave Christianity that has equated *black* ethnic and cultural pride with carnality.

Protect the Woman!

In the beginning, God created the man. It was not good that the man be alone and for this reason woman was created from the body of the man [Genesis 2.7, 18-25]. God could have gathered a second handful of dust to create her, but he did not. Thus, mankind is a whole of two parts, two poles. Man and woman are completed in one another and the two are the basis of God's creative purpose.

The woman was placed in submission to the man *before* the fall.[clvii] His place in front of the woman was to provide leadership.[clviii] This leadership signifies guidance[clix] and authority, but it also denotes *protection*. The man cannot protect the woman from behind her, God placed him before her.

> 1 Corinthians 11:3 (KJV 1900)
> 3 But I would have you know, that the head of every man is Christ; and the head of the woman *is* the man; and the head of Christ *is* God.

In forcefully placing the black man *behind* the woman, the slave system deprived her of his protection. The slave master became the protector of the black woman, which proved to be no protection at all. Since slavery, the imposition of mass unemployment and mass incarceration, augmented by psychological programming, maintains this rearward position, and magnifies the difficulty of doing what God has called black men to do for their wives and families [1 Timothy 5.8].

The fact of the equality of men and women before God does not change the reality of male authority and his responsibility as leader and protector of the woman. Paul wrote Galatians 3.28 as well as Colossians 3.18. There is a

---

[clvii] Genesis 2.18; 1 Corinthians 11.7-10; 1 Timothy 2.12-14
[clviii] Ephesians 5.22; Colossians 3.18
[clix] Adam knew that the arguments of Lucifer were false, and he was not deceived by them [1 Timothy 2.12-14]. There was no discussion between he and his wife recorded. She acted independently of both he and God. Adam accepted the role-reversal and deliberately disobeyed God in full knowledge of what he was doing. He chose Eve over his Maker and is given full responsibility for the fall of mankind, because he was in authority over the woman. Thus, Paul refers to "the offense of Adam" [Romans 5.14; 1 Corinthians 15.22].

common belief today that submission equals inferiority. This is a concept that finds its origin in Lucifer, who convinced Eve that her position was her problem, and that the fruit of the Tree of Knowledge would elevate her to godhood [Genesis 3.4-6]. That submission is not inferiority is demonstrated in the Godhead where Christ submits to the Father and the Spirit to the Father and the Son in complete equality.

> John 6:38 (KJV 1900)
> [38] For I came down from heaven, not to do mine own will, but the will of him that sent me. [1 Corinthians 11.3]

Since the fall of mankind, the woman has been one of the greatest victims of the sinful tendencies of man. Far from the lying promise of Lucifer, the woman has desired but not achieved the position that she sought that day in Eden. To this very day slave religion and scientific racism continue where the serpent left off, convincing many black women of their superiority to black men, debasing him while elevating her in the home, the workplace[149] and even the pulpit.[150]

However, the pre-eminence of the black woman,[151] initiated and maintained by systems of oppression, beginning with slavery, has been at the expense of her protection. The *primary target* of Satan in oppression is the spiritual information available to the oppressed.[152] The *secondary target* is the relation between the man and the woman. In the subjugation of humanity, the devil attacked both targets simultaneously. To conquer a people without military action, it is helpful if their males can be feminized,[153] and their females masculinized.[154] Healthy relationships between men and women will tend to produce stronger families, making oppression far less profitable by making it more difficult to enforce. Role confusion will ruin marriages, which in turn destroys the family, leading to the virtual or real destruction of a people. This is also the pattern of Eden. The Fall of mankind, due to the role reversal of Adam and Eve, led directly to Abel's death and Cain's exile. This led just as surely to the Flood and the destruction of civilization.

A key factor in black disunity is conflict between black men and women. Once the institution of marriage is damaged, a people may be more easily oppressed. No people can survive the destruction of their marriages.

In modern times, black women have been deprived of the protection of black men by multiple, simultaneous campaigns aimed at returning him to a virtual slavery, or a very real death. The collection of strategies put in place to accomplish this end are so powerfully coordinated that nothing short of massive spiritual power can reverse their effects. Fortunately, such power is at the disposal of the Christian.

While lynching and castration instilled terror in black men in the past, it did not stop them from taking responsibility for their families. Mob violence against black success was temporarily successful and advanced the aim of maintaining fear through terrorism, but black men worked and raised families at a much higher rate during the first half of the 20th century than today, even under grossly inferior and segregated housing and school systems.[155] In the old days, black women and men suffered together in mutual financial and social insecurity. Today a synchronized policy of high-tech oppression closely manages social, economic, and psychological outcomes among black people and especially black men and boys.

In media, a stereotype of the black male as a predator incapable of family leadership has influenced generations of Americans. For the last forty years this stereotype has been supercharged by the creation of a "thug culture" specifically designed for black youth that is financed and promoted by the entertainment industry, which is neither owned nor operated by black people. Fatherless, leaderless, and spiritually starved black youth consume this poison and emulate its destructive lifestyle. The outcome is two generations of fatherless children due to irresponsible sex and the reduction of the potential pool of husbands through the imprisonment and/or premature death that the entertainment industry promotes through "thug culture."[156]

Lately, the media has changed course, and the black male image has been dramatically *feminized* in movies, television series and even commercials, where gay black men are shown in acts of intimacy up to and including intercourse.

The high percentage of single female led households among blacks[157] and the high divorce rate,[158] produce boys who are raised in poverty by women and who go to public schools to be taught by women, many of whom are white with little knowledge of black people beyond stereotypes.[159] These factors lead to the creation of men who are scheduled for incarceration, men who are of stripped of the resources to provide for their families, and men who are feminized. These trends produce men who are far less capable of defending and providing for black women.

The limiting of the black man's ability to support the family by mental programming, systematic economic discrimination and mass incarceration has made the black woman the leader and provider in the home and has caused many black women to believe, falsely, that they do not need black men. The popularization of feminist concepts among black women since the 1970's contributes to the diminution of the male role.[160] The problem is compounded because the counterweight of biblical teaching regarding authority is absent. It is too costly for Clergy to clearly teach male authority in the home and local church.

Affirmative action made black women the beneficiaries of better jobs while checking two boxes for their employers [being both black and female] seeking to comply with these rules.[161] Black men are under-employed,[162] paid much less than white men,[163] are promoted more slowly and are more subject to job loss.

The unnatural relation of the black man and woman short circuits any nationbuilding impulse at its origin. The relation of the man and woman in marriage is the basis of the family and the family is the basis of the nation. All the power necessary to correct this situation in your Community can be found in the local churches that remain faithful to Christ and the Scriptures. There can be no nationbuilding until this relationship is realigned to *biblical standards*. After commitment to Christ, black manhood must be measured against this yardstick, "Protect the Woman." No matter what qualification a man may possess, his success or failure in this area must be the most important measure of his fitness as a man or as a leader of men.[clx]

Our wives, mothers, sisters, daughters and nieces and aunts are to be protected first spiritually and then physically, intellectually, and emotionally from all threats. First, because they are our biblical responsibility [1 Timothy 5.8] and second because there will be no black national identity until they are protected. The black man must protect the women of his own family and then he must protect the women of every other black family. This means the following for the Christian Community:

> ➤ A man cannot hold a position in the local church if he is neglecting his biblical responsibility to the woman.

[clx] This is a biblical statement. The Bible does not permit male leadership that fails to lead, provide for, and protect its own wives and families [1 Timothy 3.2, 4-5, 12; 5.8; Titus 1.6-7]

1 Timothy 5:8 (KJV 1900)

⁸ But if any provide not for his own, and specially for those of his own house, he hath denied the faith, and is worse than an infidel.

This *provision*[clxi] affirms the requirement of financial and overall care but also prohibits marital offenses such as adultery and physical violence which are the opposite of provision. It also condemns the neglect of a man's own children ["*his own*"]. By neglecting his children, he is placing a greater burden upon a woman, often forcing her into poverty. This prohibition includes all male leaders in the church, but especially deacons, trustees, teachers, and Pastors/Elders [1 Timothy 3.4-5].

> Fornication must be identified not only as a sin, but as a sin that specifically prevents nationbuilding. Fornication increases the vulnerability of women, who risk childbirth without the protection of marriage. Single parenthood is a virtual guarantee of poverty or near poverty for most black women. Fornication also trains believers to disobey God, sabotaging marriage when and if it occurs. If the woman is convinced to disobey *God* by fornication prior to marriage, why should she not rebel against the authority of her husband after marriage? Fornication degrades the moral and spiritual character of young people in general, leading to the loss of commitment to the Lord.

> Policies must be developed regarding divorce and remarriage. Biblically sound doctrine on the subject must be taught over the pulpit and in other educational settings in the local church. Women are made vulnerable [or, make themselves vulnerable since they are far more likely to initiate divorce proceedings][164] through divorces that are not biblically sanctioned. Jesus taught upon divorce [Matthew 19.2-12] because it is important to families, to the witness of the Church, and to the Community which is no stronger than the families which comprise it. A non-biblical divorce or marriage must disqualify a man for the role of Pastor/Elder or deacon [1Timothy 3.2, 12].

All these restrictions are consistent with the plain teaching of scripture. They have fallen out of favor because they prevent church growth, are embarrassing

---

clxi **"Provide"** 4306 προνοέω [*pronoeo* /pron·o·eh·o/] v. From 4253 and 3539; TDNT 4:1009; TDNTA 636; GK 4629; Three occurrences; AV translates as "provide for" twice, and "provide" once. **1** to perceive before, foresee. **2** to provide, think of beforehand. 2a to provide for one. 2b to take thought for, care for a thing.

and difficult to enforce consistently and because so many Pastors have committed these sins themselves. The first step to implementing these changes is to have a legally approved church membership document that authorizes church discipline. This document must be signed by each new and existing member.

Slave religion demands that the black man commit to protect the wives of others while his own is vulnerable and abused. To protect the wives of others is considered patriotism, to protect our own is considered "black militancy" according to the doctrines of slave religion.

Protect the Family!

When the woman is protected, then the protection of the family naturally follows. When the woman is elevated and respected, the family will be respected as well. While marriage is the fundamental human institution, the family is the product of marriage and the building block of the Community and the state. One of the key functions of the family is to prepare the next generation for meaningful participation in society. The family transfers values, aptitudes, skills, and material wealth to the next generation. Peoples or cultures that do this well are strengthened, those that do it poorly become the vassals of those that do it well.

Slave theology required that the slave be committed to the master's family and not his own. A unified slave family automatically provided the slave with interests above that of the masters' wealth and security. A strong slave family, and especially a strong Christian family presented an persistent threat to the slave industry.

> "Through religious instruction the bondsmen learned that slavery had divine sanction, that insolence was as much an offense against God as against the temporal master."[165]

Thus, the Bible was manipulated to teach the slave that obedience to the master was the same as obedience to God. This was taught to slaves as Christian doctrine while American Pastors were proclaiming to white men that the King of England was *not* to be obeyed as God. Therefore, while the divinely ordained priority of the white Americans was family and freedom, the divinely ordained priority of the slave was the well-being of the family of the slave master alone. This arrangement had to exist to enable a perpetual system of exploitation based upon color.

(It should be reemphasized that as represented in the bible, slavery resulted from defeat in war, criminality, or debt. Sometimes, slavery was even voluntary. Slavery was not a color-based system built on kidnapping or upon the purchase of kidnapped individuals.[clxii] The bible did not condone excessive violence towards slaves or the rape of slaves regardless of their spiritual status. The bible did not require the return of an escaped slave and slaves were able to seek their freedom without being guilty of sin.)[clxiii]

The black church must condemn in no uncertain terms the neglect of women and children by black men. The church should also recognize that women may themselves be a source of problems to the family. The church must, in the process of the exposition of scripture, define and apply the pertinent doctrines concerning the family. These doctrines must be applied to the actual problems experienced by black families, problems that are mutated and magnified by the reality of individual and structural discrimination. The nationbuilding principles are summaries of biblical truths. We must discuss nationbuilding in the local church, because without it we eliminate the very thing that God has provided for the security of the family.

It is the state [nation] which protects the family, but the state is made of strong and effective families. When the black family is strong, Communities will be strong, and Communities make up our governmental units. Simply putting a black face into a governmental seat guarantees nothing [and usually produces little value for black people because of the black officeholder's inability to impact political and economic *systems*]. It is the continuous presence of strong families in strong Communities that can provide a pool of political candidates and demand accountability from local government based upon real economic power. Nationbuilding is biblical. It is the consequence of the proper function of divinely established institutions. When true disciples of Christ are made, marriages must automatically be strengthened, when marriages are strengthened then families are inevitably strengthened. When

---

[clxii] It will be argued by some that, in the case of American slavery, often the original kidnappers were Africans. This argument is biblically and legally irrelevant. The receipt of stolen property is not justified by the ethnicity of the original thief. European and American slavery created a large demand for black slaves. We have learned through the immoralities and illegalities [including illegal wars] stimulated by the oil markets what people and governments will do to profit off what we know as "black gold." Long before the discovery of oil, black bodies were the original "black gold" and I do not doubt that Africans exploited one another to profit from this market. Again, the theft of labor is theft regardless from whom the person was originally purchased. It is the purchase of stolen property and therefore theft in scripture [Exodus 21.16; 1 Timothy 1.9-10] and a felony under State law [N.C. G.S. 14-72].
[clxiii] See Appendix I: the Doctrine of Oppression-Oppression and Slavery.

families are strengthened, then Communities are strengthened, resulting eventually in both economic and political power. When Communities are strengthened the nation is strengthened, both America and the black constituent nation.

We should implement the following biblical standards in the local church regarding families:

> A man cannot hold an office in the church if his family is out of control. The Pastor/Elder and deacon are specifically prohibited from his office if this is the case [1 Timothy 3.4-5, 11-12; 5.8; Titus 1.6]. The leadership in the local church should exemplify the values consistent with scripture because this obedience is commanded and because it also promotes nationbuilding. Elders, deacons, and teachers whose minor children are involved in chronic rebellion, fornication, drug abuse or crime need to focus upon these issues which undermine their leadership authority.[clxiv]

> The church should have ministries organized to address the needs of single parent families in their Congregation. Women with teaching and shepherding gifts [and not single or married men] should be organized to lead such efforts to single women with children. Such ministries should address both the spiritual and physical needs of such families, with the goal of their full incorporation into the life of the local church.

> Special efforts should be made to cultivate a high-quality youth ministry leadership team. Perhaps the most gifted individuals in the church should be directed to this ministry. An entire church can experience a turnover of young adults/families in as little as ten years. A leadership development process should exist that perpetuates qualified leaders for every spiritual department.

Respect the Brotherhood!

Slave religion requires the disunity of the slave. Slave unity, especially the unity of black males, was a distinct threat to the slave system. Consequently, the association of numbers of black males was prohibited in the strongest terms.[166] Because of this and the other fruits of oppression, brotherhood

---

[clxiv] These standards will limit the expansion of church leadership and thereby limit church growth. This is not a bad thing, since the job of the church is to evangelize and make disciples, rather than grow vast ecclesial organizations. Discipleship and uncompromising bible teaching are the first casualties of the drive to become and remain large.

among blacks and especially among black males is not easily achieved. To this day, the concept of black unity is frowned upon as inconsistent with the spirit of Christianity,[clxv] this in a country where the majority of churches are segregated.[167] The irrationality of the spiritual prohibition of black unity while simultaneously enforcing a system of de facto segregation is strong evidence of the persistence of this dual system of theology.

The slave theologians use the following scripture to justify the discouragement of unity among blacks:

> Galatians 3:26–29 (KJV 1900)
> 26 For ye are all the children of God by faith in Christ Jesus. 27 For as many of you as have been baptized into Christ have put on Christ. 28 There is neither Jew nor Greek, there is neither bond nor free, there is neither male nor female: for ye are all one in Christ Jesus. 29 And if ye be Christ's, then are ye Abraham's seed, and heirs according to the promise.

The Galatians had corrupted their doctrine by making the law of Moses a basis for sanctification in the Church age.

> Galatians 3:3 (KJV 1900)
> 3 Are ye so foolish? having begun in the Spirit, are ye now made perfect by the flesh?

Paul clarified the Law as entirely separate in purpose from the Promise made to Abraham, one which pertained to earthly conduct and the other to eternal life. The Law was a means of discipleship and worship for another dispensation. Now that Christ had come, the Law, which had never given eternal life, had become obsolete as a means of discipleship, which is now accomplished by walking according to the dictates of the Spirit of God, [Galatians 5.16] and obsolete as a means of worship, which is now in Spirit and in the truth [John 4.24].

Galatians 3.28 shows that the era of Israel as the evangelistic agency of God has been set aside. It also reveals that a new era has dawned in which faith is

---

[clxv] From page 200: "It should be noted that the unity of black Christians for the purpose of addressing black *pathology* is not included in this limitation. If the reason for black Christian unity is the application of solutions to the *symptoms* of oppression (crime, single pregnancy, drug addition, family counseling, mental health) there is no difficulty. It is when this unity begins to address the systems, policies and philosophies that *cause* many of these pathologies, and when the search for solutions is beyond the confines of slave theology, this is when the alarm bells ring and the theological gatekeepers spring to their battle stations."

in Christ, resulting in an entirely new spiritual entity, the Church, in which Jew and Gentiles enjoy spiritual equality.

In the Church, the body of Christ, there is complete equality of spiritual opportunity and spiritual privilege. The old distinctions of Jew and Gentile continue to exist but have no special privileges or demerit in Christ. A person does not have to become a Jew to become a part of the people of God [Galatians 2.11-18]. The sex of an individual has no bearing upon their spiritual privilege or potential, nor does their status of slave or free.

Galatians 3:28 *does not mean* that social relations are necessarily changed by salvation. The new birth in Christ does not destroy the separate roles of males and females, neither does it abolish the relationships within the institution of slavery that were regulated for believers by the scripture. Slaves were still slaves after salvation.

Finally, the new birth did not eliminate the existence or the functions of culture. The problem between Paul and Peter in chapter two of Galatians was not because God planned to amalgamate or eliminate the cultures of the Greeks and Jews, the problem arose from attempting to make traditional Jewish practices the standard for the spiritual life of believers.

Black people do not become divested of culture after salvation. Black people do not have to stop thinking of themselves as black after they are born again. *Nor do black people need to fear working together as black people to advance black interests.* No one tells Messianic Jews that they are no longer Jewish and cannot work together as Jews to advance Jewish interests. Nor do we inform other ethnic groups that they can no longer pursue their culture or their political interests because they are saved. It would not at all be farfetched to say that American history has largely been the effort of Christian, English-speaking whites to secure and to maintain their way of life above all other peoples and to aggregate wealth and privilege along racial lines.

The predominant idea in Galatians 3.28 is that, in the context of opportunity and achievement in spiritual life, there is no distinction or limitation due to culture, sex, or legal status. It is the only place in life where this can be said to be true. The secondary idea is that one's identity in Christ should become more important than any of these other distinctions. For the Christian, every human condition becomes subject to the rule of Christ. For the Christian, culture must be subject to Christ.

It is biblically incorrect to tell black believers that now that they are saved that they are no longer black or that God does not see color. God created color, why should He not see it? Instruction such as this teaches the black believer to dismiss that which makes him who he is and to blindly enter the world which is composed of both unbelievers and Christians who will both see and evaluate him based on that which he is told no longer to acknowledge. This is a stark example of how Christendom reinforces the racial rules of society and strips away the defenses which the Bible provides for the individual's spiritual survival.

The requirement that black men deny the existence of systematic racial oppression and then suppress the *inevitable emotional consequences* of this oppression has created an environment where aggression seeks the only permissible outlet: violence towards other black men and women.[168] The American legal system appears to encourage black on black crime by punishing it less severely than crimes committed by blacks against whites.[169]

In this way black people oppress themselves, not only destroying other black lives, but also providing a(n) (unneeded) pretext for *mass incarceration* and a variety of other state-imposed aggressions against black people.

The outcome is the elegant reinstatement of slavery through the revocation of citizenship rights, eliminating these men from participation in society via their disqualification from the workforce, the vote, political office, work in law enforcement and many other deprivations.

> ➢ "More African American adults are under correctional control today—in prison or jail, on probation or parole—than were enslaved in 1850, a decade before the Civil War began.
> ➢ "In 2007 more black men were disenfranchised than in 1870, the year the Fifteenth Amendment was ratified prohibiting laws that explicitly deny the right to vote on the basis of race. During the Jim Crow era, African Americans continued to be denied access to the ballot through poll taxes and literacy tests. Those laws have been struck down, but today felon disenfranchisement laws accomplish what poll taxes and literacy tests ultimately could not.
> ➢ "In many large urban areas in the United States, the majority of working-age African American men have criminal records. In fact, it was reported in 2002 that, in the Chicago area, if you take into account prisoners, the figure is nearly 80%.

> "Those bearing criminal records and cycling in and out of our prisons today are part of a growing undercaste—not class, caste—a group of people, defined largely by race, who are relegated to a permanent second-class status by law. They can be denied the right to vote, automatically excluded from juries, and legally discriminated against in employment, housing, access to education, and public benefits, much as their grandparents and great-grandparents were during the Jim Crow era."[170]

The existence of spiritual and secular systems that collaborate to enforce oppression requires a specific application of the biblical principles of brotherhood within the black local church. The Bible teaches that Christians recognize and help the weak, poor, and oppressed. Slave theology supports and maintains the system that manufactures these categories of suffering.

> Isaiah 10:1–2 (NASB95)
> [1] Woe to those who enact evil statutes And to those who constantly record unjust decisions, [2] So as to deprive the needy of justice And rob the poor of My people of *their* rights, So that widows may be their spoil And that they may plunder the orphans.

Recognizing the existence of religiously sanctioned oppression is difficult for black believers because they are ridiculed and accused of evading responsibility since "everyone knows" that there is no such system of oppression. Blacks are simultaneously accused of departing from a gospel emphasis by asking that the Bible be *applied* to their imaginary problems. It is the responsibility of the Pastors and teachers to let their people know that they are not imagining things and to make direct application of the scriptures to the reality of oppression and its effects. This must be followed by positive actions by oppressed people to cease participating in this system. Positive actions of brotherhood must replace the harm that oppressed people do to one another. This effort can best begin in the local church. *Brotherhood must become a value that is conscientiously worked towards by Christians who fully recognize what racism and false religion has done to the black mind and Community.*

> Matthew 22:39–40 (KJV 1900)
> [39] And the second *is* like unto it, Thou shalt love thy neighbour as thyself. [40] On these two commandments hang all the law and the prophets.

> 1 John 3:14–18 (KJV 1900)
> [14] We know that we have passed from death unto life, because we love the brethren. He that loveth not his brother abideth in death. [15] Whosoever

hateth his brother is a murderer: and ye know that no murderer hath eternal life abiding in him. [16] Hereby perceive we the love *of God*, because he laid down his life for us: and we ought to lay down *our* lives for the brethren. [17] But whoso hath this world's good, and seeth his brother have need, and shutteth up his bowels *of compassion* from him, how dwelleth the love of God in him? [18] My little children, let us not love in word, neither in tongue; but in deed and in truth.

The Bible does teach the unity and brotherhood of all *believers*, and black believers are obligated to practice this concept with respect to all regardless of race and regardless of their willingness to return that love. However, black men and women are not consistently practicing this command towards our own people. Brotherhood is reserved for whites while suspicion and disrespect is too often directed towards other blacks. This also must stop. Black people must truly love their brothers, not because they are all deserving of love, but because Christ commands it and we will remain weak and exploited until we do.

> Romans 9:1-5 (KJV)
> 9 I say the truth in Christ, I lie not, my conscience also bearing me witness in the Holy Ghost, 2 That I have great heaviness and continual sorrow in my heart. 3 For I could wish that myself were accursed from Christ <u>for my brethren, my kinsmen according to the flesh</u>: 4 Who are Israelites; to whom pertaineth the adoption, and the glory, and the covenants, and the giving of the law, and the service of God, and the promises; 5 Whose are the fathers, and of whom as concerning the flesh Christ came, who is over all, God blessed for ever. Amen.

The local church must model this behavior to the larger Community. In marriage, family, government, and the local church it is believers who demonstrate the plan of God by righteous function within these institutions. This same example must be demonstrated in our dealings with one another in the black Community.

Indiscriminate Spiritual Unity

Beware of indiscriminate unity. *In spiritual matters*, indiscriminate unity is very dangerous. As Christians we are not free to pursue spiritual activities with just anyone claiming to be a believer.

Romans 16:17 (KJV 1900)
17 Now I beseech you, brethren, mark them which cause divisions and
offences <u>contrary to the doctrine which ye have learned</u>; and avoid them.[clxvi]

Since the solution to the problem of oppression is first spiritual and the
process of discipleship is the spiritual means by which the structures of
oppression are removed from the mind and replaced with the Mind of Christ,
we must be exceedingly careful with whom we align ourselves spiritually. *The
possession of black skin alone is an inadequate criterion upon which to unite on spiritual
issues.* Indiscriminate unity on *spiritual matters* inevitably leads to a departure
from the truth. The great commandment [Matthew 22.36-40] states that love
for God must precede love for man. Love for God is measured by our
adherence to an accurate Word.

John 14:15 (KJV 1900)
15 If ye love me, keep my commandments.

The primary problem of oppressed people is *not* a lack of commitment among
men but a lack of commitment to God. Love for God places fidelity to his
commands first. These facts must be recognized in spiritual matters. In secular
concerns, brotherhood is also to be sought, but never at the expense of
spiritual truth.

Spiritual good will not grow out of the ground of false spiritual teaching. Satan
precipitated the fall of humanity and the earth by a series of lies and half-
truths about spiritual matters. Incorrect teaching from the Bible will not heal
us. Incorrect teaching from scripture was essential to the construction and
maintenance of the problems that we now face.

The Bible commands the Christian to love his believing brother. It does not
necessarily command us to *follow* our Christian brother. If a believer, be it a
Pastor or layperson, is committed to false interpretations of the Bible, that
person is entitled to love, but he is not entitled to provide spiritual teaching or
spiritual support to the process of discipleship. Such a person is of no help in
the spiritual aspects of nationbuilding.

There are many black people who will say that the Church offers no solution
to black problems because we have so many religious differences among
ourselves. These people see black unity as the fundamental essential for black

---

[clxvi] 2 Thessalonians 3:6, 14. Titus 3:10. 2 John 10

deliverance from oppression. They think this way because they do not see oppression as *primarily* a spiritual problem, but primarily as a social, political, or economic problem. From the spiritual perspective the great majority of black [and white] people *are* unified: unified against God, against the proper interpretation of the scriptures and against the gospel [Romans 3.10-18]. They do not realize that it is God working through his people, the Church that prepares the conditions for emancipation and nationbuilding. Therefore, we must beware of indiscriminate spiritual unity with any individual or group that does not hold to the accurate interpretation of scriptures as their final authority.

The apostle Paul had a problem of this kind in the church in Crete, which he sent Titus to clean up. Paul instructed Titus as follows:

> Titus 1:5–11 (KJV 1900)
> 5 For this cause left I thee in Crete, that thou shouldest set in order the things that are wanting, and ordain elders in every city, as I had appointed thee: 6 If any be blameless, the husband of one wife, having faithful children not accused of riot or unruly. 7 For a bishop must be blameless, as the steward of God; not selfwilled, not soon angry, not given to wine, no striker, not given to filthy lucre; 8 But a lover of hospitality, a lover of good men, sober, just, holy, temperate; 9 Holding fast the faithful word as he hath been taught, that he may be able by sound doctrine both to exhort and to convince the gainsayers. 10 For there are many unruly and vain talkers and deceivers, specially they of the circumcision: 11 Whose mouths must be stopped, who subvert whole houses, teaching things which they ought not, for filthy lucre's sake.

The local churches today are overrun with false and erroneous teachers of scripture. To accomplish the spiritual rehabilitation of our people, we need a clear and accurate Word from the scriptures. We cannot allow the improper use of black unity to cause an amalgamation with a spiritual evil to the downfall of those people who need a clear Word from the Lord. We must not make the decision to place the second great commandment in front of the first.

> Matthew 22:35–40 (KJV 1900)
> 35 Then one of them, which was a lawyer, asked him a question, tempting him, and saying, 36 Master, which is the great commandment in the law? 37 Jesus said unto him, Thou shalt love the Lord thy God with all thy heart, and with all thy soul, and with all thy mind. 38 This is the first and great

commandment. 39 And the second is like unto it, Thou shalt love thy neighbour as thyself. 40 On these two commandments hang all the law and the prophets.

The Implications of Brotherhood

The message here is that *first*, we must have Respect for the Brotherhood, *secondly*, that this respect begins first in your own family and Community and *thirdly*, that love for the brothers does not mean that they are all suitable to unite with to pursue spiritual ends. In the final analysis black nationbuilding will be accomplished through spiritual means or it will not be accomplished at all.

The following are some implications of the priority of brotherhood for the local church:

➢ Teach the congregation the value of brotherhood among black people. Most of us believe, due to our mental programming under slave religion, that the mere discussion of such a subject is a sin. We need to see the connection between brotherly love, evangelism and nationbuilding. We cannot have an effective gospel witness if we have not proactively applied gospel principles to our relationships with our black neighbors. We are commanded to love believers, to love our neighbors and to love our enemies. Direct action upon broken relationships *in our families* are the priority which will eventually lead to brotherhood in society at large. Reinforce that brotherhood is a spiritual initiative that is commanded by scripture. It just so happens that brotherhood principles lead to nationbuilding as well. Use skits and drama to illustrate the intergenerational effects of brotherhood upon the family and the Community.

➢ The effort to inculcate the principles of biblical brotherhood and to address the unique problems of black people must begin with youth. The origins of most race-related pathologies begin in youth and are often never addressed until adulthood when they are so severe that they require professional attention. America is committed to the destruction of black boys. The entire apparatus of oppression is directed at them beginning in elementary school. Nonwhite schools begin with significantly less funding.[171] Special education classes remove them from the mainstream of learning and track them for the rest of their educational lives. Zero tolerance policies exist to place them into the criminal system as early as possible.[172] Instructional policies prevent the accurate portrayal of American history and black history to them. This same instructional policy fails to prepare them for the standardized testing through which the few blacks who will be allowed the opportunity to advance academically is provided. By the fourth grade, [173] black boys have become angry, hating school, and beginning to hate themselves as well. The church must teach extended *families* to take responsibility to fill up these deficiencies. The church itself can provide male teachers for boys that focus upon the accurate portrayal of black manhood, the extensive black presence in scripture and direct efforts to support biblical self-esteem in them.

➢ Actively develop opportunities for men to work together on projects or ministries that create the chance for them to establish relationships with other men. Men do not make friends as easily as do women.

➢ Teach semester long [10-12 week] classes which deal with the special problems of the blacks in marriage, in the workplace, in getting employment, in re-entry after serving time in prison. Accurate doctrine must be followed up with applications that address the real struggles of people. Classes should be Bible based and include real resources that will help in the situation covered.

➢ Attention must also be paid to the next generation of Pastors and teachers. Most churches have no planned succession of ministry leaders or elders. There needs to be early identification and training of young people with leadership, shepherding and teaching gifts for training and development. Society has already developed plans to place these black boys and girls into the criminal justice system, the church must catch them beforehand and make leaders of them.

➢ You cannot teach brotherhood to men who are not there. Look at your church bulletin. If your *order of service* is identical to that of 100 years ago, it's time to make some changes. Most church services are unnecessarily long: filled with activities to make people feel important rather than ministry: Moaning deacons, flamboyant women making announcements, hour-long choir concerts and other traditions subtract time from preaching and drive men away from your church.

Excellence

> Excellent: Excelling; surpassing others in some good quality or the sum of qualities; of great worth; eminent, in a good sense; superior [Webster's Dictionary 1913].

> Ruth 3:11 (NASB95)
> 11 "Now, my daughter, do not fear. I will do for you whatever you ask, for all my people in the city know that you are a woman of excellence.

> Daniel 6:3 (KJV 1900)
> 3 Then this Daniel was preferred above the presidents and princes, because an excellent spirit *was* in him; and the king thought to set him over the whole realm.

> Mark 7:37 (KJV 1900)
> 37 And were beyond measure astonished, saying, He hath done all things well: he maketh both the deaf to hear, and the dumb to speak.

God is characterized by excellence. Everything he does or has done is excellent in every way. God is perfect in His Person; therefore, his thoughts, motivation and decisions are all excellent. God is excellent in the formulation and execution of His plan for the created universe. God's creation was excellent in its beginning, until sin was added to it by a creature. Even in our fallen state, God's dealings with every creature in the universe are entirely appropriate and timely. The Lord is excellent.

As a creature formed in the image and likeness of God, man was created with an appreciation for excellence. It is praiseworthy among men that one seeks excellence in all things. Excellence is an attitude that glorifies God because excellence is a feature of holiness. Holiness is full obedience to the divine will in our intent and our actions. If the fallen human conscience can appreciate and strive for excellence, how much more the believer indwelt by the Spirit of God?

From the human perspective, excellence consists of purpose, priority, people, and persistence.

It is difficult to imagine how someone without a *purpose* could be excellent in their lifestyle. Purpose defines why one is committed to excellence. Purpose supplies the motivation for consistent excellence despite obstacles and reversals. The ultimate purpose of the Christian is the glory of God. This purpose works itself out in the spiritual transformation of the believer in sanctification. This sanctification is made manifest in one's dealings with people and institutions. Excellence must be sought in each echelon of purpose.[clxvii]

Once purpose is established and committed to, *priority* is the next most important element of excellence. One cannot be committed to doing everything yet still achieve excellence in the necessary things. Priority determines what must be done and in what order. Priority also determines what will *not* be done. This is as important as what will be prioritized. It is the ability to say no to low priority things that will enable or prevent excellence.

There is no excellence without other *people*. The Church is a body of believers spread across history and geography, from all walks of life, who work together to achieve spiritual ends.[174] Marriage involves two people who are equally important to its success. The family consists of many people who need to work together to secure a future for the next generation. Similarly, a Community is numerous people performing different functions that are essential to the well-being of all. There can be no excellence where people are not treated as important, where they are not loved and ministered to. Jesus emphasized love as a critical priority of the Church.

> John 13:35 (KJV 1900)
> [35] By this shall all *men* know that ye are my disciples, if ye have love one to another.

> 1 John 3:10 (KJV 1900)
> [10] In this the children of God are manifest, and the children of the devil: whosoever doeth not righteousness is not of God, neither he that loveth not his brother.

There can be no excellence without *persistence*. In the devil's world, godly excellence will be resisted. Life is already hard in this fallen world, the attempt to pursue excellence for the sake of the kingdom of God will encounter obstacles, reversals, and outright failure. One who would be excellent must possess the maturity to persist, the purpose that inspires persistence and the

---

[clxvii] Echelon of purpose: Purpose is executed through a *Plan*. A plan describes the steps to be taken and the schedule necessary for the purpose to be achieved. A person purposing to become a bible teacher [Ezra 7.10] must first commit himself achieve Christian maturity, he must become thoroughly educated in the Scriptures, and he must learn how to teach and to make disciples. After this, he must go wherever God sends him to teach. Each stage of this plan to achieve a purpose must be carried out with excellence.

priorities that will make persistence pay off.

> Romans 5:3–5 (KJV 1900)
> ³ And not only *so*, but we glory in tribulations also: knowing that tribulation worketh patience; ⁴ And patience, experience; and experience, hope: ⁵ And hope maketh not ashamed; because the love of God is shed abroad in our hearts by the Holy Ghost which is given unto us.

The local church must develop a value for consistent excellence in everything it decides to undertake. This is a spiritual value that has many practical benefits. We will give intense life to our culture by a commitment to excellence in all things.

Excellence should begin in the local church. The place where God is honored should reflect this characteristic both as a requirement for acceptable worship and as an example to the world. Neither wealth nor influence is required for excellence in ministry. Excellence begins in the pulpit with depth and precision in the preaching and teaching of the Word. Excellence in church administration and other ministries provides a model for the entire Community.

Excellence should be sought in the home, in the orderly function of family life and the physical upkeep of the home. Excellence should extend to the workplace and the classroom. Finally, excellence should be seen in the attitude and performance of the black Community in its civic responsibility. There is an excellence with respect to things and an excellence respecting ideals, the first requires effort and the second moral courage. We must cultivate both.

Black people should support excellence with our dollars and our time. We should vote for excellence when we choose a church, a school, a supermarket, or a barber. We should not fund racial prejudice by sending our dollars to discriminatory businesses, political candidates, or institutions.

Above all, we should not support false teaching or spiritually unsound churches and Christian organizations. Accurate Bible teaching is the most critical field of excellence because of its ramifications upon time and eternity. It is black support for false doctrine [and not whites or racism] that is the single greatest contributor to our spiritual slavery, because our deliverance is based upon our response to *accurate* biblical teaching [Jeremiah 23.28; Matthew 4.4]. Spiritual slavery always precedes physical slavery. Prolonged false biblical teaching always leads to divine judgment and the collapse of civilization. It makes no sense to provide funds and support for the very churches and ministers who are agents of our destruction. False religion is anti-holiness and anti-excellence because it teaches that we do not have to do what God has commanded us to do.

Just as we must create a value for excellence, we must also ensure that mediocrity is devalued and frowned upon. Today, many of our children value crime, sexual promiscuity, and an "you only live once" [YOLO] mentality because these are the cultural messages specially prepared for black youth by the entertainment industry. We must begin, with our young children, to eliminate access to these messages (you will have to plan for instructional time with your kids) and in their place provide culturally enriched entertainment and media which promotes achievement, genius, courage, leadership and yes, excellence.

Some of the practical implications of Excellence in the local church are as follows:

> The appearance and function of the local church should reflect excellence. The upkeep of the church is a direct reflection upon the gospel and its power. If the gospel is incapable of producing a Congregation capable of funding and maintaining their own place of worship, how then can it claim the spiritual power to save souls?

> The church must also be engaged in doing the right things and doing them well. The church cannot do everything, but what it does decide to do must be conceived and carried out with excellence. Many churches are trying to do too many things and fail to produce consistent excellence in anything.

> Excellent organization results in the ability to be on time and get things done. Job descriptions, departmental mission statements, training for specific ministry jobs within the church all promote excellence by focusing responsibility and eliminating confusion.

> Excellence is reflected in who is selected for leadership positions in the church. Many churches have been seriously damaged by spiritually unqualified, immature, and untrained appointments to leadership. The attempt to do too much results in the premature placement of people into positions of responsibility.

> Excellence is reflected in the orderly upkeep of the financial affairs of the church along with financial accountability to the membership. How often has the witness of the local church been damaged by financial irresponsibility?

> ➤ Promote excellence in our children by systematic Bible teaching and training [discipleship]. Racial programming has already begun destroying the self-esteem in black boys by the fourth grade. Christian children often experience no discipleship at all, resulting in a total lack of spiritual tools to address the pressures of sex, drugs, peer pressure and racism.

Ownership vs. Debt

Proverbs 22:7 [NASB]
The rich rules over the poor, And the borrower becomes the lender's slave.

> "Juneteenth — Emancipation Day, 1865 — was supposed to start a new era of black wealth creation. After 12 generations of being subject to slavery's institutionalized theft, 4 million African Americans were now free to earn incomes and degrees, hold property, weather hard times and pass down wealth to the next generation. They would surely scramble up the economic ladder, if not in one generation then in a few. Eight generations later, the racial wealth gap is both yawning and growing. The typical black family has just 1/10th the wealth of the typical white one.
>
> In 1863, black Americans owned one-half of 1 percent of the national wealth. Today it's just over 1.5 percent for roughly the same percentage of the overall population."[175]

> "Looking ahead, the Federal Reserve estimates the wealth gap can be eliminated if the racial income gap is closed (Figure 83). This effect would eventually negate the influences of unequal bequests, initial conditions, and unequal returns. The downside is that this might take roughly 200 years to achieve."[176]

In view of these things, we must examine our attitudes and behaviors concerning income and wealth.

It is a secret to no one that we live in a society that is driven by consumption. We are driven by American culture to find fulfillment and meaning in buying and possessing things. In fact, we are willing to live beyond our means and incur debt to live up to a vision of American life that is created by people who want to sell us things. Very few Americans truly benefit from this system of hyper-consumerism. For blacks, it is simply suicide. Obsessive consumption[177] is destructive for blacks not only because it is a form of false religion, but also because the death-dealing effects of debt.

The key function of the family is to prepare the next generation for meaningful participation in society. The family transfers values, aptitudes, skills, and material wealth to the next generation. Peoples or cultures that do this well are strengthened, those that do it poorly become the slaves of those that do it well. If we spend more than we earn we leave our children with no material inheritance and a questionable set of values regarding money and wealth. Consequently, instead of each generation building upon the sacrifices and achievements of the last, each generation must start from scratch, rolling the boulder of systematic discrimination up the same hill as their parents. This is self-enslavement.

Income vs. Wealth

No matter how lucrative your job is, you cannot pass it on to your children. You can pass on wealth such as real estate or stocks or even cash. You cannot pass your good job on to your children. Your job represents income, not wealth. The only way that job can help your children in the future is if you save, invest, or provide them with an education.

You do not have to be rich to help your children; you do have to be disciplined. Our history is filled with stories of cleaning women and janitors that put their children through college or left them a small inheritance. But these past generations knew how to limit their consumption and save their money over many years.

Blacks Investing in Slave Theology

Slave theology is based upon the concept of racial value. Race, an artificial construct, is used to invest some groups with artificial worth and real entitlement based on that imagined value. The same system of race deprives other groups of value and entitlement. This system is enforced by rules built into every institution of society. Racial value is justified by academia, media, and the church, and the principles of racial superiority and inferiority are made a part of education, entertainment, and our worship, all *while the existence of the entire system is denied.*

The point of slavery was to use enslaved persons to create wealth and well-being for white people and their *descendants*. For slavery to succeed in this purpose, slaves and their children must be prevented from *ever* sharing in the benefits of their centuries of labor. Thus, slavery is not just an institution of the dim American past. The compounded interest of generations of stolen labor and ingenuity must continue to be enjoyed by the *descendants* of the slave system and those whom they elect to include by their largesse.

228

"Black and Hispanic families continue to trail white and Asian families in accumulating wealth. Issues like lack of inheritances and barriers to entry, including to income and access to credit, appear to be working against the ability of Black and Hispanic families to amass wealth required for acquiring assets for personal financial security and community investment. Data from the Federal Reserve's 2010 and 2013 Surveys of Consumer Finances, while dated, reveal that inherited wealth significantly bolsters familial wealth, particularly for white families (Figure 77). Black families are less likely to receive (10.6 percent) or expect an inheritance (5.9 percent) relative to white families (22.9 percent and 18.8 percent). Meanwhile, easier avenues toward the accumulation of generational wealth, like home ownership and retirement benefits, are littered with obstacles for minorities, especially Black and Hispanic families."[178]

These facts help explain the consistent lack of economic progress made in the accumulation of black *wealth* relative to whites in the United States. Many explain this imbalance by citing an imaginary inability by black people to compete in the American system. Since it is argued that no system of institutional injustice exists, racial inferiority, called different things by different people, must be the answer to the problem of racial inequalities in income and wealth. The argument of black inferiority has been very handy. It is, on the one hand, used to *explain* inequality, but on the other to *promote* inequality at different points in history by preventing blacks from joining the military, from participating in professional athletics as players and as coaches, from joining labor unions, from having managerial and executive positions in the business world and from receiving deserved wage increases and promotions in even the most menial of jobs.

Because the existence of this race-based system is vociferously denied in schools, the workplace, and the pulpit, its *effects* upon black people can be relabeled as evidence of racial inferiority. These effects, however, are very real. The psychological and social effects of racism do not promote the entrepreneurial spirit but perpetuate inequality.

The Psychosocial Effects of White Racism[179]

1. Chronic Anger
2. Chronic Frustration
3. Chronic Conflict and Ambivalence
4. Displaced Aggression
5. Internalization of Racist Attitudes
6. Chronic Sense of Threat, Vulnerability and Anxiety
7. Ego Defense Orientation
8. Compensatory Striving
9. Relative Powerlessness and Fatalism

10. Consumer Orientedness (sic)
11. Restricted and Conflicting Affectionate Relations
12. Stress

Residential segregation enables a dual system of educational instruction that produces undereducated children. Residential and educational segregation produce a workforce suitable for unskilled labor and underemployment. Those who escape this future and achieve are faced with persistent workplace discrimination[180] which limits black income and wealth. All of this leads to economic insecurity and the accumulation of debt.

The real psychosocial effects of intergenerational racism influence the willingness of some black people to participate in the economy as we should. For those who have been able to overcome many of these symptoms, the systemic safeguards against the accumulation of significant black wealth creation kick in to limit success. We are reluctant to start businesses and we are reluctant to invest in or purchase from blacks that do start businesses.[clxviii] We become borrowers rather than lenders, *we pay interest rather than collect it.* We are focused upon income rather than wealth because of an incorrect self-concept and world view. Therefore, black income is not producing black wealth, because of the cumulative effects of oppression upon every aspect of black life.

> "Nationwide protests have cast a spotlight on racism and inequality in the United States. Now a major bank [Citigroup-rw] has put a price tag on how much the economy has lost as a result of discrimination against African Americans: $16 trillion.
>
> **"Since 2000**, U.S. gross domestic product lost that much as a result of discriminatory practices in a range of areas, including in education and access to business loans, according to a new study by Citigroup. It's not an insignificant number: By comparison, U.S. GDP totaled $19.5 trillion last year. [emphasis added]
>
> "…Specifically, the study came up with $16 trillion in lost GDP by noting four key racial gaps between African Americans and whites:
>
> ➤ $13 trillion lost in potential business revenue because of discriminatory lending to African American entrepreneurs, with an estimated 6.1 million jobs not generated as a result.

[clxviii] See Psychosocial Effects #5, 9, 10 above.

➢ $2.7 trillion in income lost because of disparities in wages suffered by African Americans.

➢ $218 billion lost over the past two decades because of discrimination in providing housing credit.

➢ And $90 billion to $113 billion in lifetime income lost from discrimination in accessing higher education."[181]

These are enormous numbers. The same study indicates that closing the racial inequality gaps just for black people would result in a $5 trillion-dollar savings *over a five-year period*, contributing "an average add of 0.35 percentage point to U.S. GDP [Gross Domestic Product] growth per year." To understand how much a .35 percent is, see the following chart created from World Bank data.

Year	Annual Per Capita GDP Growth %[182]
2016	.09
2017	1.6
2018	2.4
2019	1.8
2020	- 4.3

Figure 23: Annual Per Capita GDP 2016-2020. World Bank

The economic impacts of racial discrimination against blacks arrived at by Citigroup are not wild guesses. Their 100-page report is detailed and heavily documented. These are the effects of *current* discrimination, not from the dim past. It is unlikely, however, that these numbers are a surprise to the highest levels of American policymaking. *What possible motivation would be required to delay a genuine effort to close these gaps? Is it possible that the benefits of racial discrimination are worth it at any cost?*

Consequently, black income is not leading to black wealth, but it is being used to enrich every other nationality in America except blacks. White people do not feel guilty about spending their money in the Communities where they and their families reside (nor should they). Nor do they feel it their Christian responsibility to go to the black Community to spend their hard-earned dollars (nor should they). Their earnings go into businesses in their Communities. That money (most of it) becomes wealth that is invested in that Community creating jobs and opportunity for their children. It also provides taxation for public services and schools. The white Community has the benefit of their own dollars and of the majority of black dollars as well.

Home Ownership and Entrepreneurship

The single non-negotiable requirement for nationbuilding is evangelism/discipleship via the Congregations in the local churches. Only this will allow the Community to be built upon a strong substructure, which is properly functioning marriages and families. Schemes of Community development that attempt to build economic growth upon broken families are intrinsically inefficient. Only through strong families will the Community possess the health necessary for successful investment to be created and sustained. Only through strong generations of young people will the political power be developed to protect black investment in the Community. Given these caveats, two basic means of Community investment are entrepreneurship and home ownership. Blacks have the right to live wherever they want; we have paid more than most for that right. However, wherever we live, we must understand that in a largely segregated country, wealth tends to be segregated as well. We must be conscious of how we use our limited dollars.

So, we can invest in the Community through home ownership and by entrepreneurship. As Americans, we have the right to own the place where we live. We can own the land, the buildings, the businesses and banks and private schools. We can manufacture, distribute, and retail products. We can develop and sell services. Ownership of homes and businesses moves us beyond income to wealth. You can own your own business, or you can support other businesses by buying their products and services.

Ownership leads to political strength. Political leaders are hired and fired by those who own the businesses and the land. Political strength means that you no longer must accept a debilitating educational curriculum for your children. You do not have to tolerate police that routinely kill our men, or dope houses that never seem to go away.

Implications for the Local Church

Some practical suggestions to the local church to promote the shift from debt to ownership follow:

➢ Biblical instruction about money and its proper use should be a part of every annual teaching and preaching cycle. Young people should especially receive this instruction.

➢ The church should practice and model the policy of purchasing from Community businesses. The Congregation should be made aware of Community businesses with excellent commercial practices, products, or services.

---

[109] Woodward, C. Vann. American Counterpoint: Slavery and Racism in the North/South Dialogue (New York, Oxford Press,1971). 88. Cited in Anderson, Dr Claud. PowerNomics: The National Plan to Empower Black America. 1st edition. Bethesda, MD: Powernomics Corp of Amer, 2001. 16.

[110] https://govtrackus.s3.amazonaws.com/legislink/pdf/stat/1/STATUTE-1-Pg103.pdf

[111] 67 An Act for the Liberties of the People, Taken from Browne, *Archives of Maryland: Vol. i*, 41. 1638

"Be it Enacted By the Lord Proprietarie of this Province of and with the advice and approbation of the ffreemen of the same that all the Inhabitants of this Province being Christians (Slaves excepted) Shall have and enjoy all such rights liberties immunities priviledges and free customs within this Province as any naturall born subject of England hath or ought to have or enjoy in the Realm of England by force or vertue of the common law or Statute Law of England (saveing in such Cases as the same are or may be altered or changed by the Laws and ordinances of this Province)

"And Shall not be imprisoned nor disseissed or dispossessed of their freehold goods or Chattels or be out Lawed Exiled or otherwise destroyed fore judged or punished then according to the Laws of this province saveing to the Lord proprietarie and his heirs all his rights and prerogatives by reason of his domination and Seigniory over this Province and the people of the same. This Act to Continue till the end of the next Generall Assembly."

"1638: Act for the Liberties of the People (Maryland) | Online Library of Liberty." Accessed 01-06-2023. https://oll.libertyfund.org/page/1638-act-for-the-liberties-of-the-people-maryland.

[112] "Christianity became an intolerable doctrine unless translated into Southern Christianity, and in the 1840's, Southern Baptist and Methodist congregations seceded from the national groups and formed Southern denominations whose ministers and teachings would not question the rightness of the Southern course and would call God and the Bible to the defense of human slavery." Winthorp D. Jordan, White Over Black: American Attitudes Toward the Negro 1550-1812. New York: W.W. Norton and Company, 1968. 18. Cited in Anderson, Dr Claud. PowerNomics: The National Plan to Empower Black America. 1st edition. Bethesda, MD: Powernomics Corp of Amer, 2001. 74.

[113] MacArthur, John. History of the New World, 07-01-2001
https://www.gty.org/library/sermons-library/90-266/history-in-the-new-world Accessed 12-03-2022.

Also: MacArthur, John. *If Adam and Eve were the first two people, how did we get so many races?* Sept 26, 2010. Accessed 12-3-2022. https://www.gty.org/library/questions/QA52/if-adam-and-eve-were-the-first-two-people-how-did-we-get-so-many-races

Also: MacArthur, John. Bible Questions and Answers, Part 15, April 16, 1980. Accessed 12-03-2022. https://www.gty.org/library/sermons-library/1301-M/bible-questions-and-answers-part-15

And: MacArthur, John. Submission in the Workplace, Part 2. April 30,1989. Accessed 12-03-2022. https://www.gty.org/library/sermons-library/60-27/submission-in-the-workplace-part-2

This last citation demands a comment. The issue of slavery is addressed succinctly in Appendix 1 "The Doctrine of Oppression" in this work and will be completely addressed in the forthcoming book "Black Nations in Scripture" [late 2023].

1. Christianity undoubtedly freed slaves. In the United States, slaveholders that were genuinely saved freed their slaves as a testimony to the new birth. Christianity was also a key factor in the abolition of American slavery.

    ABSTRACTS OF SUSSEX COUNTY VIRGINIA MANUMISSIONS 1782-1818
    SUSSEX COUNTY DEED BOOKS 1782-1818
    Sussex County Deed Book F 1779-1786
    LVA reel #3

    (excerpt from the above)

    "p. 125 - 14 Dec 87 - Henry Moss - of Sussex after full and deliberate consideration and agreeable to our Bill of Rights am fully persuaded that freedom is the natural right of all man kind and that no law, moral, or decree hath given me a just right or property in the person of any of my fellow creatures and desireous to fulfill the injunction of our Lord and Saviour Jesus Christ by doing to all others as etc - sets free from bondage the following Negroes vizt. Peter [1 Jan 88], Ephraim [1 Jan 97], Phill [Jan 98], Becky [1 Jan 88], Dilcy [1 Jan 93], Edmund [1 Jan 07], and Salley [1 Jan 12]- desire to have their care and guardianship and instruction till they arrive at full - rec 20 Dec 87

    "p. 124 - 19 Sept 87 - William Ellis - of Sussex after mature deliberation and agreeable to our Bill of Rights am persuaded that no law, moral, or divine gives me a right to the life and property of my fellow creatures and to fulfill the injunction of our Lord and Saviour, Jesus Christ, by doing to all men as I would be done unto - sets free the following Negroes to wit Thomas (26 yrs), Sarah (23 yrs), Fanny (20 yrs) [10 Aug 88], Jane (16 yrs) [1 Jan 92], Philip (14 yrs) [3 Jan 94], Randolph (6 yrs) [11 March 02], Allen (4 yrs) [14 Feb 04], Alexander (2 yrs 3 mo) [22 May 06], Charlotte (2 yrs 1 mo) [14 Nov 06], Edmund (1 yr 10 mo) [17 Feb 07], Anacha (6 mo) [28 June 08] - request and desire to have the care and instruction of them till they arrive at full age – rec 19 Dec 87."

    See also: "Duck Creek Manumissions, 1774-1792..." Accessed 03-03-2023. https://digitalcollections.tricolib.brynmawr.edu/object/sc9995#page/1/mode/1up.

2. Christianity did not eliminate slavery in the new world, but neither did *true* Christianity *make* slaves. This is especially true in the case of the version of slavery practiced in Europe, America, and the Caribbean. Christ did not have to abolish slavery because he abolished *the theft of labor* ["menstealing"[G405]: Exodus 21.16; 1 Timothy 1.9-10] and *rape* [Deuteronomy 22.25-29], two legs of the three-legged stool that was American slavery, the third being other categories of violence and murder. These are the conditions that some seek to sanctify by wrongly conflating American slavery with biblical slavery. See Appendix 1- Section: Oppression and Slavery.

3. Jesus and the apostles were not moral crusaders. If they did not stamp out temple prostitution, abortion, homosexuality, and other abominations common in their day, should we now approve of these sins because of their silence? Jesus condemned sexual sin and idolatry and, in these prohibitions, presented the principle that forbad Christian involvement in institutions based upon these sins. The "argument from silence" is a logical fallacy of which the issue of slavery is a chief example.

[114] "White Christians also stand out as a group on questions related to structural injustice and perceived barriers to black social mobility. More than three-quarters of white Christians overall— including 83 percent of white evangelicals, 75 percent of white Catholics, and 71 percent of white mainline Protestants— believe that racial minorities use racism as an excuse for economic inequalities more than they should."

"Perhaps most fundamentally (see figure 5.2), more than six in ten white Christians overall *disagree* with this basic statement: "Generations of slavery and discrimination have created conditions that make it difficult for blacks to work their way out of the lower class." Sixty-seven percent of white evangelical Protestants, 62 percent of white mainline Protestants, and 57 percent of white Catholics disagree with this sentiment, compared with only 40 percent of religiously unaffiliated whites." [**emphasis added**]

"The models reveal that, in the United States today, the more racist attitudes a person holds, the more likely he or she is to identify as a white Christian. And when we control for a range of other attributes, this relationship exists not just among white evangelical Protestants but also equally strongly among white mainline Protestants and white Catholics. 24 And there is also a telling corollary: this relationship with racist attitudes has little hold among white religiously unaffiliated Americans; if anything, the relationship is negative." [emphasis added]

Jones, Robert P. White Too Long: The Legacy of White Supremacy in American Christianity (161-162; 175-176). Simon & Schuster. Kindle Edition.

[115] Citi GPS: Global Perspectives and Solutions, Accessed 01-06-2023.

[116] "As early as 1715, it was thought, and correctly, that an exclusively Negro church might become a center for conspiracy…But after the Vesey Plot in Charleston South Carolina in 1822 and the Nat Turner Rebellion in Southampton county Virginia in 1831, the assembling of purely Negro congregations and the use of Negro preachers were forbidden. "The Christianizing influence had seemingly been too effective. Negro preachers had 'distorted' the Bible into a guide or freedom and the safety of the institution was seen to hinge upon the purging of such 'heresy' from the minds of slaves. The legislature [Virginia] decreed that 'no slave, free negro, or mulatto shall preach or hold any meeting for religious purposes either day or night."

"So, what appears on the surface to be "the very best tradition of the old South" proves upon examination to be a diplomacy by which the Christian could ease his conscience by giving the Negro the gospel while at the same time preventing an insurrection against slavery. But it could hardly be expected that a church, preaching a gospel that declared the Negro essentially inferior to the white man and slavery a divine decree and using a Biblical basis for such arguments, would at the same time welcome and entertain the Negro even on the basis of spiritual equality."

Writers Program of the Work Projects Administration, Hastings House, New York, 1940, 105 cited in Haselden, Kyle. The Racial Problem in Christian Perspective. New York, Harper Bros, 1959. 26-27.

[117] Winthorp D. Jordan, White Over Black: American Attitudes Toward the Negro 1550-1812. New York: W.W. Norton and Company, 1968. 18. cited in Anderson, Dr Claud. PowerNomics: The National Plan to Empower Black America. 1st edition. Bethesda, MD: Powernomics Corp of Amer, 2001.74.

[118] MacArthur, John. Submission in the Workplace, Part 2. April 30, 1989. Accessed 12-03-2022. https://www.gty.org/library/sermons-library/60-27/submission-in-the-workplace-part-2

[119] The Bible Argument On Slavery. By Charles Hodge, D.D., of Princeton, N. J. Cited in Elliott, E.N. LL.D. Cotton is King and Pro-Slavery Arguments, Comprising the Writings of Hammond, Harper, Christy, Stringfellow, Hodge, Bledsoe, And Cartwright, on this Important Subject. Augusta, Ga: Pritchard, Abbott & Loomis. 1860.

[120] *"The decree has two aspects.* (1) The directive will of God. There are some things in which God is the author; He actively brings about the events. He creates (Isa. 45:18); He controls the universe (Dan. 4:35); He establishes kings and governments (Dan. 2:21); He elects people to be saved (Eph. 1:4).(2) The permissive will of God. Even though God has determined all things, He may actively bring them about Himself, or He may bring them about through secondary causes. Sinful acts, for example, do not frustrate the plan of God, but neither is God the author of them. They are within the scope of God's decree and are part of His eternal plan and purpose, but man is nonetheless responsible for sinful acts.

Enns, Paul P. *The Moody Handbook of Theology*. Chicago, IL: Moody Press, 1989. Logos Edition. 205.

[121] 1 Timothy 1:9–10 (KJV 1900)
[9] Knowing this, that the law is not made for a righteous man, but for the lawless and disobedient, for the ungodly and for sinners, for unholy and profane, for murderers of fathers and murderers of mothers, for manslayers, [10] For whoremongers, for them that defile themselves with mankind, for menstealers, for liars, for perjured persons, and if there be any other thing that is contrary to sound doctrine; [emphasis added]

Menstealer 435 [G405 in Strong-rw] ἀνδραποδιστής (*andrapodistēs*), οὗ (*ou*), ὁ (*ho*): n.masc.; ≡ Str 405—LN 57.187 **slave dealer**, trader in human beings, including kidnapping and then selling (1Ti 1:10+)

Exodus 21:16 (KJV 1900)
16 And he that stealeth a man, and selleth him, or if he be found in his hand, he shall surely be put to death.

Exodus 21:26–27 (KJV 1900)
26 And if a man smite the eye of his servant, or the eye of his maid, that it perish; he shall let him go free for his eye's sake. 27 And if he smite out his manservant's tooth, or his maidservant's tooth; he shall let him go free for his tooth's sake. [This applies to a Gentile slave-the Jewish slave was not to be beaten at all but was to be treated as a hired laborer Leviticus 25.39-40.]

Deuteronomy 21:10–14 (KJV 1900)
10 When thou goest forth to war against thine enemies, and the LORD thy God hath delivered them into thine hands, and thou hast taken them captive, 11 And seest among the captives a beautiful woman, and hast a desire unto her, that thou wouldest have her to thy wife; 12 Then thou shalt bring her home to thine house; and she shall shave her head, and pare her nails; 13 And she shall put the raiment of her captivity from off her, and shall remain in thine house, and bewail her father and her mother a full month: and after that thou shalt go in unto her, and be her husband, and she shall be thy wife. 14 And it shall be, if thou have no delight in her, then thou shalt let her go whither she will; but thou shalt not sell her at all for money, thou shalt not make merchandise of her, because thou hast humbled her.

[122] "Thirteenth Amendment Section 1
Neither slavery nor involuntary servitude, except as a punishment for crime whereof the party shall have been duly convicted, shall exist within the United States, or any place subject to their jurisdiction."

"U.S. Constitution - Thirteenth Amendment | Resources | Constitution Annotated | Congress.Gov | Library of Congress." Accessed 01-08-2023. https://constitution.congress.gov/constitution/amendment-13/.

The City Sun July 18-24, 1990

236

"Within five years after the Civil War, the Black percentage of the prison population went from close to zero percent to 33 percent. Then as now, the Black prison population performed an economic and political function for the benefit of Whites."

Cox, Clinton. Racism: The Hole in America's Heart. Cited in Wilson, Amos N. Black on Black Violence. 11.

Regarding the "Black Codes" [There are no *new* racial strategies, only recycled ones from the American past. This is one reason why accurate teaching regarding history is being forbidden by law. rw]

"White planters in these states denied Black people the chance to rent or buy land and paid them a pittance. The 1865 ratification of the 13th Amendment prohibited slavery and servitude in all circumstances "except as a punishment for crime." This loophole resulted in Southern states passing the black codes to criminalize activities that would make it easy to imprison African Americans, and effectively force them into servitude once more.

"First enacted in 1865 in states such as South Carolina and Mississippi, the black codes varied slightly from place to place but were generally very similar. They prohibited "loitering, vagrancy," Claybrook says. "The idea was that if you're going to be free, you should be working. If you had three or four Black people standing around talking, they were actually vagrant and could be convicted of a crime and sent to jail."" Accessed 01-07-2023 https://www.history.com/news/black-codes-reconstruction-slavery

Also: Legal Defense Fund. "Why Slavery Is Still Legal in America – And How Voters Can Take Action." Simeon Spencer. Accessed 12-03-2022. https://www.naacpldf.org/13th-amendment-emancipation/.

[123] Alexander, Michelle. The New Jim Crow. 55-58.

[124] "Black students are even more disproportionately affected. They made up nearly half of all arrests at elementary schools during the 2017-2018 school year, CBS News' analysis showed. But they accounted for just 15% of the student population in those schools."

"Handcuffs in Hallways: Hundreds of Elementary Students Arrested at U.S. Schools." Accessed 12-03-2022. https://www.cbsnews.com/news/hundreds-of-elementary-students-arrested-at-us-schools/.

[125] "Incarceration can lead to the loss of several important rights, as well as a person's physical freedom. Inmates lose their right to vote, their right to privacy, and even some of their First Amendment rights. Over the years, the Supreme Court has struggled to arrive at a consistent standard for the restriction of free speech in prisons, with some questions still unanswered today."

Free Speech Rights of Prisoners By FindLaw Staff | Reviewed by Laura Temme, Esq. | Last updated July 19, 2022. Accessed 01-10-2023. https://constitution.findlaw.com/amendment1/free-speech-rights-of-prisoners.html.

[126] "Among male prisoners in 2016, 39.0 percent were white, 41.3 percent were black, 16.6 percent were Latino, 1.4 percent were Native American, 0.6 percent were Asian, and 0.2 percent were Native Hawaiian or Other Pacific Islander.108F 109"

Collateral Consequences: The Crossroads of Punishment, Redemption, and the Effects on Communities. Briefing Before The United States Commission on Civil Rights. Held in Washington, DC. Briefing Report June 2019. Accessed 01-10-2023. https://www.usccr.gov/files/pubs/2019/06-13-Collateral-Consequences.pdf

[127] New American Standard Bible: 1995 Update. La Habra, CA: The Lockman Foundation, 1995.

[128] "Residential integration and segregation studies continually show that the degree of segregation between blacks and non-blacks is far greater than between any other two racial groups in the United

States.23 Further, outside the South, the greater the percentage of African Americans in an area, the greater the level of segregation.24 In other words, because limited contact with African Americans is preferred by most other Americans,25 increasingly higher levels of segregation are needed as the proportion of African Americans increases. What is more, unlike other groups, whose level of segregation declines with increased socioeconomic status, no strong pattern emerges for African Americans.26 Segregation is not merely separation but, in the contemporary United States, is hierarchical. Residential segregation by race, researchers show us, isolates African Americans, and concentrates poverty and social problems in their neighborhoods. This is more evidence of a black-white racialized society." [emphasis added]

Emerson, Michael O., and Christian Smith. Divided by Faith: Evangelical Religion and the Problem of Race in America. Kindle Edition. 12.

[129] "The CIA admitted in 1998 that guerilla armies it actively supported in Nicaragua were smuggling illegal drugs into the United States-drugs that were making their way into the streets of inner city black neighborhoods in the form of crack cocaine. The CIA also admitted that, in the midst of the War on Drugs, it blocked law enforcement efforts to investigate illegal drug networks that were helping to fund its covert war in Nicaragua."

Michelle Alexander, The New Jim Crow, 6.

[130] "The time I spent investigating the allegations of the "Dark Alliance" series led me to the undeniable conclusion that the CIA, DEA, DIA and FBI knew about drug trafficking in South Central Los Angeles. They were either part of the trafficking or turned a blind eye to it, in an effort to fund the Contra war."

Cong. Maxine Waters, (Foreward) Op. Cit., Webb, Gary. Dark Alliance pg. x, 14, 189-190

Also: "ATLANTA - — Wang Jun, who sipped coffee with President Clinton at the White House, heads a company that had been the subject of a federal sting investigation into its alleged scheme to sell 2,000 AK-47 assault rifles destined for gang members in California."

South Florida Sun-Sentinel Jan 05, 1997 at 12:00 am "Arms Dealer Was Subject of Sting Operation – Sun Sentinel." Accessed 02-02-2023. https://www.sun-sentinel.com/news/fl-xpm-1997-01-05-9701040227-story.html.

Also, "Sting's 18 Months of Cloak and Dagger" Reynolds Holding, Chronicle Legal Affairs Writer. https://www.sfgate.com/crime/article/Sting-s-18-Months-of-Cloak-and-Dagger-2981324.php. Accessed 02-02-2023.

[131] Entman, Robert M., and Andrew Rojecki. The Black Image in the White Mind: Media and Race in America. Repr. Studies in Communication, Media, and Public Opinion. Chicago, Ill.: University of Chicago Press, 2007. xi-xii, 41-44; 46-50, 65-68.

[132] Not only the Civil War, but the insurrection of January 6, 2021, was justified in part on "Christian" principles and Christian symbols were a part of the uprising.

Boorstein, Michelle. "A Horn-Wearing 'Shaman.' A Cowboy Evangelist. For Some, the Capitol Attack Was a Kind of Christian Revolt." Washington Post, July 6, 2021. https://www.washingtonpost.com/religion/2021/07/06/capitol-insurrection-trump-christian-nationalism-shaman/.

[133] "**Annotation:** This report examines the impact that race and stand your ground laws have on justifiable homicide rulings.
Abstract: This study used national data to examine the impact that race and stand your ground laws have on justifiable homicide rulings. The study found that White-on-Black homicides were more likely to be ruled justified (11.4 percent) while Black-on-White homicides were least likely to be ruled justified (1.2 percent). The findings also revealed that for White-on-Black, Black-on-Black, and White-

on-White homicides, the presence of a stand your ground law was associated with a statistically significant increase in the likelihood that these homicides would be ruled justified, while the change in likelihood for Black-on-White homicides was not significant."

"Race, Justifiable Homicide, and Stand Your Ground Laws: Analysis of FBI Supplementary Homicide Report Data | Office of Justice Programs." Accessed April 23, 2023. https://www.ojp.gov/ncjrs/virtual-library/abstracts/race-justifiable-homicide-and-stand-your-grounds-laws-analysis-fbi.

[134] Virginia Weapons Law 1723-Forbade blacks from keeping weapons; Virginia Incitement Law 1848-Provided death penalty for advising slaves to rebel.

Also: Ekwall, Steve. "The Racist Origins of US Gun Control," n.d.
for over thirty cases of laws enacted to keep guns out of the hands of black people.
Accessed 01-08-2023. https://www.sedgwickcounty.org/media/29093/the-racist-origins-of-us-gun-control.pdf

[135] "Constitutional Rights Foundation." Accessed 01-08-2023. https://www.crf-usa.org/brown-v-board-50th-anniversary/southern-black-codes.html.

[136] "England exerted the power of its newly found slavery-based wealth by institution the Navigation Act in the 1760's and other laws and tariffs mandated that the American colonists ship their slave-produced raw products and goods to England for processing, manufacturing and marketing. The colonists then had to purchase back the finished products at higher and inflated prices…The English crown established the first franchising system that built plantations, financed the slaveholders, supplied the slaves, and shipped and processed the slave produced goods. It took a full century for the American colonists to recognize that they were locked int an English monopoly. Once the reality set in, they began calling those monopolies "tyranny." The American colonies rejected England's plans to expropriate the fruits of slave labor and to control the politics of the colonies. The colonists knew from the English history of serfdom that any system that politically subordinates, economically exploits, and socially dominates a group of people is tyrannical because it reduces them to slaves. The colonists did not want to be England's serfs. They preferred to fight and when they did, they ignited and fought the Revolutionary War for their independence."

"…The American colonists immediately drafted the United States Constitution, which imposed on Black people the same government-sponsored tyranny, that the colonists rejected under English rule."
Anderson, Dr. Claud. PowerNomics. 11-12

[137] Ekwall, Steve. "The Racist Origins of US Gun Control," n.d. Accessed 01-09 2023.
https://www.sedgwickcounty.org/media/29093/the-racist-origins-of-us-gun-control.pdf

[138] Parshina-Kottas, Yuliya, Anjali Singhvi, Audra D. S. Burch, Troy Griggs, Mika Gröndahl, Lingdong Huang, Tim Wallace, Jeremy White, and Josh Williams. "What the Tulsa Race Massacre Destroyed." The New York Times, May 24, 2021, sec. U.S.
Accessed 01-11-2023. https://www.nytimes.com/interactive/2021/05/24/us/tulsa-race-massacre.html.

Also: Zinn Education Project. "Aug. 14, 1908: Springfield Massacre."
Accessed 01-10-2023. https://www.zinnedproject.org/news/tdih/springfield-massacre/.

Also: Zinn Education Project. "Jan. 1, 1923: Rosewood Massacre." Accessed 01-10-2023.
https://www.zinnedproject.org/news/tdih/rosewood-massacre/.

And: September 17 2020.
"Remembering Red Summer — Which Textbooks Seem Eager to Forget." Zinn Education Project.
Accessed 01-10-2023. https://www.zinnedproject.org/if-we-knew-our-history/remembering-red-summer/.

[139] Schwartz, Sarah. "Lawmakers Push to Ban '1619 Project' From Schools." *Education Week*, February 3, 2021, sec. Social Studies. https://www.edweek.org/teaching-learning/lawmakers-push-to-ban-1619-project-from-schools/2021/02.

Also: Hartocollis, Anemona, and Eliza Fawcett. "The College Board Strips Down Its A.P. Curriculum for African American Studies." The New York Times, February 1, 2023, sec. U.S. Accessed 02-25-2023.https://www.nytimes.com/2023/02/01/us/college-board-advanced-placement-african-american-studies.html.

[140] Cohen, Jennie. "7 Things You May Not Know About the Sistine Chapel." HISTORY https://www.history.com/news/7-things-you-may-not-know-about-the-sistine-chapel. Accessed January 17, 2023.

[141] The Last Supper, Leonardo DaVinci, Accessed 03-09-2023. https://commons.wikimedia.org/wiki/File:The-Last-Supper-Restored-Da-Vinci_32x16.jpg

[142] Akbar, Na'im. Breaking the Chains of Psychological Slavery. Tallahassee, FL: Mind Productions & Associates, 1996. 55.

[143] "The Statement on Social Justice & the Gospel | For The Sake of Christ & His Church." Affirmation on Culture Accessed 01-17-2023. https://statementonsocialjustice.com.

[144] Akbar, Na'im. *Breaking the Chains of Psychological Slavery*. Tallahassee, FL: Mind Productions & Associates, 1996. 57-58.

Also:

"Results...reveal that there is a tendency for the majority of these children [ages 3-7 rw], in spite of their own skin color, [blacks of light, medium and dark complexions-rw] to prefer the white doll and to negate the black doll."

Racial Identification and Preference in Negro Children, Kenneth B. Clark, Mamie P. Clark, 1947 [The Doll Test] Accessed 03-09-2023. https://i2.cdn.turner.com/cnn/2010/images/05/13/doll.study.1947.pdf

[145] Divided by Faith (p. 12). Oxford University Press. Kindle Edition. Emerson, Michael O., and Christian Smith. *Divided by Faith: Evangelical Religion and the Problem of Race in America*. Oxford: Oxford Univ. Press, 2001.

[146] Jones, Robert P. White Too Long: The Legacy of White Supremacy in American Christianity. New York: Simon and Shuster, 2020. Chapter 5.

[147] Wilson, Amos N. Understanding Black Adolescent Male Violence: Its Prevention and Remediation. 1st ed. AWIS Lecture Series. New York: Afrikan World InfoSystems, 1992. Chapter Three: Black Adolescent Masculinity and Antisocial Behavior.

[148] Ibid., 40. Wilson wrote from the perspective of a non-Christian, but his observation is still largely correct.

[149] Holzer, Harry J. "Why Are Employment Rates so Low among Black Men?" *Brookings* (blog), March 1, 2021. https://www.brookings.edu/research/why-are-employment-rates-so-low-among-black-men/.

[150] Press, Associated. "Women Breaking Through to Top Roles in US Black Churches." VOA, December 12, 2021. https://www.voanews.com/a/women-breaking-through-to-top-roles-in-us-black-churches/6348778.html.

CBN. "50 Millennial Women Preachers Get Real: #MeToo, Social Media-Depression, and Women's Role in the Church," April 18, 2019. https://www2.cbn.com/news/us/50-millennial-women-preachers-get-real-metoo-social-media-depression-and-womens-role-church.

[151] Smith, Richard V. Reeves, Sarah Nzau, and Ember. "The Challenges Facing Black Men – and the Case for Action." *Brookings* (blog), November 19, 2020. https://www.brookings.edu/blog/up-front/2020/11/19/the-challenges-facing-black-men-and-the-case-for-action/.

[152] Martin, Michel. "Slave Bible From The 1800s Omitted Key Passages That Could Incite Rebellion." NPR, December 9, 2018, sec. Religion. https://www.npr.org/2018/12/09/674995075/slave-bible-from-the-1800s-omitted-key-passages-that-could-incite-rebellion.

[153] Kunjufu, Jawanza. Countering the Conspiracy to Destroy Black Boys Vol 2. 1st ed. Chicago: Afro-Am Pub. Co, 1983. Chapter 2.

Also: Busette, Camille. "Defining a Culture of Care for Black Boys." *Brookings* (blog), November 1, 2022. https://www.brookings.edu/blog/how-we-rise/2022/11/01/defining-a-culture-of-care-for-black-boys/.

Also: NPR. "A Black Man in a Dress: No Laughing Matter." *NPR*, August 8, 2006. https://www.npr.org/templates/story/story.php?storyId=5626512.

[154] "If we had to name the most tragic failure of black people historically in the United States, we' have to point to the relations between black males and black females. Out confusion, our negligence in this area is both curious and shocking, because the relations between male and female are the most intimate and basic of all human entanglements and the most crucial for the subjugation of a people...In such a society it was historically the black male who, in the white man's mind, posed the crucial threat to his power and status...However, at the same time they endeavored to emasculate the black male, they sought to defeminize the black female. Her beauty was denied, her femininity and her virtues denigrated, and she was robbed of the chance to nestle comfortably on a pedestal of protected womanhood...She was not to be a woman any more than a black man could be a man."

Hare, Nathan, and Julia Hare. The Endangered Black Family: Coping with the Unisexualization and Coming Extinction of the Black Race. A Black Male/Female Relationships Book, no. 1. San Francisco, CA: Black Think Tank, 1984. 16-17.

[155] Variation in Percentage Currently Separated/Divorced According to Race and Ethnicity, 1940-2018

- Among ever-married women in 1940, about 2% were currently separated/divorced regardless of race/ethnicity, except for Asians (0.9%).
- In 2018, Other and Hispanic ever-married women had similar shares who were separated/divorced, at 24% and 22%, respectively.
- The percentage of Black ever-married women who were separated/divorced diverged from the other groups early in the period, rising to 33% by 2018.
- Asian ever-married women have had the lowest percentage separated/divorced at every decade since 1940, with only 11% currently separated or divorced in 2018. [emphasis added]

Schweizer, V. J. (2020). Divorce: More than a century of change, 1900-2018. Family Profiles, FP-20-22. Bowling Green, OH: National Center for Family & Marriage Research. https://doi.org/10.25035/ncfmr/fp-20-22.

[156] Walker, Richard G. Antichrist and the New World Order. A Richer Walk Ministries, 2022. 293-300.

[157] Holzer, Harry J. "Why Are Employment Rates so Low among Black Men?" Brookings (blog), March 1, 2021. Accessed 12-18-2022. https://www.brookings.edu/research/why-are-employment-rates-so-low-among-black-men/.

[158] American Sociological Association. "Women More Likely Than Men to Initiate Divorces, But Not Non-Marital Breakups," September 18, 2015. Accessed 03-21-2023. https://www.asanet.org/women-more-likely-men-initiate-divorces-not-non-marital-breakups/

"Black women were the only group that had a higher divorce rate than marriage rate, with nearly 31 divorces per 1,000 married women aged 15 and older and only 17.3 marriages per 1,000 unmarried women." Schweizer, V. (2019). Marriage to divorce ratio in the U.S.: Demographic variation, 2018. Family Profiles, FP-19-27. Bowling Green, OH: National Center for Family & Marriage Research. Accessed 11-26-2022. https://doi.org/10.25035/ncfmr/fp-19-27.

[159] "Female teachers, especially white ones, are integral in the development of black boys in America. Since the Brown vs. Topeka case of 1954, desegregation has more than ever brought Black boys into contact with White females. In light of this, it can be noted that 83 percent of all elementary teachers are females. Black children constitute 17 percent of all students but comprise 41 percent of all special education placements, primarily as Educable Mentally Retarded [EMR] and Behavioral Disorder [BD]. Of Black children placed in special education 85% are boys. African American males lead the nation in suspensions."

Kunjufu, Jawanza. Countering the Conspiracy to Destroy Black Boys. 1st ed. Chicago: Afro-Am Pub. Co, 1983. Volume II. 11. See Volume One of the same title, Chapter Two, for a description of the *Fourth Grade Syndrome* in black boys.

Also: Figlio, David. "The Importance of a Diverse Teaching Force." Brookings (blog), November 16, 2017. Accessed 01-16-2023. https://www.brookings.edu/research/the-importance-of-a-diverse-teaching-force/.

Also: Brookings. "How We Rise: How Social Networks in Charlotte Impact Economic Mobility," October 16, 2020. Accessed 01-16-2023. https://www.brookings.edu/essay/how-we-rise-how-social-networks-in-charlotte-impact-economic-mobility/.

[160] Hare, Nathan, and Julia Hare. The Endangered Black Family.

[161] Smith, Richard V. Reeves, Sarah Nzau, and Ember. "The Challenges Facing Black Men – and the Case for Action." *Brookings* (blog), November 19, 2020. https://www.brookings.edu/blog/up-front/2020/11/19/the-challenges-facing-black-men-and-the-case-for-action/.

"Moreover, peak earnings for Black women are about $5,000 higher than for Black men."
Citi GPS. 32

[162] "Black men have the highest unemployment rates of any race/gender group, and the lowest labor force participation and employment rates among men; and

"Black women work more than white and Latina women, and Black male participation and employment rates are just a bit higher than those of Black women (while white and Latino men work more than women in each group).

"While these Black male employment outcomes are already disturbing, they obscure another important fact: *the official BLS statistics don't count many Black men with low employment, and adjusting for this fact further reduces measured Black male employment and earnings rates.*

"…There appear to be two additional factors accounting for the lower observed civilian noninstitutional population of Black men: 1) The "undercount" of such men in such surveys; and 2) The large population of Black men incarcerated at any time. Of the 15 percentage-point gap in the Black male and female populations for ages 25-54, about 7 points are due to incarceration and 8 to the undercount among those non-incarcerated.

"Including those incarcerated in population counts with no employment or labor force activity lowers the measured education and employment outcome statistics of Black men relative to Black women and all other race/gender groups. For instance, adding the currently incarcerated to the populations of Black men and women renders their employment-population ratios roughly equal – at about 59 percent and 56 percent in January 2020 and 2021 respectively. And, if the undercounted (but not currently incarcerated) population of Black men has worse employment outcomes than those counted – which appears likely to be the case – then the employment of Black men falls below that of Black women.[5] Indeed, Black male employment is lower than that of Black females despite the fact that women also provide the vast majority of the child custody and care in this population.[6]" [emphasis added]

Holzer, Harry J. Why Are Employment Rates so Low among Black Men?

[163] Citi GPS. 36

[164] American Sociological Association. "Women More Likely Than Men to Initiate Divorces, But Not Non-Marital Breakups," September 18, 2015. Accessed 03-21-2023.
https://www.asanet.org/women-more-likely-men-initiate-divorces-not-non-marital-breakups/

"Black women were the only group that had a higher divorce rate than marriage rate, with nearly 31 divorces per 1,000 married women aged 15 and older and only 17.3 marriages per 1,000 unmarried women."

Schweizer, V. (2019). Marriage to divorce ratio in the U.S.: Demographic variation, 2018. Family Profiles, FP-19-27. Bowling Green, OH: National Center for Family & Marriage Research. Accessed 11-26-2022. https://doi.org/10.25035/ncfmr/fp-19-27.

[165] Stampp, Kenneth M. The Peculiar Institution: Slavery in the Ante-Bellum South. Vintage Books ed. New York: Vintage Books, 1989. 158.

[166] Throughout American history, black unity that resulted in economic or political strength has been responded to with legal action or with violence. "Racial Violence in America: 60 Years of Whitewashing." Accessed December 6, 2022. Accessed 12-06-2023. https://www.cnn.com/interactive/2021/05/us/whitewashing-of-america-racism/

[167] Smietana, Bob. "Sunday Morning in America Still Segregated–and That's OK With Worshipers." Lifeway Research, January 15, 2015. https://research.lifeway.com/2015/01/15/sunday-morning-in-america-still-segregated-and-thats-ok-with-worshipers/.

[168] Wilson, Amos N. Understanding Black Adolescent Male Violence. 1-20.

[169] "A quarter century later, many blacks share this same perception. To them, concentrations of drug abuse and criminal violence are not impersonal incidents of socioeconomic dynamics but rather the consequences of purposeful designs to deprive blacks of legal protections and the benefits that flow from them."

"…Since Mangum's study scholars in various disciplines have produced a steady flow of increasingly sophisticated empirical studies on race and capital sentencing. Most of them strongly suggest that, because of race, defendants who kill whites are more likely to be sentenced to death than defendants who kill blacks. The most comprehensive of these studies investigated the disposition of over two thousand murder cases in Georgia between 1973 and 1979. It found that even after accounting for every nonracial variable that might plausibly have mattered, the odds of being condemned to death were 4.3 times greater for defendants who killed whites than for defendants who killed blacks…"

Kennedy, Randall. Race, Crime, and the Law. 1st ed. New York: Pantheon Books, 1997. 71, 74

[170] Quoted from Ohio State Journal of Criminal Law [Vol. 9:1] Accessed 03-09-2023. https://kb.osu.edu/handle/1811/73367

[171] "Funding K-12 Schools The racial education gap begins with widespread underfunding of schools with high concentrations of children of color. The average difference in funding of predominately white school districts and predominately minority school districts sums to $23 billion, despite serving roughly the same number of children, according to a study by nonprofit think tank EdBuild. In the U.S., 27 percent of students live in non-white districts, while 26 percent live in white districts. In white districts, 5 percent of students live in high-poverty areas, while in non-white districts 20 percent of student live in high-poverty areas (Figure 69). Even relative to high-poverty white districts, well-off non-white districts receive less money." Op. Cit. Citi GPS. 44.

[172] CBS News, Handcuffs in Hallways.

[173] Kunjufu, Jawanza. Countering the Conspiracy to Destroy Black Boys. 7-31.

[174] The Church began at the first Pentecost after the resurrection of Christ and will be completed at its own future resurrection (known as the Rapture).

"CHURCH

"**The Beginning of the Church**. That the true church as the Body of Christ began on the Day of Pentecost may be demonstrated in various ways. (1) Christ Himself declared it to be yet future. (2) It was founded upon the death, resurrection, and ascension of Christ, and such an accomplished fact was not possible until Pentecost (Gal 3:23-25). (3) There could be no church until it was purchased with Christ's precious blood (Eph 5:25-27), until He arose to give it resurrected life (Col 3:1-3), until He ascended to be head over all things to the church (Eph 1:20-23), and until the Spirit came on Pentecost, through whom the church would be formed into one body by the baptism of the Spirit. (4) The baptism of the Spirit prophesied by John (Matt 3:11; Mark 1:8; Luke 3:16-17; John 1:33) was still future at Acts 1:5. That it occurred between 1:5 and 11:16 is evident by a comparison of these two verses. It is obvious that the Holy Spirit, who came at Pentecost, arrived to perform among His various ministries of regenerating, sealing, indwelling, and filling, His distinctive ministry for this age of baptizing into Christ, that is, into His Body, the church (1 Cor 12:13). It was just as impossible, considering the baptizing work of the Holy Spirit, that the church would have been formed before Pentecost as it was impossible that it should not have been formed after that date."

"**Purpose and Completion of the Church**. There is abundant Scripture that points to God's principal purpose in this particular age as the outcalling of the church, the Body of Christ, from both Gentiles and Jews (Acts 15:14-18). This pivotal passage from Acts indicates God's divine purpose for this age in taking out from among the Gentiles a people for His name. The gospel has never anywhere saved all but in every place it has called out some. The church is thus still in the process of formation, principally from among Gentiles with comparatively few Jews, who constitute the remnant according to the election of grace (Rom 11:5). When the Body of Christ is complete, it will be removed, or translated, from the earthly scene (1 Cor 15:51-53; 1 Thess 4:15-17; 2 Thess 2:1; Rev 3:10). After the out-taking of the church, the end-time apocalyptic judgments will fall upon Gentiles and unbelieving Jews. However, a remnant will be saved out of this "time of Jacob's distress" (Jer 30:7), and the advent of Christ in glory will mark the setting up of the millennial kingdom with the nation Israel reinstated in priestly communion and blessing (Zech 3) as the light of the world (4). Three views are held among premillennialists as to the time of Christ's return: before, in the middle of, and at the end of the Tribulation.

(from The New Unger's Bible Dictionary. Originally published by Moody Press of Chicago, Illinois. Copyright © 1988.)

[175] "Calvin Schermerhorn: Why the Racial Wealth Gap Persists More than 150 Years after Emancipation – Twin Cities." 11-04-2022. https://www.twincities.com/2019/06/27/calvin-schermerhorn-why-the-racial-wealth-gap-persists-more-than-150-years-after-emancipation/. *Calvin Schermerhorn is professor of history in Arizona State University's School of Historical, Philosophical and Religious Studies and author of "The Business of Slavery and the Rise of American Capitalism, 1815-1860." He wrote this column for the Washington Post.*

[176] Citi GPS. 50.

[177] Wilson, Amos N. Understanding Black Adolescent Male Violence. 14-15.

[178] Citi GPS. 48.

[179] Wilson, Amos N. Understanding Black Adolescent Male Violence 11-16/

[180] "Workplace discrimination has been so great a problem that a law had to be written to address it. Title VII of the Civil Rights Act of 1964 protects individuals against employment discrimination on the basis of race and color as well as national origin, sex, or religion.

"Workplace discrimination is so persistent that the government saw fit to strengthen workplace discrimination laws in 1971, creating the Equal Employment Opportunity Act and again, in the Civil Rights Act of 1991.

"While all racial and ethnic groups are suffering from the fall-out of the pandemic, data reveal the burden is falling more heavily on certain demographics. Black persons, in particular, appear to have suffered greater job losses amid government ordered shutdowns; found themselves in industries that are essential but low paying…"

CitiGPS. 9.

[181] Akala, Adedayo. "Cost Of Racism: U.S. Economy Lost $16 Trillion Because Of Discrimination, Bank Says." *NPR*, September 23, 2020, sec. National. https://www.npr.org/sections/live-updates-protests-for-racial-justice/2020/09/23/916022472/cost-of-racism-u-s-economy-lost-16-trillion-because-of-discrimination-bank-says.

[182] GDP per capita growth (annual %) - United States World Bank national accounts data, and OECD National Accounts data files. Accessed 12-12-2022. https://data.worldbank.org/indicator/NY.GDP.PCAP.KD.ZG?end=2021&locations=US&start=1961&view=chart

19. The Third Nationbuilding Principle

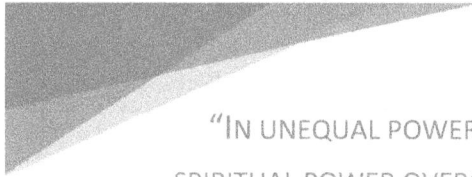

"IN UNEQUAL POWER RELATIONSHIPS, SPIRITUAL POWER OVERCOMES WORLDLY POWER. GOD CAN AND DOES OVERCOME THE ADVANTAGE OF THE POWERFUL ON BEHALF OF THOSE WHO HAVE HIS FAVOR."

Figure 24: The Third Nationbuilding Principle

Authority is a necessary element of civilization as designed by God. Human organization: marriages, families, government, the military, and businesses all require a system of authority to properly function. The Bible establishes human authority and governs it both by conscience and the written Word of God.

Romans 13:1 (KJV 1900)
1 Let every soul be subject unto the higher powers. <u>For there is no power but of God</u>: the powers that be are ordained of God.

Fallen humanity seeks to subvert authority to serve the ends of sin.

Isaiah 10:1 [KJV]
Woe unto them that decree unrighteous decrees, and that write grievousness which they have prescribed;

Exploitation of individuals and systems to obtain a better quality of life is commonplace. People cheat, they join conspiracies and commit violence to obtain authority which is then misused to oppress others. The word "oppress" and its cognates occur over 100 times in the Authorized Version, demonstrating that the abuse of authority is recognized by God as a significant problem in the world.

Satanic involvement in the world only amplifies the problem of unauthorized or misused authority. Satan fell from his original estate due to a lust for unauthorized authority: he wanted to be as God. Satan tempted Eve with an appeal the identical desire, "ye shall be as gods." Satan in his role as the temporary god of this world sponsors the abuse of genuine authority as well as imposition of illegitimate authority by wicked men and women.

The descendants of slaves in the United States have been the constant victims of systems of oppression, the abuse of authority, because of their original purpose in American society. That purpose was to create wealth and well-being for white people by taking upon themselves the most onerous aspects of the curse of Adam. The American system ensured that black people were to be separated from the fruit of their labor in perpetuity. The percentage of American wealth enjoyed by black people today is comparable to the period immediately following slavery. This achievement did not occur by accident, nor is it a result of the purported inferiority of black people. This outcome requires the careful management of a generational system of oppression. This system *requires* the abuse of authority in every institution in every era of the nation's history.

The Third Principle of Nationbuilding acknowledges the requirement that God himself be directly engaged in the plight of the oppressed for their fortunes to be reversed. Again, we emphasize that oppression is a spiritual initiative. *Secular efforts, well-conceived and executed, can reduce black misery but cannot reverse the abusive power relationships that are supported by spiritual agencies.* The good news is that God has shown himself willing to reverse these relationships for his glory and for the benefit of those who through faith and obedience, have his favor.

Biblical Examples of the Third Nationbuilding Principle

Joseph in Egypt [Genesis 37-47]

Joseph experienced extreme injustice at the hand of his brothers and the Egyptians. God reversed an unequal power relationship when He catapulted Joseph to the mastery over the people of Egypt and made him the savior of both the *nation* of Egypt and the patriarchs of the *nation* of Israel.

Samson and the Philistines [Judges 13-16]

The Philistines exercised oppressive power over the Israelites during the time of the Judges. God raised up a single man, Sampson, who, by himself, through extraordinary acts of strength, delivered the *nation* of Israel from the hands of an entire nation of oppressors. In his death, Sampson inflicted more destruction upon the Philistines than in his life.

Israel and the Exodus [Exodus 1-14]

Israel had gradually become nation of slaves, living under oppression in Egypt, the strongest and richest nation in the world. They had no wealth, no political clout, no weapons, or military organization. Nonetheless, God destroyed Egypt economically and militarily and delivered the Israelites with great riches in fulfillment of his promise to Abraham. God then constituted Israel as a *nation* in its own land.

The Twelve Disciples [Ephesians 2.20 Revelation 21.14]

The Twelve were a group of very fallible believers (except Judas, who was not a believer at all). They were not politically powerful or wealthy. At first, they did not have a very good understanding of the Old Testament, nor did they possess great spiritual maturity. At the time of their master's greatest danger, they all fled in fear. Despite the opposition of the Roman Empire and the religious hierarchy of Israel, that small group of men carried out the Great Commission [Matthew 28.18-20] to make disciples of the nations, established the Church, and were reputed to have "turned the world upside down" [Acts 17.6]. In the resurrection, the wall of the New Jerusalem will have its foundations named after these Twelve men.

In the first half of this book, we outlined the activities within the local church that lead to spiritual revival, actions which place the believer on God's side, so that He can deliver them by reversing oppressive power relationships. Everything begins with the man of God, who must first be in proper alignment with God. He prepares the Congregation through discipleship to become spiritually self-sustaining. The Congregation then ministers to the Community through the dual witness of their holy lifestyle and their verbal proclamation of the gospel. These two spiritual witnesses eventually transform the Community.

But beyond this process, God is free to personally intervene in history on behalf of those persons who are rightly related to him and walking in obedience to the scriptures. There is no limit to what God can do to rescue the faithful.

We will now look at the spiritual concepts which underlie the Third Principle of Nationbuilding.

Spiritual Concepts Beneath the Third Nationbuilding Principle

The Invisible Precedes the Visible

> Psalms 127:1–2 (NKJV) 1 Unless the LORD builds the house, They labor in vain who build it; Unless the LORD guards the city, The watchman stays awake in vain. 2 It is vain for you to rise up early, To sit up late, To eat the bread of sorrows; For so He gives His beloved sleep.

This scripture reveals that the physical world is governed by the spiritual world ("except the Lord build the house"). In Psalms 127.1 beneficial economic activity ("build the house") and national security ("guards the city") of a nation depends not upon the industry of man but the invisible activity of God on its behalf.

It was noted earlier that as a spiritual initiative, oppression is maintained by spiritual power. The secular actions of a nation ultimately succeed or fail based upon the impact of invisible spiritual forces. We see this process in action in the book of Daniel, chapter 10, where the nations of the world are influenced by both righteous and evil spiritual entities. At the battle of Jericho [Joshua 6] spiritual forces were decisive in the military victory of the Jews. There are several principles that can be derived from these examples:

> The activities of this world are related to and a part of the prosecution of a larger, more ancient conflict in the spiritual realm. Both elect and fallen angels, God and Satan are directly involved in human affairs. From the Garden of Eden this interaction between the spiritual and earthly realms can be seen.[clxix]

> Actions taken in the spiritual realm have concrete and decisive consequences in the physical world. In fact, actions taken in the spiritual realm produce the effects [political, economic, diplomatic, environmental] generally attributed to the works of men alone [Psalms 127.1; 2 Corinthians 4.18; Book of Revelation].

> The execution of the of the spiritual way of life: personal spiritual growth, followed by effective ministry in one's own marriage and family, and effective ministry to the Community through one's Christian walk, evangelism and discipleship are how the Christian engages in the spiritual warfare. Every believer is involved in the spiritual war, either as a victim or a victor.[clxx] The Christian's aim is to be transformed by the power of God into a mature believer who is capable of being blessed by Him. *Because of his relationship to God, the believer has a disproportionately powerful effect upon historical trends, positively or negatively. [2 Chronicles 16.9].*

> Spiritual warfare consists in influencing the issues in the spiritual realm to bring about consequences in the physical realm.[clxxi] Believers influence these issues, not by dabbling in the currently popular but false concepts of spiritual warfare, but by their obedience to the Word of God. In this way God acts on the behalf of the weak, both through the spiritually strong believer and by His own sovereign activity.

These are the reasons why plans for nationbuilding which simply alter the landscape of this world through social, economic, or political actions, even if initially successful, do not produce fundamental qualitative change. We are

---

[clxix] Genesis 3; Deuteronomy 28.15-44; Joshua 6; Daniel 10; Ephesians 3.10.
[clxx] 2 Corinthians 10.4-6; Ephesians 6.12
[clxxi] Genesis 3:1, Daniel 10:13, Matthew 4:8

bringing a knife to a gun fight. If we want lasting change in the world, we must influence the spiritual conflict. God has specifically authorized the mature believer to do this very thing.

Strength Out of Weakness

God is glorified when he uses the weak who serve Him to overturn the strong that live in opposition to his will. Weakness is a disability in Satan's world. However, weakness: physical, economic, political, or military can and does glorify God when accompanied by faith in the Word of God.

> 2 Corinthians 12:10 (KJV 1900)
> [10] Therefore I take pleasure in infirmities, in reproaches, in necessities, in persecutions, in distresses for Christ's sake: <u>for when I am weak, then am I strong</u>.

The weakness of a people cannot defeat them when God is with them. The strength of a people cannot deliver them when God is against them. Weakness, as men count it, is a spiritual principle by which God manages history to his glory.

The world under the administration of the devil is not merely a sinful place. It is an evil place where men in arrogance and pride erect philosophies and spiritual concepts to directly oppose God and to call into question the wisdom of his Word.[clxxii]

These same men, by overt action or by covert agreement, erect systems of oppression by which they evade the worse consequences of the Fall by the exploitation of others. Oppression is a spiritual strategy, but it is also a strategy of men by which they take upon themselves an artificial glory in imitation of God.

God glorifies himself in overturning the apparent wisdom of the wise by using the despised of this world. The weak, the poor, the marginalized are made into instruments of divine power to decisively demonstrate the wisdom of divine grace and the strength of divine righteousness.[clxxiii] Christ was slain in

---

[clxxii] Genesis 6.5; Psalms 2; 2 Corinthians 10.5

[clxxiii] There have been false theologies of liberation erected upon the idea of liberation from oppression as an end in itself. In these theologies, the Word of God is disfigured in a way similar to that which slave theology achieves. The bible teaches that God is against oppression because he is *holy*. The purpose of history is the *glory* of God, not the wellbeing of man. The Bible upholds the *integrity* of God

apparent weakness, as this world counts strength. The conspiracy that plotted his death ignorantly implemented God's plan to save the lost [1 Corinthians 2.7-8], *most of whom are the weak and the oppressed.*

> 1 Corinthians 1:26–29 (KJV 1900)
>
> [26] For ye see your calling, brethren, how that <u>not many</u> wise men after the flesh, not many mighty, not many noble, *are called.* [27] But God hath chosen the foolish things of the world to confound the wise; <u>and God hath chosen the weak things of the world</u> to confound the things which are mighty; [28] And base things of the world, and things which are despised, hath God chosen, *yea,* and things which are not, to bring to nought things that are: [29] That no flesh should glory in his presence.

In college I met a man who had recently spent 20 plus years as an inmate at Leavenworth Prison. He lived for a time in the basement of a house I lived in off campus with some other students. He had acquired several notable skills while in prison. One of them was chess. He could defeat anyone in our house in chess simply using his two rooks. Because of his years of practice, he could use two limited pieces to defeat an opponent who was utilizing more and superior pieces. In the same way God is glorified using weak and limited individuals who are "under the radar" of this status-conscious world.

The world measures power by its ability to manipulate external things: people and events, in visible ways. God exerts extraordinary power in history by applying power to change men and women invisibly and inwardly. Through spiritual power, God effects spiritual changes in and through those who have little worldly power. Then, through the faith of those individuals, God reverses oppressive power relationships for individuals, Communities and even nations.

> Isaiah 40:29–31 (KJV 1900)
>
> [29] He giveth power to the faint; And to *them that have* no might he increaseth strength. [30] Even the youths shall faint and be weary, And the young men shall utterly fall: [31] But they that wait upon the Lord shall renew *their* strength; They shall mount up with wings as eagles; They shall run, and not be weary; *And* they shall walk, and not faint.

---

which is the only sure guarantee of justice to anyone. Although oppression is a part of this world, the *character* of God demands that his people become neither oppressor nor oppressed [Psalms 103.6; 146.7; Luke 4.18 gk.].

"But they that wait upon the LORD..."

The believer must eventually realize that the essential skill for spiritual function is that of faith. Faith is a skill in that it requires practice to be learned and to be skillfully used. Faith is the means that God has provided to the believer to become a partaker of His "great and precious promises [2 Peter 1.4]." Faith makes the believer a participant in God's plan for mankind. True faith is directed at the proper object, which is the Word of God, the Bible. True faith is transformational. A person with faith is transformed by God through it. Those movements that seek to make faith separate from this transformational aspect are not practicing Christianity but another religion. That religion is Magic, where a strong desire for something can attract it to you and where visualization and magic words, words infused with 'power', can bring things into existence. This is Paganism and not Christianity. It was James who said that the one who truly has faith is not the same as he used to be.

> James 2:17–20 (KJV 1900)
> [17] Even so faith, if it hath not works, is dead, being alone. [18] Yea, a man may say, Thou hast faith, and I have works: shew me thy faith without thy works, and I will shew thee my faith by my works. [19] Thou believest that there is one God; thou doest well: the devils also believe, and tremble. [20] But wilt thou know, O vain man, that faith without works is dead?

The man or woman who believes the Scriptures will know that God directs history on behalf of his servants. These are the primary human agents of nationbuilding. Without them, there will be no rebirth of black America.

Oppressed people are often crippled by a fixation upon the physical resources that they lack: funds, numbers, power, connections, etc. This is natural since these are the physical means by which oppression is maintained in the world. Thus, those who would defeat oppression are exclusively focused upon obtaining resources, dismantling oppressive systems, or changing the minds of the oppressors themselves. Although these things are helpful for the temporary alleviation of suffering, the truth is that oppression is still a spiritual operation. Everything that creates, and sustains, disrupts, or dismantles oppression originates in the spiritual world.

In scripture, weakness that submits itself to God for solutions is invincible. Those solutions are found in the Bible, when rightly divided. Therefore, it is imperative that those with a mind to oppress spare no effort to keep accurate Bible teaching out of the hands of the victims of oppression. From Babel to the golden calf, from Jeroboam to the Charismatic Renewal,[183] people have manipulated the Word of God to acquire and maintain power over their brothers.[184]

The weakness of the apostle Paul, when combined with faith in the truth, qualified him to be the greatest theologian and missionary of the Christian faith.

> 2 Corinthians 12:8–10 (NKJV)
> 8 Concerning this thing I pleaded with the Lord three times that it might depart from me. 9 And He said to me, "My grace is sufficient for you, for My strength is made perfect in weakness." Therefore most gladly I will rather boast in my infirmities, that the power of Christ may rest upon me. 10 Therefore I take pleasure in infirmities, in reproaches, in needs, in persecutions, in distresses, for Christ's sake. For when I am weak, then I am strong.

Paul had a physical weakness [G769] "my infirmities"] that impacted his ability to minister. There are several theories, one of which was that it was a disease of the eyes [Galatians 4.13-14; 6.11]. It also may have been that his speaking ability was not up to par with some others [2 Corinthians 10.10]. God took Paul, an enemy of the faith, with these physical limitations, to demonstrate his glory and power to the Gentile world, apostate Judaism, the Church, and to history.

It is possible that Sampson might have had a normal appearance, build, and stature. There is no way to know this, but it would be consistent with God's dealings with us to demonstrate His power not through a muscle-bound specimen, but through a normal looking person capable of extraordinary deeds. It would be an apt description of every believer's spiritual potential, a potential that most believers do not appreciate or properly cultivate.

Another truth arises from the example of Paul. A relatively small stone can be used to move a much larger object using a lever. God uses weak individuals as fulcrums by which He influences and controls history. It is those believers [like Paul] who see difficulty and pain as an *opportunity* to utilize divine strength that can win the day for the masses of people who are not equipped to fight in the spiritual warfare.

The unbeliever and the spiritually immature believer think, "when I am weak, I am weak." The believer aware of God's purpose and his plan for the Christian as his agent in the world thinks. "I am weak therefore I am strong."

A relatively small group of spiritually mature believers can become the fulcrum upon which a much larger mass of people may be delivered in any age or geography. You cannot see it in its entirety because it is a spiritual process that occurs over time and across many lives. However, we can see the principle of the spiritual fulcrum in retrospect. It is illustrated in the case of Sodom and Gomorrah [Genesis 18], where one believer was heard by God and only 10 believers would have saved the entire metropolitan area of Sodom and Gomorrah. We see the principle in the story of Gideon [Judges 6] where 300 men defeated a much larger force of Midianites and saved Israel, providing peace for years. Had such a fulcrum of believers existed among the Jews at the time of Christ, the Kingdom would have been inaugurated in Israel. Israel itself is the best illustration of the fulcrum: a tiny nation, surrounded by larger and mightier nations that hated it, but being preserved and used by God to provide the world with His revelation and His Son, the written and the living Word.

How to Activate Power Reversals: King Asa of Judah

God acts in history on behalf of the weak when appropriate spiritual preparations have been made by believers in that nation.

King Asa of Judah was in danger of being strategically outmaneuvered by Baasha the king of Israel. Instead of seeking the help of the Lord as he had done in the past, Asa made an alliance with Syria, the historic enemy of the Jews. He gained temporary relief from the Northern Kingdom of Israel, but in the process, he enriched rather than defeated a national threat, the kingdom of Syria. God sent a prophet to rebuke King Asa and this prophet was the source of the following prophecy:

> 2 Chronicles 16:7–9 (KJV 1900)
> 7 And at that time Hanani the seer came to Asa king of Judah, and said unto him, Because thou hast relied on the king of Syria, and not relied on the Lord thy God, therefore is the host of the king of Syria escaped out of thine hand. 8 Were not the Ethiopians and the Lubims a huge host, with very many chariots and horsemen? yet, because thou didst rely on the Lord, he delivered them into thine hand. 9 For the eyes of the Lord run to and fro

throughout the whole earth, to shew himself strong in the behalf of *them* whose heart *is* perfect toward him. Herein thou hast done foolishly: therefore from henceforth thou shalt have wars.

The verses indicate that the Lord is constantly alert for opportunities to exercise spiritual power on behalf of his people. However, we must rely, trust, and lean upon the Lord because he helps those "whose heart is perfect towards Him." The word "perfect" means complete or whole. The believer who would have God's strong support needs to be wholly committed to Him. It is because of a lack of commitment to Him that we cannot claim the many scriptures that tell us to "ask whatever we will." The Apostle John says it plainly:

> 1 John 3:22 (KJV 1900)
> 22 And whatsoever we ask, we receive of him, because we keep his commandments, and do those things that are pleasing in his sight.

To those who wonder why we do not see more reversals of oppressive power relations, the reason is straightforward. *We are still committed in some way to the system that we want to see overcome.* Asa used the Syrians to do what he had once asked God to do: to defeat his enemies. Now he is asking his enemy to defeat his enemies! So long as we are having cordial relations with Satan's system, we have no place asking God to defeat *a part of it* on our behalf.

> James 4:4 (KJV 1900)
> 4 Ye adulterers and adulteresses, know ye not that the friendship of the world is enmity with God? whosoever therefore will be a friend of the world is the enemy of God.

James is speaking to *believers* when he says this. In the very next verse, he says that they have the Spirit dwelling within them. Asking God for assistance on these terms is like a woman asking her husband to beat up her boyfriend.

The First Nationbuilding Principle secures the process that creates believers with true faith, by its focus upon the man of God. The Second Nationbuilding Principle teaches these persons [the Congregation] the importance and power of their decisions to mold their destiny. It also shows them that faith consists in the responsible decisions about the Word of God. The Third Nationbuilding Principle is the working of the divine strategy which transmutes human weakness into divine glory through faith in God and his promises.

In unequal power relationships, spiritual power overcomes worldly power. God can and does overcome the advantage of the powerful on behalf of those who have his favor.

In the years before the failure of chapter 16, Asa experienced many years of spiritual success, leading to the blessing of Israel by God.

> 2 Chronicles 14:2–6 (KJV 1900)
> [2] And Asa did *that which was* good and right in the eyes of the Lord his God: [3] For he took away the altars of the strange *gods*, and the high places, and brake down the images, and cut down the groves: [4] And commanded Judah to seek the Lord God of their fathers, and to do the law and the commandment. [5] Also he took away out of all the cities of Judah the high places and the images: and the kingdom was quiet before him. [6] And he built fenced cities in Judah: for the land had rest, and he had no war in those years; because the Lord had given him rest.

Spiritual Revival Occurs when Behavior Changes

> 2 Chronicles 14.2
> And Asa did that which was good and right in the eyes of the Lord his God:

Divine favor does not come in a vacuum. Today's pagan focus upon the power of a person's words to create reality, the mechanical operation of magical incantation, the disconnection of "faith" from righteousness has blinded many to the fact that we must have lives that are in alignment with the Word of God before we can enjoy special favor [1 John 3.22]. *To obtain divine favor you must examine your spiritual condition.* There are no blind principles of spirituality in God's economy that will grant favor to an individual who disregards the Word of God in their daily living. In applying this principle on the national level, Asa evaluated the spiritual condition of the nation in comparison to the demands of scripture and made the necessary changes.

In like manner we must compare our lives and our households to the standard of the Word of God and make the necessary changes. Asa may have been afraid, but whether he was afraid of not, he made the changes. Asa may have encountered resistance, but he made the changes.

All of this presupposes that Asa knew what God required. Many believers today do not know what the Bible says. They cannot consistently implement the necessary changes in their lives and families to get on track with God.

Many are subject to the instructions of false teachers who do not follow the Scriptures. Many others follow well-meaning Pastors who do not know the Bible, or who are afraid to follow it for fear of losing their members or their jobs. This lack of availability of accurate teaching prevents the operation of the Third Principle of Nationbuilding because God blesses obedience to Scripture, and you must know the Bible before you can obey it. This is why power reversals are seldom witnessed by us.

Asa understood that the invisible precedes the visible. In other words, it is the invisible spiritual victory that enables the visible victory of the people. Spiritual development (the invisible) makes social, economic, and military progress (the visible) possible. Asa's religious reforms laid the foundation for the prosperous development of the nation of Israel.

> 2 Chronicles 14:5–8 (KJV 1900)
> 5 Also he took away out of all the cities of Judah the high places and the images: and the kingdom was quiet before him. 6 And he built fenced cities in Judah: for the land had rest, and he had no war in those years; because the Lord had given him rest. 7 Therefore he said unto Judah, Let us build these cities, and make about *them* walls, and towers, gates, and bars, *while* the land *is* yet before us; because we have sought the Lord our God, we have sought *him*, and he hath given us rest on every side. So they built and prospered. 8 And Asa had an army *of men* that bare targets and spears, out of Judah three hundred thousand; and out of Benjamin, that bare shields and drew bows, two hundred and fourscore thousand: all these *were* mighty men of valour.

There is a direct connection between national righteousness and national prosperity.[clxxiv]

> Proverbs 14:34 (KJV 1900)
> 34 Righteousness exalteth a nation: But sin *is* a reproach to any people.

[clxxiv] National prosperity, by itself, is not a sign of divine blessing. There is also the prosperity of the wicked. Satan, as temporary prince of this world [John 12.31] has power to prosper his servants [Luke 4.5-7]. There is a hierarchy of demonic principalities [Daniel 10; Ephesians 6.12-13] that exist to support the nations that are committed to the Mystery of Iniquity [Psalms 2; Thessalonians 2.8].

Negative and Positive Actions Must be Taken to Secure God's Favor

Negative Actions

> 2 Chronicles 14:3 (KJV 1900)
> [3] For he took away the altars of the strange *gods*, and the high places, and brake down the images, and cut down the groves:

To obtain divine favor you must examine your spiritual conviction. Sometimes the willingness is present to make changes to get in line with what God's Word says, but there are obstacles which cause the believer to hesitate to make the changes that God requires. Often these obstacles are family members, loved ones and friends. Gideon was told to tear down his father's idols [Judges 6], Jonathan had to disobey his father Saul to save David [1 Samuel 20] and Asa had to tear down the idols of his father and grandmother [1 Kings 15.11-13]. Often obedience to God requires jeopardizing *human relationships*. The human tendency is to place love for man before love of God, to place the Second Great Commandment before the First [Luke 14.26]. To truly effect change in the world around us, we must have more than correct doctrine, we must also have correct convictions, that is we must *believe* our doctrine. *Doctrine that is not followed is doctrine that is not believed.*

When Asa destroyed the idols of the previous generation, he totally destroyed them and rendered them *of no further use* to his or to any future generation. A commitment to the rule of God requires a total break with Satan's *systems* of religion. A contemporary example may be found in the tendency of churches to submit to the current ecumenical spirit. This spirit encourages sound churches to fellowship with other churches regardless of their doctrine or their practices. Doctrinally sound churches are fellowshipping with Catholic churches, charismatic churches, Mormon churches, ecumenical organizations, churches that ordain women as elders, and churches with rampant sin problems. The scripturally sound churches, although they possess a proper doctrinal statement, demonstrate a profound lack of spiritual discernment and are rebelling against the clear teaching of the Bible when they do these things.[clxxv] The proper action would be for the Pastors and Elders to publicly condemn such alliances and explain the biblical reasons why they are unacceptable. Then they should discuss this issue with other sound churches that have been exercising the same ecumenical behavior. They should cease

---

[clxxv] Romans 16.17-18; 2 Corinthians 3.6, 14; Titus 3.10

from fellowship with the offending bodies, including any otherwise sound ministries that insist upon continuing the practice. In this way they smash the idol and make it impossible for their members or friends to continue the practice without outright rebellion against the clearly proclaimed Word.

The difficulty of taking complete measures like this explains why oppressive power relationships are not being reversed for black people in America.

How can we expect God to change relationships of power in the devil's world for us when we will not sever our own relations with it?

There are those who will argue that the ministry or the individual that addresses matters in this way is "negative" and is not showing Christian love and is "judging" when he has no right to judge. All these sentiments are non-biblical. Gideon, Jonathan, and Asa were not being negative from the standpoint of the Word of God. Nor was Phinehas, a grandson of Levi, who went a great deal further than we are asked to go today in separation [Numbers 25.1-15].

Common sense informs the farmer that if he loves corn, he must hate weeds. The actions that are recommended in the New Testament to address the problems of false teaching that victimizes the people of God are far more lenient that those of the Mosaic dispensation, but it is the same God.

Positive Actions

> 2 Chronicles 14:4 (KJV 1900)
> 4 And commanded Judah to seek the LORD God of their fathers, and <u>to do the law and the commandment</u>.

Abijah, Asa's father, knew the right thing but didn't do it. Abijah tried to please both God and the people.[clxxvi] Asa knew the right thing and did it, both the negative and the positive.

Asa recognized that actions in the spiritual realm produce concrete results in the physical world. There is no way to have God's favor without submitting to God's Law. The heathen relied upon the devil to provide them with prosperity and therefore they submitted themselves to *his* law. You cannot submit to the devil and then expect deliverance and nationbuilding from God.

[clxxvi] 1 Kings 15.3,12,13,15 c.f. 2 Chronicles 13. 1-22

Asa also understood that we seek the Lord by "do[ing] the law and the commandment." Asa was not free to improvise with the Scripture, mixing it with his own ideas and the religion of the nations around him. Theology is the most important science to man, but ministry leaders behave as if it is a matter of taste rather than precision. Today people are taught that you can "praise" your way into divine power and deliverance and that you can "declare" your way into it or that you can "speak" your way into spiritual victory. All these methods omit submission to God through obedience to His Word which is why they have been massively successful among the public. The unsaved world wants national blessing, but they want it outside of submission to God.

God Provides the Conditions for Nationbuilding

> 2 Chronicles 14:6 (KJV 1900)
> 6 And he built fenced cities in Judah: for the land had rest, and he had no war in those years; because the LORD had given him rest.

Having met the spiritual conditions for divine favor, *God creates the conditions* that enables the empowerment of Israel. God has the wisdom and the power to order circumstances that enable the strengthening of the national entity. In the case of Israel in the 10th century B.C., God provided freedom from war. This peace enabled a shift of resources from war to national infrastructure. Such a shift benefitted business and created a measure of prosperity. Further, a new generation of men entered adulthood who were not killed in warfare. This had a long-term impact upon prosperity and stability by maintaining the strength of the family. The effect of war as a destroyer of generations of the best men in a society is underestimated. This fact is used by those who understand war as a means of limiting population growth and destroying the nationbuilding capacity of a people. The same can be said of the effects of crime as generations of young men are killed and incarcerated. Oppressing nations use both war and crime to this end.

The building of cities enabled the growth of the nation and expanded opportunities for those with ambition in commerce or government. In peace time Asa also prepared the national defense by building fortified cities and his army.

> 2 Chronicles 14:7–8 (KJV 1900)
> 7 Therefore he said unto Judah, Let us build these cities, and make about them walls, and towers, gates, and bars, while the land is yet before us;

because we have sought the LORD our God, we have sought him, and he hath given us rest on every side. So they built and prospered. 8 And Asa had an army of men that bare targets and spears, out of Judah three hundred thousand; and out of Benjamin, that bare shields and drew bows, two hundred and fourscore thousand: all these were mighty men of valour.

The provision of peace was the provision of *time*. Asa used this time wisely by providing for all aspects of national development. The people of God must be ready to take advantage of divine favor when it comes. *The most powerful preparation is the strengthening of marriages and families as this is the basis of all that will be built afterwards.* Nationbuilding requires many categories of skills and aptitudes to implement divine favor in practical ways. While we are waiting and trusting God for blessing, we must also prepare ahead of time so that when the divinely appointed opportunity arises, we are in position to take advantage of it.

God creates the conditions that enables the empowerment of those He favors. Once the doctrinal and ethical obstacles to God's working are removed, *God is free to create power for the powerless.* The prevalence of false teachers among oppressed people prevents this process from taking place by convincing people to place their faith in bad doctrine and dangerous alliances. False doctrine keeps the oppressed powerless-God is not free to create power for the weak due to incorrect behavior based upon incorrect beliefs about Himself and his Plan. Blessing the powerless under these conditions would cause him to violate his own holiness, which he will never do.

The Third Nationbuilding Principle Illustrated by King Asa

- ➤ **Cause** [Believers]: Know, obey, and lead with an accurate understanding of Word of God
- ➤ **Cause** [Believers]: Remove the doctrinal and ethical barriers to divine blessing.

- ➤ **Effect** [God]: God brings about the conditions necessary for the creation of power: Peace, economic conditions, prosperity, health, longevity, children or whatever is needed.
- ➤ **Effect** [God]: Power and deliverance to the oppressed in whatever category required.

Therefore, when local churches, led by the Elders, obey, defend, and teach (discipleship) the Word of God, then God creates the environment for the reversal of oppressive power relationships.

> "In unequal power relationships, spiritual power overcomes worldly power. God can and does overcome the advantage of the powerful on behalf of those who have his favor."

Summary of Revival and Nationbuilding

Black America is in a social and a spiritual crisis. Despite the presence of many local churches and many professed believers, the basic institutions of black America are in a desperate condition. Sin, the embrace of false religion and the lack of conscientious disciple making based upon sound Bible doctrine have precipitated the decay of the institutions of marriage and family and with it the loss of rights won by earlier generations.

These spiritual weaknesses have resulted in the reanimation of vicious forces that oppose black well-being. For example, the resurgence of both attitudes and movements dedicated to the re-enslavement of black people in the United States and elsewhere. This re-enslavement initiative is seen in the successful efforts to criminalize as many black men as early in life as possible (mass incarceration), thus removing them from the home (social effects), preventing meaningful participation in the workforce (economic effects), depriving them of the right to vote or to enter law enforcement (political effects). The efforts towards re-enslavement are seen in the efforts to feminize the black male and reverse sexual roles between black men and women. This new conception of slavery is also seen in the all-out effort to disenfranchise all black people by a coordinated effort within the states consisting of laws and rules designed to limit black voting or to diminish the value of votes that are cast. There is also the strengthening of anti-black hate groups that promote racial violence and have become a political power bloc, seeking mainstream acceptance.

The Bible teaches that civilization is advanced through the invisible spiritual impact of the local church. It is the local church that provides light to the Community through its moral example and through its witness to the gospel of Christ. This dual witness of the Congregation through faithful disciples results in the strengthening of the institutions of marriage and family, producing generations of mentally healthy, socially adjusted, and productive youth.

The Three Nationbuilding Principles are a summary of the essential biblical principles that when obeyed, will lead to the freedom of any people. They have been tried and proven in Scripture where there are many examples of the weak overcoming the strong by the will and power of God. It is a spiritual truth that the weakness of the weak cannot defeat them if God is on their side, and the strength of the strong cannot deliver them if the Most High opposes them.

The First Nationbuilding Principle reveals the origin of both slavery and freedom to be the spiritual world. Oppression is a spiritual initiative and the people that ignore this truth will suffer for it.

The Second Nationbuilding Principle establishes the priority of personal human decisions in determining human destiny. Oppressed people are convinced as a part of their psychological programming that their decisions do not matter. However, one's personal decisions matter a great deal because there is a God who can make them matter.

The Third Nationbuilding Principle forces the believer to determine if God is on his side by asking himself if he is on God's side. Many peoples in history have chosen slavery to men over slavery to God and his Word [Matthew 27.22-26]. The Third Principle encourages the believer that God can and will do what seems to be impossible.

If you put these principles to work personally and in your own local church, you can see their effects in your families and in your neighborhoods in your own lifetime

---

[183] For example, the Charismatic Movement has become increasingly indistinguishable from Evangelicalism. Charismatic theology diminishes the authority of the scriptures by its emphasis upon experience and its use of poor exegesis to justify its beliefs and practices. Modern churches may not openly promote charismatic doctrine, but the concepts and nomenclature of the movement have permeated Evangelicalism. The ordination of women, a practice popularized by this movement, is common in black churches today. Defunct spiritual gifts and offices have been revived, spiritual gifts bearing no resemblance to their New Testament counterparts are sought and practiced. Biblical faith has been redefined and praise turned into a means of getting what we want. The declarations of men are considered equal to those of God in Scripture. Charismatic doctrine and practice have become the modern "high places," *untouchable* by Pastors because the people love them so [Leviticus 26.27-31; 2 Kings 14.1-4; 15.32-34].

Also: MacArthur, John F. Strange Fire: The Danger of Offending the Holy Spirit with Counterfeit Worship, Thomas Nelson. Kindle Edition, 2013. xiv-xvi.

The Barna Group wrote the following in 2008, *fourteen years ago*:

"It is assumed faith trends in America are dictated by white churches, which represent about 77% of the nation's Protestant congregations. However, only 16% of the country's white Protestant congregations are Pentecostal, compared to 65% of the Protestant churches dominated by African-Americans."

"Is American Christianity Turning Charismatic? - Barna Group." Accessed 02-02-2023. https://www.barna.com/research/is-american-christianity-turning-charismatic/.

Also: Walker, Richard G., The Spiritual Gift of Tongues, The New Fundamental Series: Book One. A Richer Walk, 2020

[184] "On display now at the Museum of the Bible in Washington, D.C., is a special exhibit centered on a rare Bible from the 1800s that was used by British missionaries to convert and educate slaves.

"What's notable about this Bible is not just its rarity, but its content, or rather the lack of content. It excludes any portion of text that might inspire rebellion or liberation.

"Anthony Schmidt, associate curator of Bible and Religion in America at the museum, says the first instance of this abridged version titled, Parts of the Holy Bible, selected for the use of the Negro Slaves, in the British West-India Islands, was published in 1807.

"As people come from a multitude of backgrounds, Anthony Schmidt of the Museum of the Bible says how they encounter the Bible can vary greatly from person to person.
Elizabeth Baker/NPR
"About 90 percent of the Old Testament is missing [and] 50 percent of the New Testament is missing," Schmidt says. "Put in another way, there are 1,189 chapters in a standard protestant Bible. This Bible contains only 232."

"Schmidt says passages that could have prompted rebellion were removed, for example:

""There is neither Jew nor Greek, there is neither bond nor free, there is neither male nor female: for ye are all one in Christ Jesus." Galatians 3:28"

Martin, Michel. "Slave Bible From The 1800s Omitted Key Passages That Could Incite Rebellion." NPR, December 9, 2018, sec. Religion. https://www.npr.org/2018/12/09/674995075/slave-bible-from-the-1800s-omitted-key-passages-that-could-incite-rebellion.

20. Epilogue

Revival and Nationbuilding describes the spiritual processes whereby the people of God influence the nations of this world. Just as individual believers influence their families and Communities by their gospel witness and sanctification, so do larger numbers of Christians influence the state. The end of Revival and Nationbuilding is not a Christian state, but the optimal function of the secular state in the devil's world. These spiritual processes are how the black American sub-nation may be revitalized and made powerful.

The presence of mature believers anywhere is a potential blessing to that place. The spiritual processes through which the people of God, by their normal spiritual function, revive and purify the institutions of society, also serve to limit, or remove oppression. God is against oppression and oppressors and removes their influence and power for the sake of obedient believers.

Revival and Nationbuilding is God's response to obedient believers. When Christians are compliant to the accurate teaching of the Word of God, He blesses them and makes them a blessing to those in their periphery. The basic institutions of civilization are strengthened. When marriage and family are refreshed and fortified, consciences are recalibrated, and society is reset.

Under these conditions, the power of oppressors can be weakened even if the apparatus of oppression remains intact. God can render exploiters impotent without changing their attitudes towards their victims.

Racism is a major category of oppression and has a central role in Satan's systems of world management. Racial oppression causes the corruption of the psychological and spiritual function of believers. In this way, racial oppression is an effective means of neutralizing the local church, or worse, making it ground zero for a negative spiritual chain reaction in society.

Consequently, it is imperative that this problem is specifically addressed by Pastors and teachers in their ministry of the Scriptures to the Church. When the appropriate teaching is directed at the real problems caused by racial oppression, then the Word of God does what it always does when believed: minds are renewed and eventually, power relations are modified.

Three Nationbuilding Principles have been presented which organize the pertinent information on this subject in the Bible. Other concepts relating to the character of racial oppression and its effects have also been introduced. Pertinent definitions have been offered for the purpose of providing a framework for conceptualizing what is really happening in the world: a biblically derived schematic for interpreting reality.

It is the local church and its spiritual leadership that are the responsible parties for the initiation of Revival and Nationbuilding. Revival is a commitment to true biblical values demonstrated by a change in behavior. Nationbuilding is the irresistible structural outcome of obedience to an accurate interpretation of God's Word.

Richard G. Walker

Appendix 1:
The Doctrine Of Oppression

The Definition and Description of Oppression

> Oppression is the treatment "of a disadvantaged member of society
> unjustly with the effect of causing him to suffer ill-treatment." Also, to
> "defraud, extort, cheat, formally, oppress or mistreat. i.e., steal or rob
> from a disadvantaged person...and so creating suffering and undue
> torment of the poor or disadvantaged."[185]

Therefore, oppression may be seen as *the improper use of power over
another to deprive them of justice* The primary injury to those under
oppression is the loss of justice.[clxxvii] Oppression is the opposite of
justice.

Oppressors also exploit unequal power relationships. Oppression is
the exploitation of the dependent by those in a position of power,
the abuse of those who by virtue of their weak condition are first
to be exploited.[clxxviii] The fact that oppression often deprives a *class
of persons* of justice tends to perpetuate their disadvantaged status.

In the scriptures, the tendency of oppressors to seek out a weakened class of

---

[clxxvii] Psalms 103.6; Isaiah 10.1-2; Ecclesiastes 5.8
[clxxviii] Deuteronomy 24.14-15; Proverbs 22:22–23; Amos 4.1

individual is illustrated by the oppression of foreigners [strangers],^{clxxix} *the oppression of women without husbands [widows] and children without fathers [orphans].*^{clxxx}

Racial or ethnic oppression is a special category of oppression which targets whole people groups by their appearance, nationality, or culture, spreading the disadvantages of oppression across an entire class or caste, while in many cases *spreading the benefits of oppression* across the entirety of the oppressing group [Exodus 3.9; Judges 6.1-6]. The Jews in ancient Egypt experienced firsthand being an oppressed ethnic minority [Exodus 3.9; 22.20; 23.9]. Despite this experience, oppression within the nation of Israel was common.^{clxxxi}

The Origin of Oppression

Oppression and the Fall of Man

Oppression is a feature of the Fall of angels and the Fall of mankind. Oppression is the corruption of the original instinct for dominion given to man in his innocence.

> Genesis 1:26–28 (KJV 1900)
> [26] And God said, Let us make man in our image, after our likeness: and let them have dominion over the fish of the sea, and over the fowl of the air, and over the cattle, and over all the earth, and over every creeping thing that creepeth upon the earth. [27] So God created man in his *own* image, in the image of God created he him; male and female created he them. [28] And God blessed them, and God said unto them, Be fruitful, and multiply, and replenish the earth, and subdue it: and have dominion over the fish of the sea, and over the fowl of the air, and over every living thing that moveth upon the earth.

In the Fall, mankind's rejection of divine authority led to the

---

^{clxxix} Stranger: 1731 [H1616 Str. rw.] גֵּר (gēr): n.masc.; ≡ Str 1616; TWOT 330a—LN 11.55–11.89 alien, stranger, foreigner, i.e., one who is of a different geographical or cultural group, often with less rights than the reference group (Ge 15:13), see also LN 85.67–85.85; note: for NIV text in Isa 5:17, see 1531."
^{clxxx} Exodus 22.21; 23.9; Exodus 22.22-23; Jeremiah 7.6; Ezekiel 22.7
^{clxxxi} Ezekiel 22.7, 29; Malachi 3.5; Zephaniah 3.1-2; John 4.9; 8.48

malfunction of human authority in every institution, beginning in marriage and the family with the role reversal of Adam and Eve, and the murder of Abel by his brother. From that point forward, the abuse of authority, the basis of oppression, became common within human relationships and human institutions.

Oppression and the Fall of Angels

Lucifer's fall was caused by the abuse of the authority given him by God.

> Ezekiel 28:15–18 (KJV 1900)
> [15] Thou *wast* perfect in thy ways from the day that thou wast created, till iniquity was found in thee. [16] By the multitude of thy merchandise they have filled the midst of thee with violence, and thou hast sinned: therefore I will cast thee as profane out of the mountain of God: and I will destroy thee, O covering cherub, from the midst of the stones of fire. [17] Thine heart was lifted up because of thy beauty, thou hast corrupted thy wisdom by reason of thy brightness: I will cast thee to the ground, I will lay thee before kings, that they may behold thee. [18] Thou hast defiled thy sanctuaries by the multitude of thine iniquities, by the iniquity of thy traffick; therefore will I bring forth a fire from the midst of thee, it shall devour thee, and I will bring thee to ashes upon the earth in the sight of all them that behold thee.

Lucifer, by this sin becomes Satan the Adversary, and commits himself to the overthrow of divine authority and to usurp the rule of heaven and earth.

> Isaiah 14:12–17 (KJV 1900)
> 12 How art thou fallen from heaven, O Lucifer, son of the morning! How art thou cut down to the ground, which didst weaken the nations! 13 For thou hast said in thine heart, I will ascend into heaven, I will exalt my throne above the stars of God: I will sit also upon the mount of the congregation, in the sides of the north: 14 I will ascend above the heights of the clouds; I will be like the most High. 15 Yet thou shalt be brought down to hell, to the sides of the pit. 16 They that see thee shall narrowly look upon thee, and consider thee, saying, Is this the man that made the earth to tremble, that did shake kingdoms; 17 That made the world as a wilderness, and destroyed the cities thereof; That opened not the house of his

prisoners? [Hebrews 2.14-15]

What began as an upward focus upon divine worship and a downward stewardship [dominion] over that which God had created was corrupted by sin into an unholy urge by angels and men to dominate their peers.clxxxii The outcome of this obsession could not be anything but oppression. In the fall of Lucifer, he makes himself the implacable enemy of God, of the people of God and of humanity in general.

Oppression Against the People of God

Because of Satan's position as the temporary prince of this world [John 12.31; 2 Corinthians 4.4] oppression against the people of God can arise from a variety of sources. It can arise from the actions of the State, as it does in the case of Israel in Egypt. The reasons for that oppression were complex, involving the growing fear of an immigrant population that through their expansion were perceived as at least a threat to the Egyptian way of life and perhaps even to the national security [Exodus 1.7-10]. Satan used these political insecurities to instigate the oppression of the people of God.

There was the oppression of Israel during the period of the Judges when the neighboring city-states of Canaan and the vicinity fought against what could have been seen by them as an invading power that had wiped out much of the inhabitants of that land. Add to this God's desire to punish Israel for their rapid departure from the Covenant of Moses once in the land of Canaan [Judges 2.1-5, 10-15].

There was the persecution of the infant church by the Romans who saw Christianity as an illegal religion, unsanctioned by Roman

---

clxxxii This is the desire for unauthorized authority, the will to power over men, angels, and God Himself. Satan sought to rise above the "clouds" and inspired angelic rebellion [Ezekiel 28.16, 18; Revelation 12.1-4]. He also makes "prisoners" of men [Isaiah 14.17]. The devil tempted Eve with the offer of unauthorized authority ("ye shall be as gods"). Cain sought to dominate Abel and eventually the entire world was filled with oppression and violence [Genesis 6.11-13]. Once infected, the lust for unauthorized authority metastasized among men, resulting in the spiritual surgery of divine judgment in the worldwide flood that destroyed mankind but for one family.

law. This illegal status would eventually change, but until it did, there are recorded ten major persecutions of the Church in the empire.[186]

Oppression can originate from competing religions or sects. Perhaps the most vicious of persecutions occur from these motivations. Jesus himself was put to death because of such religious oppression [John 11.45-53]. After the Roman persecutions, the true Church was oppressed by that portion of Christendom that had assimilated into Rome, resulting in far more suffering than that inflicted by the Roman state.

God also uses the oppressive tendencies of the nations to correct his own people. For example, the scriptures specifically state that oppression would be a consequence of the breaking of the Law of Moses by the Jews [Deuteronomy 28.28-33]. Israel was judged for its determined disobedience to the Mosaic Covenant by nations like the Philistines, Assyrians, and Babylonians.[clxxxiii] Israel had become an oppressing nation in violation of the Mosaic Covenant.[clxxxiv] After much patience, and many cycles of discipline executed by the Gentiles tribes that surrounded Israel, God sent cataclysmic judgment through Gentile conquest and colonization of the Jewish nation by the Assyrians and the Babylonians. The fall of Jerusalem at the hands of Nebuchadnezzar in 586 BC. began what is called in prophecy the Times of the Gentiles.[187]

Oppression is a permanent characteristic of the fallen world and *believers* can find themselves its victims. Nothing need be done for oppression to find believers. The presence of oppression does not imply the guilt or innocence of its victim. The believer must be sure that he does not become the perpetrator of oppression or the protector of oppressors.

Oppression Against Humanity in General

In addition to state-sponsored or religious oppression, mankind may be oppressed spiritually. Satan and his demons can enforce

---

clxxxiii Jeremiah 6.6; Zephaniah 3.1, 5-6
clxxxiv Deuteronomy 24.14 c.f., Jeremiah 6.6

degrees of spiritual bondage upon people. The intensification of a person's existing sinful practices, the introduction of new depravities into the Community, demonically induced illnesses and disabilities, and the bodily possession of demonic spirits are all possible under this category of oppression. Demonic oppression comes about through extended and willful disobedience towards God, through engagement with other demonically involved individuals or groups, by generational spiritual commitments or by direct appeals to Satan for pleasure, power, or insight. Jesus himself was tempted by the devil to achieve the kingdom, power, and glory by capitulation to Satan's authority [Luke 4.5-7].

There is oppression that is based upon factors such as race or ethnicity. This category of oppression approximates the experience of the Jews in Egypt, which is why Egyptian slavery was a recurring theme of the sermons and songs of black believers during the slavery era in the United States. The oppression of the Samaritans by the Jews of Israel is an example of ethnic oppression that was disguised as religious zeal. As we have noted, God does not assign judgment to races, because race is not valid basis for human categorization, but an artificial concept designed to control society and isolate wealth and power to specific groups. Divine judgments are applied to the categories that God Himself created such as individuals, families, nations, and lands. The question of race-based slavery will be addressed later in this Appendix.

There are oppressions which originate with God as a judgment against unbelievers or believers that fail to respond to the ethical light that they have been provided by Him. God is free to impose any and all kinds of calamity upon mankind and sometimes this takes the form of oppression.[clxxxv]

Oppression and the Nations

God holds the Gentile nations responsible for their adherence to conscience.[clxxxvi] God expects the nations to do right and punishes them when they do not. God administers judgment upon the

---

[clxxxv] Judges 2.10-14; 3.5-8; Isaiah 10.1-6
[clxxxvi] Romans 1.18-21; 2.14-16

oppressing nations by periodically turning the oppressor into the oppressed. God himself orchestrates the overthrow of oppressing nations by successively stronger empires.[clxxxvii]

Human history is the story of national empires seeking world domination through force and oppression [Daniel 2; 8; 9]. Human history will culminate with the appearance of the first true world empire since Babel, led by a man who will most faithfully represent Satan's thinking in economics, religion, politics and social organization, the Antichrist. This leader will represent his dominion as the fulfillment of mankind's spiritual aspirations, the Kingdom of God. However, his kingdom will be quickly revealed to be a rule of oppression by demonic despotism [Revelation 13].

Oppression and the fear of oppression defaces civilization. Satan uses fear to rule men and oppression produces a soul-disfiguring fear [Hebrews 2.14-15]. The devil uses this fear to divide or to unite men as he sees fit. Because of the Fall, the urge to oppress is a feature of the sin nature. This predisposition is exploited by Satan and made into a spiritual system by which the nations are ruled by him. Oppression is a spiritual initiative of Satan, which is why there is no combination of secular factors that can remove it. Although oppression is administered by human systems, it can only be removed by spiritual action. God can deprive oppression of its power to debilitate his people, this is the meaning of the Third Nationbuilding Principle. God allows the believer to participate in the defeat of oppression via spiritual warfare.

God is Opposed to Oppressors

> Psalm 72:1–4 (KJV 1900)
> 1 Give the king thy judgments, O God, And thy righteousness unto the king's son. 2 He shall judge thy people with righteousness, And thy poor with judgment. 3 The mountains shall bring peace to the people, And the little hills, by righteousness. 4 He shall judge the poor of the people, He shall save the children of the needy, And shall break in pieces the oppressor.

[clxxxvii] Assyria and Babylon: Jeremiah 46:14–24; 50:15-18.

God is implacably opposed to the oppressor, whom He judges in this life and in the life to come.[clxxxviii] No one will get away with anything. The oppressors will pay for their oppression and the oppressed believer will be rewarded for obedience to the Word of God while under oppression.[clxxxix]

God judges' oppressors among His people.[cxc] Regardless of how oppressive they are, believers seldom recognize themselves as oppressors. The holiness of God demands the severe judgment of all oppressors. Just as the sin nature demands that oppressors exist, so the essence of God demands their judgment [Malachi 3.5].

The people of God are to be holy for they live in God's presence and have been purchased as His possession [1 Peter 1.16]. Holiness is anti-oppression, anti-exploitation, anti-abuse of the weak. *Oppression by believers is evidence of the malfunction of sanctification.* Oppression also involves a disrespect for the Word of God which so plainly condemns exploitation of others. Sanctification results in a person who is like God. Such a person will not practice oppression or justify those that do.

> 1 John 3:10 (KJV 1900)
> [10] In this the children of God are manifest, and the children of the devil: whosoever doeth not righteousness is not of God, neither he that loveth not his brother.

The restoration of justice for the weak is a fruit of repentance.[cxci] The righteous person sets the oppressed free.[cxcii] This is an apt commentary on the psychological disposition of "Christian nations" that practice oppression, constantly discovering innovations that will enable the most efficient exploitation of the weak. Oppression is consistent with Satan's philosophy and system of world administration.

[clxxxviii] Exodus 22.21-24; Psalms 10.15-18; Proverbs 22:22–23; Isaiah 49:26; Jeremiah 6.5-7
[clxxxix] This also applies to believers who are involved in oppression. Not only will such Christians suffer divine discipline in this life, but they will also suffer a loss of eternal reward in the life to come [2 Corinthians 5.9-10].
[cxc] Jeremiah 6.5-7; Zephaniah 3:1–4
[cxci] Psalms 82:1-4; Isaiah 1.16-18
[cxcii] Isaiah 58.6-7; Luke 4.18

The relief of oppression was a part of the ministry of Christ in his first advent.

> Luke 4:18 (KJV 1900)
> [18] The Spirit of the Lord *is* upon me, because he hath anointed me to preach the gospel to the poor; he hath sent me to heal the brokenhearted, to preach deliverance to the captives, and recovering of sight to the blind, to set at liberty them that are <u>bruised,</u>
>
> **Bruised 2575** θραύω (*thrauō*): vb.; ≡ Str. 2353; LN 22.22 **oppress**, (pass.) be oppressed, be downtrodden [188]

The Psychology of the Oppressor

Jeremiah 22:17 [KJV]
 But thine eyes and thine heart are not but for thy covetousness, and for to shed innocent blood, and for oppression, and for violence, to do it.

According to the Scriptures, the psychology of the oppressor is characterized by:

1. *The fear of death*
2. *Worship of consumption*
3. *Violence, Pride and Blasphemy.*

You Only Live Once

The *doctrine* of the oppressor is that this life is all there is.[cxciii] The hope of the wicked is in this life alone: "You Only Live Once" is his motto. Therefore, he has little fear of God until the very moment of judgment. If he is a believer, his sin-induced spiritual blindness results in self-justification until he finally perishes under terminal divine judgment [1 John 5.16]. Because of this earthly focus, both his heaven and hell are found here on earth. Because of

---

[cxciii] Psalms 14.1,4; Hebrews 2.14-15; 2 Peter 3.3-4

this conviction His conscience is calibrated to justify all that promotes the achievement of his best life now, by any means necessary.

Worship of Consumption [Lust]

The *worship* of the oppressor is the fulfillment of lust by consumption. By *consumption* is meant the satisfaction of lust, of whatever category it might be.

> 1 John 2:16 [KJV]
> For all that is in the world, the lust of the flesh, and the lust of the eyes, and the pride of life, is not of the Father, but is of the world.

A chief means of acquiring what the oppressor consumes is by oppression [Amos 3.15-4.1]. The wicked view whatever power they have as ability to satisfy their covetousness which is the purpose that provides them with meaning. Many oppressors are likely to clothe their lust with ideology to justify *to others* the ruthlessness that oppression entails. They have no need for internal self-justification because they have reversed their conscience. To do good is an abomination to them, in that it is lost opportunity to oppress[cxciv] and importantly, because genuine good is a reproach to their corrupted conscience. "Good" is of value only to the extent that it enables a greater oppression to be perpetrated.

Once general revelation[189] is rejected as the foundation of the human conscience, the character of humanity becomes fixed upon the exploitation of others.

> Romans 1:28-32 [KJV]
> And even as they did not like to retain God in their knowledge, God gave them over to a reprobate mind, to do those things which are not convenient; 29 Being filled with all unrighteousness, fornication, wickedness, covetousness,

---

[cxciv] Micah 2.1-2; Proverbs 13.19; 29.27

maliciousness; full of envy, murder, debate, deceit, malignity; whisperers, 30 Backbiters, haters of God, despiteful, proud, boasters, inventors of evil things, disobedient to parents, 31 Without understanding, covenantbreakers, without natural affection, implacable, unmerciful: 32 <u>Who knowing</u> the judgment of God, that they which commit such things are worthy of death, not only do the same, but have pleasure in them that do them.

Oppression is the fallback religion of men who, due to their sinful commitments, cannot trust in God. Consumption [lust] is the chief value of the oppressor, his spiritual objective [1 John 2.15-16]. Since they find life in this world only, acquiring, storing up and consuming is the objective of their religion [Psalms73.7-9]. Oppression therefore is the process of extorting the weak for the purpose of ever-growing consumption.

It is important not to limit the lust/consumption of the oppressor to physical things. Asa's *pride* [the maintenance of self-esteem, the "pride of life"] was the reason for the oppression in 2 Chronicles 16:7–10. The Egyptians profited from the enslavement of the Jews, but their initial issue was *fear* of Israel's growing power and influence [Exodus 1.7-10] because of the potential *loss of control* of their nation. American slavery was the origin of a system that not only steals labor, but also addicted the people to the narcotic of *racial superiority*. Even the commitment of the power elite to the establishment of the ultimate expression of oppression, the consummation of the Mystery of Iniquity under the coming world ruler [2 Thessalonians 2.1-10] is the fulfillment of lust through the permanent administration of *universal demonic despotism* promised them.[cxcv] It is fascinating to note that this coming world ruler, the Beast and his kingdom, is also described in these same terms of consumption, oppression and violence.

[cxcv] Genesis 3.4-5 "ye shall be as gods"

> Daniel 7:23 [KJV]
> Thus he said, The fourth beast shall be the fourth kingdom upon earth, which shall be diverse from all kingdoms, and shall <u>devour</u> the whole earth, and shall <u>tread it down, and break it in pieces</u>. [c.f. Revelation 13.1-2]

Violence

Violence is the *modus operandi* of oppression; without it, or the threat of it, oppression cannot be maintained. Regardless of the cultural facades oppression might utilize, behind them all is the threat of violence. Love is the underlying motivation and interpersonal tool of the believer and God. Violence is the agency and interpersonal tool of the wicked.[cxcvi]

> Psalms 12:5 [KJV]
> 5 For the oppression of the poor, for the sighing of the needy, now will I arise, saith the Lord; I will set him in safety from him that puffeth at him.

The word for *oppression* in Psalms 12.5 can be interpreted as *violence*. The root of much, if not all violence is lust, the desire to acquire. Violence is the strong right arm of injustice. Violence is the domain of the devil who was a "murderer from the beginning" [John 8.44]. Satan incited the first human to sin in full knowledge of its lethal consequences for mankind.

Pride and Blasphemy

The apparent "prosperity of the wicked" exists because judgment is delayed.[cxcvii] The trust of the wicked in riches is a trust in their own ability over against the ability of God, whom they do not trust. Because of the [merciful] delay in God's judgment upon sin, men

---

[cxcvi] Psalms 73.6; Jeremiah22.17; Ezekiel 28.15-16
[cxcvii] Psalms 73.3-5; Ecclesiastes 7:15; 8.11

of power will have space to use that power to oppress others. Health, peace, longevity, sons, and other factors will work to their advantage enabling wickedness to prosper.

> Psalms 73:3–9 (KJV 1900)
> 3 For I was envious at the foolish, When I saw the prosperity of the wicked. 4 For there are no bands in their death: But their strength is firm. 5 They are not in trouble as other men; Neither are they plagued like other men. 6 Therefore pride compasseth them about as a chain; Violence covereth them as a garment. 7 Their eyes stand out with fatness: They have more than heart could wish. 8 They are corrupt, and speak wickedly concerning oppression: They speak loftily. 9 They set their mouth against the heavens, And their tongue walketh through the earth.

Because of divine probation upon mankind, the wicked become proud, which is the result of freedom of movement to oppress and the apparent success of their efforts.[190] Their success causes them to conclude that their philosophy and methods are effective and validated by experience [Psalms 73.6]. They see themselves as "self-made men." The one who oppresses does not perceive any eternal consequences for his oppression [Psalms 73.11] because his corrupt conscience affirms him and because, to him, this life is all there is. Arrogance prevents him from considering consequences in this life until they are upon him, and even then, he often does not understand them as consequences of his actions.

Case Study: Satan

> "His own terrible sin before God would not be condemned in the eyes of the world, for it is that which they most idealize and praise. In his sin he aspired to that which is highest, and proposed to realize his ideal by his own self-sufficiency and strength...

> "Yet this unholy ambition and disregard for the Creator is a most commendable thing according to the standards of the Satanic order. In the language of the world, Satan is simply "self

made" and every element of his attitude toward his Creator is, as a principle of life, both commended and practiced by the world."[191]

The word *corrupt*[192] in Psalms 73.8 (above) means to mock or to blaspheme. These men mock and scoff at true religion, since they are impressed only with the success and the proceeds of oppression. Therefore, they extol the science of corruption and contemplate even more grandiose schemes to defraud and rob others. This includes racism which is simply a method of extorting wealth [and other things] from a weaker group.

> "Racism is the calculated introduction of discrimination into the institutions of society. Racism is a conspiracy to scientifically marginalize or destroy a specific racial group by the manipulation of the organs of society such as the family, government (including legislation, law enforcement and the courts), academia, the media, and the church. Racism is cultural warfare, or the extension of conventional warfare to the cultural sphere."[cxcviii]

In biblical terms, racism is the deliberate and organized exploitation of the stranger and the foreigner.

These men are cognizant of the fact that their religion is opposed by heaven [Psalms 73.8b-9]. However, their unbelief and relative freedom from divine rebuke has made them reckless in their attitudes and actions against God.

Romans 9:22–23 (KJV 1900)
22 What if God, willing to shew his wrath, and to make his power known, endured with much longsuffering the vessels of wrath fitted to destruction: 23 And that he might make known the riches of his glory on the vessels of mercy, which he had afore prepared unto glory,

---

[cxcviii] Definition from Chapter Two

The Psychology of the Oppressed:

Oppression affects every part of the life of the oppressed person. To achieve optimal effectiveness, oppression must impair the soul. Oppression can result in categories of mental illness [Deuteronomy 28.28-34!].[cxcix]

Oppression can interfere with proper spiritual function.[cc] Oppression puts pressure upon the properly functioning spiritual life, especially in its effect upon the self-concept of the oppressed and the oppressor [Romans 12.1-3].[cci]

Oppression is related to terror.[ccii] Some modern translations use the word *terror* for the final reference to oppression in Psalms 10.18. The oppressor has as his aim the terror of the victims of oppression. He strives to create a mental condition in the oppressed which facilitates oppression. Terror reduces the costs of exploitation by producing self-oppression in its victims. Terrorism in support of oppression can defeat the deployment of spiritual resources by the oppressed.

The process of spiritual disarmament is advanced by the planting of false Bible teachers among the oppressed. False teachers are an essential feature of exploitation because spiritual truth defeats oppression by re-establishing the proper spiritual and psychological function of the soul. The spiritually healthy believer can combat

---

[cxcix] Chapters Six and Seven
[cc] Psalms 119.134; Isaiah 58:6; Luke 1.74
[cci] Oppressors who purport to be Christians tend to scoff at concern for the self-concept of the oppressed for obvious reasons. The efficient execution of oppression depends upon a manipulated self-concept resulting in psychological self-oppression. Thus, it was important for the slave to be *broken* and in modern times, systems of retaliation exist for members of the oppressed group who *break* their programming. Slave theology posits that to be a good Christian, oppression, the neurotic self-concept, and semi-functional Christian experience that comes with it must be accepted. To the extent that slave theology concedes any damage to the black soul, it is falsely believed that the gospel can heal these psychological wounds without directly addressing their source or the processes which create new psychological disability to the souls of black folk.
[ccii] Psalms 10.18 (NASB); Isaiah 54.14

terror with faith in God and his Word.

Oppression destroys human capacity. By terror it destroys the capacity for self-defense, it damages productive capacity by stealing the products of labor, and it devastates psychological well-being of the people through the mental programming designed to maintain oppression in the soul, and as stated, it cripples spiritual capacity by the teaching of false Christian doctrine and the misapplication of accurate doctrine.

Oppression and Slavery

Slavery is a system of oppression. Slavery is inconsistent with the *divine purpose* for man at creation [Dominion], it is incompatible with the *concept of man as the image and likeness of God* [Genesis 1.26-28] and it is in conflict with the *position of the believer* who is in Christ [1 Corinthians 7.23]. Therefore, slavery is not benign, in fact, it is the symbol of that institution from which man is set free by the new birth.

> Galatians 4:3 [NASU]
> Therefore you are no longer a slave, but a son; and if a son, then an heir through God

Slave theology has created a doctrine of slavery which contradicts that presented by Scripture. The purpose of this slave theology is to justify American slavery by:

> ➤ Justifying American slavery by falsely equating it with the regulated institution established in the Law of Moses.
> ➤ Using the argument from silence of the prophets, apostles, and Jesus, regarding the pagan practice of slavery in their day to prove that the institution was outside the scope of the gospel and Christian sanctification.
> ➤ In this way, the bible teachers and Christians justify the permanent separation of the oppressed from the continually compounding proceeds of their stolen labor, while commanding their silent acceptance of the

continued exercise of oppression in its more advanced forms.

Slavery Is Oppression

> Deuteronomy 23:15–16 (KJV 1900)
> 15 <u>Thou shalt not</u> deliver unto his master the servant which is escaped from his master unto thee: 16 He shall dwell with thee, even among you, in that place which he shall choose in one of thy gates, where it liketh him best: <u>thou shalt not oppress him</u>.

Israel, the nation in which God resided, was apparently a *nation of refuge* for any escaped slave. In this passage, to return an escaped slave is equated with oppression. To fail to return a slave to his master was not considered a crime. Not only are the Jews commanded not to return him to his owner [if he were merely an employee, why would he need to escape?], but neither are the Jews permitted to oppress him by re-enslaving him or exploiting his vulnerability in other ways.

Slavery is oppression. The Jews were oppressed as slaves in Egypt. God delivered them from slavery *without compensation* to the Egyptians.[193] On the contrary, the Jews plundered the Egyptians on their way to freedom [Exodus 12.36].

God regulated the institution of slavery in Israel. In so doing, he removed the oppressive elements from it. Gentile slaves could be held as property, even intergenerationally [Leviticus 25.46], but they could not be obtained by kidnapping, or as stolen property.[cciii] Slaves could not be injured or raped without severe consequences.[194]

> Exodus 21:16 (KJV 1900)
> 16 And he that stealeth a man, and selleth him, or if he be found in his hand, he shall surely be put to death.

[cciii] Exodus 21.16, 20, 26-27 Deuteronomy 21.10-14; 1 Timothy 1.8-11

Exodus 21:26–27 (KJV 1900)
26 And if a man smite the eye of his servant, or the eye of his
maid, that it perish; he shall let him go free for his eye's sake. 27
And if he smite out his manservant's tooth, or his maidservant's
tooth; he shall let him go free for his tooth's sake.

Exodus 21:20 (KJV 1900)
²⁰ And if a man smite his servant, or his maid, with a rod, and he
die under his hand; he shall be surely <u>punished</u>.

Punished 5358 נָקַם [naqam /naw·kam/] v. A primitive root; TWOT
1413; GK 5933; 35 occurrences; AV translates as "avenge" 18 times,
"vengeance" four times, "revenge" four times, "take" four times,
"avenger" twice, "punished" twice, and "surely" once. 1 to avenge, take
vengeance, revenge, avenge oneself, be avenged, be punished. 1A (Qal).
1A1 to avenge, take vengeance. 1A2 to entertain revengeful feelings. 1B
(**Niphal**). **1B1 to avenge oneself. 1B2 to suffer vengeance.** 1C (Piel)
to avenge. 1D (Hophal) to be avenged, vengeance be taken (for blood).
1E (Hithpael) to avenge oneself. James Strong, Enhanced Strong's
Lexicon (Woodside Bible Fellowship, 1995).

Slavery in the ancient world could occur because of defeat in
warfare, debt, criminal punishment, from birth to a slave or by
voluntary agreement. There were also illegal or immoral ways of
ending up a slave, which the scriptures prohibited to the people of
God.

God regulated in the Law human systems which were harmful to
mankind if left unregulated, such as polygamy [Exodus 21.10-11],
divorce [regulated by Moses, Deuteronomy 24.1-2], and
manslaughter [Numbers 35.22-29, 32].

God's regulation of slavery within Israel was an alternative to
worse alternatives that existed amongst the Gentiles. Slavery in the
Bible as regulated by God for Jew or Gentile, kept the institution as
a solution for the situations described above, while removing the
sinful elements. God does not regulate sin, he prohibits it. It was an
imperfect solution applied to sinful men, but it was not, in the
form commanded by God a sin, or oppression. *God did not create a*

situation where Jews were free to commit sin against Gentile slaves. On the other hand, the Gentile slave system that God replaced, was denominated by the abuses that the Law of Moses discouraged. An example of these abuses is readily found in American slavery, which was a race-based institution founded upon men stealing, the theft of labor, rape, and severe forms of violence.

Slavery is entirely incompatible with the divine ownership of His people. Israelites could not be made slaves by fellow Jews because they were already the slaves of God. They were not even to be referred to as slaves, but as hired servants [Leviticus 25.40]. Therefore, because of their relation to God, the status of the Jewish slave was different from the Gentile slave. He was not considered property, his service was temporary, he was not to be treated with the cruelty that characterized their treatment in Egypt. Even the Gentiles residing in Israel did not have the right to permanently hold a Jewish slave if the slave himself or another Jew could redeem him [Exodus 25.39-55].

In the Church Age, this same principle is in force. The new birth does not eliminate the institutions of this world such as slavery, under either Testament, but it does modify them for believers. Christians are not allowed to make slaves of their brethren in Christ for the same reason that the Jews of the Old Testament were not allowed to do so. *Slaves in Israel did not possess a greater privilege under salvation than the members of the Body of Christ who were slaves to believers.* The failure to make this distinction under American slavery is yet another artifact of Slave Theology.

In the book of Philemon, Paul sent the slave Onesimus back to Philemon as a courtesy, not out of legal necessity. Deuteronomy 23.15-16 was still a valid principle to be applied, even if Onesimus was an unbeliever. *A fortiori*, the *conversion* of Onesimus absolutely changed the character of slavery that was heretofore to be practiced by Philemon.

Philemon 1 (KJV 1900)

1 PAUL, a <u>prisoner</u> of Jesus Christ, and Timothy our brother, unto Philemon our dearly beloved, and fellowlabourer,

> **Prisoner 1198** δέσμιος [*desmios* /des·mee·os/] . From 1199; TDNT 2:43; TDNTA 145; GK 1300; 16 occurrences; AV translates as "prisoner" 14 times, "be in bonds" once, and "in bonds" once. **1** bound, in bonds, a captive, a prisoner.[cciv]

Philemon 8–9 (KJV 1900)

[8] Wherefore, though I might be much bold in Christ to enjoin thee that which is convenient, [9] *yet* for love's sake I rather beseech *thee*, being such an one as Paul the aged, and now also a prisoner of Jesus Christ.

Paul begins his letter to Philemon stating that he himself was *under bonds*, to the Lord.[195] He immediately intimates the principle taught in the Old and New Testament regarding the ownership of believers by God. Although he was a prisoner of the secular authorities in Rome, he identifies himself as a prisoner of Jesus Christ.

He continues that he has the power to command Philemon to do what he will ask because of his Apostleship, since his demands will be scriptural and therefore constitute Philemon's duty [v 8-*convenient*], but rather, he prepares him for a request that he will make in the letter concerning Onesimus.

Philemon 10–11 (KJV 1900)

[10] I beseech thee for my son Onesimus, whom I have begotten in my bonds: [11] which in time past was to thee unprofitable, but now profitable to thee and to me:

Paul says that Onesimus has been born again through his evangelistic ministry. Divine providence led the slave to Paul, who happens to not only know his master, but who is the spiritual

---

[cciv] James Strong, *Enhanced Strong's Lexicon* (Woodside Bible Fellowship, 1995).

287

authority in the life of Philemon. Onesimus has been saved, he is now the property of God, like the Israelites, but enjoys a greater privilege because of the enhanced position of the Christian as a member of the Body of Christ.

> Ephesians 5:30 (KJV 1900)
> [30] For we are members of his body, of his flesh, and of his bones.

Although Onesimus remained in the same economic relation to Philemon, this is all that remains the same. Under the inferior economy of the Law, Paul would not have been required to return Onesimus at all, regardless of his spiritual condition [Deuteronomy 23.15-16]. How much less reason to return him now?

> Philemon 15–16 (KJV 1900)
> [15] For perhaps he therefore departed for a season, that thou shouldest receive him for ever; [16] not now as a servant, but above a servant, a brother beloved, specially to me, but how much more unto thee, both in the flesh, and in the Lord?

Paul has specifically identified the biblical principle that the saved individual is no longer a slave but a brother, even if original economic arrangements remain intact. Philemon was not simply a Gentile slave owner, but a believer and a an Elder in the local church [Philemon 2]. Even so, Paul did not return Onesimus because of those secular arrangements, but out of respect for his relationship with Philemon. There was no spiritual obligation to return a runaway slave.

The fear of American Christian slave owners that the salvation of Africans would invalidate slavery was at least partially true. Salvation made the slave the property of God, His chattel preceding the legitimate but secondary claim of the of the Christian slave owner, who is now the brother of the slave and obligated to treat him as a such, just as commanded under the Law and clarified here in the New Testament. This idea was directly contrary to the character of American slavery, which was the perpetual theft of labor based upon race and enforced by terror. The Christian slaveholder properly understood that he could no longer work the Christian slave to an early death to avoid elderly care, could no longer mercilessly whip, castrate, and lynch the slave and could no longer borrow his wife or daughter at night. The only way to reconcile the new status of the believing slave with the wants and needs of the slaveholding system *was to change Christianity*, and this is what happened.

> Leviticus 25:55 (KJV 1900)
> 55 For unto me the children of Israel *are* servants; they *are* my servants whom I brought forth out of the land of Egypt: I *am* the Lord your God.

> 1 Corinthians 7:21–23 (KJV 1900)
> 21 Art thou called *being* a servant? care not for it: but if thou mayest be made free, use *it* rather. 22 For he that is called in the Lord, *being* a servant, is the Lord's freeman: likewise also he that is called, *being* free, is Christ's servant. 23 Ye are bought with a price; be not ye the servants of men.

Christian Leadership Enables Oppression

In Section One it was established that the spiritual leadership of the people of God can be the source of a positive or negative chain reaction in the Congregation and the Community. A departure from the Word of God among the spiritual teachers (prophets, priests)[ccv] facilitates oppression within the civil leadership structure (princes) [ccvi] and the eventual debasement of the people, who are also sold to oppression.[ccvii] This conspiracy of teachers leads to the people failing to hear faithful prophets [Zechariah 7:8-13] and following the "commandments of men," worldly philosophies and trends [Hosea 5.11]. Israel was trained in oppression by its spiritual

---

[ccv] Ezekiel 22.23-31
[ccvi] Ezekiel 22.6-7; Zephaniah 3:1–4
[ccvii] Isaiah 30.9-12; 59.12-15; Hosea 12.1-7

leadership.

Today, the infiltration of political philosophy into practical theology has led to a weakening of belief in the authority of the scriptures. The Pastors and teachers still proclaim their allegiance to biblical authority, but they are willing to ignore or change the Word of God for the sake of political expedience. They are unwilling to stand for simple right and wrong except where it is in alignment with their political tribe. Moral unbelievers look upon this kind of Christianity with justifiable contempt. Unsurprisingly, this kind of compromise kills the spiritual effectiveness of the local church because it euthanizes the spiritual lives of the Congregation.

This same process in ancient Israel did not result in the loss of an election, but the loss of hundreds of thousands of lives in futile wars, the three conquests of Israel[ccviii] and the diaspora of hundreds of thousands more.

Although the judgment of America for its departure from the Word of God in service to racial apartheid has been going on since at least the Civil War, when an entire generation of men were wasted in death and incapacitating wounds, most of Christendom does not even perceive that it is under divine judgment, because they do not believe that they are wrong. This is solely because of the corrupt spiritual leadership of the nation. Because of this the Community and the nation are stripped of spiritual protection and suffering under intensified demonic oppression.

> Isaiah 1:4–7 (KJV 1900)
> [4] Ah sinful nation, a people laden with iniquity, A seed of evildoers, children that are corrupters: They have forsaken the Lord, They have provoked the Holy One of Israel unto anger, They are gone away backward. [5] Why should ye be stricken any more? Ye will revolt more and more: The whole head is sick, and the whole heart faint. [6] From the sole of the foot even unto the head *there is* no soundness in it; *But* wounds, and bruises, and putrifying sores: They have not been closed, neither bound up, neither mollified with ointment. [7] Your country *is* desolate, Your cities *are* burned with fire: Your land, strangers devour it in your

---

[ccviii] Israel Northern Kingdom 722 BC., Judah Southern Kingdom 586 BC., Jerusalem and Judah 70 AD.

presence, And *it is* desolate, as overthrown by strangers.

The Duration of Oppression

The *duration* of oppression depends upon the spiritual disposition of the oppressed and hidden purposes of the plan of God [Psalms 42:9]. It does not primarily depend upon the thinking of the oppressor.

It is both interesting and important to note that the Bible presents very few examples of oppressor groups or nations that repent of their oppression. In almost every case, the nation continues to oppress all the way until its final destruction and deletion from history. Only Assyria in the days of Jonah comes to mind as a minor, brief exception. The United Kingdom of Israel, with the benefit of the Word of God, the priesthood and the prophets immediately departed from the Lord after the death of Joshua's generation, becoming a nation of oppressors. In the Southern Kingdom of Judah, God's gracious provision of several godly kings led the nation to short seasons of repentance, while the Northern Kingdom of Israel lacked any righteous kings. Despite many faithful prophets, the nation of Israel continued until John the Baptist in a state of spiritual rebellion, ultimately conspiring to kill the prophesied Messiah who was authenticated by scripture, signs, and wonders.

This is one good reason [but not the only reason] why the oppressed should not look to their oppressor for deliverance from oppression. God need not change the attitude of the oppressor to deliver the oppressed.

> Psalm 23:5 (KJV 1900)
> [5] Thou preparest a table before me <u>in the presence</u> of mine enemies: Thou anointest my head with oil; my cup runneth over.

It was not necessary for God to make the Egyptians love or respect the Jews for Him to deliver them for slavery. God did not need to change the attitude of Haman and the Persian people to deliver Esther and the Jews of that day. Neither was it necessary that the Southern States change their attitudes regarding black people and slavery for African people to be emancipated in the United States.

Deliverance can be delayed because the people rely exclusively upon secular solutions, because they persist in their own sins, because of *divine grace towards the oppressor*, or because of many other purposes in the plan of God.

God delayed the judgment of the oppressive Canaanites for four hundred years to fill up their judgment [Genesis 15.16]. He gave the entire world, which was filled with violence and oppression, one hundred twenty years of grace before the flood [Genesis 6.3]. The martyred saints beneath the throne of God wail "how long?" awaiting God's vengeance [Revelation 6.10].

Deliverance from Oppression

Oppression is not the exploitation of the strong, but the weak. The Jews were warned not to oppress the widow, the orphan, or the foreigner in their gates because they too were once socially disadvantaged aliens in Egypt. By its very definition, deliverance from exploitation must come from a stronger party and that party, for the believer, is God.

> Matthew 12:28–29 (KJV 1900)
> [28] But if I cast out devils by the Spirit of God, then the kingdom of God is come unto you. [29] Or else how can one enter into a strong man's house, and spoil his goods, except he first bind the strong man? and then he will spoil his house.

Israel is criticized and punished in scripture for looking to the nations: Syria, Egypt, Assyria, and Babylon for rescue rather than to God. God restores justice to the oppressed.[ccix] God Himself is the only guarantor of justice to anyone [Psalms 119.122].

God delivers people *from* oppression, and he delivers people *in* oppression. *Believers are not guaranteed freedom from physical oppression, but deliverance from it.* Deliverance can mean complete rescue from oppression, or the ability to prosper while under oppression. Every

[ccix] Psalms 10:18; 12.5; 17:7–10; 103.6; Ecclesiastes 5.8; Proverbs 22:22–23

believer will not experience physical deliverance from oppression. The entire testimony of scripture attests to this fact.

> Hebrews 11:35–40 (KJV 1900)
> 35 Women received their dead raised to life again: and others were tortured, not accepting deliverance; that they might obtain a better resurrection: 36 And others had trial of cruel mockings and scourgings, yea, moreover of bonds and imprisonment: 37 They were stoned, they were sawn asunder, were tempted, were slain with the sword: they wandered about in sheepskins and goatskins; being destitute, afflicted, tormented; 38 (Of whom the world was not worthy:) they wandered in deserts, and in mountains, and in dens and caves of the earth. 39 And these all, having obtained a good report through faith, received not the promise: 40 God having provided some better thing for us, that they without us should not be made perfect.

In considering deliverance from oppression, one must first ask what is the believer's responsibility when under oppression? Is the Christian's first obligation to escape oppression, or is it to accomplish something while under it?

The first responsibility of the believer is to glorify God by his sanctification and by his verbal witness of the Gospel, irrespective of the conditions under which he finds himself. Modern Christianity has made the well-being of the believer the purpose of the new birth. The believer's happiness in this life and the next is the sole objective of the Cross, according to the modern understanding of the Christian faith. This way of thinking leads to the perception that God is here for our benefit, rather than we here for His benefit.

The truth is that God is accomplishing something in the heavens and the earth, among angels and men, into which he has invited elect angels and men to participate. Our assignment upon the earth is to make God, his power and grace, known in whatever situation we are assigned, recognizing that he has placed us in history where he has chosen. The silver lining in all this is that the believer's obedience to God's commands in scripture are the very means by which God accomplishes deliverance from oppression. The Three Principles of Nationbuilding are the distillation of doctrinal truths that can prepare a family, Community, or nation for freedom when God determines that it is time to provide it.

Normally, the oppressed want to find an avenue of liberation that does not include submission to God. This includes many who call themselves Christians. The most serious categories of oppression are nullified in the new birth. When we comprehend that oppression is a spiritual initiative then it will be understood that spiritual redemption of the soul *is* the deliverance of the oppressed.[ccx] Every unsaved individual is living under *spiritual* oppression, which is the source of every other kind of exploitation. Spiritual oppression is defeated in the new birth. Redemption through faith in Christ frees the believer from the debt and guilt of sin, but also from the oppression of the devil and of the dominion of sin in the flesh.

> Hebrews 2:14–15 (KJV 1900)
> 14 Forasmuch then as the children are partakers of flesh and blood, he also himself likewise took part of the same; that through death he might destroy him that had the power of death, that is, the devil; 15 And deliver them who through fear of death were all their lifetime subject to bondage.[ccxi]

Even under worldly forms of oppression the faithful can find refuge and protection in the Lord. The awareness of God's provision in trials is essential to establishing the framework in which God may provide physical deliverance. Oppression is a test that produces spiritual growth and accrues future blessing for the Christian [1 Peter 4.12-16]. The testimony of the faithful under

---

[ccx] Jeremiah 31.11; 50.33-34; Luke 4.18
[ccxi] **Bondage**: 1397 δουλεία [douleia /doo·li·ah/] n f. From 1398; TDNT 2:261; TDNTA 182; GK 1525; Five occurrences; AV translates as "bondage" five times. 1 slavery, bondage, the condition of a slave.

oppression is evangelistic, resulting in the conviction and salvation of the lost who witness the provision of God for the believer who is under oppression yet thrives via divine resources.

God provides physical as well as spiritual support for his people. He provides for the logistical support [food, clothing, shelter, Bible instruction] of every believer regardless of his status under freedom or oppression. Both spiritual deliverance and physical provision belong to every believer, everywhere and at every stage of history.

> Psalm 37:25–26 (KJV 1900)
> 25 I have been young, and *now* am old; Yet have I not seen the righteous forsaken, Nor his seed begging bread. 26 *He is* ever merciful, and lendeth; And his seed *is* blessed.

Believers can delay their deliverance from oppression by disobedience to God, by ignorance of how God delivers from oppression and of how God sustains the Christian while under oppression.

When group oppression is a consequence of sustained disobedience against the Lord, the judgment of the unfaithful becomes the testing of the faithful. The same God who provides the unfaithful believer with punishment simultaneously provides the faithful believer with pressure that forms Christian character and accrues a surpassing weight of glory [2 Corinthians 4.17-18]. The oppressed can proclaim praise within oppression because they know that the character of God remains intact, along with His promises and His plans. The praise of the believer is not based upon His circumstances but upon His realization of the Person and the Work of God in his own life and in the world. The obedient believer can be certain that God is working all things for good regardless of his situation. Therefore, God will be glorified, His purposes accomplished, and His people blessed and rewarded even under oppression.

Because oppression is a spiritual initiative of Satan, the believer's spiritual function under forms of oppression constitutes an intensification of spiritual warfare. Spiritual warfare is the conscious effort to accomplish spiritual aims through everyday affairs.[ccxii] It is for this reason that under oppression, the importance of Pastoral ministry, discipleship, marriage, the family, and evangelism are elevated in importance. Seen in this way, for the spiritually mature person, oppression, as awful as it, is an opportunity. In it the believer operates "undercover" as a powerful spiritual resource for the Lord.

It is permissible for the believer to seek to escape oppression. The problem is seeking to achieve justice outside the auspices of the Lord and his Word. Moses delayed the deliverance of the Jews by his killing of the Egyptian [Acts 7.23-30]. By contrast, David refused to rid Israel of Saul by killing the Lord's anointed [1 Samuel 24.1-8]. At the proper time David ascended the throne and at the end of his life wrote the following regarding justice and injustice:

> 2 Samuel 23:1–4 (KJV 1900)
> [1] Now these *be* the last words of David. David the son of Jesse said, And the man *who was* raised up on high, The anointed of the God of Jacob, And the sweet psalmist of Israel, said, [2] The Spirit of the Lord spake by me, And his word *was* in my tongue. [3] The God of Israel said, The Rock of Israel spake to me, He that ruleth over men *must be* just, Ruling in the fear of God. [4] And *he shall be* as the light of the morning, *when* the sun riseth, *Even* a morning without clouds; *As* the tender grass *springing* out of the earth By clear shining after rain.

The true Christian is in the justice business, the liberation business. First by liberating people from spiritual bondage through the gospel of the grace of God in Christ. Secondly, by condemning

---

[ccxii] The life of Jesus is a wonderful example of this principle. No one would doubt that Jesus was constantly involved in spiritual warfare, but he battled, for the most part, through ordinary living: obedience under the Law of Moses, loving and serving others, teaching the disciples, suffering mistreatment including conspiracy leading to unjust capital punishment. His performance in the everyday affairs experienced by all formed a significant part of his spiritual warfare.

oppression in word and in deed. Opposing oppression in word is to expose it when it is found, as the Word of God commands the believer.

> Ephesians 5:6–11 (KJV 1900)
> 6 Let no man deceive you with vain words: for because of these things cometh the wrath of God upon the children of disobedience. 7 Be not ye therefore partakers with them. 8 For ye were sometimes darkness, but now *are ye* light in the Lord: walk as children of light: 9 (For the fruit of the Spirit *is* in all goodness and righteousness and truth;) 10 Proving what is acceptable unto the Lord. 11 <u>And have no fellowship with the unfruitful works of darkness, but rather reprove</u> *them*.

To oppose injustice *in deed* is accomplished by laying the appropriate spiritual groundwork [the Nationbuilding Principles] initiating a spiritual chain reaction that creates a combustion of repentance, life, and national healing.

---

[185] James Swanson, Dictionary of Biblical Languages with Semantic Domains: Hebrew (Old Testament) (Oak Harbor: Logos Research Systems, Inc., 1997) H6231.

[186] Foxe's Book of Martyrs, Chapter II: The Ten Primitive Persecutions.

[187] "2:29–30. Daniel asserted at the outset that the king's dream was prophetic (cf. v. 45, "what will take place in the future"), about **things to come** and what was **going to happen**. Nebuchadnezzar's dream covered the prophetic panorama of Gentile history from his time till the forthcoming subjugation of Gentile powers to Israel's Messiah. This time period is called "the times of the Gentiles" (Luke 21:24). This dream was given to Nebuchadnezzar, the first of many Gentile rulers who would exert power by divine appointment during the times of the Gentiles."

Pentecost, J. Dwight. "Daniel." The Bible Knowledge Commentary: An Exposition of the Scriptures, edited by J. F. Walvoord and R. B. Zuck. Wheaton, IL: Victor Books, 1985.

[188] Swanson, James. *Dictionary of Biblical Languages with Semantic Domains: Greek (New Testament)*. Oak Harbor: Logos Research Systems, Inc., 1997.

[189] REVELATION

By general revelation is meant that which is given to all men, in nature and history, and in the nature of man himself. The reality and validity of revelation in this sense is declared in Scripture verses such as Ps 19:1; Isa 40:26; Rom 1:19-20; Ex 9:16; Acts 14:15-17; Rom 2:14-15; Matt 6:22-34. But the actual power of this revelation over men has, in numberless cases, been reduced or nullified by sin (see Rom 1:18-21). And, besides, the coming of sin into the world and the establishment of the economy of redemption has necessitated the making known of truths not made known by general revelation. Therefore God has given the special revelation brought to us in the holy Scriptures. The Scriptures reiterate the truths proclaimed in nature, in history, and in man himself; and, in addition, declare the salvation that God has provided for mankind in Jesus Christ.

Unger, Merrill. The New Unger's Bible Dictionary. Chicago: Moody Press of Chicago,1988.

[190] Shedd regarding Rom 9.22 sq. "Notwithstanding the immanent and eternal indignation of God against the wickedness of men like Tiberius and Cæsar Borgia, there was in their history a long-continued and strange forbearance to punish them. This is sometimes so marked, as to be painful to the human conscience, leading men to cry out: "How long, O Lord, how long?" If God bears patiently for a time with such persons, not destroying them at the first moment, but deferring the punishment prepared for them, what ground for complaint have they before the bar of eternal justice?"

Shedd, William G. T. A Critical and Doctrinal Commentary upon the Epistle of St. Paul to the Romans. New York: Charles Scribner's Sons, 1879.

[191] Lewis Sperry Chafer, Satan. New York: Gospel Publishing House, 1909. 73.

Corrupt [192] OT:4167
muwq (mook); a primitive root; to jeer, i.e. (intens.) blaspheme:
KJV - be corrupt.

(Biblesoft's New Exhaustive Strong's Numbers and Concordance with Expanded Greek-Hebrew Dictionary. Copyright © 1994, 2003, 2006 Biblesoft, Inc. and International Bible Translators, Inc.)

[193] Unlike in Washington D.C where slaveholders were paid reparations for the loss of slaves. Accessed 01-30-2023. https://www.archives.gov/exhibits/featured-documents/dc-emancipation-act

[194] 1 Timothy 1:9–10 (KJV 1900)
9 Knowing this, that the law is not made for a righteous man, but for the lawless and disobedient, for the ungodly and for sinners, for unholy and profane, for murderers of fathers and murderers of mothers, for manslayers, 10 For whoremongers, for them that defile themselves with mankind, for menstealers, for liars, for perjured persons, and if there be any other thing that is contrary to sound doctrine;

Menstealer 435 ἀνδραποδιστής (andrapodistēs), οὖ (ou), ὁ (ho): n.masc.; ≡ Str 405—LN 57.187 slave dealer, trader in human beings, including kidnapping and then selling (1Ti 1:10+)

Exodus 21:16 (KJV 1900)
16 And he that stealeth a man, and selleth him, or if he be found in his hand, he shall surely be put to death.

Exodus 21:26–27 (KJV 1900)
26 And if a man smite the eye of his servant, or the eye of his maid, that it perish; he shall let him go free for his eye's sake. 27 And if he smite out his manservant's tooth, or his maidservant's tooth; he shall let him go free for his tooth's sake. [this applies to a Gentile slave-the Jewish slave was not to be beaten at all, but was to be treated as a hired laborer.]

Deuteronomy 21:10–14 (KJV 1900)
10 When thou goest forth to war against thine enemies, and the LORD thy God hath delivered them into thine hands, and thou hast taken them captive, 11 And seest among the captives a beautiful woman, and hast a desire unto her, that thou wouldest have her to thy wife; 12 Then thou shalt bring her home to thine house; and she shall shave her head, and pare her nails; 13 And she shall put the raiment of her captivity from off her, and shall remain in thine house, and bewail her father and her mother a full month: and after that thou shalt go in unto her, and be her husband, and she shall be thy wife. 14 And it shall be, if thou have no delight in her, then thou shalt let her go whither she will; but thou shalt not sell her at all for money, thou shalt not make merchandise of her, because thou hast humbled her.

Exodus 21:20 (KJV 1900)
20 And if a man smite his servant, or his maid, with a rod, and he die under his hand; he shall be surely punished.

[195] Paul was a prisoner when he wrote Philemon (vv. 1, 9). This epistle is therefore included among the so-called "prison epistles," and was written during his first Roman imprisonment, a.d. 61–63. Because Onesimus accompanied Tychicus, who carried the letter to Colosse, it is evident the two epistles were written at about the same time, probably in the summer of a.d. 62.

Deibler, Edwin C. "Philemon." In The Bible Knowledge Commentary: An Exposition of the Scriptures, edited by J. F. Walvoord and R. B. Zuck. Wheaton, IL: Victor Books, 1985.

Appendix 2:
Theologians On The Issue Of Race

I have defined racism as a conspiracy to marginalize a people by scientifically introducing discrimination into the institutions of society. This conspiracy ultimately serves Satan's overall strategy to control history and to neutralize the Church. Technically, racism is not merely having hateful feelings against a race;[ccxiii] it may not be related to one's emotions at all. Racism is a calculated strategy to exploit and harm that draws its power and genius from Satan, it is a spiritual enterprise. Human beings administer the earthly systems that exploit the weak or disadvantaged, but the origin of the strategy is Satan.

God and scripture are therefore opposed to racism and oppression and supply the remedy for it. Through the sacrifice of Jesus Christ for sin, individuals may be rescued from the spiritual and psychological bondage that is required to perpetuate oppression. By the new birth: the creation of a new nature and the indwelling of God in the soul of the new believer, he is given the mentality and the power to reverse racism's *effects* in his own soul. Furthermore, the Bible provides the principles whereby, over time, Congregations and Communities may even be freed from the physical restraints of oppression.

Because of the irreversible character of the new birth, Satan must find a way to cause the malfunction of the Christian in his discipleship. Otherwise,

---

[ccxiii] The realm of *attitudes* is addressed by the word "prejudice" in Chapter 2.

oppression as a system of world rule would be in jeopardy anywhere that sound biblical teaching could be found. His answer was to promote *versions* of Christianity that did not radically change the content of Christian dogmatics but changed the way those truths are *applied* to different races. This is what we called Slave Religion or Slave Theology in an earlier chapter. In this way, the human systems necessary to maintain the isolation of privilege could not only be maintained, but Christian ministers could inoculate both Christians and the secular Community with the values that support racism.

1. The presentation of the concept of race as a legitimate biblical concept.
2. The notion that some races are cursed (inferior, handicapped, underdeveloped, primitive) and other races bequeathed permanent hegemony over mankind.
3. That the cursed races are endowed with genetic characteristics that are the cause of their misery and disadvantage.
4. That there are no systems that exist primarily to maintain the status of those unfortunate races (or: that such systems existed long ago, but no longer, or: that the people who administered them are long dead, or a hundred other excuses.)
5. The assertion that these points do not conflict with scripture and should be accepted themselves as spiritual truth.
6. That efforts to ameliorate the conditions of the cursed races by changing the *systems* that perpetuate their oppression are anti-gospel and a departure from the true priorities of spiritual practice. Such efforts constitute a revolt against the Bible and Christ who will himself establish universal righteousness. On the other hand, the freedom and well-being of the blessed races may be maintained by every legal or illegal means, up to and including violence and insurrection.

The incorporation of these ideas into Christian doctrine have occurred throughout American history so that today they no longer need to be taught but are a part of the Christian heritage of this country. Violators of this heritage are reprimanded as necessary, but the teaching long ago became a part of the religious and racial history which are integral to American culture.

After an in-depth statistical analysis of survey responses, Robert P. Jones [2020] summarized a portion of his findings:

> "Across a range of questions, the overall pattern that emerges is abundantly

clear. On the one hand, white Christians explicitly profess warm attitudes toward African Americans. At the same time, however, they strongly support the continued existence of Confederate monuments to white supremacy and consistently deny the existence not only of historical structural barriers to black achievement but also of existing structural injustices in the way African Americans are treated by police, the courts, workplaces, and other institutions in the country. And, notably, Christian affiliation remains a powerful differentiator among whites, with differences between white Christians and religiously unaffiliated whites running from 20 to nearly 40 percentage points across these questions. In every case, it is religiously unaffiliated whites who stand closer than white Christians do to their African American Christian brothers and sisters."[196]

The following quotations are a small sample of the documented positions of Christian scholars and teachers regarding black people.

Keil and Delitzsch

"In the sin of Ham[197], "there lies the great stain of the whole Hamitic race, whose chief characteristic is sexual sin."[198]

Willmington's Guide to the Bible

"...but the wider scope of Noah's words accurately foretell that the descendants of Ham would in some measure be subjected to the descendants of both Shem and Japheth. History attests to this."[199]

Matthew Henry

"He pronounces a curse on Canaan the son of Ham (v25) in whom Ham himself is cursed."[200]

Jamieson, Fausset and Brown

"Cursed be Canaan-This doom has been fulfilled in the destruction of the Canaanites, in the degradation of Egypt and the slavery of the Africans, the descendants of Ham."[201]

Dake's Reference Bible

Regarding Genesis 9.19 Finis Dake says in Dake's Annotated Reference Bible: "All colors and types of men came into existence after the flood.

All men were white up to this point, for there was only one family line-that of Noah who was white, and in the line of Christ, being mentioned in Lk3.36 with his son Shem."[202]

Regarding the Sons of Ham, Dake continues: "The above study concerning the sons of Shem, Ham and Japheth gives on an idea of the origin of the various races of men and shows clearly that Gods' original plan was to have separate races of various colors and distinct types after the flood. It is plainly evident that God segregated and scattered the people abroad on the face of the earth..."[203]

Again, from Dake's Study Bible:

"3o Reasons for the segregation of the Races"

"4. Miscegenation means the mixture of races, especially the Black and white races, or those of outstanding type or color. The Bible goes ever further than opposing this. It is against different branches of the same stock intermarrying such as Jews marrying other descendants of Abraham..."[204]

Unger's Bible Dictionary

Entry: Nimrod

"In the Bible Nimrod appears as a great personality in whom earthly imperial power first appears in human history. That this character is evil appears from several observations. 1. Earthly kingship initially comes into existence, among the Hamitic peoples, upon one branch of which a prophetic curse was pronounced, and in the entire family of which, there is an absence of divine blessing."[205]

Pentateuch and Haftorahs, J.H. Hertz Ed.

Genesis 10.6 "Ham. The most ancient name for Egypt was 'Chem', meaning 'black', alluding no doubt to the dark colour of the Egyptian SOIL."[206] (emphasis added)

Jamieson, Fausset and Brown

Genesis 2:3

"In some cases it is not secreted at all; and hence, the strange anomaly of white negroes, which, though rare, are not unknown. It has been remarked that America affords a better development of the African race, even though they continue in a condition of servitude; and we learn, on the high authority of Dr. Prichard, that in the third generation of those slaves who are regular residents in houses, many of the negro characteristics begin to disappear: the depressed nose rises, the mouth and lips assume a moderate form, while the hair becomes longer at each family gradation. What has been said regarding the physical peculiarities of the negro is still more applicable to his mind. Born in a country where they do not require to labour for supplying themselves with food, clothing, or habitations, and living under a climate whose enervating influence produces mental indolence and sensuality, there is no wonder that the negroes appear in a state of intellectual debasement which has been regarded as the indication of an inferior race."[207]

Fausset's Bible Dictionary

ISRAEL

"Similarly, the Santhals on the W. frontier of lower Bengal derive themselves from the Horites who were driven out of mount Seir by the Edomites. Their traditions point to the Punjab, the land of the five rivers, as the home of their race. They say their fathers worshipped God alone before entering the Himalayan region; but when in danger of perishing on those snowy heights they followed the direction whence the sun rose daily, and were guided safe; so they hold a feast every five years to the sun god, and also worship devils. They alone of the Hindu races have negro features, and the lightheartedness and also the improvidence of the race of Ham.[208]

Dr Anthony Evans notes that even some of the best-known religious leaders of early America justified slavery by theology, laying the foundation for the efforts of secular intellectuals devising a scientific doctrine of race. These religious men cited by Dr Evans included Jonathan Edwards, George Whitefield, John Davenport, and Evera Stiles, President of Yale.[209]

Basil Manley Sr.[210]

"One window into the worldview of Christian white supremacy is the ardent defense of slavery and the Confederacy that was proffered by Reverend Basil Manly Sr. As founder of Southern Baptist Seminary and chaplain to the Confederacy, Manly was one of the most prolific and tireless Christian defenders of slavery. While Manly was one of the most prominent purveyors of white supremacist theology, he was not unique among Southern Baptists, and he had counterparts in the southern branches of the other major Protestant denominations, such as William Capers, a Methodist, and James Henley Thornwell, a Presbyterian. Like his fellow defenders of slavery, Manly grounded his arguments with generous citations from the Bible."[211]

Charles Hodge

Princeton theologian Charles Hodge exclaimed in his paper, "The Bible Argument for Slavery (1860),

"If the present course of the abolitionists is right, then the course of Christ and the apostles were wrong."[212]

John MacArthur

> When asked about the racial issues represented by the Charlottesville Va. march and the Black Lives Matter movement Dr. John MacArthur stated that, in the church, it is "in a sense a non-issue, it doesn't exist as an issue."[213] See also the following endnote. [214]

Racism as a Stabilizer of American Culture

Whereas the divine institutions (marriage, family, nation) are the mechanisms of stability in a nation, *biblical sources of stability were replaced* in America, in part, by an utterly sinful mechanism, that of racism. There was a strong movement towards racism in the eighteenth and nineteenth centuries in the western hemisphere. This movement was motivated by the Atlantic slave trade and the rise of European imperialism throughout the world. The European world, fundamentally impacted by the Bible and Christianity, found it necessary to compromise this set of beliefs to justify the systematic subjugation of out-races. It is suggested that racism did in fact provide a false sense of security among Americans which contributed to the apparent stability of marriage, family, and nationhood, while materially prospering the country. Racism became an unofficial religion which secretly displaced Christianity by subtly contradicting, and thus nullifying the theological content of *biblical* Christianity. Carl F. Ellis refers to this emasculation of biblical Christianity as "Christianity-ism."

> "...negative religious practices (including racist ones) expressed in the language of Christianity. Christianity-ism strips institutional Christianity of its theological content-God's solution to the problem of human unrighteousness-and leaves only the institution itself which is treated as the object of faith."[215]

The theology of race, promoted by Pastors and theologians, performed a psychological function in America by providing "automatic self-esteem" which served to stabilize the young institutions of the developing American civilization.[216]

---

[196] Jones, Robert P. White Too Long: The Legacy of White Supremacy in American Christianity (p. 162). Simon & Schuster. Kindle Edition.

[197] See Appendix 3 "The Curse of Noah" for a refutation of the alleged Curse of Ham.

[198] Keil Karl Freidrich, Delitzsch, Franz, "Commentary On The Old Testament, New Updated Edition, Electronic Database," Peabody, Hendrickson Publishers, 1996. 134.

[199] Willmington, Harold, Dr., "Wilmington's Guide to the Bible." Tyndale, 1981. 34.

[200] Henry, M., "Matthew Henry's Commentary on the Whole Bible: Complete and unabridged in one volume." Peabody, Hendrickson, 1994. Genesis 9.24-27.

[201] Jamieson, R., Fausset, A. R., & Brown, D., "Commentary Critical and Explanatory on the Whole Bible." Oak Harbor, Logos Research Systems, Inc., 1997. Genesis 9.25.

[202] Dake, Finis Jennings, "Dake's Annotated Reference Bible." Lawrenceville, Dake Bible Sales, 1987. 8.

[203] Ibid. 40.

[204] "30 reasons for the segregation of races" Dake, Finis Jennings. "Dakes' Annotated Reference Bible." Dake Bible Sales Inc, Lawrenceville Ga., 1963. 159 [New Testament].

[205] Unger, Merrill, "Unger's Bible Dictionary." Chicago, Moody, 1979. 794.

[206] Hertz, J.H., "Pentateuch and Haftorahs, Second Edition," (1966) Genesis 10.6.

[207] Jamieson, Fausset, and Brown Commentary, Electronic Database. Copyright © 1997, 2003, 2005, 2006 by Biblesoft, Inc. All rights reserved. Genesis 2.3.

[208] Fausset's Bible Dictionary, Electronic Database Copyright © 1998, 2003, 2006 by Biblesoft, Inc. All rights reserved. Israel.

[209] Sweet, William W. "The Story of Religion in America." 170, 285. Cited in Evans, Dr. Anthony "Are Blacks Spiritually Inferior to Whites." Renaissance Productions Inc. 1992. 26.

[210] "Manley's most systematic defense of slavery was encapsulated in one of eight "Sermons on Duty," a series he honed and preached at various venues across the South. Notably, his discussion of slavery was embedded in a larger theological framework of the patriarchal family, which he saw as central to God's plan for human society. Different members of the family have divinely ordained differentiated roles, he argued, and the practice of slavery should be understood within this hierarchical context. Thus, the divine order for accomplishing social needs "naturally lead to different occupations— some to labor, some to plan, and to direct the labor of others." 13 Like a symbiotic ecosystem, genders and races had their roles to play, and when all parts functioned as designed, the ecosystem thrived, and individual members— whatever their lot— were content, since they were fulfilling their created purpose."

Jones, Robert P. White Too Long: The Legacy of White Supremacy in American Christianity (p. 82). Simon & Schuster. Kindle Edition.

[211] Ibid.

[212] The Bible Argument On Slavery. By Charles Hodge, D.D., of Princeton, N. J. cited in Elliott, E.N. LL.D Cotton is King and Pro-Slavery Arguments, Comprising the Writings of Hammond, Harper, Christy, Stringfellow, Hodge, Bledsoe, And Cartwright, on this Important Subject. Augusta, Ga: Pritchard, Abbott & Loomis.1860.

---

[213] John MacArthur, The Gospel, Racism and Black Lives Matter. Accessed 03-03-2023.
https://www.youtube.com/watch?v=s3QZcVEDEPl

[214] MacArthur, John. Submission in the Workplace, Part 2. April 30, 1989. Accessed 12-3-2022
https://www.gty.org/library/sermons-library/60-27/submission-in-the-workplace-part-2

This citation demands a comment. [See also "Oppression and Slavery in Appendix I] The issue of slavery will be completely addressed in the forthcoming book "Black Nations in Scripture" [late 2023].

1. Christianity undoubtedly freed slaves. In the United States, many slaveholders who were genuinely saved freed their slaves as a testimony to the new birth. Christianity was a key factor in the abolition of American slavery.

   ABSTRACTS OF SUSSEX COUNTY VIRGINIA MANUMISSIONS 1782-1818
   SUSSEX COUNTY DEED BOOKS 1782-1818
   Sussex County Deed Book F 1779-1786
   LVA reel #3

   (excerpt from the above)

   "p. 125 - 14 Dec 87 - Henry Moss - of Sussex after full and deliberate consideration and agreeable to our Bill of Rights am fully persuaded that freedom is the natural right of all man kind and that no law, moral, or decree hath given me a just right or property in the person of any of my fellow creatures and desireous to fulfill the injunction of our Lord and Saviour Jesus Christ by doing to all others as etc - sets free from bondage the following Negroes vizt. Peter [1 Jan 88], Ephraim [1 Jan 97], Phill [Jan 98], Becky [1 Jan 88], Dilcy [1 Jan 93], Edmund [1 Jan 07], and Salley [1 Jan 12]- desire to have their care and guardianship and instruction till they arrive at full - rec 20 Dec 87

   "p. 124 - 19 Sept 87 - William Ellis - of Sussex after mature deliberation and agreeable to our Bill of Rights am persuaded that no law, moral, or divine gives me a right to the life and property of my fellow creatures and to fulfill the injunction of our Lord and Saviour, Jesus Christ, by doing to all men as I would be done unto - sets free the following Negroes to wit Thomas (26 yrs), Sarah (23 yrs), Fanny (20 yrs) [10 Aug 88], Jane (16 yrs) [1 Jan 92], Philip (14 yrs) [3 Jan 94], Randolph (6 yrs) [11 March 02], Allen (4 yrs) [14 Feb 04], Alexander (2 yrs 3 mo) [22 May 06], Charlotte (2 yrs 1 mo) [14 Nov 06], Edmund (1 yr 10 mo) [17 Feb 07], Anacha (6 mo) [28 June 08] - request and desire to have the care and instruction of them till they arrive at full age – rec 19 Dec 87"

   See also: "Duck Creek Manumissions, 1774-1792..." Accessed March 3, 2023.https://digitalcollections.tricolib.brynmawr.edu/object/sc9995#page/1/mode/1up.

2. Christianity did not eliminate slavery in the new world, but neither did true Christianity *make* slaves. This is especially true of the version of slavery practiced in Europe, America, and the Caribbean. Christ did not have to abolish slavery because he abolished theft of labor [menstealing Exodus 21.16; 1 Timothy 1.9-10] and rape [Deuteronomy 22.25-29], two legs of the stool that was American slavery, the third being other categories of violence and murder, which are also abolished. Without these things, there could be no slavery in the New World.

3. Jesus and the apostles were not moral crusaders. They did not stamp out temple prostitution, abortion, or homosexuality either, should we now approve of these sins because of their silence? Jesus condemned sexual sin and idolatry and, in these prohibitions, presented the principle that forbad any institutions based upon these sins. The "argument from silence" is a logical fallacy of which the issue of slavery is a chief example.

---

[215] Ellis, Carl F. "Beyond Liberation, The Gospel in the Black American Experience" Inter Varsity Press 1983. 16 (note).

[216] "The most difficult, because unpleasant, fact that we must face is that for all its malevolence, racism served a stabilizing function in American Culture for many generations. Indeed, it was a source of gratification for whites. It defined a social universe, absorbed aggression, and facilitated a sense of virtue in white America-a trait which contributed to Americas' material success. Racism was an integral part of a stable and productive cultural order. Because of the incompatibility of this old order with advanced industrial life, with our ideals, and with the will of black people, we must try to eradicate racism and move away from its decisions. But this change of direction brings in its wake instability, and a set of anxieties and counter-responses which threaten the advances our culture has made."

Kovel, Joel "White Racism-A Psychohistory." Vintage, 1971. 4.

Appendix 3:
The Curse Of Noah

1. To learn the circumstances surrounding the so-called curse of Ham.
2. To understand the racial attitudes of Bible scholars and how these attitudes impacted their interpretation of Genesis 9.
3. To distinguish a true from a false curse.

Genesis 9:18–21 (KJV 1900)
18 And the sons of Noah, that went forth of the ark, were Shem, and Ham, and Japheth: and Ham *is* the father of Canaan. 19 These *are* the three sons of Noah: and of them was the whole earth overspread. 20 And Noah began *to be* an husbandman, and he planted a vineyard: 21 And he drank of the wine, and was drunken; and he was uncovered within his tent.

Great Men Aren't Always Great

Noah and his sons were the cultural bridge from the old world before the flood to the new world afterwards. They carried both good and bad things across this bridge with them.

Noah was a righteous man before God. This was the basis of his election to the new world beyond the flood.

> Genesis 6:9 (KJV 1900)
> 9 These *are* the generations of Noah: Noah was a just man *and* perfect in his generations, *and* Noah walked with God.

Noah possessed the judicial righteousness ["just"] possessed by all who have adjusted to the second person of the Godhead, Jesus Christ, by faith in any age. Noah also walked with God. In other words, he lived out his faith in obedience to God in his daily life. His living was consistent with his profession.

Even though Noah was justified before God, even though he walked with God, he was capable of sin and capable of improper motives. No one in this life is ever free of the possibility of sin, therefore we are warned to take heed.

> 1 Corinthians 10:12–13 (KJV 1900)
> 12 Wherefore let him that thinketh he standeth take heed lest he fall. 13 There hath no temptation taken you but such as is common to man: but God *is* faithful, who will not suffer you to be tempted above that ye are able; but will with the temptation also make a way to escape, that ye may be able to bear *it*.

Every believer is vulnerable to the attack of sin. Spiritual victory, as in the case of Noah, is a very special kind of vulnerability, the vulnerability of spiritual prosperity.

We must say these things before we read the commentaries that interpret this passage. Not only can the righteous believer suffer from spiritual vulnerability, but also the Bible teachers and scholars.

All commentators and preachers teach and preach from a context. That means that we all are impacted by our backgrounds and the circumstances of our times. The challenge of biblical interpretation is to separate our cultures and our personal biases from our interpretation of the scripture.

Unfortunately, in the case of this passage of scripture, these biases and human limitations have resulted in interpretations of this passage that are erroneous.

The backgrounds and historical contexts of many commentators resulted in a treatment of Genesis 9, that would not have been tolerated if used to explain

John 3 or Psalms 23, a treatment that was demanded not by the text, but by the historical setting and the special temptations of that time, and apparently, temptations that remain today.[217]

The incorrect teaching of Genesis 9 has contributed to the worst excesses of oppression and tyranny. Sin and the loss of human freedom are the perennial fruits of false teaching. The concept of the curse of Noah as normally taught is nothing less than false doctrine.

> Genesis 9:20 (KJV 1900)
> [20] And Noah began *to be* an husbandman,[ccxiv] and he planted a vineyard:

Let's note what commentators have to say about this passage.

Albert Barnes suggests that Noah may have accidentally invented the cultivation of wine and was unaware of its effects.

> Genesis 9:18-29 "The cultivation of the vine and the manufacture of wine might have been in practice before this time, as the mention of them is merely incidental to the present narrative. But it seems likely from what follows, that, though grapes may have been in use, wine had not been extracted from them. "And was drunken." We are not in a position to estimate the amount of Noah's guilt in this case, as we do not know how far he was acquainted with the properties of wine."[218]

The mention in the biblical text of Noah becoming a husbandman and planting a vineyard was not simply "incidental to the present narrative" as we shall see. Regarding the assignment of "guilt in this case," Noah is the only person in the narrative for which clear evidence is provided from which to make such an assignment. Neither is there any good reason to assume that Noah did not know what wine was.

Adam Clarke in his Commentary suggests the same thing-that wine had not been thought of in the thousands of years before the flood and Noah was caught unawares by its effects.

> Genesis 9:21 It is very probable that this was the first time the wine was cultivated; and it is as probable that the strength or intoxicating power of the expressed juice was never before known. Noah, therefore, might have drunk it at this time without the least blame, as he knew not till this trial the effects it would produce.[219]

Noah did not invent agriculture.[220] Cain worked the ground, as did Adam. It is

---

ccxiv Husbandman: H376 H127 a man of the soil

311

also highly unlikely that Noah invented wine. It is doubtful that in all the sinning and perversity that existed in the centuries prior to the Flood, that drunkenness from wine had not secured its place among a population that is described thus:

> Genesis 6:5 (KJV 1900)
> 5 And God saw that the wickedness of man *was* great in the earth, and *that* every imagination of the thoughts of his heart *was* only evil continually.

> Matthew 24:38 (KJV 1900)
> 38 For as in the days that were before the flood they were eating and drinking, marrying and giving in marriage, until the day that Noe [Noah] entered into the ark,

It is profitable to look at all the references to the phrase "eating and drinking" in scripture. These appear not to simply refer to drinking in general but includes [but not exclusively] the idea or alcoholic beverages, most likely wine.

> Luke 7:33–34 (KJV 1900)
> 33 For John the Baptist came neither eating bread nor drinking wine; and ye say, He hath a devil. 34 The Son of man is come eating and drinking; and ye say, Behold a gluttonous man, and a winebibber, a friend of publicans and sinners!

These expositors attempt to soften the single sin[221] that is noted in the entire passage. Even those who are forced to acknowledge the sin attempt to explain it away. It appears that they do this to clear the way for the interpretation that Noah's son Ham or grandson Canaan performed an act that condemned a significant percentage of the world's population, forever.

The Bible does not hide the weaknesses of great men-and Noah is a great man by God's own admission. Great men of God commit sins and commit errors of judgment.

David numbered the people of God.

> 1 Chronicles 21:1 (KJV 1900)
> 1 And Satan stood up against Israel, and provoked David to number Israel.

Solomon forsook the Lord to serve false gods.

> 1 Kings 11:4–8 (KJV 1900)
> 4 For it came to pass, when Solomon was old, *that* his wives turned away his heart after other gods: and his heart was not perfect with the Lord his God,

as *was* the heart of David his father. ⁵ For Solomon went after Ashtoreth the goddess of the Zidonians, and after Milcom the abomination of the Ammonites. ⁶ And Solomon did evil in the sight of the Lord, and went not fully after the Lord, as *did* David his father. ⁷ Then did Solomon build an high place for Chemosh, the abomination of Moab, in the hill that *is* before Jerusalem, and for Molech, the abomination of the children of Ammon. ⁸ And likewise did he for all his strange wives, which burnt incense and sacrificed unto their gods.

Hezekiah unnecessarily exposed the people of God to their enemies. Afterwards he was told by the prophet Isaiah:

> 2 Kings 20:16–19 (KJV 1900)
> ¹⁶ And Isaiah said unto Hezekiah, Hear the word of the Lord. ¹⁷ Behold, the days come, that all that *is* in thine house, and that which thy fathers have laid up in store unto this day, shall be carried into Babylon: nothing shall be left, saith the Lord. ¹⁸ And of thy sons that shall issue from thee, which thou shalt beget, shall they take away; and they shall be eunuchs in the palace of the king of Babylon. ¹⁹ Then said Hezekiah unto Isaiah, Good *is* the word of the Lord which thou hast spoken. And he said, *Is it* not *good*, if peace and truth be in my days?

At issue here is not whether Noah was a great man, certainly he was, but that the entire series of events was precipitated by the sin of Noah. We will see that this sin of drunkenness is to continue in its effects throughout the narrative.

The unrealistic attempt by teachers to ignore or deflect this origin of the entire course of events guarantees the improper interpretation of the passage.

The Firstfruits of Sin

> Genesis 9:21–22 (KJV 1900)
> ²¹ And he drank of the wine, and was drunken; and he was uncovered within his tent. ²² And Ham, the father of Canaan, saw the nakedness of his father, and told his two brethren without.

Noah did not just plant grapes, ferment them and drink wine. Many of the Old Testament believers drank wine. In fact, it was so common that when a particular group of Jews did not drink wine, it was considered unusual.

In Jeremiah 35:12-16, the descendants of Jondab the son of Rechab had been forbidden by their father to drink wine. Due to their unique obedience to the wishes of their father God used them as an example of obedience in contrast to Israel's disobedience.

God did not make an issue of the wine in this passage, but the fact that the Rechabites listened to their father after the flesh, but Israel would not listen to their God. Similarly, the Nazirite was commanded not to drink wine or eat grape products, because this was a part of their temporary separation from the rest of Israel unto the Lord.

> Numbers 6:1–4 (KJV 1900)
> [1] And the Lord spake unto Moses, saying, [2] Speak unto the children of Israel, and say unto them, When either man or woman shall separate *themselves* to vow a vow of a Nazarite, to separate *themselves* unto the Lord: [3] He shall separate *himself* from wine and strong drink, and shall drink no vinegar of wine, or vinegar of strong drink, neither shall he drink any liquor of grapes, nor eat moist grapes, or dried. [4] All the days of his separation shall he eat nothing that is made of the vine tree, from the kernels even to the husk.

Therefore, the issue here is not drinking, but drunkenness. Although there was no written scripture in the days of Noah, the mind of God on the subject is clear.

> Proverbs 23:29–33 (KJV 1900)
> [29] Who hath woe? who hath sorrow? Who hath contentions? who hath babbling? Who hath wounds without cause? Who hath redness of eyes? [30] They that tarry long at the wine; They that go to seek mixed wine. [31] Look not thou upon the wine when it is red, When it giveth his colour in the cup, *When* it moveth itself aright. [32] At the last it biteth like a serpent, And stingeth like an adder. [33] Thine eyes shall behold strange women, And thine heart shall utter perverse things.

The argument that Noah didn't know what wine was, or did not understand its effects, is not acceptable. This episode of drunkenness must be remembered to understand what happens later in the story.

Even here, the commentators deflect attention from Noah to his sons. A modern commentator does an excellent job overall on the passage, even describing the offensiveness of Noah's drunkenness, but when it comes to this critical point, the "goal of the story" is identified in a way moves the focus from Noah.

"It is not Noah's drunkenness and misdeed per se that are the goals of the story; it is the consequence of the infraction. Noah's curse and blessing foreshadow the relationship of the nations that the three brothers originate"[222]

This narrative should be examined from the perspective of the ill-advised decisions of Noah from his drunkenness to his actions after he awoke. These actions form an unbroken chain of improprieties that marked off the last mention of Noah in scripture, the end of whose life was characterized by divine silence. It is by moving the "goal of the story" from these facts to *speculations* about the actions of his sons that the groundwork is laid to create a doctrine, the Curse of Ham, which would provide biblical support to a variety of evils for hundreds of years.

Noah was drunk enough to lie naked in an open tent. We can know that it is open because there is no evidence in the text that Ham made any special effort to enter the tent. This statement, that Noah was uncovered in his tent, is described by Strong's Lexicon as follows:

Uncovered OT:1540

to denude (especially in a disgraceful sense); by implication, to exile (captives being usually stripped); figuratively, to reveal:[223]

This is no casual loss of a garment, but a degrading exhibition that was a direct outcome of drunkenness. This gives us an idea of how drunk Noah was. This word "uncovered" is used in a context like the one here in 2 Samuel, where David's wife falsely accuses him of shamelessly exposing himself before the people of Israel.

2 Samuel 6:14–16, 20 (KJV 1900)
[14] And David danced before the Lord with all *his* might; and David *was* girded with a linen ephod. [15] So David and all the house of Israel brought up the ark of the Lord with shouting, and with the sound of the trumpet. [16] And as the ark of the Lord came into the city of David, Michal Saul's daughter looked through a window, and saw king David leaping and dancing before the Lord; and she despised him in her heart. [20] Then David returned to bless his household. And Michal the daughter of Saul came out to meet David, and said, How glorious was the king of Israel to day, who uncovered himself to day in the eyes of the handmaids of his servants, as one of the vain fellows shamelessly <u>uncovereth</u> himself!

The Second Act

> Genesis 9:22 (KJV 1900)
> [22] And Ham, the father of Canaan, saw the nakedness of his father, and told his two brethren without.'

Regarding the word "saw"[ccxv] in our passage:

> Genesis 9:22 (KJV 1900)
> [22] And Ham, the father of Canaan, <u>saw</u> the nakedness of his father, and told his two brethren without.

This same word [saw] in the same form is used 139 times in the Old Testament and means to see, perceive to look upon or observe.

> Genesis 1:4 (KJV 1900)
> [4] And God <u>saw</u> the light, that *it was* good: and God divided the light from the darkness. [also vss. 10, 12, 18, 21, 25, 31 same morphology]

> Genesis 6:5 (KJV 1900)
> [5] And God <u>saw</u> that the wickedness of man *was* great in the earth, and *that* every imagination of the thoughts of his heart *was* only evil continually.

This word is infused with all kinds of wicked intent by some expositors, shown below. Ham was in the tent and observed his father in his condition, which all may agree was inappropriate and disrespectful.

Regarding the word "without"

> Without OT:2351

> from an unused root meaning to sever; properly, separate by a wall, i.e. outside, outdoors:[224]

It appears that Ham was in the tent. There is no evidence that the tent was closed. However, there is also no good reason given for Ham to have been within the tent. Even today, it is not considered proper for one's offspring to enter the private quarters of their parents uninvited. Noah was in no condition to have invited Ham into the tent. I believe that it is fair to say that Ham had no business inside the tent.

[ccxv] VaW3MS--- Strong's H7200

He then told his brothers what he saw. He made no effort himself to cover his father, nor did he attempt to hide the information from his brothers to protect his father's dignity. These actions would have been preferable and honestly, the more honorable actions.

Nonetheless, the scriptures go no further than this. No motives or other actions are attributed to Ham or to Canaan by the Word of God.

But such is not the case with the commentators. As willing as the scholars are to understate the sin of Noah, they are even more eager to create motives for Ham [and Canaan][225] that are not given in the Bible.

Keil and Delitzsch

Genesis 9:18-25 This trifling fall served to display the hearts of his sons. Ham saw the nakedness of his father, and told his two brethren without. Not content with finding pleasure himself in his father's shame… he just proclaimed his disgraceful pleasure to his brethren, and thus exhibited his shameless sensuality.[226]

"In the sin of Ham, "there lies the great stain of the whole Hamitic race, whose chief characteristic is sexual sin""[227]

Matthew Henry

Genesis 9:18-23 He pleased himself with the sight, as the Edomites looked upon the day of their brother (Obad 12), pleased, and insulting. Perhaps Ham had sometimes been himself drunk, and reproved for it by his good father, whom he was therefore pleased to see thus overcome. Note, It is common for those who walk in false ways themselves to rejoice at the false steps which they sometimes see others make. But charity rejoices not in iniquity, nor can true penitents that are sorry for their own sins rejoice in the sins of others. 2. He told his two brethren without (in the street, as the word is), in a scornful deriding manner, that his father might seem vile unto them. It is very wrong, (1.) To make a jest of sin (Prov 14:9), and to be puffed up with that for which we should rather mourn, 1 Corinthians 5:2. [228]

Adam Clarke

Genesis 9:22-24 Ham, and very probably his son Canaan, had treated their father on this occasion with contempt or reprehensible levity. Had Noah not been innocent, as my exposition supposes him, God would not have endued him with the spirit of prophecy on this occasion and testified such marked disapprobation of their conduct. [229]

These are not the worst of the lot. There are those who accuse Ham and Canaan of even greater sins than this. However, none of the preceding accusations ["contempt, reprehensible levity," for example] can be verified from the Hebrew nor the context of the passage.

> Genesis 9:23 (KJV 1900)
> 23 And Shem and Japheth took a garment, and laid *it* upon both their shoulders, and went backward, and covered the nakedness of their father; and their faces *were* backward, and they saw not their father's nakedness.

The two brothers exhibited the proper attitude and behavior. In this they also reveal the error of Ham's actions.

> Jamieson, Fausset, and Brown
>
> -Genesis 9:23 The characters of these two brothers, as manifested by their conduct in this transaction, stand in favourable contrast to that of Ham, whose lack of filial reverence and indecent levity indicate his strong assimilation to the gross propensities and habits of the antediluvian race with which he had allied himself by marriage (see Genesis 4:22). [230]

Here the commentator introduces the actual motivation for his interpretation, the issue of race. Apparently, the authors by their citation of Genesis 4.22, wished to associate Ham with the offspring of Cain, who was believed by some expositors to be the father of a line consisting of fallen men, in contrast to the line of Seth, populated exclusively by godly offspring. Cain was also believed by some at the time [without evidence] to have been cursed with the mark of blackness [Genesis 4.15]. Noah and all his offspring and their wives were of the "antediluvian[ccxvi] race." Their citation proves nothing about Ham or his wife, begging the question of where his brothers or even their father got their own wives since eight persons entered the ark [1 Peter 3.20].

Although Cain was cursed by God (Genesis 4.11), Ham is cursed by Noah and the expositors.

The Third Act

> Genesis 9:24 (KJV 1900)
> 24 And Noah awoke from his wine, and knew[ccxvii] what his younger son had

---

[ccxvi] ANTEDILU'VIAL, ANTEDILU'VIAN, adjective [Latin ante and diluvium, a flood. See Lave.] Before the flood, or deluge, in Noah's time; existing, happening, or relating to what happened before the deluge. Websters Dictionary 1828 Accessed 02-01-2023
https://webstersdictionary1828.com/Dictionary/Antediluvial
[ccxvii] The NIV84, HCSB and NET Bibles uses the words "found out," "and learned," and" he learned" in the place of the word "knew."

done unto him.

There is no certainty of the meaning of "his little son" in the original according to Keil and Delitzsch.

However, we are not yet done with the effects of the drunkenness of verse 21. It is mentioned again in verse 24.

Noah awakened from his wine. In other words, he awakened from a drunken night to a somewhat less drunken next day. Any intoxication sufficient to produce naked unconsciousness is sufficient to produce a hangover. The effects of drunkenness are not eliminated in a single night's sleep.

There are professions where you are not allowed to work with a hangover: airline pilots, surgeons, certain kinds of machine operators and prophets, to name a few.

Nonetheless Noah immediately leapt into a prophetic posture, pronouncing an unwise judgment that would yield tainted and sinful fruit for a hundred generations.

> Genesis 9:25–27 (KJV 1900)
> [25] And he said, Cursed *be* Canaan; A servant of servants shall he be unto his brethren. [26] And he said, Blessed *be* the Lord God of Shem; And Canaan shall be his servant. [27] God shall enlarge Japheth, And he shall dwell in the tents of Shem; And Canaan shall be his servant.

There are six observations that must be made regarding this pronouncement by Noah.

1. The curse was made by the principal offender.
2. The one making the curse did not witness the alleged offense.
3. The pronouncement of perpetual slavery upon an entire people was an overreaction, inconsistent with divine behavior[ccxviii] and evidence of human motivation.
4. God (not the expositors) never ratifies this curse in Scripture despite many opportunities to do so.
5. History does not attest to the validity of the curse.

[ccxviii] The cases where God condemned a posterity based on the actions of a single person are few and the persons precipitating the multigenerational curse committed egregious acts e.g., Adam [Genesis 3], Eli [1 Samuel 3], Jeconiah [Jeremiah 22]; Judas [Psalms 69.22-28 c.f. Acts 1.20. Even the curse upon Cain was upon him alone.

6. This leaves us with only the Bible scholars who make unbelievable claims based on no textural evidence; and the Bible teachers who uncritically repeat these to generation after generation. Thus, this *false* curse is given artificial but malignant life by the propagation of false teaching.

First, the curse was made by the principal offender.

The foremost and clear-cut sin in this entire story is that of Noah. It is this sin which creates the opportunity for Ham's ill-advised action, and which also issues into the ill-advised remarks by Noah.

Second, the one making the curse did not witness the alleged offense.

It is not indicated how Noah came to know what had happened. We do not know whether he received a correct or an incorrect story. We do know that when Ham was in or around the tent, Noah was still too drunk to know it.

Whatever story he heard, it apparently involved Canaan. There is no mention of any offense by Canaan in this entire narrative, or elsewhere in scripture. It is Bible expositors who have created the imaginative tales without the benefit of proper exegesis. Ham was not cursed, and the curse of Canaan brings into question the source of Noah's information.

Third, perpetual slavery of an entire people was an overreaction and evidence of human motivation.

The longer it is examined, the more unreasonable this "curse" appears. There is no offense in the text that deserves the punishment meted out by Noah.

One is forced to ask the penalty for Noah's own sinful behavior. Apparently, he decided to allow himself to go free. It calls to mind those in John 8.4 who caught the woman in *the very act* of adultery, but not the man.

An unknown assailant (Canaan, according to Noah) commits an unknown crime (nothing is mentioned in the scripture passage) that the victim (Noah) did not see. The penalty is everlasting slavery for Canaan[ccxix] and for the many nations who would descend from him. It is reasonable to inquire if this curse is a valid one.

[ccxix] And according to the expositors, slavery for Ham as well.

Fourth, God never ratifies the curse despite many opportunities to do so.

God had many opportunities in scripture to ratify the curse but did not. This curse is never used to explain divine judgment against Canaan or any son of Ham in the Bible. The Canaanites were scheduled for destruction, as many peoples have been, (even Judah 2 Kings 21.10-15) because of their incorrigible idolatry and abominable cruelty.[ccxx] God would have destroyed Nineveh for the same reasons had they not repented [Jonah 3]. God did destroy Sodom and Gomorrah for the same reasons [Gen 19]. Egypt/Cush; Assyria; Babylon; Persia, Greece and Rome fell because God holds nations responsible for actions that violate conscience.

Noah's curse is not mentioned in connection with the many nations descending from either Canaan or Ham in scripture. These peoples suffered severe judgment without reference to the fulfillment of the alleged curse of Noah. The absence of mention of the curse in references to the judgment of the Canaanites is especially noteworthy when we are aware of the eagerness of biblical scholars to point to it as the great fulfillment of the curse.

The so-called curse of Ham has been a justification for the oppression of blacks for centuries [see below]. Ham is correctly associated with many [but not all] black peoples and nations in history. This curse sanctified the theft of labor, rape, and violence against blacks in Europe and America by citing the divine sanction in Noah's curse.

Perhaps more revealing of the faulty foundation of the curse of Ham or of Canaan is the fact that the Jews themselves descended from a man, Abram, who came from a black [Hamitic] nation, Chaldea [Genesis 11.31]. Abraham and his sons lived in Canaan [Hamitic], moved to Egypt [Hamitic] where they intermarried with the Africans [Yes, Egyptians were Africans and Hamites] for 400 years. The wife and children of the first Hebrew to enter Egypt and the last to leave: of Joseph and of Moses were black [Genesis 41.45; Numbers 12]. After this, Israel was returned to Canaan, where they continued to disobediently intermarry with the idolatrous Canaanites [Hamitic]. Were the Jews also subject to the curse of "Ham," or the even the curse of Canaan?

Fifth, history does not attest to the validity of the curse.

There is no evidence of historical judgment against Ham or Canaan based on

---

[ccxx] Deuteronomy 7.1-10; 12.28-32; 20.16-18

Noah's curse.

On the contrary, four great empires of the ancient world, the Cushites, Babylonians, Hittites,[231] and the Egyptians, were all Hamitic. Many other *Hamitic* nations [the sons of Ham were Cush, Mizraim, Phut and Canaan] existed in the biblical world and in the ages which preceded Abraham.

> "Bunsen concludes by saying, 'Cushite [eldest son of Ham-rw] colonies were all along the southern shores of Asia and Africa and by archaeological remains along the southern and eastern coasts of Arabia. The name Cush was given to four great areas, Media, Persia, Susiana and Aria, or the whole territory between the Indus and the Tigris in prehistoric times. In Africa the Ethiopians the Egyptians, the Libyans, the Canaanites and Phoenicians were all descendants of Ham. They were a Black or dark colored race and the pioneers of our civilization. They were emphatically the monument builders on the plains of Shinar and the valley of the Nile from Meroe to Memphis. In southern Arabia they erected the wonderful edifices. They were responsible for the monuments that dot southern Siberia and in America along the valley of the Mississippi down to Mexico and in Peru their images and monuments stand as voiceless witnesses.'"[232]

It can be demonstrated throughout the Bible and secular sources[233] that the sons of Ham provided all the elements of civilization to the world after the flood. Language, art, science, technology, architecture, philosophy, and law are all developed to high levels by the blacks. These contributions formed the basis of modern civilization.

> "Bunsen says in his Philosophy of Ancient History, "The Hamitic family as Rawlinson proves must be given the credit for being the fountain of civilization. This family comprised the ancient Ethiopians, the Egyptians, the original Canaanites and the old Chaldeans. The inscriptions of the Chaldean monuments prove their race affinity. The Bible proves their relationship."[234]

Daniel's interpretation of Nebuchadnezzar's dream of the giant statue (Daniel 2) shows at even God believes that the quality of civilization has declined since those days.

If the flood occurred in roughly 2800 B.C., then the families of Ham were dominant for 2000 years. This does not indicate divine discipline against Ham.

The manner of the fall of the Hamitic nations parallels the fall of the Persians, Greeks, and Romans. All nations have departed from divine standards and fallen under divine discipline. So, if Ham is cursed because his nations fell, so then were the Greeks and Romans also.

Sixth, this leaves us with only the Bible scholars who make unbelievable claims based on no textural evidence; and the Bible teachers who uncritically repeat these false teachings to generation after generation. To them we will return momentarily.

About False Curses

Noah is not the only person to pronounce an ill-advised curse. The Bible teaches that a false curse will not prevail.

> Proverbs 26:2
> 2 Like a fluttering sparrow or a darting swallow, an undeserved curse does not come to rest. NIV

➤ Shimei cursed King David and it eventually cost him his life [2 Samuel 16; 1 Kings 2.44]
➤ The famous curse of Balaam failed to alight on Israel [Numbers 23].
➤ Saul pronounced a foolish curse upon the man that would eat food before Israel's enemies were defeated [1 Samuel 14.24].

The curse of Canaan/Ham, however, is the prototype of false curses. It illustrates so many of the characteristics of a false curse. Perhaps this is why it is the first of its kind in scripture.

The Necessity of Black Inferiority

There is a cultural and historical background to why the doctrine of the curse of Ham gained the popularity that it did.[235]

The European development of this doctrine of the curse of Ham coincided with the development of colonial ventures in non-white nations. There was a *need* to reconcile the obvious contradiction of the theft of labor based upon race, not to mention the other atrocities that accompanied slavery and the slave trade, with Christianity which the Europeans knew opposed it.

> Exodus 21:16 (KJV 1900)
> 16 And he that stealeth a man, and selleth him, or if he be found in his hand, he shall surely be put to death.

> 1 Timothy 1:9–10 (KJV 1900)
> 9 Knowing this, that the law is not made for a righteous man, but for the lawless and disobedient, for the ungodly and for sinners, for unholy and profane, for murderers of fathers and murderers of mothers, for manslayers,

[10] For whoremongers, for them that defile themselves with mankind, for menstealers, for liars, for perjured persons, and if there be any other thing that is contrary to sound doctrine;

Menstealers 57.187 ἀνδραποδιστής, οὖ: one who sells persons as slaves, including one who kidnaps persons and sells them—'slave dealer, kidnapper.' ἀρσενοκοίταις, ἀνδραποδισταῖς, ψεύσταις 'sexual perverts, kidnappers (or 'slave dealers'), liars' 1 Tm 1:10.[236]

Menstealers 405 ἀνδραποδιστής [*andrapodistes* /an·drap·od·is·**tace**/] From a derivative of a compound of 435 and 4228; GK435; AV translates as "manstealer" once. **1** a slave-dealer, kidnapper, man-stealer. 1a of one who unjustly reduces free men to slavery. 1b of one who steals the slaves of others and sells them.[237]

The mythology that developed because of this need became the justification of a new thing, world conquest based upon a relatively new concept, racial identity.

Martin Bernal in his book, Black Athena, acknowledges the existence of a curious change in the intensity of racism that existed before and after the seventeenth century, the catalyst being the apogee of the Atlantic slave trade.

"a more clear cut racism grew up after 1650 and that this was greatly intensified by the increased colonization of North America, with its twin policies of the extermination of the native Americans and enslavement of Africans. Both of these presented moral problems to Protestant societies in which the equality of all men before God, and personal liberty, were central values which could only be eased by strong racism."[238]

The task was to devise a scientific doctrine that would alleviate the moral problem presented by slavery by placing the African to a lower rung of the family of humanity. If the African was not quite a human being, then slavery would not be a sin. In fact, slavery might be an asset to the slave, civilizing and Christianizing him. Slavery could be the best thing that ever happened to the slave.

Martin Bernal identifies thinkers such as John Locke, David Hume, and Benjamin Franklin as racists[ccxxi] [239] and demonstrated their use of racist arguments to justify and perpetuate exploitative policies towards Africans and Native Americans. For example,

"Locke's consistent disparagement of Native Americans was essential to his politics

---

[ccxxi] Bernal's choice of words

because the land the indigenous population inhabited was needed to provide a wilderness available for English and other settlers."[240]

Also

"To recapitulate: it is certain that Locke and most 18th-century English speaking thinkers like David Hume and Benjamin Franklin were racists: they openly expressed popular opinions that dark skin color was linked to moral and mental inferiority. In Hume's case, racism so transcended conventional religion that he was a pioneer of the view that there had been not one creation of man, but many different ones...[241]"

It is fascinating to note that the concept of polygenesis, or multiple creations, used to justify the argument that blacks are not of the same species as whites, did not originate with the Nation of Islam.

The term "white" as a racial designation was not used in the Americas until the 1680's[242], and the term "Caucasian" was not coined by Blumenbach until 1795.[243] New racial attitudes and nomenclature resulted from historical necessity. The desire to reconcile the slave trade with Christian teachings, the need to justify the economic exploitation of African and other nations *because* they were non-white, resulted in the social, theological, then scientific concepts of race.

American society, ostensibly dedicated to Christian principles, resorted to the economic exploitation of Africans to navigate the early pressures of nationhood. There developed a legacy of national strength based upon theft and arrogance rather than the Word of God. To justify that sin, a racial folklore, then a racial theology and finally a racial science emerged. Christianity was *modified* to accommodate these priorities. It is by taking a hard look at these realities that we can begin to understand the systems of inequality that are directed at blacks in the twentieth and twenty-first centuries, long after the pretext of slavery has been eliminated.

To continue our review of the attitudes that led to the modern concept of race, I quote from Bernal.

"...the notion of European superiority increased with European economic and industrial progress, and expansion into other continents."[244]

And

"These intellectual and educational changes can be related to specific national configurations of European colonization and expansion into other continents. For instance, the initial development of ancient Indian studies in the 17th and 18th centuries grew out of the East India Companies need to understand their subjects and 'native' allies."[245]

W.E.B. DuBois wrote,

"It is especially significant that the science of Egyptology arose and flourished at the very time that the cotton kingdom reached its greatest power on the foundation of the American Negro slavery…"[246]

Prior to the development of systems of pseudoscience which would classify blacks right out of history,[247] theologians took the lead in justifying the profitable but immoral practices of that time.

"In the eighteenth century and early nineteenth century southern Baptists and Methodists exhibited considerable anti-slavery sentiment. Many slaveholders were therefore reluctant to have the preachers and missionaries of these denominations work among their slaves. But when the southern wings of these churches changed their positions, when southern clergymen became ardent defenders of slavery, the master class could look upon organized religion as an ally. Church leaders now argued "that the gospel instead of becoming a means of creating trouble and strife, was really the best instrument to preserve peace and good conduct among the negroes."[248]

"One window into the worldview of Christian white supremacy is the ardent defense of slavery and the Confederacy that was proffered by Reverend Basil Manly Sr. As founder of Southern Baptist Seminary and chaplain to the Confederacy, Manly was one of the most prolific and tireless Christian defenders of slavery. While Manly was one of the most prominent purveyors of white supremacist theology, he was not unique among Southern Baptists, and he had counterparts in the southern branches of the other major Protestant denominations, such as William Capers, a Methodist, and James Henley Thornwell, a Presbyterian. Like his fellow defenders of slavery, Manly grounded his arguments with generous citations from the Bible."[249]

Dr Anthony Evans notes that even some of the best-known religious leaders of early America justified slavery by theology, laying the foundation for the efforts of secular intellectuals devising a scientific doctrine of race. These religious men cited by Dr. Evans included Jonathan Edwards, George Whitefield, John Davenport, and Evera Stiles, President of Yale.[250]

These citations are a small sample of the extensive record[251] of the role of Christian theology in creating an American *version* of Christianity. This modified Christianity facilitated oppression by uniting itself with the concept of white supremacy to create the American personality and culture embraced by so many today.

The curse of Ham was one of several modifications to Christianity [see Chapter 18] that made racial prejudice and discrimination impervious to the effects of sanctification, effectively *redefining the gospel*, when it came to race relations.

The *biblical* gospel created a new nature in the believer, gave him a new power in the Spirit and commanded him in the Great Commission to obey "all things whatsoever I [Jesus Christ] commanded you" [Matthew 28.20]. The *modified* gospel of American Christianity separates the act of belief in Christ from the effects it should have in the life when confronted with the issue of race relations. Therefore, persons seeking to get many white believers to apply the principles of sanctification to their dealings with blacks individually and collectively, respond, "let's just stick to the [modified] gospel."

Since the blacks were cursed by God (note how Noah was replaced by God) then colonial power was merely the hand of God at work. In fact, the colonial/slave power was a blessing to the dark races since they now could be evangelized. Never mind that the Christian church was in Africa almost since its inception and that African theologians stabilized the early church, which itself was neither "white" nor European.

The modified Christianity of the United States explains the current political upheaval in Christendom and the nation at large. Religious conservatism is largely this modified Christianity, which has displaced the old liberalism as a force for political change. Neither has the spiritual power to address the true spiritual needs of the nation, any more than the Pharisees and Sadducees did in the times of Christ. Both then and now, false religion has power, but for the purpose of corrupting the truth and sustaining oppression.

> Mark 12:38–40 (KJV 1900)
> [38] And he said unto them in his doctrine, Beware of the scribes, which love to go in long clothing, and *love* salutations in the marketplaces, [39] And the chief seats in the synagogues, and the uppermost rooms at feasts: [40] Which devour widows' houses, and for a pretence make long prayers: these shall receive greater damnation.

> Matthew 3:7–8 (KJV 1900)
> [7] But when he saw many of the Pharisees and Sadducees come to his baptism, he said unto them, O generation of vipers, who hath warned you to flee from the wrath to come? [8] Bring forth therefore fruits meet for repentance:

---

[217] See Appendix 2: Theologians on the Issue of Race

[218] (from Barnes' Notes, Electronic Database. Copyright (c) 1997 by Biblesoft)

Also, from Lange on this same passage,

"The wine-garden of Noah is a mild reflex of paradise in the world of the fallen human race; and this enjoyment, in its excessively sinful use, to which Noah led the way, although he was not aware of its effect, has become a reflex of Adam's enjoyment of the tree of knowledge; with this difference, however, that Noah erred in ignorance, and not in the form of conscious transgression" [emphasis added]

Lange, John Peter, Philip Schaff, Tayler Lewis, and A. Gosman. *A Commentary on the Holy Scriptures: Genesis*. Bellingham, WA: Logos Bible Software, 2008.

[219] (from Adam Clarke's Commentary, Electronic Database. Copyright (c) 1996 by Biblesoft) Genesis 9.21

[220] Mathews, K.A. The New American Commentary. Genesis 1-11:26, vol. 1A, (Nashville: Broadman & Holman Publishers, 1996), 414–415

[221] The correspondences between the events of this passage and the events in the Garden of Eden are striking and point directly to the culpability of Noah for the events that followed. The one significant correspondence that is *not emphasized* in the following commentary is that both Adam and Noah committed the original sin that resulted in divine judgment and set into motion the downward spiral of the human race. Even this author softens Noah's guilt, transferring it to a "corrupt seed." (rw)

"The telling of Noah's drunkenness, which results in the patriarch's invocation for curse and blessing, recalls the language of the world before the flood, especially Adam's story, but also Cain's rivalry with brother Abel.151 We have seen in the flood story that the creation and garden accounts (1:1–2:3; 2:4–4:26) are re-presented, especially 9:1–7, so as to picture Noah as the second Adam, the father of the postdiluvian world. In this concluding episode, the parallels are also unmistakable: Noah and Adam share in the same profession (2:15; 9:20); the language of "curse" (3:14, 17; 4:11; 5:29; 9:25) and "blessing" (1:28; 5:2; 9:26) are heard again; both experience the shame of "nakedness" (3:7, 10–11; 9:22–23); and, like Adam, Noah's transgression results in familial strife among his descendants, resulting in fratricide for Adam's sons (4:8) and slavery for Noah's youngest (9:25–26). There are many allusions to the garden sin: the tree of knowledge "in the middle of [bĕtôk] the garden" (2:9; 3:3, 8) and Noah "inside [bĕtôk] the tent" (9:21); the woman "saw" (rāʾâ, 3:6), and Ham "saw" (rāʾâ, 9:22), though the brothers did not "see" (rāʾâ, 9:23); Adam and Eve "knew [yādaʿ] they were naked" (3:7), and Noah "knew [yādaʿ] what his youngest son had done to" him (9:24); and God asked, "Who told [nāgad] you that you were naked?" (3:11), and Ham "told" (nāgad) his brothers. Indeed, Noah is the second Adam both as recipient of divine blessing and as father of a corrupt seed.152" [emphasis added].

K. A. Mathews, Genesis 1-11:26, vol. 1A, The New American Commentary. Nashville: Broadman & Holman Publishers, 1996. 417.

[222] Ibid.

[223] (Biblesoft's New Exhaustive Strong's Numbers and Concordance with Expanded Greek-Hebrew Dictionary. Copyright (c) 1994, Biblesoft and International Bible Translators, Inc.)

[224] (Biblesoft's New Exhaustive Strong's Numbers and Concordance with Expanded Greek-Hebrew Dictionary. Copyright (c) 1994, Biblesoft and International Bible Translators, Inc.) H2351.

[225]Jamieson, Robert, A. R. Fausset, and David Brown. Commentary Critical and Explanatory on the Whole Bible. Oak Harbor, WA: Logos Research Systems, Inc. 1997. Genesis 9.24-25.

[226] (from Keil & Delitzsch Commentary on the Old Testament: New Updated Edition, Electronic Database. Copyright (c) 1996 by Hendrickson Publishers, Inc.) Genesis 9.18-25.

[227] Zeigler cited in Keil and Delitzsch Commentary of the Old Testament. 134.

[228] (from Matthew Henry's Commentary on the Whole Bible: New Modern Edition, Electronic Database. Copyright (c) 1991 by Hendrickson Publishers, Inc.) Genesis 9.18-23.

[229] (from Adam Clarke's Commentary, Electronic Database. Copyright (c) 1996 by Biblesoft) Genesis 9.22-24.

[230] (from Jamieson, Fausset, and Brown Commentary, Electronic Database. Copyright (c) 1997 by Biblesoft) Genesis 9.23.

[231] The Hittites descended from Canaan [Gen 10.15]. "**Heth**—dread, a descendant of Canaan, and the ancestor of the Hittites (Gen. 10:18; Deut. 7:1), who dwelt in the vicinity of Hebron (Gen. 23:3, 7). The Hittites were a Hamitic race. They are called "the sons of Heth" (Gen. 23:3, 5, 7, 10, 16, 18, 20)." Easton, M. G. *Illustrated Bible Dictionary and Treasury of Biblical History, Biography, Geography, Doctrine, and Literature.* New York: Harper & Brothers, 1893.

[232] Bunsen, Philosophy of Ancient History 52. Cited in Houston, Drusilla D. Wonderful Ethiopians of the Ancient Cushite Empire, Book 1. Baltimore, Md.: Black Classic Press, 1985. 20.

[233] See Black Nations in Scripture late 2023.

[234] Houston, Wonderful Ethiopians of the Cushite Empire. 19.

[235] See the following article from "Answers in Genesis" where a well-meaning bible ministry essentially ratifies many of the points about the Curse of Canaan that are herein refuted.

Lacy, Troy. "The Curse of Canaan" October 12, 2012 Answers in Genesis, Accessed 11-13-2022. https://answersingenesis.org/bible-characters/the-curse-of-canaan/

That the "Curse of Ham" would have to be denied and refuted at all in the 21st century is evidence of its pernicious longevity.

[236] Johannes P. Louw and Eugene Albert Nida, Greek-English Lexicon of the New Testament: Based on Semantic Domains. New York: United Bible Societies, 1996. 578.

[237] James Strong, Enhanced Strong's Lexicon (Woodside Bible Fellowship, 1995).

[238] Bernal, Martin. Black Athena: The Afroasiatic Roots of Classical Civilization. First Edition. New Brunswick, N.J: Rutgers University Press, 1987. 201-202.

[239] Racist in this sense does not mean mere prejudice, but the systematic and scientific brand of discrimination that seeks to obtain global aims.

[240] Bernal, Martin. Black Athena, Vol. 1. 202.

[241] Ibid., 203.

[242] Dunston, Bishop Alfred G. "The Black Man in the Old Testament and its World." Trenton: Africa World Press,1992. 6.

[243] Bernal, Martin. "Black Athena" Vol. 1. 219.

[244] Ibid., 198.

[245] Ibid., 237.

[246]. DuBois, W.E.B" The world and Africa: an enquiry into the part which Africa has played in world history", (New York, International Publishers 1946/1965) 99, 106. Cited in, "Bringing Maat, Destroying Ifset: The African and African Diasporan Presence in the Study of Ancient Egypt", Asa G. Hilliard III in Egypt: Child of Africa, ed. Ivan Van Sertima, (Transaction 1995). 138.

[247] Charles Darwin was one of many scientists involved in this effort. The helpful website, "Answers in Genesis" has this to say and more about the doctrine of evolution and its impact upon thinking regarding race:

"Evolutionary thinking, on the other hand, provides support for racism. Darwin, in his world-changing tomes The Origin of Species by Means of Natural Selection or the Preservation of Favored Races in the Struggle for Life and The Descent of Man, proclaimed his belief that some people groups are more highly evolved than others. In The Descent of Man, Darwin repeatedly called people with darker skin "degraded" and hundreds of times described them as "savages." In fact, Darwin actually predicted in The Descent of Man that civilized people would someday exterminate such savages. Darwin's own words provided "scientific" justification for the next century of "racially" based atrocities. Though evolution is not the cause of racism, the late evolutionist Stephen J. Gould noted, "Biological arguments for racism may have been common before 1859, but they increased by orders of magnitude following the acceptance of evolutionary theory."2

"Evolution, despite claims to the contrary,3 cannot rescue the world from the scourge of racism. Rightly accepting what the Bible actually says about the origin of people groups and about God's love for all is the basis on which to build a better tomorrow.

"AiG President Ken Ham has a written a blog item this weekend about the non-existent "curse of Ham." You can also learn more about the ways evolutionists like Darwin, Ernst Haeckel, and even James Watson (of DNA fame) have promoted extreme racial prejudice."

[Ken Ham's Blog: "Was Ham Cursed"] "Creation Museum Does Not Support the Curse of Ham" by Dr. Elizabeth Mitchell, January 26, 2013, Answers in Genesis Accessed 11-13-2022.
https://answersingenesis.org/ministry-news/creation-museum/creation-museum-not-support-curse-of-ham/

[248] Stampp, Kenneth M., The Peculiar Institution, Slavery in the Ante-Bellum South. Vintage, New Your, 1956. 157-158.

[249] Jones, Robert P. White Too Long: The Legacy of White Supremacy in American Christianity (p. 82). Simon & Schuster. Kindle Edition.

[250] Evans, Dr. Anthony "Are Blacks Spiritually Inferior to Whites."

[251] "While belief in Ham's curse can be traced to early Judaism, Christianity, and Islam, its popularity grew exponentially in America prior to 1865. The curse served as a prooftext for pro-slavery preachers, enabling them to make heavenly sounding justifications for the hellish enslavement of dark-skinned image-bearers.

"Baptist Pastor and Southern Seminary trustee Iveson L. Brookes (1785–1868) taught that "Negro Slavery is an institution of heaven and intended for the mutual benefit of master and slave, as proved by the Bible. . . God himself . . . authorized Noah to doom the posterity of Ham."

"Patrick Mell (1814–1888), the fourth president of the Southern Baptist Convention, proposed: "From

Ham were descended the nations that occupied the land of Canaan and those that now constitute the African or Negro race. Their inheritance, according to prophecy, has been and will continue to be slavery . . . [and] so long as we have the Bible . . . we expect to maintain it."

"Sadly, quotes like these were commonplace across denominations in the 1800s. And though slavery was abolished in 1865, echoes of this false doctrine continued to reverberate throughout America's culture and churches. Prominent Pastors used it to support segregation, and its sentiments fuel modern-day white supremacist theology. Just recently I had to take down racist posters promoting these lies near our church building."

Kell, Garrett. Damn the Curse of Ham: How Genesis 9 Got Twisted into Racist Propaganda, The Gospel Coalition, January, 9 2021. Accessed 11-13-2022.
https://www.thegospelcoalition.org/article/damn-curse-ham/